# THE FIRST DUTY

*"I think the first duty of society is justice."*

ALEXANDER HAMILTON

# THE FIRST DUTY

*A History of the*
*U.S. District Court for Oregon*

Edited by
Carolyn M. Buan

With contributions by
Caroline P. Stoel, Ralph James Mooney,
Todd A. Peterson, Jack G. Collins, Randall B. Kester,
and Laurie Bennett Mapes

U.S. District Court of Oregon Historical Society
Portland, Oregon

Printed in the U.S.A.

ISBN 0-9635156-0-8

Library of Congress Catalog Card Number 92-063268

# CONTENTS

# PREFACE

T he U.S. District Court of Oregon Historical Society began with a picnic at the home of the Hon. James M. Burns, a site on the banks of the Willamette River appropriately close to Champoeg, the historic riverside village where the Provisional Government of Oregon was organized in 1843. That Saturday afternoon, August 20, 1983, the Honorable Robert F. Peckham, chief judge of the U.S. District Court for the Northern District of California, visited with assembled Oregon lawyers, judges, and their family members and told them about his court's historical society— the first such organization in the country. On the basis of what they heard, those assembled determined to form the second district court historical society and did so the on January 23, 1984. The governing board was made up of members from the bench and the bar, as well as private citizens from around the state.

The Oregon district has a tradition of outstanding and colorful judges including Matthew P. Deady, James Alger Fee, John F. Kilkenny, and Gus J. Solomon. You'll meet them in this book.

The society's first bulletin, written by Caroline P. Stoel, cited these judges and announced the aim of the society as the collection, preservation, study, and dissemination of the history of the Oregon court. The bulletin also announced that the society had begun "collecting" by hiring Rick Harmon of the Oregon Historical Society to take the oral histories of Judges John Kilkenney, Gus Solomon, and William West. Warren McMinimee and Arlene Schnitzer were co-chairs of the first oral history committee.

It was particularly appropriate that Judge Kilkenny, one of the founding fathers of the society, recognized as the savior of Portland's Pioneer Courthouse, wrote about "his" courthouse in the first bulletin. The article reflects Judge Kilkenny's love of that fine old building and knowledge of its minutiae (the hat and coat racks, for example, came from a courthouse in Butte, Montana). The bulletin advised members to attend the exhibit honoring pioneer Portland attorney C.E.S. Wood, opening

September 1984 at the Oregon Historical Society, and also invited members to a reception to be held immediately prior to the president's reception at the Oregon State Bar convention in Portland.

And so it's gone with the society. Friends and colleagues, lawyers, judges, and citizens (Arlene Schnitzer is an art patron and businesswoman) over the years have collected, met, learned to take oral histories, presided over investitures. We've recorded history as it was passing. We've made history as we've practiced law in the federal courts and honored the courts as we marked transitions in the life of the courthouse. The society's first event occurred on August 30, 1985, when it sponsored the ceremony rededicating the district courthouse in Portland and two courtrooms (once a post office) on the first floor. The portrait of the Honorable Alfred T. Goodwin, Ninth Circuit Court of Appeals and formerly a district court judge, was dedicated that day. Judge Goodwin made some remarks as did Senator Mark O. Hatfield, Judge Owen M. Panner, and Judge James R. Browning, presiding judge of the Ninth Circuit.

Judge Owen M. Panner succeeded Judge Burns as chief judge and chair of the society. The picnic at Judge Burns' home evolved into board meetings in the first floor conference room of the courthouse and brown bag lunches for the executive committee in Judge Panner's chambers. The society has greatly benefitted from the wisdom and perseverence of both men. Randall B. Kester was our first president, followed by Norman J. Wiener, Wayne Hilliard, and Don S. Willner. Caroline Stoel, Randall Kester, and Don Willner have served on the board since its founding. Arlene Schnitzer continued as chair of oral histories and chair of several gala annual dinners through 1991.

Now we have this book, the most important product of our society's work, for it makes the court's history widely available. (The book, incidentally, is part of a larger project designed to educate the public about the court's history through free lectures to schools and community groups, as well as through this publication.)

Like the history of our court, the book does not speak with one voice. In fact, it is a collection of essays from six authors:

• Caroline P. Stoel, adjunct associate professor of the history of law at Portland State University, writing on *Oregon's First Federal Courts, 1849–1859*;

• Ralph James Mooney, a professor at the University of Oregon School of Law, writing on *The Deady Years, 1859–1893*;

• Todd A. Peterson, a Portland attorney with Bullock & Regier, P.C., and Jack G. Collins, who heads the forfeiture division of the U.S. attorney's office in Portland, writing on *Years of Growth, 1893–1927)*;

• Randall B. Kester, a partner in the Portland firm of Cosgrave, Vergeer & Kester, writing on *A Time of Change, 1927–1950*;

• Laurie Bennett Mapes, a faculty member at the Northwestern School of Law of Lewis and Clark College, writing on *A Period of Complexity, 1950–1991*.

Thanks to these authors—and to historian Terence O'Donnell, who wrote the introduction, for adding their voices to the history of our court and making that history accessible to the general reader.

We are especially indebted to the Meyer Memorial Trust, which provided initial funding for our project and enabled us to place our book in each high school in Oregon free of charge. Without the Meyer Trust and its trustees' interest in this educational endeavor, there would be no book. Thanks also to the Rose E. Tucker Charitable Trust, the Jackson Foundation, Norman J. Weiner, and the firms of Miller Nash Wiener Hager & Carlsen; Lane Powell Spears Lubersky; Pozzi Wilson Atchison O'Leary & Conboy; Cosgrave, Vergeer & Kester; Stoel Rives Boley Jones & Grey; Black Helterline; Lindsay Hart Neil & Weigler; Sussman Shank & Watnick; Kennedy King & Zimmer; Heller Ehrman White & McAuliffe; Bogle & Gates; Ball Janik & Novack; Perkins Coie; and Schwabe Williamson & Wyatt for their contributions, which have allowed us to complete our project. Another thank you goes to Arlene and Harold Schnitzer for underwriting the book's handsome four-color dust jacket, as well as a promotional brochure. We are also grateful to our society's lifetime members—Robert Belloni, Owen Blank, Raymond Conboy (membership given in memoriam), Paul T. Fortino, George H. Fraser, Edwin A. Harnden, Wayne Hilliard, Daniel O'Leary, Chester E. McCarty, Jeffrey S. Mutnick, Owen M. Panner, Frank Pozzi, Arlene

Schnitzer, John Schwabe, Norman Sepenuk, Gayle L. Troutwine, William White, and Donald Wilson—whose significant monetary contributions have been matched by service to the society.

A tap of the gavel recognizes William F. White, book committee dynamo and a collector of anecdotes and "sea stories," for his work on the book project. We are grateful, as well, to board member George Fraser, an afficiando of legal history, for reviewing the book manuscript; to Norman J. Wiener for help with fund raising; to Kirk Hall, executive director of the Professional Liability Fund, for early planning help and for managing the book distribution effort; to Cynthia Harrison and Beverly Hudson Wirtz of the Federal Judicial Center for use of their research materials; and to Paula Hammer for editorial assistance. Our sincere thanks to Chet Orloff, executive director of the Oregon Historical Society and former executive director of the Ninth Judicial Circuit Historical Society; Virginia Linnman, OHS press sales and marketing manager; and Bruce Hamilton, director of the OHS press, for offering excellent advice about marketing.

The project was guided by book committee members Caroline Stoel, Albert Bannon, William White, and Carolyn Buan. These individuals learned a great deal from one another, but I and the three other lawyer members have learned the most from our editor, Carolyn Buan, whose professional skills, patience, and perseverence resulted in the publication of this book.

Katherine H. O'Neil
President, U.S. District Court
of Oregon Historical Society
Portland, Oregon
November 1992

# INTRODUCTION

## BY TERENCE O'DONNELL

J ustice is a woman holding in her hand a scales in perfect balance. Such is art. Then there is life.

Some years ago a young Dubliner penetrated the inner courtyards of Dublin Castle, the then seat of British authority in Ireland. Reaching the castle's Hall of Justice—Justice herself in bronze above the portal—the young man placed a ladder against a wall, ascended to the scales, and in the bottom of one of the two pans drilled a tiny hole. Thus did the young man bring reality to the ideality of art—for it rains a lot in Dublin.

*The First Duty* is a history of the scales as held in the hands of the federal judiciary of Oregon. The pans of these scales were not always in perfect balance either, for after all, and again, they existed in reality, not art—the hands holding the scales were flesh and blood, not bronze. Thus the rains of faction and ideology, of avarice and ignorance may on occasion have thrown the balance off. Still, and despite these forces of asymmetry, the federal judiciary more often than not has kept the scales in balance. How that was achieved is the subject of this book.

American law, in the form of the admiralty statutes, first appeared in what we now call Oregon on a May morning in 1792. The occasion was the crossing of the bar of the fabled Great River of the West by Captain Robert Gray of Boston. Gray was the first known white to enter the river (long sought by Spanish and British explorers), and he named it for his little ship, the *Columbia.*

After a week or so of trading buttons and beads for sea otter pelts, Captain Gray and his crew sailed away, taking with them their laws as well as some good impressions of the natives with whom they had traded and, no doubt, consorted too. "The Men at Columbia's river," wrote 17-year-old John Boit, "are strait limb'd, fine looking fellows, and the women are very pretty."

American law next came to the Columbia with Lewis and Clark. The reports of Gray and other traders drove to an even higher pitch the curiosity of that already exceedingly curious man, President Thomas Jefferson. It was to satisfy this curiosity in its many aspects that Jefferson dispatched the two army officers overland to the Columbia in the spring of 1804. Even before starting out, Clark noted the nature and operation of the expedition's law in a journal entry of May 17:

> ...John Collins Charged...for behaving in an unbecoming manner at the ball last night [and] for speaking in a language...tending to bring into disrespect the order of the Commanding officer....The Court are of opinion that the Prisnoir (sic) is Guilty of all the charges alleged against him it being a breach of the rules and articles of War and do sentence him to receive fifty lashes on his naked back.

Lewis and Clark, after a damp winter on the Columbia—it rained every day but six—gratefully returned to the U.S. in 1806. Their reports, together with lucrative markets for Northwest pelts in China, persuaded the German-born John Jacob Astor to establish a fur-trading post at the mouth of the Columbia. Here, again, the admiralty statutes obtained for the first Astorians arrived by ship. However, Captain Thorn as judge was as capricious in his observance of the statutes as the ocean winds themselves, for the simple reason that he was, in the opinion of all, a madman. Indeed the whole Astor enterprise ended in failure, Astoria eventually passing to the ownership of the British Hudson's Bay Company, which in 1824 established a new headquarters up river at a place they called Fort Vancouver.

Ten years later Americans appeared once again on the scene, this time bringing with them not the codes of the admiralty or military but rather the very laws of God—or so at least the American missionaries asserted. The native people, however, were less certain of the divine nature of these American "sacred" laws. (A confusion between the divine and the secular sometimes occurred then, and sometimes now, too.) "Where are these laws from?" asked Yellow Serpent, chief of the Walla Walla. "Are they from God or from the earth? I think that they are from the earth because from what I know of white men, they do not honor these laws."

These several American presences in the Northwest—Captain Gray, Lewis and Clark, the Astorians, the missionaries, together with the promise of a salubrious climate, free and fertile land and, of course, the endemic American restlessness—all these combined to encourage border-state Americans to migrate to the Oregon Country, beginning in the 1840s. Since the wagon trains on leaving Missouri passed through a region without government or law, it was incumbent on the pioneers to create an ad hoc code until such time as they would reach their destination.

Depending on their make-up, different wagon trains created different laws. Some required that every man carry a Bible while others specified the quantity of whisky each wagon would be permitted. Common to all the codes were penalties for specific crimes. Murder earned a hanging; rape, 39 lashes three days in succession; fornication the same but for one day only. There were in addition a number of minor offenses—sleeping while on guard duty, for example, or engaging in "obscene conversation." In general the concern was, as one pioneer put it, "that we not degenerate into a state of barbarians."

On reaching the Willamette Valley the immigrants' first task was to find land on which to settle. Considered ideal were those border regions between the valley prairies and the wooded foothills: prairie land to till and on which to graze their herds, timbered slopes to provide lumber for their barns and houses. Concurrent with this settlement came the establishment of towns, little ensembles in the white and simple manner of the classic revival style, each proudly proclaimed by a church spire, the bell tower of a school house, and in some cases the cupola of a pillared courthouse. For the pioneers these farmsteads with their orchards, fields, and flocks, these towns with their merchants, preachers, schoolmasters and—sometimes—a judge signified a great achievement: the domestication of the wilderness.

The discovery of gold in California in 1848 greatly augmented this process. Now, at last, there was a market for Oregon produce as well as capital for the Oregon farmers and merchants returning from the gold fields. It meant as well the purifying of the Oregon community, for some of the gold seekers did not return—good riddance, for those who would choose to remain in California could not be persons of true respectability. Further, and as an Oregon historian of the time wrote,

*This distance of Oregon from the Sierra Foothills proved at this time the greatest of blessings, being near enough for commercial communication, and yet so far away as to escape the more evil consequences attending upon the mad scramble for wealth...social dissolutions, the rapine of intellect...a delirium of development...robbery, murder, and all uncleanness.*

From such wickedness Oregon, unlike its unfortunate neighbor to the south, had been preserved.

There were, however, two disturbing elements in this period of the 1840s and 50s: war between the settlers and the native Oregonians and war between the two political parties of the time, the Democrats and those precursors of the Republicans, the Whigs.

Indian hostilities began with the Cayuse War of 1849-50, waged to punish the Cayuse murderers of the Whitman missionaries at Walla Walla. The second war, or rather cluster of wars called the Rogue River wars, occurred in 1853-55. In general these hostilities between native Oregonians and whites developed when government offered free land to the immigrants before arranging for its purchase from the native Oregonians. The matter was settled, at least in the Willamette Valley, when treaties providing for purchase were finally ratified and the natives moved to reservations. But the wars, and in particular the call on the part of many for the total extermination of the native Oregonians, stained with blood our beginnings.

Though usually lacking in bloodshed, the political wars of the period were disruptive as well. This arose in part from the fact that in the nineteenth century, party loyalty, defense of party, was a fighting matter and in part from the fact that politics was the trough in which the slop of spoils flowed. It was the crowding at this trough that accounts for much of the rough and tumble of Oregon politics in the 1850s.

There were other issues too—the handling of Indian affairs, prohibition, the location of the capital, statehood, and the fact that the Democrats represented agrarian interests while the Whigs represented the merchant class. These animosities and conflicting interests were expressed most vividly in the party newspapers, the Democrats' *Oregon Statesman* and the Whigs' *Oregonian*. The *Statesman* consistently referred to the *Oregonian* as *The Sewer* while the *Oregonian* favored the *Statesman*'s editor with the title of "Pimp Generalissimo."

In all this turmoil of settlement and town-building, Indian wars, gold strikes, and political strife, how did the law fare and what kind of law did the immigrants find on reaching Oregon? This is the subject of Caroline Stoel's "Oregon's First Federal Courts: 1849–1859."

By way of background, Stoel summarizes the laws enacted by the Provisional Government of Oregon, an ad hoc structure formed in 1843 by settlers, retired trappers, Hudson's Bay personnel, and missionaries. It was to serve until such time as the conflicting claims of the British and Americans to the Oregon Country might be determined. This occurred with the boundary agreement of 1846 and the creation of the Oregon Territory in 1848.

Stoel next reviews the territory's legal corpus and the appointment of federal judges to administer it, at the same time providing a profile of each of the judges and the rancorous relations between them. She concludes with an examination of six cases that illustrate the general character of the court when confronted with some of the important matters of the day.

Stoel's conclusions are not of great credit to the federal bench during this period. "Not until the end of the territorial period was some degree of judicial proficiency achieved." In other words, the rainfall in Oregon at this time was especially heavy.

Oregon passed—reluctantly—from territory to statehood in 1859. This, the end of Caroline Stoel's period, is the beginning of Ralph James Mooney's in "The Deady Years: 1859–93."

No period in Oregon history saw more change than occurred in the years of Mooney's study. First there was statehood itself, accepted "reluctantly" as noted above. After all, had not the people voted *against* admission to the Union on three previous occasions, seeming to prefer the looser, freer territorial connection? That the proposition now succeeded was due not so much to a sentiment toward union but rather to the maneuverings of the Democratic party, which had the most to gain from statehood.

This aloofness, this penchant for separation—what John Gunther a century later called the "deep-rooted insistence of a state to grow its own way without regard to its neighbors"—explains in part the indifference of most Oregonians to the next important event following statehood: the Civil War. It is true that the issue of slavery gave birth to Oregon's Republican party ("a collection of old grannies and niger-struck (*sic*) dames," the Democrats' *Statesman* called these founding members of the party), and it is true as well that the Albany Democrats threw the town cannon in the river to prevent its being fired in celebration of Lincoln's inauguration. In general, however, Oregonians were concerned with their own affairs and their state's development rather than with the travail of the nation.

One of these developments was the spread of settlement out of the Willamette Valley up to eastern Oregon and down to the seacoast. Gold strikes in Baker and Grant counties in the early 1860s drew thousands of miners, some of whom settled in the region. Of more lasting importance were the cattle driven up from the valley to feed the miners, the cattle flourishing on the High Country's then abundant bunchgrass. Thus began the great cattle ranches, and later sheep ranches, of eastern Oregon.

It was gold finds as well that initiated settlement on the coast, particularly at Port Orford and Gold Beach in the 1850s. In the following decade the federal government began building lighthouses to protect ships from one of the world's most treacherous coastlines. These too brought little settlement along the coast. In the same decade the first salmon cannery began operation at Astoria, the forerunner of what for a time would be the coast's major industry.

The most sizable development, however, was taking place in the Willamette Valley. By the end of the 1850s, over 30 towns had been established. The most important stood at the final bend of the Willamette and was called Portland. "A small and beautiful village," wrote a local judge. "Rather gamey" wrote a lady, visiting from California. Whatever it was called, by the time of statehood Portland had 100 shops and a population of about 2,000. This growth was not surprising, for Portland at the juncture of the two rivers was now the principal port of the Northwest coast and also the center of the lucrative outfitting trade that serviced both the Indian wars and gold strikes. By the 1870s, when these profits had diminished, a new bonanza—wheat—came along. Initially the wheat carted to the Portland wharves came from the Valley but soon the upper Columbia Basin, opened to settlement by the gold strikes, began to grow wheat on a vast scale, which led to a great multiplying of the Portland wharves.

The final important development of Judge Deady's years was the arrival in Portland in 1883 of the first transcontinental train. Until then Oregon had been a very isolated place, requiring a journey of several months by wagon or ship. Now immigration was much facilitated, for as the Portland Board of Trade announced, "We are at last incorporated with the rest of the world."

The coming of the railroad had two other significant effects. Farming was no longer dependent on access to waterways for the transport of produce but might occur wherever the soil was good and the rails ran— and by the end of the period they ran almost everywhere. Secondly, among the places the rails ran were the Oregon forests—a development that was to have a massive impact on the state's economy as well as on its environment.

Nothing illustrates better the changes that occurred during these years of Judge Deady's tenure, the 1860s to the 1890s, than what was at this time the major statewide event of the year: the Oregon State Fair.

There in the oak groves of the capital, Oregonians gathered to view and acclaim the astonishing progress made by the state in the few years since settlement. When young Mathew Deady had arrived in Oregon in 1849 he had found oxen, a few milk cows, a paucity of fowl, practically no sheep. Now the number, variety, and breeds of livestock had increased enormously—a development of the greatest significance to the farmers who made up the majority of the Oregon population. There had been a similar increase in the variety and strains of fruits and vegetables, a cornucopia compared to the wild berries, peas, and boiled wheat of the pioneer years. Also, due to the toil of Chinese laborers, thousands of acres of Willamette Valley stump and brush land had been cleared for the planting of hops, one of the state's major crops.

But what impressed the fair-goers most, and reflected the greatest and most welcome change, were the exhibits of farm machinery, devices undreamed of when the pioneers arrived with their hoes and crude plowshares. Now "gorgeous in red paint," there were mowers, reapers, cultivators, and—most marvelous of all—steam-driven threshers.

The fair also reflected the development of manufacturing. From a few crude sawmills and cooperages, manufacturers had gone on to produce the necessities of everyday Oregon life: cloth, paper, soap, pottery, leather, furniture, wagons, beer. Now, too, exports of Oregon products had increased from 3 million in the 1850s to 18 million by the end of the 1870s: wheat, flour, lumber, wool, salmon, potatoes, gold, and silver.

Along with these material advances, there had been progress of a cultural nature. A walk away from the fairgrounds, there was a four-year college,—one of four in the state—schools of medicine and pharmacy, and institutions for the blind and simple. By now, too, the state prison had been moved from Portland to Salem, much to the gratification of the *Oregonian* for the prison would be handily convenient to the Democratically controlled state house. As for the insane asylum, it remained for some years in Portland, where it was believed there was more need for it—though one commentator of the 1870s was at pains to point out that most of the inmates were not only not Portlanders but indeed were from out-of-state, which is to say not even Oregonians!

As in any period of such rapid and fundamental change, the demands on the legal system increased accordingly. Thus Oregon was fortunate in having as its first U.S. district judge a jurist of the stature of Mathew Deady. This former seminarian and blacksmith served as district judge for more than three decades with a distinction that earned him a national reputation. In addition to his cultivation, humor, and charm, his devotion to good works made him an ornament of the Oregon community. One of his greatest contributions, in historical terms, was the diary he kept from 1871 to 1892, which deservedly makes him the Pepys of Oregon, providing about the best account we have of the character of Oregon life in the last quarter of the nineteenth century.

Ralph James Mooney begins his study of Judge Deady with a summary of the judge's early life and then goes on to his legal philosophy and his most outstanding accomplishments. He next examines a number of Deady's cases in the four catagories of federal public land law, admiralty law, disputes related to industrial enterprise, and judicial responses to racism. He concludes with a summary of the career of a jurist whose "record of achievement and public service...may never be equalled...[who] personified to a remarkable degree the civilizing force of federal law in the early Far West."

Oregon entered the twentieth century with a grand flourish in the form of the Lewis And Clark Exposition and Oriental Fair of 1905. Ostensibly created to celebrate the centenary of the great explorers, the exposition had origins of a more mundane nature. Seattle, that coarse and wicked settlement to the north, was fast approaching Portland in population. What could be done to avert such a catastrophe, which is to say Seattle passing Portland in the census and thus becoming the Northwest's principal city? Why not, the boosters argued, hold a great fair in Portland to which all the world would come and, overwhelmed by paradise, would settle and invest in. The people in general, however, showed little interest in playing host to strangers. "Indifference, inertia, self-sufficiency, the wish to be alone," thundered the editor of the *Oregonian* in exasperation at his complacent fellow citizens.

But in time the boosters prevailed and the fair opened to reveal "a scene of unparrelled splendor," particularly with all its roses and its thousands of electric lights: Eden up to date.

And indeed the fair was a colossal success and in its success prefigured aspects of Oregon's course for the coming quarter century. Despite an occasional "squeeze," as recessions were then called, the economy prospered. The vast wheat lands of the Columbia Basin made Portland one of the major grain ports in the world. Also the depletion at this time of eastern forests, combined with Oregon's enormous stands of virgin timber, as well as the rails, rivers, and developing roads to harvest and ship the timber, made lumbering Oregon's major industry. Finally the cattle and sheep ranches of the High Country were now fully established and contributed significantly to the economy.

The distribution center for this economy of timber, wheat, and cattle was Portland with its stockyards and flour mills, its harbor crowded with ships loading wheat and lumber. All this, of course, contributed greatly to Portland's growth. In 1900 it had been a good-sized town of 90,000. By 1910 it was a city of almost a quarter of a million.

Portland was not alone in its growth, for urbanization—facilitated by the railroads and Oregon's Good Roads movement ("Get Oregon Out of the Mud!")—had increased the population of many Oregon towns, making them important centers of economic, political, and cultural life, whether they lay in the Valley, at the coast, or in the High Country. In Judge Deady's last years 73 percent of Oregon's population lived in the country. By 1910 almost half the population lived in towns and cities.

The dynamism of the period with its expanding economy and population shifts was reflected as well in another area: reform. The reform movement, though cresting now in the first quarter of the century, had its beginnings in the 1870s with the protests of farmers (through the Oregon Grange) over the high freight rates imposed by the railroads. Initially the Grange was defeated due to the corrupt alliance between the railroads and government. In time, however, the protest movement broadened to include businessmen as well as farmers and in addition gained strength by allying with a new political party, the Populists. With the election of the colorful Populist, Sylvestor Pennoyer, to the governorship in 1886 (he who wired President Cleveland to mind his own business), reform achieved a significant victory. With the appearance of William S. U'Ren and his Direct Legislation League in 1898, political corruption was finally at bay.

It was U'Ren and his supporters who in the first years of the century enacted the then-famous and later much-emulated Oregon System: the initiative and referendum in 1902; the direct primary in 1904; a corrupt practices act in 1908, following the conviction of Oregon's long-time Republican senator, John H. Mitchell, for both bigamy and bribery; and the recall in 1910.

There was also reform in the societal sphere, particularly with respect to women. In 1912 women's suffrage was finally secured in the constitution. In the same year, in an attempt to suppress prostitution, the Portland Ministerial Association published a vice report which asserted that in every downtown Portland block there was an average of three brothels or hotels and rooming houses welcoming short-time guests. A far more successful reform, however, occurred the following year when the legislature enacted the nation's first effective minimum-wage and maximum-hour law for women.

A generally thriving economy and a reform movement touching many aspects of Oregon life might suggest that this first quarter of the twentieth century in Oregon was a golden age. Not quite, for the gold was shot through with the base metal of bigotry. It is an old and recurring element in the otherwise equitable character of Oregon society, beginning with our treatment of the Native Oregonians. At about the same time the territorial legislature enacted a law prohibiting the immigration of blacks to Oregon. In the following decade the Know Nothings, a political party that would have denied citizenship to all foreign-born Americans, gained considerable support. The 1870s saw the first of the anti-Chinese riots, occurring again and more seriously in the 1890s. It was in the 1890s, too, that the *Oregonian Handbook* was gratified to report that "The beauty of the city and the purity of its municipal government are not marred by the debasing influence of foreign paupers."

Anti-foreign sentiment continued into the twentieth century, particularly with respect to Asians. World War I shifted the focus to persons of German descent (German street names were changed to the names of presidents and flowers) and to those opposed to the war such as the Portland librarian who as a Quaker refused to buy war bonds and was drummed from her position. Socialists who publicly opposed the war, Dr. Marie Equi and Floyd Ramp, among others, were simply jailed.

The intolerance of the war years extended into the next decade as well. The Portland Police Department created a" Red Squad" that in its enthusiasm tended on occasion to overlook the law. Also, anti-Japanese sentiment surfaced in Klamath Falls, Redmond, and Hood River while in Portland the flaming crosses of the Ku Klux Klan flared from the eastside buttes. In the end, discriminatory legislation was passed during this prosperous decade which effected both Orientals and Roman Catholics. It was an unlovely combination, the bigotry and boom.

It might be said of this period, as Dickens said of another, that "it was the best of times and the worst of times." Todd Peterson and Jack Collins in "Years of Growth: 1893 –1927" hold a mirror to the time, reflecting its many aspects and thus a mirror both clear and clouded.

Together with profiles of Charles Bellinger, Charles Wolverton, and Robert Bean, the three judges who span the period, the authors summarize the considerable expansion in the federal court's jurisdiction and the "new and broader segments of society now affected by its rulings." As illustrative of the above, the authors review the extraordinary variety of cases that came before the court—many concerned with attempts by railroads and others to defraud the government of its public lands. Other cases responded to the issues raised by the new food and drug and antitrust legislation. Perhaps the most controversial was the litigation surrounding those laws devised to address the social issues of the day: Asian immigration, the Mann Act, the Sedition Act, and Prohibition.

Peterson and Collins end their story with an examination of the Oregon Legislature's Compulsory School Bill of 1922, which denied parents the right to send their children to private schools (legislation sponsored by the Ku Klux Klan and aimed at Catholic education). No public act better reflects the bigotry of the period. However, when the matter came before the court, Judge Wolverton "found that the schools and parents…had constitutional rights protected by the Fourteenth Amendment," and thus did that other aspect of this period, the fairness reflected in the spirit of reform, prevail.

The lighter aspects of the 1920s—its prosperity, aplomb, and vivacity— fell with the 1929 fall of the stock market. Oregon, with the rest of the country, entered the Great Depression. "Oregon is dead broke," Governor Julius Meier pronounced in 1934, with a succinctness and candor rare in present-day political discourse.

Though various New Deal policies and the construction of Bonneville Dam in 1938 did prove partial panaceas, true economic recovery did not occur until World War II. As in World War I, shipbuilding, lumber (Oregon now the major lumber-producing state in the nation), and food production were greatly stimulated. Now, too, an important, new industry—aluminum— came to Oregon.

There was also an important change in the character of the state's population, a change that had begun in the 1930s with migrants from the dustbowl states and the South. Now in the 1940s, 160,000 out-of-state workers were drawn to the war-time industries. Many of these workers were black, giving to the state for the first time a black population of significant proportion. Likewise changing conditions in food production and harvesting offered jobs to Spanish-speaking migrants, many of whom settled as well. In the 1950s significant migration from the East began, which increased in the 1960s and 1970s. The following decade saw the arrival, in large numbers, of Southeast Asians. Thus has the state's old homogeneity been diversified and enriched.

Another significant change in the state came with post-war highway construction. On the one hand, urban centers were radically affected by the proliferation of suburbs. On the other hand, small-town Oregon began to go into decline, for now it was often no more than a half-hour drive to the malls and professional services of the larger towns.

Randall Kester, in "A Time of Change: 1927–1950," reviews the increased purview of the court during this period, as reflected in the addition of judges and the building in 1933 of a new and larger courthouse. After profiles of the judges of the period—James Alger Fee, John H. McNary, Claude McColloch, Gus J. Solomon, and Bankruptcy Judge Estes Snedecor—Kester examines the major issues the court confronted.

Kester first deals with the new Federal Rules of Civil Procedure, which took effect in 1938, and examines several cases affected by the rules. He next scrutinizes cases stemming from the Great Depression—bankruptcies, for example, and cases consequent on such New Deal legislation as the National Industrial Recovery Act and the Agricultural Adjustment Act.

World War II also created a number of new issues calling for the court's attention: the Selective Service Act and draft evasion, violations of the economic regulations of the Office of Price Administration, and the Japanese Exclusion Orders.

The remainder of Kester's study is devoted to a review of the court's other significant cases in a variety of areas: probate, admiralty, and antitrust, to name a few. The chapter ends with a tribute to Judge Fee, the period's "dominant figure from the standpoint of both the force of his personality and his contribution to the jurisprudence of the court."

Any object held in close proximity to the eyes cannot be clearly seen. The same holds true for the recent past. Still some events and developments do penetrate the blur. It may be, of course, that in the future these happenings will be considered inconsequential, whereas others barely glimpsed—if seen at all—will be judged of the greatest significance. Bearing these reservations in mind, certain developments during the 41 years covered by Laurie Mapes' concluding chapter seem important, albeit from the fallible vantage point of *now*.

As noted earlier, the 1960s and 70s saw a large influx of easterners to Oregon. These newcomers brought with them an energy which, from the beginning, outside commentators on the Oregon scene have found rather lacking in the Oregon character. Also, this new ingredient in the population—together with the continued residency of many 1940s war workers—appears to explain the ascendance of the Democratic party in the state after nearly a century of Republican rule.

Another important development in these years was an increasing concern with the environment. From the time of the pioneers, the majority of people coming to Oregon have been "Eden seekers," to use the late Malcolm Clark's instructive phrase. For most of the state's history, Oregonians were simply content to appreciate their environment. In this period they also became its protectors, for two reasons. First, increases in population and development began to blemish and diminish the natural environment. Second, Oregon had become primarily an urban community (nearly 70 percent of the population living in cities and towns), and urbanites, denied the pleasures of the natural environment in their everyday lives, tended to give it a special importance—which may account for the fact that today so many environmentalists are city dwellers.

Whatever the reasons, the above mentioned or others, this concern for the environment led to strong measures for its protection. As Oregon at the beginning of the century led the nation with the Oregon System of legislative reform, so in the area of environmental protection it now took the lead with such citizen-supported measures as the Scenic Rivers Act, the Beach Bill, the ban on aerosol sprays, the Bottle Bill, and a bill establishing a Land Conservation and Development Commission.

The beauty of Oregon's natural environment has led to two other developments as well. One is the establishment in the state of the electronics industry, considered to be relatively harmless to the environment. But the most significant addition by far is tourism.

Tourism has its roots in the enormous increase in the private ownership of automobiles following World War II, the consequent upsurge in highway construction and improvement, and the now-common provision for two-and three-week paid vacations. These changes, together with a natural environment worth traveling to see, have made tourism the state's second largest source of revenue.

As might be expected, tourism, as well as recreation, has had effects on regions of eastern Oregon and the coast. The coast, for so long inaccessible (there was no serviceable road to the north coast and no highway along the coast itself until the 1930s) now benefits from an extensive resort economy. As for the High Country and in particular the Deschutes region—called by a pioneer "a barren and God-forsaken place—this region is now described in the weather reports and travel brochures as the Central Oregon playground!"

These then, from the blurred perspective of the present, would seem to be some of the noteworthy developments in Oregon's recent past. There were too, of course, as in the nation as a whole, profound societal changes. Perhaps no area illustrates these changes better than Oregon's federal court and the multiplicity of vexing issues with which it was confronted in these agitated years of 1950 to 1991.

Laurie Bennett Mapes begins her study of these years with a general statement on the growth of the court, as signalized by the fact that by the end of the period six judges sat on the ever-lengthening federal bench. Like the preceding authors, she profiles all the judges who served during the period, 14 in all. She also surveys the procedural matters dealt with by the court—class action suits and sentencing practices, for example, and the great part played by Judge Solomon in streamlining court procedures.

Mapes next goes on to the bewildering number, variety, and complexity of the cases heard by the court. In environmental matters there were suits over herbicides, dams, timber lands, and the Mt. Hood Freeway. In the criminal area, drug violations and the often associated bank robberies greatly increased the number of cases. Added to these were cases involving race and gender discrimination, prisoners' rights, Indian fishing rights, product liability, abortion, and, with Vietnam, draft and freedom-of-expression cases. And then, as if the judicial plate were not piled high enough, who should appear in the courtroom but the be-turbaned figure of the Bhagwan Shree Rajneesh!

In reviewing these cases, Mapes points out that in many of them the judges were obliged to master all manner of technical information in order to reach their decisions and, having reached them, found themselves acting as managers in various areas—the prisons, forests, and fisheries, for example.

The layperson reading Mapes' summaries of these cases cannot help but wonder how the court refrained from throwing up its hands and crying out with St. Augustine, "Oh God, we are lost among the multiplicity of things." And in view of the constantly increasing load, it would be most understandable if the court had resorted to the eighteenth-century American custom of the "busk." At a busk a whole community would turn out to build a great bonfire, throw upon it everything they found encumbering (including the legal codes), and then dance about the fire, rejoicing in their lightened load.

Yet somehow the court kept its collective head and prevailed, for as Mapes writes, "The judges who served in the district of Oregon between 1950 and 1991 met these demands admirably and were known for their hard work and diligence. In the federal system, Oregon was considered a strong district with good administration."

It is now two centuries since American law first came to the Oregon Country, crossing the bar with Captain Gray into the Great River of the West; nearly a century and a half since President Polk appointed the first three judges to the Oregon territorial court; and somewhat less than that since Oregon achieved statehood and Matthew Deady became the judge of the U.S. District Court for Oregon. A commentator qualified—as this writer is not—to do a true critique of the U.S. District Court for Oregon and its predecessor, the Oregon territorial court, would probably find that on occasion the scales of Justice have dipped. Nonetheless, it would seem from a reading of the instructive and cogent studies in this book that, by and large, the hands that held the scales were steady, kept the pans in balance, and accomplished that "first duty" of society so vital to all of us.

## CHAPTER 1

∾

# OREGON'S FIRST FEDERAL COURTS 1849–1859

By CAROLINE P. STOEL

*A* mericans had lived in the Oregon Country for more than *two decades before they were able to count on the protection of laws enjoyed by their countrymen in states and territories to the east. During those years they existed in a kind of no-man's land, a place where citizens of different nationalities lived alongside the Indians, without formal government or law. It was not until after Oregon officially became a territory that a system of courts was established, charged with the administration of both federal and local laws.*

*In the early years of the territorial courts, justice depended on men who followed the westward trail for various reasons—some for profit and adventure, others to establish homes and settle down. Then, as today, a federal judgeship was a prestigious position and most of the appointees were well trained by the standards of the day. Even so, some proved to be unsuited to the role of pioneer judge and to be unreliable dispensers of justice.*

*A mixture of national and frontier politics, of integrity and occasional greed makes up the story of Oregon's early federal courts. It is, however, a story that led finally to a system of justice based on the same principles that ruled the courts throughout the nation.*

∾
# HISTORICAL BACKGROUND

At the beginning of the nineteenth century, four nations—the United States, Great Britain, Spain, and Russia—were competing for territorial and trading rights in the Pacific Northwest, in what was known as the Oregon Country. By 1825 Spain and Russia had retired from the competition, leaving the United States and Great Britain to vie for a vast territory that stretched from the summit of the Rocky Mountains to the Pacific Ocean, and from approximately 42º to 54º 40' north latitude. Both nations based their claims on early exploration and on settlement.

Great Britain's claims rested chiefly on the explorations of Captain George Vancouver (1792), Alexander McKenzie (1789-95), Simon Fraser (1806-08), and David Thompson (1807-12), and upon the enterprises of the Hudson's Bay Company and its predecessor, the North West Company. The establishment in 1824 of the Hudson's Bay Company headquarters west of the Rockies at Fort Vancouver (present-day Vancouver, Washington), with Dr. John McLoughlin as its chief factor, gave the British a strong claim based on actual occupation at a time when there were virtually no American residents in the entire area.[1]

Early records indicate that by 1841 the population of Fort Vancouver was between 700 and 800 inhabitants, including Indians. Great Britain, however, was primarily interested in the fur trade, and permanent settlement by the company's employees was discouraged. In spite of this policy, in the early 1830s retired employees who had married native women began to take up land in an area near Champoeg, known as French Prairie, where a group of independent French-Canadian trappers were farming.

The claims of the United States were based to a large extent on Robert Gray's discovery and exploration of the Columbia River (1792), on the Lewis and Clark expedition to the Northwest (1804-06), and on the activities of the Pacific Fur Company, whose founder, John Jacob Astor, established a trading post at Astoria at the mouth of the Columbia (1811). After the Louisiana Purchase (1803) the United States also relied on the principle of contiguity to support western expansion.[2]

The presence of agricultural settlements in the Willamette Valley strengthened American claims. As the fur trade collapsed, independent American trappers and hunters began to cultivate the land, and missionaries, who came to convert the Indians, stayed and became important figures in early Oregon government and politics. During the 1830s these settlements were small. It has been estimated that in 1841 there were only 137 Americans and 63 French Canadians living in the Willamette Valley, including women and children.[3]

American colonization began in earnest when the first typical wagon train of settlers to the Pacific Northwest arrived in 1842 under the guidance of Elijah White. The number of immigrants increased so rapidly during the following three years that by the summer of 1845, the white population south of the Columbia River was estimated at more than 2,000. When the international boundary line was established in 1846, between 8,000 and 9,000 people, excluding Indians, lived in the whole of the Oregon Country, and of those, two thirds were located in the Willamette Valley.[4]

Despite the rapidly growing population and the settlers' frequent petitions, the United States government was slow to establish authority over the area. Many in Congress thought it was too remote and not worth the anticipated problems of administration and defense. Furthermore, territorial status could hardly be seriously debated until the border between the United States and British Canada was settled.

Under the terms of the Joint Occupation Agreement, entered into on October 20, 1818, the border east of the Rocky Mountains had been established at the 49th parallel, but it was agreed that no decision on the border west of the Rockies would be made for a period of ten years. During that time the country was to remain "free and open" to exploration, trade, and settlement by both nations. In 1827 this agreement was renewed for an indefinite period and by the 1840s, when American settlers began clamoring for laws and clear title to the land they were farming, there was still no definite boundary.

Fortunately, although the region lacked a formal government, it had never been subject to widespread disorder and lawlessness. The small population lived in groups whose leaders exercised considerable control over their conduct and activities, and the Indians, particularly those in the Willamette Valley whose population had been greatly reduced by disease, posed no serious threats to the white settlers. Thus, not much thought was given to organizing a government until the large influx of settlers in the mid-1840s.[5]

## McLoughlin As Lawmaker and Judge

More than any other individual, John McLoughlin, chief factor of the

*John McLoughlin, chief factor of the British Hudson's Bay Company's Department of the Columbia, maintained law and order in the Oregon Country from 1825 to 1843. (Oregon Historical Society Negative #ORHI248)*

British Hudson's Bay Company's Department of the Columbia, was responsible for the unusual measure of law and order that prevailed in the Oregon Country from 1825 until the establishment of the Provisional Government in 1843.

The Hudson's Bay Company occupied a unique place in the early development of the Northwest. It was a self-governing organization, operating under a license from the British government, with exclusive rights to trade with the Indians within its allotted territory. The company's Department of the Columbia extended from the Russian settlements in the north to the Spanish claims in the south, and from the Rockies to the Pacific. As chief factor of this vast domain, McLoughlin, from the Fort Vancouver headquarters, was responsible for the administration of the company's business and for the conduct of its employees, over whom he had limited civil and criminal jurisdiction. An act of Parliament of July 1821 had extended the laws of Upper Canada to British subjects residing in the Oregon Country, and justices of the peace had been appointed for the area.

By the judicious exercise of his powers, McLoughlin firmly established his authority throughout the area, often over those who were not strictly subject to his jurisdiction as well as those who were. Because the Hudson's Bay Company was the chief source of goods and supplies, he was able to exert considerable economic pressure in addition to moral persuasion to maintain order and settle disputes. This he did with aplomb. His firm, even-handed treatment of the Indians earned their respect, and his influence among the French Canadians, most of whom were former company employees, was always strong. Even the American settlers, who resented him as British and Catholic, credited his generosity and fairness. As a result, in spite of the fact that he had no legal authority over the Americans,

McLoughlin was frequently able to resolve disputes with them and sometimes among them.

## The Provisional Government

As the number of settlers in the Willamette Valley increased, the
Americans became more and more dissatisfied with their status, insisting
that some form of government was necessary for civil and military protection.[6] Above all, they wanted assurance their land claims would be protected. Furthermore, many resented McLoughlin's authority and the
British presence he represented. In an attempt to solve these problems,
the settlers considered two proposals: one for an independent state, and
the other for a provisional or temporary government that would function
only until the boundary line was settled and Oregon became a territory.
At a meeting at Champoeg on May 2, 1843, by a narrow vote, a move to
organize a provisional government was approved. Those supporting
organization were primarily Americans, joined by a few French
Canadians, while the rest of the Canadians present opposed the proposal.
By no means all of the settlers attended, and while the record is not clear,
there may have been some present who did not vote. The Hudson's Bay
Company officials, including McLoughlin, did not actively participate in
the meeting, but it was well known that company policy opposed any
organization set up in anticipation of United States control. In July 1843
the Provisional Government was formed and basic laws adopted. These
original laws were extensively amended in 1845.[7]

The Organic Law contained a bill of rights for the protection of civil
liberties, prohibited slavery, and mandated humane treatment of Indians.
The statutes of Iowa Territory were adopted as the law to be applied in
civil, military, and criminal cases, and where no statute was applicable,
principles of common law and equity were to govern. Of primary importance to the settlers, however, was the section relating to land claims.
Under this provision "any person now holding or hereafter wishing to
establish a claim to land in this territory" was required to mark the
boundaries of his claim and record it within 20 days. Within six months
of recording a claim, the claimant had to make permanent improvements
on the land, and within a year, become an occupant. Old settlers already
in possession of land were allowed one year from the passage of the act to
file a description of their claims in the recorder's office. Claims were limited to 640 acres per person.[8]

5

## The Territory of Oregon

On June 15, 1846, the "Oregon question" was finally settled when the United States ratified an agreement with the British government setting the international boundary west of the Rockies at the 49th parallel—with the exception of Vancouver Island, which was to be part of British Canada. The treaty further provided that the Hudson's Bay Company should have navigation rights on the Columbia River south of the line and that its posts and lands in the United States territory should be protected.

The border settlement meant that the United States now had the authority to extend its jurisdiction over the Oregon Country. But Congress was not to be hurried, and for two years the settlers fretted while the matter was being considered. Finally, on August 14, 1848, Congress passed "An Act to Establish the Territorial Government of Oregon".[9] Its boundaries included "all that part of the territory of the United States which lies west of the summit of the Rocky mountains and north of the forty-second degree of north latitude." This extensive area covered the present states of Oregon, Washington, Idaho, and parts of Montana and Utah.

**Territorial Government.** A territory of the United States is a hybrid governmental form, with characteristics of both state and federal government. Its executive officers and its judges are appointed by the president; its laws may be enacted either by Congress or by the state legislature (depending on the method chosen), although the ultimate legislative authority is the Congress. Its courts are a part of the federal court system, but unlike other federal courts they perform all the functions of state courts as well. The fundamental law of the Oregon Territory included the Oregon Territorial Act, the Northwest Ordinance, and the United States Constitution. In addition Congress passed several acts relating to public lands in Oregon, notably the Oregon Donation Act of 1850, amended in 1853 and 1854.

The Northwest Ordinance,[10] enacted July 13, 1787, and amended in 1789 to conform to the recently ratified United States Constitution, was the basic law of all territories northwest of the Ohio River; Section 14 of the Oregon Territorial Act specifically extended that law to Oregon. Article II of the ordinance guaranteed freedom of religion, basic civil liberties, proportionate representation and judicial proceedings according to the course of the common law. Article VI forbade involuntary servitude or slavery. Because Congress was unwilling to delegate to territorial legislatures control of federal lands, it denied the legislature power "to interfere with the primary disposal of the soil,…to tax lands of the United States…(and) to interfere with the claims to land within the territory." (Article IV)

**Legislative Power and Laws.** The power to legislate for the territories is specifically given to Congress by the United States Constitution.[11] Congress may exercise this power by directly enacting statutes or, more commonly, by delegating to the territorial legislature the power to pass laws, subject to Congressional disapproval. Section 4 of the Oregon Territorial Act provided that the legislative power should be vested in the territorial legislative assembly, and section 6 applied that power to "all rightful subjects of legislation not inconsistent with the constitution and laws of the United States."

Under the Territorial Act the laws of the Provisional Government were to continue in effect except where incompatible with the United States Constitution, but they could be modified or repealed by the territorial legislature. In accordance with the Northwest Ordinance, however, those laws of the provisional government which related to land claims or grants were declared null and void. Thus, the claims of settlers were still in limbo.

At long last, on September 27, 1850, the eagerly awaited Congressional Act validating Oregon land holdings became effective.[12] It granted 320 acres of land to all white settlers or occupants of the public lands, including American halfbreed Indians, who were above the age of 18 years and citizens of the United States and who had "resided upon and cultivated the same for four consecutive years." Even those who declared an intention to become a citizen before December 1, 1851, were eligible. A married man could claim one section or 640 acres, half of it to be held by his wife "in her own right." Interestingly, the term "single man" was interpreted later to include an unmarried woman.[13]

**Territorial Courts.** As has been indicated, courts of the territories occupy an anomalous position. While the other federal courts are established under the authority of Article III of the United States Constitution, the territorial courts owe their existence to an act of Congress. Hence they are properly described as legislative rather than constitutional courts.[14] Although they administer both federal and local law, these courts are not governed by federal rules of procedure but by rules enacted by local legisla-

7

tures. Such rules are subject to congressional disapproval and must be consistent with the U.S. Constitution and statutes. The same basic procedure is followed whether a case arises under federal or state law.

The Oregon Territorial Act provided for a system of courts similar to that established in other territories. The judicial power was vested in a supreme court, district courts, probate courts, and justices of the peace. The supreme court consisted of a chief justice and two associates, any two of whom constituted a quorum. In addition to his duties as a supreme court justice, each of the judges presided over one of the three judicial districts into which the territory was divided. From the district courts an appeal went to the territorial supreme court. Appeals were allowed to the United States Supreme Court "in the same manner as from the circuit courts of the United States," where the value of the property or the amount in controversy exceeded $2,000. The act provided that each of the district courts "shall have and exercise the same jurisdiction in all cases arising under the constitution and laws of the United States, as is vested in the circuit and district courts of the United States, and also of all cases arising under the laws of the said territory, and otherwise." [15]

Territorial judges were appointed by the president of the United States, and at the time Oregon became a territory, the term of office was four years, replacing the earlier tenure of "during good behavior". The change made it possible for the president to get rid of an unsatisfactory judge by not reappointing him. The judges, who were given their posts primarily for political reasons, usually came from outside the territory and, as was true of many territorial appointees, they were often regarded as interlopers by the local bar and citizenry. In turn, some of the judges considered their appointments solely an opportunity for political and financial gain and showed little interest in performing their duties in a responsible manner. The judicial careers of the judges of the Oregon Territory, examined briefly below, clearly illustrate this point.

∾

# THE JUDICIARY OF
# THE OREGON TERRITORY

On August 14, 1848, President James K. Polk appointed three judges to the Oregon territorial court: William P. Bryant, chief justice, and Peter H. Burnett and James Turney, associates. Of the three, only Bryant accepted

8

the commission. William A. Hall, appointed shortly thereafter, also declined. The court roster was not complete until Orville G. Pratt, a Polk appointee, and William Strong, appointed by President Zachary Taylor, received their commissions in the fall of 1849. Governor Joseph Lane declared the territorial government established on March 4, 1849, and in April the courts of the provisional government were officially replaced by those of the territory.

For the first two years—from March 1849 until April 1851—the attendance record of these pioneer judges was so erratic that not more than one of them was present for 18 of the 25 months. That one judge was responsible for hearing all cases at the district level and for administering the court system. It was also his duty to hear appeals, but this he could not do since two judges were required to convene the supreme court. Two judges were present for only seven months during the entire period, and at no time were all three in residence. It is no wonder that a memorial was sent to the president by a group from Portland, protesting the judges' failure to hold court and to discharge their other duties. The situation was somewhat relieved with the arrival of Thomas Nelson, whom President Fillmore had appointed to replace Bryant. Although there was now a full bench, the judges' failure to act in a responsible and mature manner continued to impede the court's work.

## The First Four Judges

A brief examination of the lives and careers of the territorial judges tells us much about life, law, and politics on the frontier.

**William P. Bryant.** The first chief justice of the Oregon Territory was William P. Bryant, about whom almost nothing complimentary has been written.[16] He was born in Mercer, Kentucky, August 3, 1806, and raised as a Shaker. Having no fondness for Shaker customs, he moved from his father's home first to Lancaster, Kentucky, and then to Rockville, Indiana, where he began to practice law in 1825 and embarked on an undistinguished career as a state legislator and local judge. In 1840, because his law partner, General Tilghman A. Howard, was running for governor on the Democratic ticket, Bryant switched his allegiance to that party. In August 1848, as a reward for supporting Polk's successful 1844 campaign for the presidency, Bryant was appointed chief justice of the Oregon court. In Oregon he joined another Indianan, General Joseph Lane, the recently appointed territorial governor.

Although Bryant was expected to serve the normal four-year term, he was in Oregon for less than seven months. He did not arrive until April 9, 1849, and departed in October of that year, having held only one term of court in his district, one term of the supreme court, and one special term. On August 20 Bryant opened court at Oregon City in the most populous first district, which included Clackamas, Champoeg,[17] and Linn counties. It was a short session and apparently only routine business was considered. One thing Bryant failed to do was resolve McLoughlin's disputed land claim at Willamette Falls in which the judge himself had acquired an interest. After discussing the matter with Bryant, McLoughlin furnished the court a complete description of the claim, but nothing had been decided when the session ended on August 22.

On August 30, 1849, the sole session of the supreme court was convened in Oregon City for only one day, with Bryant and Associate Justice Orville Pratt sitting as judges. The chief activity of that brief session seems to have been the delivery of an oral opinion in a case that had been transferred from the supreme court of the provisional government.

The only other court Bryant held was a special session at Steilacoom (now in the state of Washington) in the third judicial district, to which no judge had been assigned. There he heard the trial of six Snoqualamie Indians for murder. According to his report to Lane of October 10, 1849, four were found not guilty by the jury, two were convicted and hanged.

Bryant left Oregon apparently expecting to return. We next hear of him testifying against McLoughlin before Congress in connection with the donation land law bill. Even though ill health and personal problems kept him from resuming his duties in Oregon, he did not resign from the court until October 1850, a full year after his departure. He returned to Indiana and served one term there as circuit judge from October 1852 until November 1858. When his try for a second term failed, he resumed his law practice in Rockville, where he died on October 10, 1864, at the age of 58.

**Orville C. Pratt.** Judge Pratt arrived in Oregon in January 1849, several months before Chief Justice Bryant and Governor Lane. He was born in Rushville, New York, and received his education in New York schools and at West Point, where he was enrolled for two years. After practicing law in Albany and Rochester from 1841 until 1843, he decided to move west to try his fortune. While in Illinois he became involved in Democratic politics, leading to his appointment by President James

Polk on November 22, 1848, to the Oregon territorial court.

When Pratt discovered how much higher prices were in the west than in the east, he determined to find ways to supplement his meager territorial judge's salary of $2,000. His first venture took him to San Francisco, where he bought articles that were in short supply in Oregon. He then chartered a vessel to bring the merchandise to Portland and resold it for a handsome profit of some $40,000! Next he bought lumber being loaded in Portland for $20 per thousand feet and sailed with it to San Francisco. Almost as soon as he arrived, he was offered $250 per thousand feet for the shipment. However, believing he could do better, he refused this offer and a little later sold it for $400 per thousand, adding another $40,000 to his profits.[18] Throughout his career as judge and lawyer Pratt continued to add to his wealth in this fashion, eventually becoming a millionaire. Today it would be considered unethical for a judge to be so actively involved in business affairs, but the standards of judicial conduct on the frontier were much more lax.

Pratt was assigned to the second district, which contained the counties of Benton, Polk, Yamhill, and Tualatin (or Tuality).[19] However, from October 1849, when Bryant departed, until just prior to the arrival of Judge William Strong in August 1850, Pratt was the sole judge in the territory and as such had to sit in all districts.[20] From May 13 to May 25, he presided over the court in Bryant's first district at Oregon City, where he conducted one of the most important trials of the territorial period—that of five Cayuse Indians accused of the murder of Marcus and Narcissa Whitman and other members of their mission.

As a judge, Pratt conducted himself in a dignified manner, commanding respect and praise. Matthew P. Deady, later a territorial judge and the first United States district court judge, made his debut as an Oregon attorney in Pratt's court at Lafayette. He had this to say of the occasion:

> The court was held in a large unoccupied room in Jacob Hawn's tavern. The bench and furniture was improvised for the occasion. But the dignity of the court…would not suffer from a comparison with Westminister Hall.[21]

Had Pratt not let himself become involved in partisan advocacy in what is known as the Location Case, he would be remembered as an honest judge who understood and administered the law with considerable ability. Instead he sabotaged his judicial career by openly supporting the Democratic party machine, the "Salem clique," with such passion that any objective solution to the problem of whether the territorial capital should be located at Oregon City or Salem became impossible. The result of his uncompromising position and of his animosity toward fellow judges Thomas Nelson and William Strong was that the work of both the supreme court and the legislature came to a virtual halt during the last two years of his tenure.

Pratt's term expired officially on December 18, 1852, but because Charles Train refused the appointment as his successor, he continued on the bench until the inauguration of President Franklin Pierce. Pratt was elated when in April 1853 Pierce appointed him chief justice of the court, particularly since neither Nelson nor Strong was reappointed. His elation changed quickly to disappointment, however, when he was charged with corruption and the appointment was withdrawn.[22] Complaining bitterly at the unfairness of the charges, Pratt tried to rehabilitate himself in Oregon. His efforts failed, however, and he moved to California in June 1856, where he finished his long career as lawyer and judge. He died in 1891 at the age of 72.

**William Strong.** Judge William Strong was appointed to the territorial court by President Zachary Taylor in September 1849. He and newly appointed Governor John P. Gaines arrived in Oregon in August 1850 after a long, arduous journey with their families from the east coast around Cape Horn to San Francisco and then up the Pacific coast to Astoria. When they learned it would be at least three weeks before transportation to Oregon City would be available, Governor Gaines sent an Indian messenger by canoe to notify Chief Factor Peter Skene Ogden of the Hudson's Bay Company at Fort Vancouver of their predicament. Ogden promptly dispatched a large bateau to the rescue, and in due course the group arrived safely at Oregon City. Such was Judge Strong's introduction to Oregon.[23]

Strong, one of seven sons of a Presbyterian minister, was born in Vermont in 1817, though he lived most of his early life in New York state. A graduate of Yale University, he studied law at Ithaca, New York, and was practicing in Cleveland, Ohio, when he learned of his appointment to the territorial court. Shortly before Strong's arrival, Pratt had left for the east, and as Judge Bryant had been gone since the preceeding October, again only one judge was present for several months.[24]

Strong had been assigned to the third district, which until now had had no judge. By far the most extensive, the third district included Clatsop County and all of the country that now comprises the states of

William P. Bryant

Orville C. Pratt

William Strong

Thomas Nelson

*The first four judges were William P. Bryant and Orville C. Pratt, appointed by President James K. Polk; William Strong, appointed by Zachary Taylor; and Thomas Nelson, appointed by Millard Fillmore. Erratic attendance and failure to act in a responsible manner impeded the court's effectiveness during this period (1848 to 1853). (Oregon Historical Society Negatives #ORHI37489, #9176, #ORHI63248, and #ORHI37492)*

Washington, Idaho, and Montana north of the 46th parallel and west of the Rockies. The enormous area north of the Columbia River was divided into two counties, Vancouver and Lewis, with a total population of only 1,049 in 1850.[25]

Courts were held at Vancouver and at the headwaters of the Cowlitz River in Lewis County. Strong wrote that the thirty-mile trip up the Cowlitz took five days in a Hudson's Bay Company boat manned by a "good Indian crew," while the return trip in a canoe with two Indians took only five hours.[26] It is apparent from his writings that Strong enjoyed the wilderness and the rugged journeys. He settled in Cathlamet (later in Washington state), which has been described as "one of the loneliest places on earth."[27]

Strong held court in all of the districts during his tenure, but apparently did not find the work intellectually challenging.

*The principal business of the courts was not largely of a commercial character....There were a good many homicides...most of them arose from disputes about land under the donation land law. There were also some cases of assault....*[28]

As a supreme court justice, Strong was involved with Pratt and Chief Justice Nelson in the Location Law controversy. His position was considerably more objective than Pratt's, but nonetheless his judgeship was tainted by the dispute.

From experience, Strong knew that the third judicial district, though sparsely populated, was an area too vast for one judge to administer properly. He led a successful movement to separate the portion north of the Columbia River from the rest of the Oregon Territory and on March 2, 1853, Congress passed an act establishing the Territory of Washington. Five years later Strong was appointed to its supreme court, where he served as associate justice for three years. After his term expired in 1861, he moved to Portland to practice law. There he attracted a number of important clients, among them the Oregon Steam Navigation Company, the largest business organization in the Pacific Northwest at the time.[29] Judge Strong died in 1887, leaving four sons and two daughters, several of whom were prominent in Oregon affairs for years to come.

*Strong was scholar, lawyer, jurist, codifier, legislator and soldier. He was mediocre in none of these fields and he excelled in most of them. As a lawyer he stood among the leaders of his profession.... But it was in the role of pioneer judge that he made his greatest contribution.*[30]

**Thomas Nelson.** Judge Thomas Nelson has been described as "a man of substance in worldly goods, in mental attainments, in professional ability.... "[31] Indeed, he was a man of many talents: a Latin scholar who was conversant in French and versed in history, English literature, and anatomy. Born in Peekskill, New York, in January 1817 and graduated from Williams College, he spent most of his life in New York City, where he practiced law, first in partnership with his father and finally with his son 67 years later.

This long residency in New York was interrupted for a brief two-year interval when he came to Oregon to serve as chief justice of the territorial court, having been appointed by President Fillmore in January 1851 to fill Chief Justice William Bryant's unexpired term. He arrived in Oregon City in April to complete the supreme court bench of three judges. Nelson sat as trial judge in the first district—the counties of Clackamas, Marion, and Linn.

His decisions reflected the prevailing attitudes of the time. In a case heard at Oregon City in July 1851, he held that the testimony of Indians against whites was inadmissible except in cases involving the sale of liquor to Indians.[32] Racial issues were involved in two other cases coming before him and again he took a racist stance.

In *Magruder v. Vanderpool*, Theophilus Magruder filed a complaint in Nelson's court demanding that Jacob Vanderpool, a mulatto living in Oregon City, be forced to leave the territory. Vanderpool asserted that a 1849 territorial exclusion law forbidding blacks or mulattoes to settle in Oregon violated both the federal Constitution and the Northwest Ordinance. In his decision, Nelson upheld the statute and ordered the defendant to leave the territory within 30 days.[33] In the case of *Holmes v. Ford*, Nelson avoided making a decision in a case that involved one of the burning issues of the day: whether or not slaveholders could carry their slaves into the territories and hold them there as property. Instead, he procrastinated until his term of office expired, leaving the burden of deciding the case to his successor, Chief Justice George Williams. In avoiding the issue, Nelson may have been torn between making an unjust decision or an unpopular one.[34]

Because of the controversies swirling around the Location Law and the "Blue Books," which will be discussed later, there was no *esprit de corps* among the judges during Nelson's term. He and Strong, both with Whig leanings, were constantly opposed by Pratt, a Polk appointee and a staunch Democrat. Rancor not only affected the supreme court to the extent that the court never sat as one body but soured relationships between the judges as well. In one instance, Nelson freed an attorney Pratt had found guilty of contempt. Pratt was rightly infuriated, since the chief justice had the power to exercise trial jurisdiction only in his own district and the contempt proceeding had taken place in Pratt's district in the court where he was presiding as district judge. (There was no question here of appellate jurisdiction.)

*Nelson appears not to have consulted with Judge Pratt on the matter, neither in trying to have Pratt stay the contempt order, nor in ascertaining Judge Pratt's reasons for having issued an order. Nelson's action amounted to a public rebuke of a fellow judge.* [35]

Although at times Nelson was guilty of injudicious conduct of this kind, he viewed the location controversy generally as an unfortunate issue that should be settled by Congress. That body did act to resolve the conflict on May 4, 1852. Salem was declared the capital—a victory for Pratt and the Democrats. In spite of Nelson's attempts to remain objective, he was singled out for severe criticism by the local Democratic press. In addition, because he had opposed the Democrats on the issue, the legislature reduced his judicial district to only Clackamas County and added Marion and Linn to Pratt's district. Nelson was incensed when he went to Marion County to hold court on the day previously set, only to find Pratt had preceeded him and there were no cases to be heard. [36]

Resentful of this treatment, Nelson contemplated resigning from the court, but was persuaded by his supporters to remain until his term expired in April of 1853, when he returned to New York. Thirty-six years later (1889) he visited Oregon where "his old friends were extremely glad to see him. At the age of 70 years (*sic*) he is still in good health, and looks as if he yet has many years of life before him." [37] He died in New York in 1907, a gentleman and a scholar, who was perhaps unsuited to the rough and tumble of frontier politics.

## The Last Three Judges

When Franklin Pierce succeeded Millard Fillmore to the presidency he swept the judicial slate of the Oregon territorial court clean and in April 1853 appointed three new judges. After withdrawing the name of Orville C. Pratt, he named George H. Williams as chief justice, Matthew P. Deady and Cyrus Olney as associates. Due to an error, Deady's name appeared on the commission as "Mordecai P. Deady." Since there was no such person, Obadiah B. McFadden was appointed instead. The mistake was eventually corrected and Deady took his seat on the court in February 1854. After Washington became a territory in 1853, the judicial districts were rearranged. Williams sat in the first district, composed of Marion, Linn, Lane, Benton, and Polk counties; Olney in the second district— Clatsop, Clackamas, Columbia, and Washington; and Deady in the third—Jackson, Douglas, and Umpqua.

**George H. Williams.** Chief Justice Williams, described as "one of the most colorful characters in the political and legal history of Oregon and of the nation," was born on March 26, 1823, in a log cabin in rural northern New York.[38] He received his education in Pompey, New York, and at the age of 21 was admitted to the bar at the Court of Common Pleas in Onondaga County. Soon thereafter he emigrated to Fort Madison, Iowa, and was elected a circuit court judge while still in his twenties. In 1852, having been chosen by the Democratic Party as a presidential elector, he cast his vote for Franklin Pierce. As his reward he was appointed chief justice of the Oregon Territory.

Williams' immediate task as chief justice was to bring order to the court from the chaos created by his predecessors. One reason for dissension among the judges was that as a supreme court, they had to rule on decisions each had made in the district courts. Williams' solution was to set up a system whereby most of the litigation coming before the district courts could be brought into the supreme court for determination.[39] In other matters, Williams allowed the district judges full control within their districts. The result of these practices was a better relationship among the judges and greater uniformity in court decisions. Between terms of the supreme court, Williams made it a point to keep in touch with his associates through correspondence, giving advice when it was sought.[40]

One of Williams' important achievements was the formalization of court records. Until this time there had been no official written report of decisions made either in the supreme court or in the district courts. Cases were often reported in newspapers, sometimes at length and at other times in summary fashion. Williams recognized that formal publication of the court's decisions would make them available as precedent and would educate the citizens of the territory as to their rights and obligations. Williams' efforts in this area culminated in the publication of the *Oregon Reports*, beginning with the December term, 1853.

During Williams' tenure as chief justice, the supreme court decided 66 cases and Williams wrote the opinions in 43. These opinions show him to be a pragmatic man, concerned with the proper application of the law and also with its practicality. This is illustrated in the case of *O'Kelly v. Territory of Oregon*.[41] The defendant appealed a verdict finding him guilty of murder and his attorney asked for a reversal on nine technical grounds. In affirming the verdict Williams, writing the opinion for the supreme court, said:

> ...it is no hardship to say that, if they [prisoners] have any objection to the acts of the tribunal before which they are tried, they shall make these objections known to such tribunal, or forever after hold their peace...criminal laws were made to prevent crime, and their firm enforcement by courts is a duty as plain as it is painful...if judicial compassion now bends the laws to suit a seemingly hard case, a door may be opened through which the midnight assassin and mercenary murderer may escape from the punishment due to their crimes.[42]

Another interesting opinion is one Williams wrote in the case of *Vandorf v. Otis*.[43] A white settler, who was married to an Indian woman, had claimed 640 acres under the Oregon Donation Act. A claim jumper attempted to settle on 320 acres of the claim, asserting that an Indian wife did not qualify for land under the act. In upholding the rights of the wife, Williams said that if a man was married and competent, that was sufficient; he did not have to explain his family affairs in order make his claim.

> Now, is not a man married to an Indian woman, as much a "married man," to all intents and purposes, as though his wife were the "fairest of the fair?" Is not an Indian woman, married to a white male citizen of the United States, "a wife in every sense of the law?"...When the donation act was passed, congress must have known that many of the early settlers of Oregon had married Indian women; and if it was not intended to place men so married upon the same footing with other married men, why did not congress say so, instead of using language by the terms of which they were clearly embraced?[44]

*Marlin v. T'Vault*, another case decided by the court in 1854, involved claims to townsites.[45] Here Williams demonstrated his considerable ability by successfully juggling three potentially conflicting federal statutes to achieve a result both legally sound and in keeping with settlers' expectations.

Sitting as a district judge in Polk County, Williams decided the important case of *Holmes v. Ford*, involving the question of slavery. The case, discussed later in this chapter, was a legacy from the previous territorial court that both Nelson and Olney had managed to avoid deciding.

*In April 1853 President Franklin Pierce appointed three new judges—George H. Williams (left) and Cyrus Olney (right) and Matthew P. Deady (the subject of Chapter 2). During the three men's time on the bench, they generally handled cases in a careful manner. All three were important figures in the community.* (Oregon Historical Society Negatives #018333 and #ORHI3540)

Shortly after the Oregon constitution was approved by the voters in November 1857, Williams, anticipating statehood, resigned from the court to prepare himself for an active life in the political arena. His subsequent achievements were significant: he served in the United States Senate, he helped draft the Fourteenth Amendment, he was selected by President Grant as United States attorney general, and he was nominated by Grant for the position of chief justice of the United States Supreme Court. The nomination was withdrawn, however, amid charges of incompetency and corruption. According to the *Portland Oregonian*, one charge alleged "Williams had used some $1,600 out of a contingent fund of the Department of Justice to supply himself for family use a handsome landaulet, and some $750 for a pair of horses." It was further asserted he "paid out of government moneys the wages of two liveried servants." [46] Much of the blame for Williams' troubles was placed on his second wife, an ambitious woman and a social climber who was unpopular in both Washington and Portland. [47]

Williams returned to Portland to practice law in 1881. Twenty years later, at the age of 79, he was elected mayor for a three-year term. When his bid for reelection failed, he resumed practice with his old firm, then called Williams, Wood and Linthicum, one of the leading law firms in Oregon. He remained active in his practice and in community affairs until his death on April 4, 1910. In spite of his faults, Williams will be remembered as a good judge and a colorful, if not skillful, politician.

**Cyrus Olney.** Judge Olney was born in Geneva, New York, on October 11, 1815. In the 1830s the Olney family—father, mother, and 11 children (with another yet to come!)—migrated to Ohio, where for two years Cyrus attended Marietta College. After ten years in Ohio, the family pushed farther west, this time to Iowa. Here Cyrus passed the bar, began to practice law, and served as a circuit judge in Fairfield. Intrigued by accounts of the Oregon Country told him by a brother living in The Dalles, Olney arrived in Oregon in August 1851. Four months later he was admitted to the Oregon bar, and as an attorney made frequent appearances in the courts. In April 1853 he was appointed to the territorial supreme court by President Pierce.[48]

Olney was serving on the court with Matthew P. Deady when the news came that there had been a mistake in the name on Deady's commission and that Obadiah B. McFadden had been appointed in his place. Olney felt so strongly Deady deserved the judgeship more than he that he wrote a letter to Joseph Lane, the territorial delegate in Washington, offering to resign his position if it was the only way Deady could be reappointed. Lane made this recommendation to the attorney general, but as it turned out Olney's resignation was not necessary: Judge McFadden received an appointment to the supreme court of the newly formed territory of Washington, and Deady was issued a new commission to the Oregon court.

When Judge Olney's term expired in 1857, he declined reappointment. He went into business with his brother Nathan, who was a farmer and trader. On one occasion they spent several weeks in the Hawaiian Islands, having taken a cargo of furs there for the China trade. After his brother's untimely death,[49] Olney settled in Astoria, where he prospered. All of his immediate family—his wife and seven children—predeceased him, and he himself died at the relatively early age of 55. In his will he left his fortune "in perpetuity for the Town of Astoria," but his relatives—brothers, sisters, nephews, and nieces—broke the will and divided his estate of some $100,000.

During his term, Olney wrote 16 opinions for the supreme court, more than Deady and McFadden together, but fewer than Chief Justice Williams. While not precedent making, Olney's opinions are clearly written and show a good understanding of both substantive law and legal procedure. He refused, as Nelson had, to make a decision on the hotly debated issue of slavery presented in the case of *Holmes v. Ford*, leaving that task for Williams. Of Olney's judicial prowess, Williams wrote:

> *…I have never met but one who, in my judgment, could dovetail the facts and circumstances of a case together with more completeness and more convincing effect than Cyrus Olney: but, notwithstanding this, my opinion is that his qualifications for a judge were not equal to those possessed by Judge Deady.*" [50]

Although Olney did not play as important a part in the history of the State of Oregon as did his colleagues, his interest in civil affairs and local politics was noteworthy. He served as a trustee of Willamette University and in 1866 was elected to the state senate from the district composed of Clatsop, Columbia, and Tillamook counties. In 1870 he was chosen to represent the same district in the state house of representatives, where he served with distinction, even though he was suffering from a terminal illness. According to Williams, Olney was "a modest, retiring and rather eccentric, but no ordinary man." [51]

He was replaced on the territorial court bench by Reuben P. Boise, who served briefly until statehood when he was elected to the Oregon Supreme Court. He became chief justice of that court in May 1861.

**Matthew P. Deady.** Matthew Deady's career as Oregon's first United States district court judge will be fully covered in the succeeding chapter, "The Deady Years, 1859-1893." Before statehood, however, Deady sat on the territorial court, assigned to the southern district, and shortly after his appointment in April 1853 he moved to the Umpqua Valley. In September he opened court at Jacksonville, the first to be held south of the Umpqua. At about this time he learned that there had been an irregularity in his commission, which had been issued to "Mordecai Deady."

The mistake appears to have been the result of an attempt at levity by the *Oregonian* and the fact that "the *Oregonian* is the only paper from Oregon which is read at Washington." [52] Judge Olney only added to the confusion by declaring from the bench that Matthew Deady was indeed Mordecai and therefore a judge of the supreme court. [53] This decision is probably the only Oregon case holding that a judge was not who he claimed to be.[54] Because Deady was a member of the controlling Democratic party, and because he deserved the appointment, a loud outcry went up—resulting, as we have seen, in McFadden's removal to the Washington territorial court and Deady's reappointment.

For the next six years, Deady faithfully held court in his district and sat on the supreme court when it was in session. He was held in high esteem by his colleagues and friends, admired for his judicial ability and his brilliant mind. However, the supposed error over his commission—there was always some suspicion that it had not been an error, but a deliberate act— was not forgotten by him.

> It…left a lasting impression upon Deady, and thenceforth, notwithstanding his judicial demeanor and unbiased attitude, he continued his political activity, and he retained a partisan temper and character which stayed with him during his entire career.[55]

As these brief biographies show, the territorial judges were men of considerable ability and training, measured by the standards of the day. But until Williams arrived, little effort was made to establish a workable court system. Whether this was due to the conditions encountered on the frontier, or simply to a desire to profit from what the new land offered, is difficult to determine. What is evident, however, is that most of the judges had no clear sense of judicial decorum and responsibility and that for some of them, personal ambition was more important than professional integrity. Under Bryant and Nelson as chief justices, the supreme court never achieved a cohesiveness sufficient to make it worthy of the name. During that period the behavior of the judges toward each other was not only contentious, it was petty and absurd. Not until the end of the territorial period was some degree of judicial proficiency achieved.

Five cases will illustrate more specifically the activities of the court and some of the important issues confronting it.

# THE McLOUGHLIN LAND CLAIM: THE CASE THAT WAS NEVER HEARD

It has been said that the arrival of Chief Justice William P. Bryant at Oregon City on April 9, 1849, began one of the most dismal episodes in the history of the courts of Oregon.[56] This "most dismal episode" involved a successful conspiracy to deprive John McLoughlin of his land claims at Oregon City—a conspiracy in which the chief justice of the territorial court, the governor of the territory, the territorial delegate to Congress, and several members of the Methodist mission all actively participated.

## Origin of the Claim

The controversy over McLoughlin's claim had deep roots, dating back to 1829, when he first took possession of the property in what is now Oregon City. The claim was in McLoughlin's name, although it had been made at the instruction of George Simpson, governor of the Hudson's Bay Company. In 1827 the Joint Occupation Agreement with Great Britain had been renewed for an indefinite period, during which the country was to remain "free and open" to settlement by both nations. Simpson and McLoughlin knew that England did not seriously intend to claim any part of the Oregon Country south of the Columbia River and believed the area would eventually become a part of the United States. McLoughlin later stated he had decided to settle in the Willamette Valley when he retired, and his claim was to be "for his old age, for the benefit of himself and children." [57]

McLoughlin's claim included both town property and a small island—later called Abernethy, or Governor's, Island—situated near the crest of the Willamette (later Oregon City) falls. The island was the most valuable part of the claim, since its location was well suited to the development of water power. McLoughlin began to make improvements on the property and in 1832 blasted a mill race on the island. Although his residence was in Fort Vancouver, he continued to maintain a presence at the falls property for the next 11 years, during which time there were no adverse claimants. Trouble started, however, in 1840, when the Methodist mission took up a nearby 640 acres and began to cast covetous eyes on McLoughlin's holdings.

## McLoughlin and the Methodist Mission

As soon as the mission began operations on its claim, McLoughlin wrote to the Reverend Jason Lee, superintendent of the mission, setting out in detail the extent of his claim, and Lee in turn assured him his rights would be respected. In spite of this exchange and in spite of McLoughlin's substantial assistance to the mission— including the gift of a part of his land for the erection of a mission house—disputes and controversies arose. In 1841 an employee of the mission, Felix Hathaway, began to build

23

a house on the island. When McLoughlin complained to the Reverend
Alvan F. Waller (whom Lee had placed in charge of the Oregon City operations), the activity ceased. Even so, later that year Hathaway conveyed to
the newly formed Oregon Milling Company, composed primarily of
members of the mission, "all his right and title to the island." When the
company erected a saw mill on the island and announced its intention to
set up a flour mill, McLoughlin countered by building a saw mill on the
river bank near the island and also projecting a flour mill.

At that point the plot began to thicken. In 1842 McLoughlin had the
town claim (which he now called Oregon City) surveyed and laid out in
blocks and lots. Some of these he deeded to settlers. On Lee's advice,
Waller, wishing to use a part of this land for mission purposes, refused to
recognize McLoughlin's deeds. Lee wrote:

> *I considered his Deeds good for nothing and especially as we were the*
> *first permanent residents at the Falls. I resolved to set up no opposi-*
> *tion claim to anyone to land in that place, but simply to occupy it till*
> *government made some disposition of it....*[58]

The situation had developed into a genuine dispute over the claim,
which only a court of law could resolve. Unfortunately, however,
McLoughlin had no judicial recourse since the only courts in the territory
were those of the Provisional Government, whose authority he had not
accepted.[59] In the absence of a legal remedy, he was forced to enter into an
agreement with Waller to pay him $500 and to convey to him and to the
mission certain lots and blocks of the property. In return, Waller agreed to
relinquish all claims he might have to the island. [60]

McLoughlin believed the agreement would end the dispute, but he
was mistaken. The Oregon Milling Company continued to operate and
to assert claims to the island, and in 1846 George Abernethy, the provisional governor, became the company's owner. In these circumstances it
was impossible to resolve the affair until the Oregon Territory was established and the territorial court convened. McLoughlin hoped his complaint would be heard and resolved through the normal judicial process,
but this expectation proved too optimistic. Chief Justice Bryant's actions
shortly after his arrival made it clear there would be no impartial hearing
for McLoughlin.

## Chief Justice Bryant and the Oregon City Claim

One of Bryant's first duties as territorial judge should have been to
hear and determine conflicting land claims that had arisen during the

period of the Provisional Government and to set out rules by which titles could be established. He not only failed to fulfill these duties but quickly put himself in a position of conflict. In addition to his being chief justice of the territory, he was also the judge assigned to the first judicial district, which included Oregon City. On May 29, 1849, several months before he held the first term of the district court, Bryant purchased from Abernethy all of Abernethy's rights to the property at the falls. At the time of the transaction, Bryant was fully aware that Abernethy's claim was contested by McLoughlin and that the dispute would have to be settled by a lawsuit brought in his district.

During this period there were only two judges in the territory: Bryant and Associate Justice Orville C. Pratt, who was assigned to the second district covering the counties west of the Willamette and south of the Columbia. Although Bryant might have assigned Pratt to hear the case, that would not have solved the problem completely, for in the likely event of an appeal to the territorial supreme court, Bryant would have to disqualify himself, leaving only one judge to sit, whereas two were required. It is difficult to believe Bryant did not realize how unethical his conduct was. In a letter published in the *Oregon City Spectator* on September 12, 1850, McLoughlin writes of his dilemma.

> …*I deferred bringing the case to trial, til the government extended its jurisdiction over the country; but when it had done so, a few days after the arrival of Judge Bryant and before the courts were organized, Judge Bryant bought the island of George Abernethy, Esq.…and as the island was in Judge Bryant's district and as there were only two judges in the Territory, I thought I could not at the time bring the case to a satisfactory decision. I therefore deferred bringing the case forward until a time when the bench would be full. In July or August, 1849, Gov. Lane told me Judge Bryant would speak to me in regard to my claim on the Island; the Judge did so and asked me to state the extent of my claim.* [61]

At Bryant's request, McLoughlin furnished him with a complete written description of the claim. Even though the district court at Oregon City was in session from August 20 to 25, the judge made no statement on the matter, nor did he take action to divest himself of his recently acquired interest. In October of 1849 Bryant left for Indiana, ostensibly to bring his family to Oregon, but whatever his intentions may have been he never returned. Before he left, he sold his interest in the Oregon Milling Company to the territorial governor, Joseph Lane.

## Thurston and the Oregon Donation Act

In addition to the chief justice and the governor, there was a another prominent Oregonian determined to oust McLoughlin from his claim. In June 1849 Samuel R. Thurston was elected Oregon's territorial delegate to Congress by a narrow margin, with heavy support from the Mission party and opposition from McLoughlin and others with close ties to the Hudson's Bay Company. Soon after taking over his congressional duties, he became active in pushing through the House of Representatives a bill to secure the land claims of the Oregon settlers. The result was the Oregon Donation Act of 1850.[62] Due to Thurston's efforts, the bill included a section stripping McLoughlin of all his rights.

One of the questions debated in Congress was the extent to which claims of British subjects would be honored. Article III of the boundary treaty of 1846 provided that the "possessory rights of the Hudson's Bay Company and of all British subjects who may be already in the occupation of land or other property lawfully acquired within the said territory, shall be respected." [63] Although McLoughlin was a British subject, he had broken his ties with the Hudson's Bay Company and declared his intention to become an American citizen. For this reason, he expected to have his claim validated under section 4 of the donation land act relating to citizens and intended citizens.

Thurston, however, denied the validity of McLoughlin's declaration of citizenship. He used this along with other false statements to secure the passage of section 11 of the law, which effectively abrogated McLoughlin's claim. His language was extravagant and undoubtedly persuasive.

*The Oregon City Claim is located here (in the) county seat of Clackamas County. It is unquestionably the finest water power in the world....This claim has been wrongfully wrested by Dr. McLoughlin from American citizens. The Methodist Mission first took the claim, with the view of establishing there their mills and Mission. They were forced to leave it under the fear of having the savages of Oregon let loose upon them....Having at his command the Indians of the country, he (McLoughlin) has held it by violence and dint of threats up to this time....He has already made half a million out of the claim.... He is still an Englishman, still connected in interest with the Hudson's Bay Company, and still refuses to file his intentions to become an American citizen, and assigns as a reason to the Supreme Judge of the Territory, that he cannot do it without prejudicing his standing in England...."[64]*

26

*Joseph Lane, the territorial governor, and Samuel R. Thurston, territorial delegate to Congress, were among those who tried to oust John McLoughlin from his Oregon City land claim. Five years after McLoughlin died, the Oregon Legislature vindicated him. The McLoughlin land grab was one of the most shameful incidents in the early history of Oregon and its courts.*
(Oregon Historical Society Negatives #ORHI1703 and #CN020665)

Section 11 divested McLoughlin not only of the disputed site at the falls, but also of his town property, which had been uncontested since his agreement with Waller. This part of his claim was put "at the disposal of the legislative assembly to the establishment and endowment of a university."

To pull off such an outright steal, Thurston needed an ally and he found one in Chief Justice Bryant, who had come to Washington to lobby for the donation land law and was willing to testify falsely confirming some of Thurston's accusations. (It has been suggested that Bryant's willingness was impelled by his wish to have Lane's claim to Abernethy Island confirmed, so that Lane would be able to pay off the notes he had given Bryant in payment for the property.) [65] Particularly upsetting to McLoughlin was Bryant's testimony that McLoughlin had never declared his intention to become a citizen.

> *I declared my intention to become an American citizen on the 30th May, 1849, as anyone may see who will examine the records of the court....I am astonished how the Supreme Judge could*

27

*have made such a statement as he had a letter from me pointing
out my intention....* [66]

News of the passage of the Oregon Donation Act was greeted in
Oregon with great rejoicing. The settlers would receive legal title to their
lands; the title to Abernethy Island was "confirmed to the legal assigns of
the Wilamet milling and trading companies"—to the delight of Lane and
the Mission party; and John McLoughlin's town lots were taken from him
without compensation for the benefit of a university. During the next 12
years, however, in spite of this valuable property's location in the heart of
the town, no move was made to develop it. Thus the effect of section 11
was not only to deprive McLoughlin of the lots, but also to end any real
growth of Oregon City. [67]

Although the conspirators believed they had achieved complete success, their rewards were to be few. When the news of Thurston's villany
finally reached Oregon, reaction set in. He was condemned for his lies and
treachery, and there was talk of other candidates for the position of congressional delegate. Whether or not he would have been defeated became
a moot point when in April 1851, at the age of 35, he died at sea while
returning to Oregon. He has been described as a man of considerable
ability and accomplishment but one who allowed his ambition and passion to override his judgement. His letters, speeches, and actions against
McLoughlin are viewed as the one great blot on his career.[68]

Nor did the other conspirators fare much better. Both Chief Justice
Bryant and Governor Lane believed the island claim would bring them
great wealth, but subsequent events proved otherwise. Bryant had difficulty collecting on the notes Lane had given him in payment for the property, and Lane suffered a devastating loss when the mill on Abernethy
Island was severely damaged by a great surge of water sweeping down the
Willamette. The *Oregon City Spectator* reported the loss at $75,000 and
estimated repairs in the thousands of dollars. [69]

Dr. John McLoughlin died on September 3, 1857. In October 1862,
five years after his death and twelve years after the passage of the donation
land law, the Oregon Legislature passed an act that officially vindicated
him. The act conveyed to his son David and to his daughter Eloisa and
her husband Daniel Harvey the "McLoughlin or Oregon City land
claim," excepting Abernethy Island, in return for the nominal sum of
$1,000, to be paid to the University Fund of Oregon. [70] At long last a sem-
blance of justice was done, though it was too late to be of solace to
McLoughlin himself.

One writer has succinctly described the conspiracy against McLoughlin in this way:

> Bryant conducted a "holding action" in the territory while Thurston labored mightily in Washington to secure the stamp of Congressional approval. Lane gave the efforts approval by purchasing Bryant's interest and then writing Thurston supporting the confirmation of the island claim to himself. Taken as a whole, these efforts amounted to a conspiracy to obstruct justice by precluding McLoughlin from ever litigating the validity of his claim. The chief justice's conduct was the cornerstone of the entire operation, and it is under this shabby cloak of conduct that the judiciary of the territory began its institutional life. [71]

The McLoughlin land grab represents a shameful incident in the history of Oregon and its early courts. Unfortunately it is recorded for all time in our statute books—in section 11 of the Oregon Donation Act.

∾

# SHORT v. ERMATENGER: THE LOCATION CASE [72]

*Amos M. Short v. F. Ermatenger*, decided on December 2, 1851, was a strange case in which two of the judges of the United States Supreme Court of the Territory of Oregon held that the seat of government for the territory was at Oregon City and that a law providing for the location of the seat of government at Salem was unconstitutional. The validity of the decision itself depended on whether the court had convened at the proper place— in the words of Associate Justice Strong, "...our actual sitting and transacting business as a court, at Oregon city, being of itself a virtual decision." [73]

The involved and prolonged location controversy stemmed from an act passed by the legislative assembly of the Territory of Oregon on February 1, 1851, entitled "An act to provide for the selection of places for location and erection of public buildings of the Territory of Oregon." Section 1 of the act located the seat of government at Salem in Marion County; section 2 provided that a penitentiary be located in Portland in Washington County; section 3 located a university at Marysville in

Benton County. Other provisions related to the construction and financing of the buildings.[74]

This seemingly straightforward enactment fell into difficulty because of two provisions in section 6 of the act of August 1848 establishing the Territory of Oregon.[75] One of these provisions enumerates certain subjects on which the legislative assembly is forbidden to act and states, "all such laws and any law or laws inconsistent with the provisions of this act shall be utterly null and void." The other provides:

> To avoid improper influences, which may result from intermixing, in one and the same act, such things as have no proper relation to each other, every law shall embrace but one object and that shall be expressed in the title.

Two days after the location law was passed, Governor John Gaines told the legislative assembly that in his opinion the enactment conflicted with the Territorial Act because it embraced more than one object and the title was not clear.[76] A similar opinion was rendered by the United States attorney general, John J. Crittenden, who stated that in his view the act "is

*When the territorial assembly tried to move the seat of government from Oregon City (pictured here) to Salem, a bitter political battled ensued. When the case came before the territorial supreme court, even the judges' positions split along party lines. Ultimately, Congress decided the question in favor of Salem. (Oregon Historical Society Negative #ORHI801)*

null and void in all its parts, and consequently can give no legal validity to anything done under color of its authority." [77]

In normal circumstances it would seem that the situation could have been easily remedied by having the legislative assembly convene at Oregon City, the seat of the Provisional Government, and passing an act to locate the capital henceforth at Salem without including any other subject matter. But such a simple solution was not acceptable to those involved, who were far more eager to pursue a political agenda than the business of government. The Oregon Democrats, known as the "Salem clique," refused to accept the opinion of either Governor Gaines or Attorney General Crittenden, both of whom were Whigs. The governor was accused of "unwarranted executive interference," and Asahel Bush, editor of the *Oregon City Statesman*, characterized Crittenden's letter as "but the opinion of a lawyer, based on an *ex parte* statement." [78]

Since the Oregon Territorial Act required the supreme court to meet at the seat of government, the court was also affected by the controversy. Like the legislature, the court was divided along party lines. Associate Justice Orville Pratt had been appointed by President Polk and was associated with the Salem clique, while Chief Justice Thomas Nelson, appointed by Fillmore, and Associate Justice William Strong, by Taylor, supported the position of Governor Gaines and the Whigs. None was willing to assume a conciliatory position.

Matters came to a head in December 1851, when all but five members of the legislative assembly met at Salem and were sworn in by Judge Pratt. The remaining five met at Oregon City but could not convene for lack of a quorum. They were joined by the governor, the district attorney, and Judges Nelson and Strong. With a quorum of two judges, the supreme court opened in Oregon City on December 1. As was expected, Judge Pratt was not in attendance. The court's jurisdiction was immediately challenged in *Short v. Ermatenger* on the ground that the court was not convened in the proper place—the seat of government.

Those who have studied the case have generally regarded the opinions of the judges as little more than sophistry justifying a political position. On closer examination, however, these opinions show that the judges had a full understanding of the applicable law as well as the ability to argue with ingenuity in support of their conclusions. Nelson and Strong, who handed down a decision in the name of the territorial supreme court, found the legislative act unconstitutional and declared Oregon City the capital. Pratt's opinion, delivered at the request of the legislative assembly, ridiculed the decision of his fellow judges and upheld the act. Nelson's and Pratt's opinions are summarized below.

## The Opinion of Chief Justice Nelson[79]

Nelson begins by stating, "The supreme court of Oregon Territory is required to hold a term in the first Monday of December in each year, at the seat of government, and the question is now raised: Where is the seat of government?" [80] He points out that section 14 of the Territorial Act provides that the laws of the Provisional Government shall remain in force until changed and asserts that "by the law of that government the legislative body was required to meet at Willamette Falls, now Oregon City." [81] Therefore, Nelson says, Oregon City is still the seat of government unless it has been relocated by a subsequent law.

Nelson's second question is: Has the law been changed? Section 15 of the act gives the territorial legislature the power to establish the seat of government, and on February 1, 1851, a law was passed locating the seat of government at Salem. But because the act contained additional provisions relating to other matters, Nelson finds it is in conflict with section 6 of the Territorial Act, which prohibits the intermixing of "objects" of legislation and is therefore void. His conclusion is that the law of the Provisional Government has not been changed and the seat of government is still Oregon City.

He then responds to the argument that legislation should be presumed valid until the courts have ruled otherwise. He asserts that the part of section 6 that made all legislation contrary to the act "null and void" applies here, making the law in question void whether or not the courts held it to be so.

*A void act is none the more void because the court has so judicially determined; the court does not make the law void, it only settles the question and removes the uncertainty.* [82]

A confusing part of Nelson's opinion is his attempt to counter the allegation that the judges should go to Salem to render the decision.

*But if the court shall go to Salem, and there, as a court, decide that Salem was not the seat of government, it would, in effect, convict itself of a violation of the law. And even if it was not unlawful for it to do so, what good purpose could it serve if it should proceed there—it would be a mere piece of useless formality, and the law never requires an idle ceremony.* [83]

Nelson concludes by saying that he respects the legislative assembly and regrets the necessity of calling its proceedings into question. However, he asserts that respect and obedience is first due to the Congress and that "courts are not to sacrifice duty to etiquette. They are bound to follow the law and not expedience." He expresses the hope that reason will prevail and that the citizens of the territory will show enough good sense and patriotism to "uphold with a steady hand…the law of the land as settled by the authoritative tribunal." [84]

On these grounds Nelson held that the plaintiffs' objections to the court's jurisdiction should be overruled.

## Pratt's Opinion[85]

The legislative assembly of the territory requested Pratt to give his opinion on several questions relating to the location law. This Pratt did at great length—27 pages of small print, dated December 25, 1851. One of the questions posed was whether any law in force in the territory authorized the supreme court to convene at Oregon City. In his response, Pratt points out that the Territorial Act did not specify the time and place for holding court, but left that choice to the legislative assembly. The first legislative session was convened by Governor Gaines at Oregon City, a place chosen because it was convenient, not because it had been the seat of government of the Provisional Government. Furthermore, subsequent sessions were held there by consent, not by necessity, and at the third session a law was passed locating the capital at Salem. In Pratt's view this law is valid and Nelson and Strong acted illegally in convening the supreme court in Oregon City.

In reaching this conclusion, Pratt holds that in spite of section 14 of the Territorial Act, a law of the Provisional Government establishing the seat of government at Oregon City would be incompatible with section 15 of that act, which gives the legislature the power to locate the capital. This is true, he says, because the act uses the words "to locate", whereas if the seat of government were already "located" under the laws of the Provisional Government, the words used should have been "to alter" or "to change".[86]

A second question Pratt was asked was "whether by any law now in force the Legislative Assembly is legally authorized to assemble at Salem…?" His answer is that the act of February 1, 1851, making Salem the seat of government is constitutional and is the proper place for the legislature to convene.

In making this response, Pratt cleverly weaves his way around the requirement of section 6 of the Territorial Act that each law have but one "object." First, he says, it is a well-known principle of statutory construction that statutes may be good in part and bad in part.

> *...good for so much as the lawmaker had authority over the subject matter, and bad for so much as relates to that where such power is wanting....When certain portions of a statute conflict with a constitution, while other parts do not, the latter will be sustained and enforced if they can be separated from that which is constitutional.*[87]

In applying this principle to the present case, Pratt finds that the part of the law locating the seat of government and the university is voidable—not void—since the legislature had the sole power to enact such a law. However, the provision relating to the penitentiary is void, since the legislature and the governor shared the authority to locate it. In line with this somewhat convoluted reasoning, Pratt concludes that the location of the seat of government at Salem is valid unless and until it is voided by a court having the authority to do so.

He then turns to the argument that *all* of the law is invalid under that part of section 6 of the act which makes laws "inconsistent with the provisions of this act...utterly null and void." This mandate, he asserts, does not apply to the clause in the same section requiring that every law have but one object. He points out that the words "shall be absolutely null and void" not only *precede* the words requiring every act to have but one subject, but they are in a different sentence. The failure to adhere to the requirement that every law shall have but one object is a mere irregularity, not a *usurpation of power* that renders a law null and void.[88] Thus he neatly removes the primary objection to the law.

The decision in *Short v. Ermatenger* created much sound and fury both in Salem and in Oregon City, but it failed to change the situation either legally or politically. The question of the location of the seat of government remained deadlocked. On January 1, 1852, Governor Gaines wrote to President Fillmore asking whether the enactments of the legislative assembly meeting in Salem had the force of law. And again Attorney General Crittenden advised the president that the law was "utterly null and void." He continued:

> *...I see no proper remedy for the state of things existing in Oregon but that which must be found in the wisdom of Congress.... Congress can put an end to the disputed question about the seat of government, and can dispose of all the other minor or incidental*

*questions which have sprung up and contributed to the disorder
and confusion that now prevail in Oregon.*[89]
This advice was heeded and on May 4, 1852, Congress approved a
joint resolution which "ratified, approved, and confirmed" the act of the
Oregon territorial legislative assembly "establishing and locating the seat
of government of said territory at Salem." [90]

The location controversy was primarily a political and not a legal battle. The winners were the Salem clique, including Matthew Deady, who
had probably helped Pratt fashion his opinion, and Asahel Bush, whose
*Oregon City Statesman* led the fight for the Salem location. The governor
and the Whig faction that had fought for Oregon City as the seat of government lost political power and prestige.

But the big loser in the dispute was the territorial court. The controversy revealed a court still lacking the attributes of a judicial institution
worthy of respect and confidence. None of the judges had been willing to
consider the matter fully in a rational, conciliatory manner. Instead,
their conduct had been injudicious and undignified, as each stubbornly
upheld his own point of view. Nelson, scholarly and steeped in eastern
tradition, felt the sting of criticism and rejection keenly, even to the point
of considering resignation. Strong, although his views were overruled as
well, quickly turned his attention to promoting the establishment of the
Territory of Washington. For awhile Pratt rode on the crest of victory
but, as we have seen, was ultimately disappointed with his judicial career
in Oregon.

## The Battle of the Blue Books

A controversy similar to the location law dispute, known as "The
Battle of the Blue Books," concerned which of two Iowa codes was law in
the Oregon Territory. The Provisional Government had adopted the
1839 Iowa code, known as the "Little Blue Book" (because of the color of
the boards with which it was bound). The territorial legislature adopted
the newer code, that of 1843, known as the "Big Blue Book." Amory
Holbrook, attorney general for the territory, claimed the statute adopt-
ing the 1843 code conflicted with section 6 of the Territorial Act in the
same manner as did the location law.

The judges were similarly divided. Nelson and Strong used the Little
Blue Book in their decisions, while Pratt used the Big Blue Book in his.
The problem was not solved until January 1853, when the legislature
authorized the drafting of a new code. [91]

# THE TRIAL OF
# THE CAYUSE INDIANS

The trial of five Cayuse Indians indicted for the November 29, 1847 murder of Marcus and Narcissa Whitman and seven other members of the Waiilatpu Mission (near the present site of Walla Walla, Washington) was one of the earliest and most important cases to be tried by the United States District Court for the Territory of Oregon. Many of the documents relating to the case are stored in the Oregon State Archives, still in their original state—on thin crumbling paper, in spidery, difficult-to-decipher handwriting. The case file contains the indictments and statements of the witnesses, and the District Court Order Book sets out each step of the trial proceedings.[92] Nonetheless, the court record as a whole seems incomplete and enigmatic, leaving unanswered many questions about the case. The account of the trial in the *Oregon City Spectator* adds a few details, but also some contradictions.[93]

There is no doubt the murders were committed, and there is no doubt they were committed by Cayuse Indians. But were the five indicted the guilty ones? Were they the only guilty ones? Why were two Indians indicted but never tried? Was the jury selection fair? Was the evidence presented by the prosecution clear and convincing? Was the judge's charge prejudicial? Why was no new trial allowed and no appeal filed? It is doubtful if the answers to these questions will ever be fully known. Yet the case is worth reexamining. It reveals two tragic tales —that of the victims and that of the hanged.

## The Cayuse Indians

The Cayuses' name for themselves meant "superior people" and, indeed, they have often been described as proud, haughty, and arrogant. Respected as fierce fighters by both friend and foe, they killed the braves of defeated tribes and took the women and children as slaves. Primarily hunters and gatherers, living in lodges of poles covered with mats, their domain lay east of the Cascade Mountains on the Columbia River plateau along the Umatilla and John Day rivers. The acquisition of horses brought mobility and prestige, enabling them to wander widely and to dominate many of the smaller bands of Indians living along the Columbia. Their chief ally was the Nez Perces, with whom they intermarried and whose less complicated dialect they eventually adopted. At annual fairs the Cayuses socialized with the Nez Perces and other friendly tribes, engaging in athletic competition and extensive trading.

Intrigued by the variety of goods the white man brought, they were eager to trade with him. They wanted tools, utensils, beads, rings, and other trifles, but above all guns to fight enemy tribes. In return they were able to offer beaver skins and, more importantly, horses—always the chief measure of their wealth. Because they controlled the routes over which much of the fur trade passed, the fur trading companies were anxious to stay in their good graces. Even John McLoughlin, chief factor of the Hudson's Bay Company, who was known as a strict disciplinarian of offending Indians, used a light hand in his dealings with them.

It is probable that the Cayuses' first exposure to Christianity was through the Catholic French-Canadian trappers and the employees of the Hudson's Bay Company. These men regularly associated with the Indians and frequently married Indian women. The Cayuses were fascinated by the rituals of the Christian Church and sometimes combined them with Indian rites in conducting their own devotions. They were anxious to have missionaries, both Protestant and Catholic, come to their lands to teach them more of this "magic."[94]

## The Mission at Waiilatpu

In late 1836, under the auspices of the American Board of Commissioners for Foreign Missions, Dr. Marcus Whitman, a medical doctor by training, and his wife Narcissa arrived at Waiilatpu to set up a mission among the Cayuses. The site had been chosen a year earlier by the Reverend Samuel Parker at a meeting with three of the Cayuse chiefs, "as a place to build a preaching house, to teach them to live and to teach school to their children."[95] Whitman was a sincere and dedicated man who sought to teach the Indians not only principles of Christianity but also the ways of civilization. He believed they were an inferior race whose culture was destined for extinction unless they settled down to an agricultural rather than a nomadic existence.[96]

The task Whitman set for himself proved more difficult than he had expected. The Cayuses, never as friendly toward white men as many other tribes, mistrusted the Whitmans almost from the start.[97] Further, the choice of a site for the mission was unfortunate because Waiilatpu was destined to become an important stop for immigrants on the Oregon Trail. Helping the immigrants not only took up much of Whitman's time

37

and resources, but the newcomers' passage through Cayuse territory antagonized the Indians, who saw it as a threat to their lands and way of life.

The Cayuses knew Whitman was encouraging immigration, and many were convinced he intended to rob them of their lands. Among these were Chief Telokite and his band, on whose land the mission was established. From an initial attitude of respect and tolerance the mood of the Indians gradually changed to one of anxiety and suspicion, and increasingly they resorted to threats and violence.[98] Whitman was fully aware of the Indians' dislike and their desire to have the mission abandoned. On several occasions he had been urged by McLoughlin and others to move to the Willamette Valley for safety, but he could not bring himself to abandon the mission.

The precipitating cause of the massacre at Waiilatpu was a season of severe sickness in the fall of 1847, when half the Cayuse people living near the mission died, many of a particularly virulent form of measles brought by the immigrants of that year. In contrast, the white settlers' death rate was much lower, most having acquired at least a partial immunity to the diseases from which the Cayuse suffered. Whitman had done his best to cure both Indians and whites, but the striking difference in mortality

*Tensions between settlers and Indians erupted in November 1847 when the Whitman Mission (near present-day Walla Walla, Washington) was attacked by Cayuse Indians. Despite a trial in district court, conducted with all the standard legal formalities, the five Cayuse accused of the murders were doomed to die. The fanciful scene pictured here appeared in 1870 in Frances Fuller Victor's* River of the West. *(Oregon Historical Society Negative #ORHI1644)*

made the Indians suspicious of Whitman's medications and his intentions. They were convinced he was dispensing two kinds of medicine—one for whites, which cured, and another for Indians, which killed. The Cayuses, like many primitive peoples, held their medicine men to high standards, believing that if their cures failed they were sorcerers who dispensed bad medicine. A strange tale is told of Whitman's betrayal by Joe Lewis, a mixed blood whom he had befriended. Lewis told some of the Cayuses that he had overheard Dr. and Mrs. Whitman and the Reverend H.H. Spalding plotting to poison the Indians so the missionaries could have their lands, horses, and cattle.

> *Yet this devil incarnate did not convince his hearers at once of the truth of his statements; it was resolved in the tribe to make a test of Dr. Whitman's medicine. Three persons were selected for the experiment; two of them already sick, and the third quite well. Whether it was that the medicine was administered in too large quantities, or whether an unhappy chance so ordered it, all those three persons died.… It was then that the decree went forth that not only the Doctor and Mrs. Whitman, but all the Americans at the mission must die.*[99]

On November 29 a crowd of Cayuse Indians entered the mission and with guns, tomahawks, and axes began to terrorize the 75 people living there. In the melee that followed, Marcus and Narcissa Whitman were among those slain. Some of the Indians protested the senseless violence, but their voices went unheeded. Only a small portion of one band of Cayuses—that of Chief Telokite—was actively involved in the massacre, but because of the savage fury of those few, the Cayuse nation was doomed.

## The Trial: *U.S. vs. Telokite et al.*

The trial of the Cayuse Indians opened on May 21, 1850, in the U.S. District Court for the County of Clackamas at Oregon City, with Judge Pratt, the only judge in the territory at the time, presiding. According to the court Order Book, the grand jury returned three indictments: one against Telokite et al.—Tomahas (the murderer), Clokomas, Isiaasheluckas, Kiamasumkin—one against Frank Escaloom, and a third against Clokomas. The case files contain six other indictments filed by the district attorney, Amory Holbrook, but these do not appear in the Order Book. All of the indictments are dated May 13, 1850, and in each the accused is charged with the killing of one or more persons, either by striking with knives, tomahawks, and axes; by shooting with guns; or both. The victims named are Marcus and Narcissa Whitman, Emmon Stevens, Luke M. Saunders, Jacob H. Hoffman, Andrew Rogers, Francis Sager, one Gillon, and one Kimball.[100] The prosecutor proceeded on only one of the indictments, that against Telokite et al. for the murder of only one of the victims, Marcus Whitman.

On May 22, the second day of the trial, the defendants came into court, and by their counsel—Kintzing Pritchette (the territorial secretary), R. B. Reynolds, and Captain Thomas Claiborne (army attorneys)—offered a plea in bar, asserting that they were Cayuse Indians and that the crimes were committed in Cayuse country, which at that time was not subject to U.S. jurisdiction or laws. In its replication, the prosecution, led by Amory Holbrook, declared that certain acts of Congress regulating intercourse with the Indians gave jurisdiction to the district courts over these crimes. The court overruled the plea in bar and ordered the defendants to plead to the indictments.[101] Each pled "not guilty" and then requested a change of venue on the ground of prejudice. After argument, this petition too was denied.

On May 23 and 24 the testimony of witnesses was presented. Witnesses for the prosecution were persons who had been present at the mission during the massacre. Eliza Hall testified that she "saw Telokite…striking Marcus Whitman in the face with a hatchet," presumably in the courtyard. On cross-examination she admitted she was a hundred yards away and that there was much fighting and confusion.[102] Elizabeth Sager, who was ten years old at the time of the massacre, said she saw Isiaasheluckas attack and shoot Saunders and saw Clokomas "sitting in the mission house…." Lorinda Chapman did not see the assaults but "heard the voice of Telokite" and the report of a gun. Josiah Osborne said he saw Tomahas armed, confronting Saunders, and that he (Osborne) then hid and from his hiding place "heard the Indians kill Mrs. Whitman, Mr. Rogers and a young man."

Dr. John McLoughlin testified for the defense. He said he had cautioned Whitman repeatedly that as long as he remained on Cayuse lands his life was in danger; further, he had warned him not to give medicine to Indians as "they kill their medicine men." Stickas, a Cayuse chief, related how he had warned Whitman on the day before the attack of what might happen. This was corroborated by Dr. Henry Spalding, who said he was present at the time of the warning. Counsel for the defendants offered to introduce testimony to prove it was the custom and usage of the Cayuse nation to kill their bad medicine men. This was denied, and the defense took exception to the ruling.

There is no official record of the judge's charge to the jury, but according to the *Spectator,* Judge Pratt made a masterful speech for an hour and ten minutes.[103] The jury retired and after little more than an hour returned a verdict of guilty. Defendants' counsel then moved for arrest of judgment and for a new trial based on several grounds: the case was not within the court's jurisdiction; the court erred in finding it was not necessary to prove that the facts given in evidence occurred in the place alleged in the indictment; the court erred in charging the jury that it might infer from the Cayuse nation's surrender of the accused that they were in fact the perpetrators of the massacre; evidence regarding the Cayuse treatment of medicine men should have been admitted. The court denied the motions for arrest of judgment and for a new trial.

*An artist's conception of Tomahas, the man accused of murdering Dr. Marcus Whitman.* (Oregon Historical Society Negative #4325)

At four o'clock in the afternoon, "the defendants being placed at the bar of the court, the Court pronounced that they having been duly convicted of wilful murder as charged…are each adjudged to suffer death by hanging…on June 3, 1850." In spite of protests and petitions for reprieve, the executions were carried out by U.S. Marshall Joe Meek on the day set.

Reports of the Indians' reactions varied. *The Spectator* indicated that after they were condemned, Telokite, Tomahas, and Isiaaskeluckas confessed to the murder of Marcus Whitman; Clokomas confessed to the death of Narcissa Whitman (for which he was not on trial); and Kiamasumkin went to his death protesting his innocence.[104] Other sources indicate that none of the defendants admitted guilt.[105] Escaloom, who had been charged with the death of "one Kimball" (Nathan S. Kimball) in one of the original indictments, disappeared from the case record. "Escaloom" was apparently another name for the defendant Isiaaskeluckas, the brother of Tomahas.[106]

## A Clash of Cultures

The trial, the verdict, and the execution have taken their place in the annals of history, but questions still remain. There is little doubt that the Cayuse nation surrendered the five Indians who were tried for Whitman's murder to avoid punishment of the tribe and another war with the white man in which defeat seemed assured. The accused were all chiefs and might easily have escaped.

> ...there was no imperative necessity upon them to suffer death, had they chosen to flee to the mountains. But with that strange magnanimity which the savage often shows, to the astonishment of Christians, they resolved to die for their people rather than fight to involve them in a war.[107]

When questioned about their submission, Telokite answered, "Did not your missionaries tell us that Christ died to save his people? So die we, to save our people!"[108]

Although the trial was conducted with all the required legal formalities, the Indians were pre-doomed to die. The prosecution appears to have relied almost entirely on the testimony of witnesses who gave incomplete and unsatisfactory accounts of the events.[109] For example, only Telokite was identified as Whitman's killer, and on cross-examination that identification seemed shaky. Even though the defense attorneys made a vigorous attempt to defend the accused (20 peremptory challenges were made during jury selection in an effort to obtain an unbiased jury), the defendants were speedily convicted on the confusing evidence presented.

Judge Pratt's rulings were uniformly in favor of the prosecution on all important issues: jurisdiction, change of venue, admission of testimony to show Cayuse custom regarding their treatment of medicine men (which might have influenced the jurors to recommend a lesser punishment than hanging), and the defendants' identity. Pratts' charge to the jury that they might infer from the Cayuse nation's surrender of the defendants that they were "in fact the perpetrators of the massacre" lightened the burden of the prosecutor considerably, especially since none of the Cayuses testified about the selection process. Further, proper identification of the defendants by the witnesses, who were for the most part unfamiliar with Indian names or language, might have proved difficult.

Finally, the motions for arrest of judgment and for a new trial were denied and no appeal was filed. Why? Several reasons were advanced: no territorial supreme court could be convened since Pratt was the only judge present in the territory; there was no jail where the prisoners could be kept while awaiting an appeal, either to the territorial supreme court or to the U.S. Supreme Court; it was widely rumored that the defendants would be lynched if there was not a swift execution. Defense attorney Kintzing Pritchette, who was acting as governor during Governor Joseph Lane's absence, wanted to reprieve the defendants until an appeal could be taken to the U. S. Supreme Court. However, Judge Pratt told him there was no firm proof of Lane's absence (though it was a well-known fact), and that such an act would be unauthorized.[110]

The case of *U.S. v. Telokite* hastened the end of the Cayuses as a nation. In less than a decade their proud culture was submerged, their lands were taken from them, and their free nomadic life style was exchanged for the confines of a reservation. The conflict between the Cayuse Indians and the Whitman mission represented an inevitable clash between two cultures—that of the white man and that of the Indian. Here, as elsewhere in America, the Indians were the losers.

ᴖ

# THE CASE OF
# *ROBIN HOLMES v. NATHANIEL FORD*

One of the most significant cases to come before the territorial court involved the question of slavery and involuntary servitude. What was the position of slaves brought into the territory from a slave state? In the case of *Holmes v. Ford*, decided on July 13, 1853, the court recognized the right of a black man to sue for custody of his children, who were being held in virtual slavery by the petitioner's former owner. The decision for the petitioner was notable because it came at a time when the law of slavery, both nationally and locally, was uncertain and many judges were reluctant to hand down an opinion that might prove to be politically unpopular. Even though the decision was advanced for the time, it was almost completely ignored by the press. Three years later it was overruled by implication in *Scott v. Sanford*, in which the U.S. Supreme Court held that property in slaves was to be protected no matter where they might be.[111]

## Oregon Laws of Slavery and Exclusion, 1843 to 1859
Although the Oregon Territory was far removed from the national political scene, the settlers could not escape questions of race and slavery.

Many of the emigrants were natives of slave or border states, and their attitudes reflected the conflicts they had hoped to leave behind.

> *(They), not having been of the privileged class of wealthy planters, well understood the evils of poverty and slavery together…. When they emigrated they determined to leave behind the clinging curse of caste, and to have for their own a free country and free institutions to leave to their children. By a curious and contradictory impulse of mind, no southern man, desiring freedom for himself from the evils of slavery, ever could be brought to look with complacency upon a free negro. The black man, though not to blame for the condition of society his presence entailed, was never forgiven for it, nor admitted to be a sufferer by it.*[112]

This dislike of both slavery and free blacks is evident in the laws enacted, from the initiation of the Provisional Government in 1843 to statehood in 1859.

**Provisional Government.** The organic laws of the Provisional Government, adopted in July of 1843, contained a provision prohibiting slavery and involuntary servitude.[113] In June of 1844 the legislative committee reaffirmed the antislavery prohibition, but added a section calling for the expulsion of all Negroes and mulattoes, both slave and freemen. Any Negro or mulatto convicted under this act faced corporal punishment every six months until he or she left Oregon.[114] At the December 1844 session the act was amended, substituting for corporal punishment a hiring at public auction with a duty on the employer to enforce his employee's departure as soon as possible.[115] In July 1845 both of these acts were repealed.[116]

**Territorial Government.** The bill for the organization of the Oregon Territory, first introduced in Congress in 1846, became embroiled in the sectional dispute over slavery. The controversy centered on whether the bill should specifically prohibit slavery. While it was not anticipated that Oregon would become a slave state, the inclusion of such a prohibition would, southerners argued, establish an undesirable precedent for future western states that might be more suited to slavery. The final bill, passed in August 1848, contained no specific provision relating to slavery, but it did include a provision making the Northwest Ordinance of 1787 applicable to the Oregon Territory. Article VI of the ordinance prohibited slavery and involuntary servitude.[117]

At its first session in September 1849, the territorial legislature reenacted the exclusion law of the Provisional Government. Negroes and mulattoes were again prohibited from settling in Oregon under penalty of fine and imprisonment, though the few already living in the area were permitted to remain.[118] This law was inadvertently repealed when it was mistakenly omitted from the new code of 1853–54. As soon as the error was discovered an almost identical exclusion act was introduced but did not pass. Succeeding legislatures similarly rejected it.

**The Constitution.** The Oregon constitution, adopted in 1857, was very much a "white man's document." Article II, section 6, denied suffrage to Negroes, mulattoes, and Chinese. Slavery was prohibited, but free Negroes were excluded. Article XVIII, section 2, posed three questions for the voters to decide: (1) Do you vote for the constitution? (2) Do you vote for slavery in Oregon? (3) Do you vote for free Negroes in Oregon? The constitution was approved by a vote of 7,193 to 3,125, slavery was rejected 7,725 to 3,125, and the admission of free Negroes was defeated by a vote of 8,640 to 1,081.[119]

**Enforcement of the Laws.** During the territorial period the number of cases involving either slavery or the expulsion of free blacks was small. This is not surprising since there were only 56 blacks and mulattoes in the Oregon Territory in 1850 and no more than 124 by 1860.[120]

The records show that the exclusion laws were not uniformly enforced and that in a number of cases, the presence of free blacks was tolerated. For example, in 1850 a black named George Washington settled in a sparsely populated area north of the Columbia River, even though he was fully aware of the exclusion law. In December 1852 his petition to the legislature to exempt him from the law was granted.[121] A different conclusion was reached, however, in the case of *Magruder v. Vanderpool* (1851), in which Chief Justice Nelson enforced the statute and ordered the defendant, Jacob Vanderpool, to leave Oregon City.[122]

In spite of the prohibitions against slavery there is no doubt that it did exist in Oregon. For example, the 1860 census of Linn County openly lists the occupation of two blacks as "slaves."[123] Most of the cases of slavery resulted when immigrants from slave states brought with them blacks who did not know they were entitled to freedom or were too timid to claim it.[124]

### *Holmes v. Ford* [125]

In deciding the case *Holmes v. Ford*, Chief Justice Williams made it clear that the antislavery laws would be enforced and that slavery in the territory would not be tolerated. Before Williams heard the case, however, it had been in the courts for more than a year. On April 16, 1852, a writ of habeas corpus was issued by the district court of Polk County ordering Nathaniel Ford to produce "the bodies of Jenny or Mary Jane Holmes, Roxana Holmes and James Holmes, by you unlawfully detained...." [126] There must have been a petition to the court by Holmes for the issuance of the writ, but it is not to be found in the existing record.

No further pleadings appear until April 5, 1853, when Ford made his "return." Here he states that he has the children in his "care and possession"; that the child Jenny, along with her parents Robin and Polly, were brought by him from the state of Missouri to this territory in 1844 "as his servants and slaves"; that the children James and Roxanna were born in Oregon; that the parents of the children "were in the possession of this Respondent, as his servants and slaves, and so continued til in or about the year 1849." He further states that when Robin Holmes returned in the spring of 1850 after a year in California, he and Holmes entered into an agreement that Holmes and his wife were henceforth to be free and that they would be allowed to take with them their recently born child. The other three children, however, were to remain with Ford until they became of age "to hold them not as slaves, but as wards." This was only fair, since having provided for them when they were young, he was now entitled to their services. As an additional argument, Ford claims that he had been advised to take the Holmes family back to Missouri where he could sell them, and that he might have done so had he not believed Robin would abide by the agreement. Further he alleges that it was better for the children to stay with him than with Holmes, "who is poor and ignorant and unfit to have the care, custody and bringing up of children."

Robin Holmes' answer, filed April 6, 1853, makes several points. First, he questions his status as a slave at the time he came with Ford to Oregon in 1844. He claims he and his wife had been sold by Ford to satisfy a debt, but the creditor had never claimed them. Ford solicited him to come to Oregon to help him "open a farm," promising that when that task was done Holmes would be free of further service. Second, he asserts he came to Oregon under an agreement with Ford that he would work for Ford for five years and at the end of that time would be "liberated and discharged absolutely from the service and control of said respondent." Third, he alleges that in the spring of 1849, when the five years of service had ended, Ford "desired" that he go to work for a year in the California gold mines with Ford's son Mark, with the understanding that as soon as Holmes returned he and his family would be set free in accordance with the agreement made in Missouri. However, on his return, Holmes says, he was told that he, Polly, and the baby could leave, but that Ford would keep three of the children. Holmes denies that he ever made an agreement with Ford for the children's services. Fourth, Holmes states that Ford often threatened to take the Holmes family back to Missouri and sell them to deter Holmes from seeking custody of his children. Finally, Holmes claims he is well able to provide for his children and is in no way unfit to have their care and custody.

On April 16 Ford requested that the hearing be delayed to await the arrival of General Joseph Lane, whose testimony he alleged would prove the existence of a contract between Ford and Holmes whereby Holmes agreed that Ford was to keep the Holmes children until they were of age. Apparently this request was granted by the presiding judge, Chief Justice Thomas Nelson. A deposition filed by Holmes on June 9 indicates that during the preceeding five weeks, Nelson had refused to act in the case and had let it be known that he would leave the matter to his successor to decide. On that date, Holmes addressed a petition to Cyrus Olney, as associate justice of the supreme court, again asking for a writ of habeas corpus for the release of his children, who he now alleged were in danger of being taken by Ford from the territory and sold as slaves.

Olney was no more willing than Nelson had been to decide this controversial issue. On June 13 he ordered Ford to place the children in the custody of the sheriff of Polk County and to proceed "at any time and any place" to take the testimony of General Joseph Lane, which Ford had claimed was essential to prove his case. In his response, dated June 23, Ford makes essentially the same allegations as in his earlier pleading, holding that he has a "legal and equitable right" to keep the children because of the agreement with Holmes and his support of the children during their early years. On June 24 Olney issued an order that the final disposition of the children await the arrival of the newly appointed Chief Justice Williams and that in the meantime Jenny, who had reached her majority, was free to leave Ford whenever she desired. Roxanna was awarded to Ford and James to Holmes until the later hearing.

The record does not show whether Jenny returned to her parents' home or whether James was released to his father. However, on July 13 another petition seeking custody of all three children was filed by Holmes in the Polk County District Court before Judge Williams, alleging once more that Ford had the children in his custody and refused to release them. Williams' order of July 13, 1853, is simple and brief: "The said children…are hereby awarded to the care and custody of their parents Robin Holmes and his wife as fully in all respects as though they…had not been in the custody of the said Ford." [127]

Judge Williams' opinion does not appear in the court record, but it was published almost two weeks later in the *Oregon City Statesman*. [128] He quickly dismissed the possibility that Ford might be entitled to Holmes and his family as slaves.

> *Respondent makes no claim to said children because their parents were his slaves in Missouri, and certainly none can exist for as soon as the laws of Oregon touched the parties the relation of master and slave was dissolved and petitioner and his wife and children were made free people.*

He found that no mutually binding contract existed between Holmes and Ford for a grant of custody of the children to Ford; he dismissed the testimony of General Lane as vague and unsatisfactory; he noted that the terms and conditions of service were not set out and that there was no consideration, since the respondent was not bound to do anything.

> *Every subsisting contract must have a good or valuable consideration to support it. The consideration by respondent for the alleged contract as shown by his answer and evidence was an attempted grant of freedom to petitioner and his wife. To convey that to a person which at the time is absolutely his by law plainly amounts to nothing.*

## Behind the Record

In reminiscing about *Holmes v. Ford* many years later, Williams wrote, "Whether or not slaveholders could carry their slaves into the territories and hold them there as property had become a burning question, and my predecessors in office for reasons best known to themselves, had declined to hear the case." [129] This is not a completely accurate statement, since both Nelson and Olney heard the case but refused to decide it.

When Williams arrived in Oregon, he determined to settle the matter quickly and with as little fanfare as possible. He did not place the case on the supreme court docket, but chose instead to hear it *de novo* in the district court in Polk County. [130] He later described the hearing in these words:

*Mr. Ford contended that these colored people were his property in Missouri...and he had as much a right to bring that kind of property into Oregon and hold it here as such as he had to bring his cattle or any other property here and hold it as such; but my opinion was, and so I held, that without some positive legislative enactment establishing slavery here, it did not and could not exist in Oregon, and so I awarded to the colored people their freedom.*[131]

This states the holding too broadly, since the issue of slavery was never squarely before the court. According to the opinion itself, Ford never claimed to hold any of the Holmes family in Oregon as slaves. The decision rested instead on the contractual issue.

It was nonetheless a landmark decision for several reasons. It recognized the right of a black man to sue in the Oregon territorial courts; it effectively put an end to attempts to hold slaves legally in Oregon; and, of greatest significance, it anticipated the ultimate result of the issue, resolved finally by the Civil War.

# *MARLIN v. T'VAULT*: TITLE TO TOWNSITES IN OREGON[132]

Free land—expected or promised—was the principal motivation for the mass migration of settlers to the Oregon Country from 1843 onward. As early as 1840, those in the national government who believed that the United States should move quickly to establish its claim to the Pacific Northwest recognized that offering free ownership of land would be the most successful way to encourage American settlement of the area. Senator Lewis Linn of Missouri, in particular, repeatedly introduced bills in Congress providing for land grants to settlers. Though none of these bills was enacted, they kept the issue before the public and were influential in inducing the migration to Oregon.[133]

For many of the immigrants arriving in 1843 and the following years, establishing a land claim by marking its boundaries and building a shelter represented their reward for overcoming the dangers and hardships of the cross-country trip. Records show, however, that a surprising number came not to settle down and raise crops, but as small-scale speculators.

*The land offices received entries from 3,134 persons qualified to receive sections (or half sections) by virtue of residence in Oregon before December 1, 1850. This is a surprisingly low number out of the possible 8000 or more adults in the Territory by this date....*

*...It is also interesting that few original claimants retained the lands they filed upon. This may have been because of the fluidity of the American frontier settlement, but it also suggests that many claimants were speculators on a small scale.*[134]

## Protection of Land Claims

Regardless of their reasons for emigrating to Oregon, the pioneers knew that only a governmental authority could protect their claims against trespassers and rival claimants. Thus the first organic laws of the Provisional Government, adopted July 5, 1843, contained articles dealing with land claims. Section 17 provided for recording claims by current and future claimants, set forth the qualifications of claimants, and generally limited claims to 640 acres per person. After amendments in 1844, this land law appeared in revised form in the Organic Law of the Provisional Government of Oregon adopted by the people on July 26, 1845.[135]

The settlers recognized that the laws of the Provisional Government were of a temporary nature and gave only limited protection to their claims. As we have seen, they were anxious to have the border with Great Britain established so that the United States could grant territorial status to the region and enact a land law upon which they could fully rely. The boundary treaty was signed in 1846, territorial status achieved in 1848, and the donation land act passed in 1850.

While the Territorial Act provided that those laws of the Provisional Government that were not incompatible with the U.S. Constitution or with the Territorial Act's provisions were to remain in force, it specifically excepted the land laws. Most threatening to the settler who had established his claim under the Provisional Government was the section declaring that "all laws heretofore passed in said territory making grants of land...shall be and are declared null and void."[136] The Oregon Donation Act did much to allay this anxiety. It allowed generous grants of land to settlers and enabled most to reestablish their claims without undue difficulty. While it changed the law of the Provisional Government by reducing the amount of land granted each settler from 620 to 320 acres, it granted an additional 320 acres to wives. Thus a family was still entitled to one section.[137] According to some sources this led to brief courtships and early weddings of brides who were often teenagers.[138]

Applying the new law was not always an easy task, in spite of its seemingly simple and straightforward provisions. For example, the Oregon Donation Act did not make clear the status of townsites. Were the donations of public lands to be made for agricultural purposes only, as some argued, or were townsites also included in the act? The status of townsites was made more uncertain because of questions regarding the application to Oregon of the Public Lands Act of 1844. Titled an act "for the relief of citizens of towns upon lands of the United States, under certain circumstances," it set out a procedure for validating claims to townsites on public lands.[139] How, if at all, was this act to be applied in Oregon? This was a question for the courts.

## Application of the Land Law

As has been described, the Oregon territorial court was driven by politically motivated differences and could scarcely be said to operate as a supreme court until the appointment of Judges Williams, Olney, and Deady in 1853. Publication of the court's decisions was one of Chief Justice Williams' important procedural reforms. The first formal publication, *Oregon Reports* Volume 1, begins with the December 1853 term of the "Supreme Court of the United States for the Territory of Oregon" and states on page one that it includes "cases argued and determined in The Supreme Court of the State of Oregon and Decisions rendered in the District Court of the United States for the District of Oregon." If appeals of minor criminal offenses and decisions on procedural issues are omitted, the cases dealing with land questions represent at least one half of what may be termed the "important" cases in which the court published an opinion. This is evidence of both the settlers' desire to have their claims verified and the court's problems in applying the various statutes.

The case of *Marlin v. T'Vault et al.* illustrates the difficulties the court encountered in reconciling the tangle of provisions in the land laws: the enactments of the Provisional Government (1843–45), the Public Lands Act of 1844 (also called the Townsite Act), the Territorial Act of 1848, and the Oregon Donation Act of 1850.

The facts in the Marlin case are relatively simple. In 1847 the plaintiff, Marlin, conveyed a land claim to the defendants in exchange for the promise (referred to as their "bond" in the opinion) to obtain title and convey to him a block of ten lots in a townsite they had created and named Columbia in the county of Vancouver. More particularly, the defendants promised, in the words of the court, "to comply with all the requisites of the act of Congress granting donations of land to settlers in Oregon, so as to acquire title to said block and then to convey, etc."[140] The plaintiff alleged that the defendants had not complied in any way with the landgrant laws and had not provided title to him. The case came before the court on defendants' demurrer—that is, the defendants alleged that even if plaintiff's facts were true, they did not state a cause of action.

## Williams' Opinion

Chief Justice Williams wrote the opinion for the court. In overruling the demurrer he demonstrated both his practicality and his determination to give controlling weight to the unique history of Oregon land grants. The defendants argued numerous grounds in support of their demurrer. Of these, Williams thought several worthy of notice and dealt with them decisively but at such considerable length that he ended his opinion by saying somewhat defensively:

> These general views, fuller, perhaps, than the necessities of the case required, have been expressed to show in what light courts of law might regard the question.[141]

The most important of Williams' responses to the defendants' arguments may be summarized as follows: The defendants asserted that at the date of the contract there was no act of Congress granting donations of land to settlers of Oregon and that the contract was unenforceable for that reason. However, Williams said that public history showed that at the time of the contract it was expected that a congressional act would authorize land grants and that the contract was made on this understanding.

Before the contract date, February 18, 1847, the defendants had laid out a townsite plan and, as described above, had sold a block of lots to the plaintiff. They argued that under the Oregon Donation Act of 1850, townsites could not be taken and held and that their failure to perform their contract obligation was excused by this legislative prohibition. Williams recognized clearly that if the defendants prevailed on this ground, many other settlers in similar situations might have their titles to land overturned, with all the resultant confusion that would follow. Therefore, he devoted the bulk of his opinion to a vigorous repudiation of the defendants' suggestion.

In support of their position, the defendants relied chiefly on a recent opinion of Commissioner Wilson of the general land office. Williams summarized the commissioner's reasoning as follows:

> lst. *The act of 14 August, 1848, establishing a territorial government for Oregon, "shuts out" all claims under the territorial laws prior to its enactment.*
>
> 2d. *By said act of Congress, the laws of the United States were declared in force in this territory, so far as the same, or any provision thereof, might be applicable.*
>
> 3d. *The act of 23d of May, 1844, relative to town sites upon the public lands, being a law of the United States, was put in force here by said act of 1848, so that town sites were to be entered by certain public authorities, and not subject to be held as donation by private persons.*
>
> 4th. *That donations of land, under the act of September 27th, 1850, are only made for agricultural purposes.*[142]

Williams would accept none of this reasoning. He recognized that Section 14 of the Territorial Act provided "that all laws heretofore passed in said territory, making grants of land, or otherwise affecting or incumbering title to lands, shall be null and void…." But he said that before the Territorial Act was passed, many persons had taken and improved claims under the laws of the Provisional Government and in his view, "Congress did not intend to leave these claims without any legal protection."[143]

In Williams' view, under a proper interpretation of congressional intent the claims were not void as between the citizens of the territory. The "null and void" provision of Section 14 simply meant that the land claim laws of the Provisional Government could not bind or encumber the title in the United States. He then pointed to several provisions of the Donation Act of 1850 which expressly recognized claims made under the Provisional Government and concluded that whatever effect the Territorial Act may have had on such claims, the act of 1850 "clearly saves and protects them." [144]

The sentence in Section 14 of the Territorial Act quoted above concludes with the statement that "the laws of the United States are hereby extended over, and declared to be in force in said territory, so far as the same or any provision thereof, may be applicable." The Public Lands Act of 1844 contained provisions granting municipal authorities special rights to townsites and restricting private persons from taking a claim to a townsite. On the ground that the Act of 1844 was a law of the United States which was extended to Oregon by the above-quoted provision of the Territorial Act, the commissioner held that townsites were "not subject to be held as donation by private persons."

Again Williams found the development of Oregon's land law under the Provisional Government to be unlike the evolution of land law of the other territories. After relating several examples of the impossibility of applying the 1844 Act to the Oregon situation, he concludes with a scornful repudiation of the commissioner on this point:

> …there never was and there never will be a time when town sites in Oregon could or can be entered in accordance with said Act of 1844…. No claims were ever taken with reference to such laws and nobody ever dreamed of being governed by them until the late decision of the Commissioner. [145]

In the concluding portion of his opinion, Williams strikes at a statement by the commissioner that "policy was as strong as the law in support of his opinion," saying:

> …people have universally acted on the belief that the Act of 1844 was not in force here. Claims have been located, improvements made and moneys loaned on this assumption, and the effect of a contrary rule is now to unsettle rights, and strike a blow at the property of nearly every town in Oregon. If policy is to be consulted in construing the donation act, it ought to be a policy as liberal to the first settlers of the country to the men who braved the perils of the then unbroken wilderness as to those who have since followed in their footsteps. [146]

As noted above, Justices Olney and Deady sat with Williams on the Marlin case and concurred in Williams' opinion. Professor Ralph James Mooney in the next chapter[18] describes how in 1861 Judge Deady, sitting as the federal district judge for the District of Oregon in the case of *Lownsdale v. City of Portland*, similarly held that the 1844 Act did not extend to Oregon. Deady referred respectfully to Williams' opinion with the comment:

> This subject is ably and intelligently examined in the Case of Marlin v. T'Vault, et al., decided in the Supreme Court of the late territory of Oregon at the June term, 1854. [147]

Finally, when the Oregon case of *Stark v. Starr* was heard by the United States Supreme Court, Justice Field strongly upheld the view of Williams and Deady that the Townsite Act did not apply to Oregon.[148] In his opinion, Justice Field quoted at length from Justice Deady's holding in *Lownsdale v. City of Portland* and said of *Marlin v. T'Vault*:

*A similar view of the subject was taken by the Supreme Court of the State, after full examination, in the case of* Marlin v. T'Vault. *That court concludes a well considered opinion by stating that the people of the State had universally acted upon the belief that the act of 1844 was not in force there, and that the effect of a contrary rule would be to unsettle rights, and strike a blow at the prosperity of nearly every town in Oregon.*[149]

As already noted, Williams' opinion in *Marlin v. T'Vault* was issued in the June 1854 term of the territorial court. Whether by coincidence or in response to the holding in that case, Congress by an act of July 17, 1854, amended the Oregon Donation Act in several respects. Included were provisions that townsites or "lands settled upon for purposes of business or trade, and not for agriculture" were to be specifically excluded from the operation of the donation act and that the 1844 Townsite Act applied to Oregon lands.[150] In the early 1860s the decisions in *Lownsdale v. City of Portland* and *Starr v. Stark*, cited above, made it clear that the Townsite Act was effective in Oregon only as to lands claimed after the passage of the 1854 amendments.

❧

# CONCLUSION

Oregon's first federal courts—those of the territory— functioned as both federal and state courts. In spite of the shortcomings described in this chapter, they met the basic needs of the society by maintaining order and settling disputes. Even though the courts were never completely free from prejudice, politics, and self-interest, the performance of the judges improved notably during the ten years from territory to statehood, and under the direction of Chief Justice George Williams much was done to organize the courts and their records.

When Oregon became a state in 1859, the territorial courts were replaced by two separate court systems—federal and state—each with its own jurisdiction and its own laws. Because many problems of great importance to the local citizenry and to the national government had not yet been settled, cases coming before the new United States District Court for the State of Oregon required it to determine a number of issues critical to the state's development. These judicial duties fell upon the capable shoulders of Judge Matthew P. Deady, the first federal district court judge for Oregon. In contrast to many of the judges who had presided over the territorial courts, Deady proved himself worthy of his heavy responsibilities.

It is fitting that the territorial period should end and the period of statehood begin with a man of Deady's caliber on the federal bench. He has been aptly described as Oregon's first citizen, who more than any other individual gave form to Oregon's political, cultural, and legal institutions.[151]

---

∾

# NOTES

1. ..."British claims based on occupation were overwhelmingly strong in 1826. Except for a few free trappers there was not a single American resident in the entire Oregon Country, while the Company had a well-knit and extensive system of permanent posts, some with farms, and maintained a veritable army of employees beyond the Rockies." J. A. Hussey, *Champoeg: a Place of Transition*, 121 (1967).

2. It was weakly contended that the Oregon Country was a part of the Louisiana Purchase. B. J. Hibbard, *A History of the Public Land Policies* 1920 (1939).

3. F. V. Holman, *A Brief History of the Oregon Provisional Government*, 13 Or. Hist. Q. 89 (1912).

4. W. A. Bowen, *The Willamette Valley* 12-13 (1978).

5. Some historians have seen the first step toward organized government in the selection of Dr. Ira L. Babcock on February 18, 1841, to act as "Supreme Judge with probate powers" to settle the estate of Ewing Young. Young had died intestate, possessed of a rather large estate, and it was realized that an impartial settlement of his affairs was necessary to avoid dissension. See: *Mirth Tufts Kaplan, Courts, Counselors and Cases: The Judiciary of Oregon's Provisional Government*, 62 Or. Hist. Q. 117, 120-22 (1961).

6. *Id.* at 119-20.

7. The 1843 organic laws of the Provisional Government are reproduced in D. C. Duniway and N. R. Riggs, *The Oregon Archives, 1841-1843*, 60 Or. Hist. Q. 211 (1959). The 1845 version appears in *General Laws of Oregon, 1843-1872*, at 46-51.

8. The Organic Law of the Provisional Government (1845), Art. III.

9. 9 Stat. 323 (1848).

10. 1 Stat. 52 (1787).

11. U.S. Const. art. 4, sec. 3.

12. Oregon Donation Act, 9 Stat. 497 (1850).

13. *Silver v. Ladd,* U.S. Sup. Ct., 7 Wall. 219 (1868).

14. *McAllister v. U.S.*, 141 U.S. 174 (1890); *Wingard v. U.S.*, 141 U.S. 241 (1890).

15. 9 Stat. 323, sec. 9 (1848).

16. See S. Teiser, *The First Chief Justice of the Oregon Territory: William P. Bryant*, 48 Ore. Hist. Q. 45 (1947).

17. Champoeg County was changed to Marion County on September 3, 1849, in honor of General Francis Marion.

18. Teiser, *First Associate Justice of Oregon Territory: O.C. Pratt*, 49 Or. Hist. Q. 171, 176-77.

19. Tualatin County was renamed Washington County on September 3, 1849, in honor of President George Washington.

20. Teiser, *supra* note 18 at 178-79.

21. *Id.* at 178.

22. 2 H. H. Bancroft, *History of Oregon* 307 n. 26 (1886).

23. S. Teiser, *William Strong, Associate Justice of the Territorial Courts*, 64 Or. Hist. Q. 293 (1964).

24. W.D. Strong, *Knickerbocker Views of the Oregon Country: Judge William Strong's Narrative*, 62 Or. Hist. Q. 57, 65 (1961).

25. C. H. Carey, *General History of Oregon* 482-83 (3d ed. 1971).

26. Strong, *supra* note 24, at 63-64.

27. T. N. Strong, *Cathlamet on the Columbia* 100 (1906).

28. Strong, *supra* note 24, at 65-66.

29. Teiser, *supra* note 23, at 304.

30. *Id.* at 306.

31. S. Teiser, *The Second Chief Justice in Oregon Territory: T. Nelson*, 48 Or. Hist. Q. 214 (1947).

32. *Oregon City Statesman*, July 22, 1851.

33. *Id.* Sept. 2, 1851.

34. See F. Lockley, *Some Documentary Records of Slavery in Oregon*, 23 Or. Hist. Q. 111, 125-26 (1922).

35. D. C. Johnson, *Politics, Personalities, and Policies of the Territorial Supreme Court, 1848–1859*, 4 Envtl. L. 11, 41 (1973).

36. J. K. Kelly, *History of the Preparation of the First Code of Oregon*, 4 Or. Hist. Q. 185, 189 (1903).

37. *Portland Oregonian*, July 26, 1889.

38. S. Teiser, *Life of George. H. Williams: Almost Chief Justice*, 47 Or. Hist. Q. 255, 417, 440.

39. *Portland Oregonian*, June 24, 1854.

40. Johnson, *supra* note 35, at 62-63.

41. 1 Or. 51 (1853).

42. *Id.* at 58-59.

43. 1 Or. 153 (1854).

44. *Id.* at 155-56.

45. 1 Or. 77 (1854).

46. *Portland Oregonian*, Dec. 25, 1873; Jan. 5, 1874.

47. Teiser, *supra* note 38, at 432-33.

48. S. Teiser, *Cyrus Olney, Associate Justice of Oregon Territory Supreme Court*, 64 Or. Hist. Q. 309 (1963).

49. Nathan was, among other things, an Indian fighter. On one occasion when he was protecting an immigrant train from an attack, an arrow lodged in his head. Doctors were unable to remove it completely, and he eventually died of its effects.

See Teiser, *supra* note 48, at 317-18.

    50. G.H. Williams, *Occasional Addresses* 174 (1895).

    51. *Id.*

    52. *Portland Oregonian,* May 21, 1853.

    53. *Id.,* June 6, 1853.

    54. Johnson, *supra* note 35, at 53-55.

    55. S. Teiser, *A Pioneer Judge for Oregon,* 44 Or. Hist. Q. 51 (1943), at 76.

    56. Johnson, *supra* note 35, at 14.

    57. F. Holman, *Dr. John McLoughlin, Father of Oregon* 103 (1907).

    58. Jason Lee to Elijah White. April 25, 1843. Quoted in R. J. Loewenberg, *Equality on the Frontier, Jason Lee and the Methodist Mission, 1834-43,* at 192 (1976).

    59. As an employee of the Hudson's Bay Company, McLoughlin believed his acceptance of the authority of the Provisional Government would be interpeted as an act of disloyalty to the company and to Great Britain. In 1845, after the Organic Law was extensively amended making it more compatible with his interests and those of the company, he was persuaded by Jesse Applegate and others to join the new government, bringing with him most of the company's employees. 1 Bancroft, *History of Oregon* 493ff.

    60. Agreement between Dr. John McLoughlin, the Reverend A. P. Waller, and the Reverend David Leslie, of April 4, 1844, reproduced in Holman, *McLoughlin, supra* note 57, at 224-28; for an account of the circumstances surrounding this agreement, see F. F. Victor, *River of the West* 355ff. (1974; originally published 1870).

    61. *Oregon City Spectator,* Sept. 12, 1850.

    62. 9 Stat. 497 (1850).

    63. 9 Stat. 869 (1846).

    64. Excerpted from Thurston's letter to the House of Representatives, published in the *Spectator,* Sept. 12, 1850.

    65. Johnson, *supra* note 35, at 23.

    66. *Spectator,* Sept. 12, 1850.

    67. Holman, *supra* note 57, at 160.

    68. *Id.* at 144.

    69. *Spectator,* Dec. 27, 1849; Jan. 10, 1850.

    70. *General Laws of Oregon, 1862,* at 90.

    71. Johnson, *supra* note 35, at 26-27.

    72. The Location Law controversy was the subject of a "Message from the President of the United States inviting the attention of Congress to the condition of things in the Territory of Oregon." This document contains materials relating to the case of *Short v. Ermatenger,* including the opinions of the judges. House Executive Documents, 32nd Congress, 1st Session, Document No. 94, May 3, 1852, hereafter cited as Doc. 94. The opinions may also be found in the *Oregon City Spectator,* Dec. 9, 1851 and Jan. 6, 1852. It should be noted that "Ermatenger" appears in other sources as "Ermatinger" or "Armitinger".

    73. Doc. 94, *supra* note 72, at 7.

    74. Or. Terr. Laws, 2nd Gen. Sess, 1851, at 222.

    75. 9 Stat. 323, sec. 6 (1848).

76. Doc. 94 *supra* note 72, at 34.

77. *Id.* at 56.

78. Quoted in: Johnson, *supra* note 35, at 37-38.

79. Doc. 94, *supra* note 72, at 14-21.

80. *Id.* at 14.

81. There was disagreement about when the law of the Provisional Government designating Oregon City as the capital was passed, if at all. Strong asserts such a law was enacted on June 27, 1844, whereas Pratt doubts one was ever passed. If such a law was enacted in June of 1844, it was never published. However, a law locating the seat of government at Oregon City was enacted on Dec. 19, 1845. *Laws of a General and Local Nature, 1843-49*, at 37 (Salem 1853).

82. Doc. 94, at 17.

83. *Id.* at 20.

84. *Id.* at 21.

85. Doc. 94, appendix, at 833.

86. *Id.* at 11.

87. *Id.* at 20.

88. *Id.* at 23 (Italics are Pratt's).

89. Doc. 94, at 32.

90. 10 Stat. 146 (1852).

91. For the complete story, see M. Deady, "The Battle of the Blue Books" (original in Bancroft Library, University of California, Berkeley; copy in Oregon Historical Society library).

92. *U.S. vs. Telokite et als.* (*sic*), U.S.D.C. for the County of Clackamas, Order Book 1 (Journal), 1849-1856, at 28-32.

93. *Oregon City Spectator*, May 30, 1850.

94. R. H. Ruby & J. A. Brown, *The Cayuse Indians, Imperial Tribesmen of Old Oregon* 63ff (1972).

95. *Id.* at 86.

96. Letter from the Rev. H. K. W. Perkins to Jane Perkins, Oct. 19, 1849. Reprinted in 2 C. M. Drury, *Marcus and Narcissa Whitman and the Opening of Old Oregon* 392 (1986).

97. A. M. Josephy, Jr., *The Nez Perce Indians and the Opening of the Northwest* 165-66 (1965).

98. Victor, *supra* note 60, at 401; Drury, *supra* note 96, vol.1, at 437-41.

99. Victor, *supra* note 60, at 404; see also Drury, *supra* note 96, vol. 2, at 211-12.

100. Other sources disagree on the number of victims. *The Oregon City Spectator* of December 9, 1847, lists nine dead, but the names are not identical with those given in the indictments. This is understandable, since on that date most of the survivors were still captives and their stories were yet to be heard. In what is to date probably the most reliable account of the massacre, 13 people are identified as having been killed by the Indians during the period November 29 through December 8: Marcus and Narcissa Whitman, Frances and John Sager, Nathan Kimball, Luke M. Saunders, Jacob A. Hoffman, Walter Marsh, Isaac Gilliland, Andrew Rodgers, James Young, Crocket Bewley, and Amos Sales. A fourteenth person listed as a victim was Peter Hall, who drowned after escaping from Waiilatpu. See Drury, *supra* note 96, at 224ff.

101. In 1834 Congress passed an act providing that all U.S. territory west of the Mississippi was "Indian Territory" and that the criminal laws of the U.S. should be in force there (4 Stat. 729, secs. 1 and 24). At that time Oregon territory was not a part of the U.S., and it was highly questionable whether the 1834 act could be properly extended to the area prior to the passage of the Territorial Act of 1848. In a case decided in 1853, Chief Justice Williams of the territorial supreme court held that, "Congress, by express enactment in 1850, extended said act to this territory, for the reason…that it was not in force here before that time." *U.S. v. Tom*, 1 Or. 26. If this decision had been made before the Cayuse trial, presumably the plea in bar would have been granted.

102. Other sources place Whitman's killing in the kitchen of the mission house, and a later account by Catherine Sager, who was present at the massacre, asserts Eliza Hall mistakenly identified Whitman as the victim of the attack she witnessed. Drury, *supra* note 96, at 225-26.

103. *Oregon City Spectator*, May 30, 1850.

104. *Id.*

105. Drury, *supra* note 96, at 327ff.

106. *Id.*, vol. 1, at 437. The case file is confused by the inclusion of an indictment against "Tomonoes" for the murder of Emmon Stevens on January 1, 1850. The name "Emmon Stevens" does not appear elsewhere in connection with the Whitman murders, and the date disproves any relationship between the two cases. Further, on May 22 an *ad capias* (a writ of arrest) was issued against Tomonoes, and the case was continued. Over a year later, on September 1, 1851, he was again indicted for murder and the case was again continued. This would indicate that Tomonoes was not another spelling for Tomahas as has been suggested.

107. Victor, *supra* note 60, at 493.

108. *Id.* at 494.

109. Because witnesses' verbatim testimony is not included in the record, the jury may have heard fuller accounts of the events surrounding the massacre than appear in the record. Drury, *supra* note 96, at 326.

110. F. F. Victor, *Early Indian Wars of Oregon* 251 (1894).

111. 60 U.S. 363 (1857).

112. Bancroft, *supra* note 59, at 483.

113. Prov. and Terr. Govt. Papers of Oregon, docs. 1582 and 1583; Duniway and Riggs, *supra* note 7, at 258, 274.

114. Prov. & Terr. Govt. Papers, doc. 12191, at 41.

115. *Laws of a General and Local Nature, 1843-49*, at 83.

116. *Oregon Acts and Laws…of 1845*, at 8.

117. 9 stat. 323, sec. 4 (1848).

118. 1859 Or. Laws 181.

119. Constitution of Oregon, Art. XVIII, sec. 2, in General Laws of Oregon, 1843-1872, at 97, n.1.

120. K. Richard, *Unwelcome Settlers: Black and Mulatto Oregon Pioneers*, 84 Or. Hist. Q. 173, at 193-99 (1983).

121. Prov. and Terr. Govt. Papers, doc. 4530.

122. *Oregon City Statesman*, Sept. 2, 1851.

123. Richard, *supra* note 120, at 37.

124. Q. Taylor, *Slaves and Free Men: Blacks in the Oregon Country*, 1840-1860, 83 Or. Hist. Q. 153, 167 (1982).

125. The original records of this case are in the Polk County courthouse; reprinted in F. Lockley, *Some Documentary Records of Slavery in Oregon*, 23 Or. Hist. Q. 111 (1922).

126. Interestingly, the writ was "allowed" by "O. C. Pratt, Atty.," but the endorsement was signed by "O. C. Pratt, 2. Jud Dist. O. Territory." Pratt served as territorial court judge from January 1849 until April 1853.

127. Lockley, *supra* note 125, at 136.

128. *Oregon City Statesman*, July 26, 1853.

129. G. Williams, *Political History of Oregon from 1863 to 1865*, 2 Or. Hist. Q. 1, 5.

130. *Oregon City Statesman*, July 5, 1853.

131. Williams, *supra* note 129, at 5.

132. 1 Or. 77 (1854).

133. Carey, *supra* note 25, at 445 ff.

134. D. O. Johansen and C. M. Gates, *Empire of the Columbia*, 232-34 (2d ed. 1967).

135. Duniway and Riggs, *supra* note 7, at 279.

136. 9 Stat. 323, sec. 14 (1848).

137. 9 Stat. 497, sec. 4 (1850).

138. Carey, *supra* note 25 , at 482.

139. 5 Stat. 657 (1844).

140. 1 Or. at 78.

141. *Id.* at 86.

142. *Id.* at 79-80.

143. *Id.* at 81.

144. *Id.* at 81-83.

145. *Id.* at 84.

146. *Id.* at 85-86.

147. 1 Or. 381, at 393.

148. 73 U.S. (6 Wall.) 402 (1867).

149. *Id.* at 417.

150. 10 Stat. 305, sec. 7 (1854).

151. See R. M. Brown, *Historical Perspectives on Matthew P. Deady*, 63 Or. L. Rev. 639 (1984).

# CHAPTER 2

❧

# THE DEADY YEARS
# 1859–1893

BY RALPH JAMES MOONEY

*"BE IT REMEMBERED that at a term of the
United States District Court for the District of Oregon
begun and holden at Salem…, on the twelfth day
of September A.D. Eighteen hundred and fifty nine,…*

*The following proceedings were had, to wit:*

*The Hon. M. P. Deady having been appointed Judge
of this Court and having taken the oath required by law,
took his seat upon the bench and his commission
with the oath of office endorsed thereon was ordered
to be entered at length in the minutes."*[1]

T hus began the United States District Court for the District of
Oregon, presided over by 35-year-old Matthew Paul Deady. Born
May 12, 1824, in Talbot County, Maryland, Judge Deady was the eldest
child of an Irish immigrant father and a mother born and raised in
Baltimore. His father Daniel, a "rather stern, self-willed man," taught
school, moving the family to and from teaching posts in West Virginia,
Ohio, Kentucky, and Mississippi. Following his mother's 1834 death
from tuberculosis, Matthew lived for two years in Baltimore with his
maternal grandparents, then returned to live on his father's southern
Ohio farm purchased to give him and four siblings the "benefit of country life and labor."[2]

But Matthew took poorly to such life and labor, preferring the books in his father's library to unrelieved toil on the farm. In early 1841 he had a disagreement with his father and left home never to return.[3] He moved to nearby Barnesville, Ohio, where he spent four years as a blacksmith apprentice and also earned a teaching certificate by attending the local academy. In late 1845 he moved to St. Clairsville, Ohio, where he taught school for a year, then read law with William Kennon, a former congressman and presiding judge of the local common pleas court. In 1847 he joined the Ohio bar and began a small practice with Judge Kennon's brother. Like many young lawyers, he "paid some attention to politics, made some speeches, and...belonged to a polemic society."[4]

In 1849 Deady moved West. Convinced by his own polemic-society argument that gold mining disadvantaged a region, he chose Oregon rather than California as his destination.[5] He arrived at Oregon City in November 1849, dazzled by the beauty of Mount Hood as he canoed down the Columbia.

Deady settled first in Lafayette, teaching school and minding a store while beginning his law practice. In June 1850 he was elected to the Territorial Assembly and six months later began compiling the territorial laws into a single, organized volume. The following year he was elected to the Council (upper house), and in 1852 he became its president. Throughout those early years, Deady was a prominent member of the Democratic "Salem Clique" which, in uneasy alliance with congressional delegate Joseph Lane, controlled Oregon politics until late in the decade.[6]

In 1853 Democratic President Franklin Pierce appointed Deady to the territorial supreme court, where he served for six years. During that time he also presided over Oregon's 1857 constitutional convention, and at statehood in 1859 voters elected him to the new state supreme court. He chose instead to accept President James Buchanan's appointment as Oregon's first United States district judge, which he remained until his death in 1893.[7]

Matthew Deady dominated the Oregon legal landscape for four decades. Even while serving as federal district judge, he drafted or compiled many of the state's early statutes, including its codes of civil and criminal procedure and its landmark corporations act. In 1864 and 1872, he reprised his role as "Oregon Justinian" by compiling and annotating major new editions of Oregon Laws. Judicial colleagues ranging from United States Supreme Court justices to Oregon's own state-court judges frequently praised his learning and ability. Even the state's general public

*The Honorable Matthew P. Deady served on the territorial supreme court, presided over Oregon's 1857 constitutional convention, and served as a federal district judge from 1859 to 1893. He drafted or compiled many or Oregon's early statues, including its codes of civil and criminal procedure and its landmark corporations act. (Oregon Historical Society Negative #ORHI77105)*

knew and respected many of his legal and law-related views, which he publicized by periodic speeches and newspaper articles.

Throughout his career, Judge Deady revered the law, especially the common law, as foundation and guardian of a rational, orderly world. A devoted Anglophile, he read widely in English history and literature, and for him Westminster Hall was the supreme "bulwark of liberty and buttress of order." In a "Law and Lawyers" lecture he delivered frequently, he explained how the common law pervaded virtually all American law and served as "source and panoply" of the nation's cherished tradition of ordered liberty:

> The common law people—the English race, wherever they go, establish limited governments, with Parliaments and juries;...[T]he common law is the source and panoply of all those features of our system, which distinguish us from the subjects of absolute governments, ancient or modern,—either by monarchs or majorities. It was made by freemen for freemen.

Deady thus strongly associated judge-made law with preservation of Anglo-American ideals of limited, enlightened self-government. Generations of "profound jurists" had defended those ideals against the tyranny of both monarch and mob, and Deady was determined to extend that tradition to the American Far West.[8]

∾

# FEDERAL PUBLIC LAND LAW IN EARLY OREGON

America's vast and rich public domain contributed profoundly to the development of its nineteenth-century economy, society, and imagination. Federal policies distributing that domain hastened settlement of communities from the Appalachians to the Pacific, promoted internal improvements ranging from local turnpikes to transcontinental railroads, and helped finance countless public buildings, public schools, and land-grant colleges. By 1880 Congress had passed nearly 3,000 statutes granting or regulating parts of the public domain, and related administrative and judicial caseloads were increasing rapidly as well.[9]

Matthew Deady contributed to this central theme of American history a remarkable series of decisions interpreting the cornerstone of early Oregon public land law, the 1850 Oregon Donation Act. Although Deady decided other public land law questions as well,[10] it is his Donation Act decisions helping determine ownership of the Portland land claim which reveal most clearly both the importance of federal law in early Oregon and Deady's own very traditional approach to land-title disputes.

The Portland land-claim cases were uncommonly difficult to resolve. They often required Deady to reconstruct complex fact patterns, then interpret and apply an opaque federal statute overlaid with ancient common-law property doctrines. Worse, they forced him to confront repeatedly, under intense public scrutiny, the abiding judicial dilemma: how best to reconcile the need for clear, general rules of uniform, predictable application with the equally compelling need for particular results consistent with individual and community conscience. Judge Deady struggled with this dilemma in the Portland cases, often having to choose between "legal" title embodied in government land patents and formal deeds and the "equitable" title claims of good-faith purchasers who actually lived and worked on the disputed parcels.

Deady's choices tended to emphasize the former, the importance to "civilized society" of secure land titles, common-law conveyancing principles, and literal interpretations of deed language. Unhappily for him, both Circuit Judge Lorenzo Sawyer and the Supreme Court tended toward the opposite point of view, ultimately ruling in most cases for good-faith purchasers of small parcels by emphasizing the "intrinsic justice" of the disputes.

## The Oregon Donation Act
## and the Settlement of Early Portland

In September 1850 Congress passed the long-awaited Oregon Donation Act. Section 4 granted to every "white settler" residing in the Oregon Territory by December 1, 1850, 320 acres if a "single man" or 640 acres if a "married man," half to his wife "in her own right." The share of a settler who died without a will and before receiving a federal land patent went to his or her "survivor and children or heirs…in equal proportions." Section 5 then encouraged future emigration by granting to certain later-arriving "white male citizens" 160 acres if single and 320 acres if married, again half to the wife "in her own right." Eventually, Oregonians patented more than 7,000 claims under the Donation Act.[11]

Seven years earlier, in late 1843, William Overton and Asa Lovejoy had pulled their canoe into a clearing on the west bank of the Willamette River, midway between Fort Vancouver and Oregon City, and founded

Portland. Overton soon sold his half interest in the resulting 640-acre claim to merchant Francis Pettygrove. By early 1845 Lovejoy and Pettygrove had enlarged the clearing, built a cabin, and named their townsite after Pettygrove's boyhood home in Maine. Later that year, Lovejoy sold his half interest to Benjamin Stark, recently arrived cargomaster on a trading vessel, but Stark soon departed, leaving the industri-

*Portland's first house was this cabin, built in 1844. A decade later the waterfront town was bustling with activity, and the seeds of many land disputes were being sown.* (Oregon Historical Society Negatives #ORHI955 and #ORHI5493)

ous Pettygrove to promote Portland to its eventual place of prominence on the Willamette.[12]

When news of California gold reached Portland in August 1848, Pettygrove sold out to tanner Daniel Lownsdale for $5,000 worth of leather and went south. Seven months later, Lownsdale sold half of his share to Stephen Coffin of Oregon City for $6,000, and in December 1849 he and Coffin sold a third to Oregon City lawyer W. W. Chapman. Lownsdale, Coffin, and Chapman thereafter became commonly known as the Portland "proprietors." In January 1850, however, Ben Stark met Lownsdale in San Francisco and reasserted *his* half interest. The two eventually agreed that Stark would receive 48 prime acres in the claim's northeast corner, subject to all prior conveyances, or sales. Two years later, in 1852, Lownsdale, Coffin, and Chapman partitioned their remaining 600-acre claim, and by 1864 all four claimants—Lownsdale, Coffin, Chapman, and Stark—had received federal patents to their land.

## The Levee Litigation

Three clusters of Portland land-claim litigation found their way to Matthew Deady's federal court between 1861 and 1880. In the first, city officials and interested citizens alleged that the early proprietors had donated a large riverfront levee area and a downtown school-house site to the public. In the second, Daniel Lownsdale's heirs sought to reclaim land he and other proprietors had "sold" before obtaining title to it. And in the third, purchasers of lots within Ben Stark's 48 acres, notably brothers Addison and Lewis Starr, sued to establish their ownership rights.

Disagreement about title to the Portland riverfront[13] began as early as 1850 when Josiah Parrish, who owned property on adjacent Water Street, sued the three proprietors in territorial court to prevent construction of private buildings along the shoreline. He alleged that Lovejoy, Pettygrove, and later Lownsdale all had assured early lot buyers, including himself, that the riverfront would remain public.

Justice Olney's opinion for the territorial court strongly affirmed this contention. Pettygrove and Lovejoy had laid out the town with a plat clearly designating all land between Water Street and the river as public. They also had made repeated oral statements to that effect, as nearly a dozen witnesses had testified. The court emphasized that the evidence strongly supported its decision and that the proprietors had simply become afflicted with "an itching palm for this attractive property."[14]

Eight years later, however, in *Lownsdale v. City of Portland* (1861),[15] Judge Deady took a very different view. James Lownsdale, son of Daniel, sued in federal court to confirm his title to three riverfront lots on which he was building wharves, and to enjoin the city from tearing down his wharves and arresting his workers.

The city responded to Lownsdale's suit with three principal defenses. First, of course, it contended that the territorial-court decision eight years earlier already had decided the matter. But Deady ruled otherwise. An earlier judicial ruling bound one party only if it bound the other as well, and Judge Olney's opinion did not bind the city (or, therefore, Lownsdale) because the city had not been a party to the earlier case.

The city's second defense was that the proprietors' entire Donation Act claim to Portland was invalid because the 1848 federal act creating the Oregon Territory had incorporated the 1844 Townsite Act, which precluded private claims within towns and cities. But Deady ruled that the Territorial Act had not extended the Townsite Act to Oregon. Congress had intended the latter act for unsettled regions, not one like Oregon with extensive settlements, a provisional government, and even its own land law. It would "tax the ingenuity of man," he declared, to find a federal land law "less applicable to the condition of Oregon…than the Townsite Act of 1844":

> *To the thrifty and enterprising settler it would have said: By your management and industry you have built up a town on your land and thereby lost it. If you had been content to live upon it in a seven-by-nine-cabin with tottering lean-to attached, and merely pastured it with a few Spanish cattle and cayuse ponies, it would have been yours.*

Thus, in picturesque language, Deady sensibly interpreted federal land legislation in light of local conditions. James Lownsdale's claim, through his father, was *not* invalid because of the Townsite Act.

The city's third defense was that Pettygrove, Lovejoy, and later Daniel Lownsdale all had in fact dedicated the levee to public use, just as the territorial court had held. Deady heard evidence on that question, but ruled once again in Lownsdale's favor. It is here that Deady's strong preference for certainty of written land titles and his reluctance to disturb them with allegations of mere oral assurances appear most clearly. Proof of any such oral dedication, he wrote, needed to be "clear and cogent," and when consisting simply of "casual and disjointed conversations and remarks,…susceptible of various interpretations," given by witnesses tainted by "prepossessions and prejudices," it had to be "closely scrutinized":

> Security and certainty of title to real property are among the most important objects of the law in any civilized community. Any act intended and permitted to affect the ownership or use of such property the law requires to be done or suffered with certain solemnities and formalities.… What is shown to have once belonged to a person he is not presumed to have parted with; the fact, if claimed, must be satisfactorily proved.

It had not been satisfactorily proved to Deady, and he perpetually enjoined the city from asserting any right, title, or interest to a sizable portion of its riverfront. His most influential contemporaries, even those who thought the decision unfortunate, generally assigned responsibility elsewhere.[16]

## The Lownsdale Heirs Litigation

Deady's several decisions determining ownership of the 180 acres belonging originally to Daniel and Nancy Lownsdale are among the most factually complex and legally difficult he ever wrote.[17] It was in those decisions that he faced squarely the fundamental tension between "legal" and "equitable" titles—between, in effect, adhering to the law as he understood and valued it and deciding each case on the basis of equity and conscience.

Abbreviated, the relevant facts were as follows. In 1852, two years after granting Ben Stark 48 acres, the three main proprietors—Lownsdale, Coffin, and Chapman—partitioned the remainder of their Portland claim. Daniel Lownsdale's parcel became approximately 180 acres extending west from the river. Daniel and his wife Nancy promptly filed their notice of claim to that parcel—east half to him and west half to her—and thirteen years later the government issued patents for the land to their heirs.

As early as 1850, however, the proprietors had begun selling lots within their claim, including many within what became the Lownsdale parcel. Nancy died without a will in 1854, leaving Daniel and four children: Isabella and William Jr. by her first husband, William Gillihan, and Millard and Ruth by Daniel. Eight years later, in 1862, Daniel also died without a will, also leaving four children: James and Mary by his first wife, Ruth, and Millard and Ruth by Nancy. In addition, two granddaughters, Ida and Emma, survived Daniel and Ruth's deceased daughter Sarah.

71

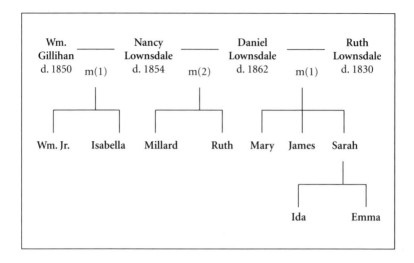

Federal-court litigation over the Lownsdale land began in 1866, when Daniel's heirs asserted title to parcels he and the other proprietors had sold a decade or more earlier. In essence, the heirs contended that promises by Daniel to transfer his later-acquired title did not bind them, and, in any event, Daniel could not have effectively sold parcels within Nancy's west half of the claim, which she had owned "in her own right."

*Oregonian* Editor Harvey Scott later recalled the "universal attention" and "multitude of opinions" lavished on the Lownsdale cases, particularly the "sympathies of all kinds" excited by the prospect that many "innocent purchasers" would be evicted. He described Judge Deady's fundamental legal dilemma this way:

*It was evident from the start that the courts must proceed in one of two ways—either to stick to the letter of the law and...recognize no title except that conferred by the United States Patent; or else to take a general view of the circumstances and necessities of the case and decide upon the general equities and common understanding of all parties, and to let possession count for all that it was worth.*[18]

In general, Deady responded again by emphasizing the "letter of the law," an emphasis which became acutely apparent in 1871 when Circuit Judge Lorenzo Sawyer arrived in Portland to announce his own quite opposite view.

Purchaser James Fields filed the first suit, alleging ownership of a parcel in the Nancy Lownsdale tract which the proprietors had conveyed to W. W. Chapman individually in June 1850 with a covenant to convey full legal title "if they should obtain [it] from the United States." Fields contended that that covenant required the Lownsdale heirs to convey to him, as Chapman's successor in interest, the title they received from the government in 1865.[19]

Deady worked his way through a maze of issues which were both "interesting in themselves" and of the "highest practical importance to this community." He first rejected a series of five technical defenses by the heirs against the proprietors' covenant to convey. One, for example, was that because no "estate" passed with the deed to Chapman in 1850, the covenant did not run with the land—that is, could not be enforced by anyone but Chapman himself.

So the covenant did bind the heirs. As written, however, it applied only to whatever title the proprietors received "from the United States." Did Daniel (and therefore the heirs) acquire any interest in Nancy's 90-acre parcel *from the United States?*

Judge Deady considered first the one-fifth interest Daniel had inherited from Nancy when she died. Had Daniel taken that interest directly from the United States, or by descent from Nancy? Again, after working his way through an "abstruse branch of the law," Deady concluded that Daniel had inherited from Nancy not her title but simply her right to *obtain* a title from the United States. Therefore, he had taken title to that first one-fifth interest directly from the United States, and the covenant to convey did indeed apply to it. So purchaser Fields prevailed with respect to one-fifth of his parcel, a result Deady believed coincided with the "justice and equity of this case."

Curiously, Deady declined to apply the same reasoning to a *second* fifth, one Daniel had purchased from Nancy's daughter Isabella in 1860, five years before the government issued a patent for the land. Deady simply asserted, without explanation, that Daniel had obtained that one-fifth from Isabella, had "in no sense obtained it from the United States," and therefore his heirs were not obliged "either in law or morals" to convey it to purchaser Fields.

The heirs also won the remaining three-fifths. Title to it had passed from the government to Nancy's other three children, not to Daniel. The Lownsdale heirs had received a patent to it only because an earlier state-court partition decree had allocated it to them.[20] So, in an opinion again emphasizing security of land title and a literal interpretation of the crucial 1850 covenant, Deady awarded purchaser Fields only one-fifth of the land he thought he had purchased, the fifth which Daniel had received "from the United States" as Nancy's heir.[21] In December 1871, the Supreme Court unanimously affirmed Deady's ruling.[22]

In May 1871, however, Circuit Judge Lorenzo Sawyer[23] arrived in Portland to preside with Deady over the pivotal case in the litigation affecting parcels in Daniel Lownsdale's own *eastern* half of the 180-acre claim. Sawyer's long, pro-purchaser opinion contrasted dramatically with both the substance and the style of Judge Deady's earlier rulings.

The underlying facts were that in June 1849 Lownsdale and Stephen Coffin had sold the disputed land to one John Marshall, with a minimal covenant that they and their heirs would never again claim the interest they were selling. I.A. Davenport eventually purchased the land and made extensive improvements on it; then almost two decades later the Lownsdale heirs sued to reclaim it.

Had Deady heard the case alone, he almost certainly would have ruled for the heirs. The 1849 sale conveyed only what the proprietors had at that time, mere possession, and the minimal covenant did not bar the heirs' later claim to full ownership rights.

Judge Sawyer, however, saw the matter very differently. In his view, the most "reasonable" interpretation of nearly all early Portland land sale contracts was that the original proprietors were later to obtain full legal title from the United States and then to convey that title to the various purchasers. Ruling for purchaser Davenport, Judge Sawyer chose to enforce that interpretation, declining to apply "purely technical principles" of land or contract law.[24] Judge Deady concurred, barely, in a very brief opinion.

Two years later, relying heavily on Judge Sawyer's reasoning, the Supreme Court affirmed. Justice Samuel Miller again reviewed the early Portland land transactions, invoked the government policy of protecting "meritorious actual settlers," and concluded that "well-settled principles of equity" required a grant of full legal title to purchaser Davenport.[25] Following that decision, most other such purchasers prevailed in federal court as well.

### Starr v. Stark

The third cluster of Portland land-claim litigation involved title to portions of Ben Stark's northern 48 acres. Once again the fundamental issue was priority between formal legal title, represented this time by Stark's 1860 patent, and the equitable, possessory claims of Portlanders who had bought and improved small parcels. Encouraged by an early

*Central figures in early Portland land-claim cases were three of the city's first landowners—Daniel Lownsdale (top left), William W. Chapman (top right), and Stephen Coffin (bottom left)—who came to be known as the Portland "proprietors." Circuit Judge Lorenzo Sawyer (bottom right) often disagreed with Judge Deady's interpretation of the cases, and it was usually Sawyer's views that prevailed. (Oregon Historical Society Negatives #ORHI72569, #ORHI4253, #ORHI82922, and #ORHI78294)*

Supreme Court decision favoring Stark, Judge Deady again sustained the legal title claim; however, again Circuit Judge Sawyer and the Supreme Court disagreed.

The 1850 Lownsdale-Stark agreement provided that Stark took his 48 acres subject to all conveyances the three principal proprietors already had made. One such conveyance had been to proprietor W. W. Chapman himself, who later sold several lots within it to brothers Addison and Lewis Starr. For more than a decade thereafter, the Starrs used and improved the lots as their own, receiving Stark's repeated assurances that he recognized their priority. Uncertainties abounded, however, and in 1860 city authorities countered Stark's patent application with one of their own under the Townsite Act. The Public Land Office responded by issuing simultaneous identical patents, excepting in each all lawful claims by the rival applicant.

Four years later, in early 1864, the Starrs sued in state court to establish their title. They alleged both *legal* title, through the city's patent, and *equitable* title, based on Stark's repeated assurances and long acquiescence. The trial judge, however, ordered the Starrs to choose between their two "inconsistent" theories. Accordingly, they chose to pursue their legal title, and prevailed: the city's patent on which they based their claim was valid, whereas Stark's patent was invalid because he had not resided on and cultivated the land for the required four years. The Oregon Supreme Court affirmed.[26]

Three years later, however, the United States Supreme Court unanimously reversed both those rulings. Justice Field's opinion for the court concluded that the Starrs lacked standing even to challenge Stark's patent because they themselves had no adequate claim to the land. Although an Oregon statute permitted anyone "in possession" to sue to establish clear title, Field ruled that mere "naked possession" (not founded upon a "claim of right") was inadequate. Even though the Starrs seemed to have just such a claim, recently upheld by a unanimous Oregon Supreme Court, Field and his colleagues saw the matter differently, concluding that the city's patent (through which the Starrs claimed) was invalid.[27]

The Starrs declined to vacate the property, however, and a year later Stark sued in federal court to force them to leave. Lewis Starr responded by alleging that he and his brother had an "equitable" title, a response which Judge Deady ordered stricken as "immaterial and frivolous": such a title, even if established, would be "no defense to an action for possession by the holder of the legal title." Because the Starrs already had lost the legal title issue in the U.S. Supreme Court, Deady ordered Lewis Starr off the land.[28]

Still Starr persisted, perhaps buoyed by references in Deady's opinion to Stark's repeated assurances and his own good faith. Rather than leave, he sued in federal court, alleging again in another way the equitable-title theory he and his brother had involuntarily abandoned six years earlier.

But again Deady declined to hear that theory. "After deliberate consideration, I am well satisfied that the former adjudication between these parties is a bar to this suit…." The state-court order to elect had been an adjudication that one theory or the other was "insufficient," and the Starrs' election had constituted a "solemn admission" that the abandoned equitable-title theory was "not well founded in fact or law, or both."[29]

Starr answered the bell for one final round, however, by changing attorneys and appealing to Judge Sawyer. Four years later, following a full trial, Sawyer delivered an opinion emphatically reversing not only Deady's prior-adjudication ruling but the Starr brothers' entire series of losses extending back to the 1868 Supreme Court decision.[30]

First, Sawyer held that the prior state-court ruling did not bar Starr's equitable-title theory. It was "quite clear" to Sawyer that the original order compelling the Starrs to elect was "erroneous." Facts supporting the two theories were "entirely consistent with each other"; only their legal implications diverged. Moreover, even if the election order had been correct, it obviously had precluded the Starrs from litigating their equitable claim.

Sawyer then proceeded to brush aside Stark's series of technical challenges to the various contracts and deeds, emphasizing again "surrounding circumstances" and the parties' "true intent." No "unprejudiced mind" could examine the evidence and fail to conclude that Stark had given the Starrs "unmistakable assurances… that if he obtained his patent to the general claim he would convey to them the lots they had purchased." Invoking the "intrinsic justice of the case," and determined to avoid "great hardship and gross injustice," Sawyer directed Stark to make such a conveyance.

Judge Deady dissented quietly, in six lines. He naturally disagreed about the effect of the earlier state-court ruling, and disagreed further about the legal effect of a conveyance "without covenants…by the donee under the donation act…prior to the passage of that act." Generally, however, he chose not to answer Sawyer's 35-page opinion reversing his decision and admonishing that no "unprejudiced mind" could fail to see its "gross injustice."

Two years later, for a unanimous Supreme Court, Justice Stephen Field affirmed both Judge Sawyer's decision and his rhetoric.[31] Field first agreed that the state-court litigation, begun 12 years earlier and decided eventually by the Supreme Court, did not preclude Starr from asserting his equitable-title claim. He also adopted Sawyer's view of the need to interpret early Portland land contracts in light of the "condition on which land in Oregon was held at that time." One important such condition was the "unwritten conventional law" of land sales:

> It was, therefore, understood by the people that, whenever the legal title was thus obtained, it should inure to the benefit of the grantees of the claimant who secured the patent of the United States.

Thus, the deeds to Starr had transferred to him the "equitable right to call for a release of the legal title."

So it was that most early Portland land purchasers finally prevailed against the original proprietors and their heirs holding federal patents to disputed parcels. District Judge Matthew Deady's view of the cases, emphasizing security of formal legal title, preservation of common-law conveyancing principles, and literal reading of early deed language, generally did not prevail. Instead it was Circuit Judge Lorenzo Sawyer's view, favoring more fact-oriented, equitable decisions even at the expense of greater legal certainty, which the Supreme Court twice affirmed.

◦◦◦

# FEDERAL ADMIRALTY LAW IN EARLY OREGON

Maritime commerce was the lifeline of early Oregon. Before the 1883 completion of Portland's first transcontinental rail link, the vast majority of travel and trade to and from the state was by sea. Thousands of passengers and millions of dollars in goods arrived at and departed Portland harbor each year. Oregon maritime exports rose to $7 million annually in 1865 and doubled again the following decade, as wheat, flour, wool, salmon, timber, and other products sailed down the Columbia toward such destinations as San Francisco, New York, Liverpool, and Hong Kong.[32]

The 1789 Judiciary Act conferred on federal district courts exclusive jurisdiction in all admiralty and maritime disputes.[33] In exercising that

*At a time when maritime commerce was vital to Oregon's economy, Judge Deady heard a wide variety of admiralty cases. In general he granted sympathetic and substantial legal protection to merchants, seamen, and passengers alike. (Oregon Historical Society Negative #ORHI35552)*

jurisdiction, district courts were to apply the fundamental principles of maritime law which English and other courts had been developing for centuries to govern disputes pertaining to navigable waters. As Chief Justice John Marshall explained in 1828: "These cases are as old as navigation itself; and the law, admiralty and maritime, as it has existed for ages, is applied by our Courts to the cases as they arise."[34]

Litigants brought a great many admiralty disputes to Judge Matthew Deady's early Oregon federal court. The issues they raised ranged from technical questions of federal admiralty jurisdiction to shipowner liability for lost or damaged goods to the rights of seamen or passengers to recover withheld wages or damages for personal injury. In general, Judge Deady granted sympathetic and substantial legal protection to merchants, seamen, and passengers alike. He felt more able in admiralty litigation than in land-law disputes to search for results he believe just, then to craft his decisions to achieve those results.

## The Limits of Federal Admiralty Jursidiction

Much disagreement existed in early America about the scope of federal admiralty jurisdiction. Authors, judges, politicians, and litigants debated the matter with unusual vigor because true "admiralty" disputes could be tried only in federal courts. Most leading treatise authors and most federal judges, including Judge Deady, construed such exclusive federal jurisdiction expansively.[35]

In *Bernhard v. Creene* (1874),[36] for example, Deady sustained his court's power to hear a suit brought by German, Austrian, and French seamen for beatings and other cruelty inflicted by a British captain. The British vice-consul protested the suit, demanding that it be left to his own "consular court." However, invoking the plenary language in both the Constitution and the 1789 Judiciary Act, Deady explained that federal admiralty jurisdiction over personal injuries inflicted on the high seas was "certain."

True, such jurisdiction was "discretionary" in cases involving foreign nationals and could be declined if "justice would be as well done by remitting the parties to their home forum." In *Bernhard*, however, the seamen and the captain were nationals of different governments, so to require the seamen to pursue the captain to a British port would have been a "mockery of justice." A decade later, Deady reaffirmed this ruling, noting that the Supreme Court had singled it out for particular praise.[37]

The issue in *The Eliza Ladd* (1875)[38] was whether a contract to furnish the propulsion mechanism for a new ship was "maritime" in nature and therefore within admiralty jurisdiction. The ship had been "launched" at Portland, then towed to the plaintiff Oregon Iron Works's yard for its propulsion machinery. The defendant shipowner, urging Judge Deady to dismiss the case, cited two Supreme Court rulings that a ship-*construction* contract was not maritime in nature. It was instead a contract "made on land to be performed on land."[39]

Deady began by criticizing such rulings as inconsistent with the "general maritime law of the civilized world." In any event, however, they did not apply. Analogizing instead to a ship-*repair* contract, which undoubtedly was maritime in nature, he concluded that a "contract made after a vessel is launched and afloat, to furnish her with a particular means of propulsion…is a maritime contract." A ship became subject to admiralty jurisdiction "at the moment when she leaves the ways, and her keel strikes the element for which she was originally designed."

Finally, in *The City of Carlisle* (1889),[40] Judge Deady once again sustained American federal jurisdiction over injuries inflicted on the high seas by foreign nationals. The facts in *Carlisle* were especially egregious. A negligently handled claw-iron had fractured the skull of a passing 16-year-old apprentice seaman. Thereafter, the captain had left the boy for days, unattended and on short rations, in an "unconscious or delirious state, sweltering and rolling in his own excrement." Six weeks later, with the wound still a "running sore" and the boy's left arm and leg partly paralyzed, the captain had ordered him "turned to" for 12-hour daily shifts on deck.

Deady responded to the "usual" objection to suits against British vessels by declaring himself unwilling to participate in a "denial of justice" by remitting the injured young sailor to a faraway British court:

> Indeed, it is shocking to think of turning this poor, helpless boy out of court in a civilized country without redress for a grievous wrong upon the theory that he has a remedy in the courts of his own country, when it is apparent that however just may be the laws of such country and impartial their administration, such remedy is, under the circumstances, to him utterly unavailable.[41]

Instead, Deady awarded the sailor $500 compensation for expenses, including a voyage home, and $1,000 for the "gross neglect and mistreatment…whereby his injury and suffering were much aggravated."[42]

## Liability for Lost or Damaged Goods

Nineteenth-century maritime law implied a promise by a shipowner accepting goods for transport to carry the goods safely to their destination.[43] However, shipowners routinely sought to negate such implied promises by inserting express liability disclaimers into their bills of lading. Judge Deady realized that owners of goods rarely if ever truly "agreed" to such disclaimers, and he generally interpreted them with appropriate skepticism.

In *The Pacific* (1861),[44] an owner of valuable mirrors had shipped them from San Francisco to Portland, where they arrived broken. The ship's freight clerk had issued a receipt acknowledging that the crate and mirrors were "in good order," but because glass was being shipped had added the words "Not accountable for contents."

Deady ruled for the owner of the mirrors. He began his opinion by explaining that a carrier acted as an "insurer," except for damage caused by an act of God or the public enemy. True, the Supreme Court had ruled that a carrier could disclaim liability (though not for its negligence) by "special agreement,"[45] but in Deady's view the handwritten words "not accountable for contents" did not constitute such an agreement. They amounted to "nothing more than a [self-serving statement] by the carrier *after* receipt of the goods, and without the knowledge or assent of the shipper." Equally unavailing for the carrier was an alleged "custom" of inserting such disclaimers in all receipts for mirrors. If courts permitted mere "custom" to "control and modify the law," common carriers could "make and unmake the law as they chose."

Three years later, Deady reached a similar result in *The Jenny Jones* (1864).[46] On a voyage from Victoria to Portland with a cargo of sugar and ale, the captain had tried to cross the Columbia bar without a licensed pilot. The ship had run aground, and to save it the crew had jettisoned the cargo.

As a defense, the shipowner relied on the bill of lading clause that disclaimed liability for damage caused by "dangers of the sea." Deady explained, however, that the law "wisely" imposed on a carrier the duty to use "all reasonable skill and prudence," and the bill of lading did not even purport to negate that duty. So the decisive issue in the case was whether the schooner had been "properly navigated" across the bar. It certainly had not: crossing the Columbia bar without a pilot betrayed either a "reckless disregard of duty" or a "want of reasonable skill and knowledge."

Following three more decisions favoring shippers of lost or damaged goods,[47] Judge Deady finally ruled for a carrier. One of five merchandise containers sent from San Francisco to Portland on the *California* had arrived empty. The owner produced evidence that all five containers had been properly packed, but offered none regarding their condition when they were actually delivered to the ship. In denying the owner recovery, Deady noted that drays carrying Portland-bound goods often waited outside the San Francisco dockyard for as long as 24 hours. Without the drayman's testimony, there was "just as much reason to believe that the embezzlement or robbery took place while the case was on the truck…as afterwards."[48]

However, such decisions favoring carriers were rare in Matthew Deady's early Oregon federal court.[49]

## Seamen's Wage Claims

Conventional nineteenth-century wisdom suggested that seamen both needed and merited special legal protection. Often poorly educated, and far from police and courts during much of their employment, they were unusually dependent on the honesty and goodwill of captains and junior officers. Matthew Deady agreed strongly with this conventional wisdom, repeatedly interpreting employment articles in seamen's favor and often awarding them compensation for deliberate or negligent physical harm.

In *The Christina* (1862),[50] a seaman had hired out of Port Townsend, Washington, for a roundtrip apple-buying voyage to Portland. He was to receive as wages one-third of the venture's anticipated profits. Once in Portland, however, the captain was unable to buy any apples, so proposed a further coastal voyage searching for another cargo. The seaman declined and sued for accrued "customary" wages.

Judge Deady explained that in the absence of a contrary agreement, a seaman was entitled to "customary wages for the voyage performed." The maxim "Freight is the mother of wages" did not apply in cases like *The Christina* because the vessel had sailed empty from Port Townsend to Portland.

The shipowner also alleged an agreement by the seaman that if the apple venture failed, the ship would sail elsewhere to search for oysters. However, Deady explained, a court's duty was to "closely scrutinize" any such alleged agreement and to "disregard" it if it was "prejudicial to the rights…of the seaman." It was neither "regular" nor "proper" for a master to enter into a new and special contract with a seaman aboard ship, when the parties plainly did not "deal upon equal terms." The seaman recovered his customary wages.[51]

The Almatia (1868),[52] six years later, was a more complicated case. Shortly after the ship arrived in Portland, the mate ordered the crew to begin work at 6:00 a.m. Sunday. They did so and worked for three hours until the mate ordered them to refurl a sail furled only five days earlier. The crew requested breakfast first, citing the custom of Sunday breakfast at 8:00. The mate then ordered them to speak to the captain, who promptly discharged them. The captain's defenses to their later suit for wages were disobedience and desertion.

Judge Deady reached the obvious initial conclusion, that there had been no desertion, but instead a "discharge by the officers." Nor was the discharge justified, which would have resulted in wage forfeiture. As Justice Joseph Story had recently explained, only "high and aggravated neglect or disobedience, importing the most serious mischief, peril or wrong" justified wage forfeiture.[53] It was "plain" that the Almatia crew's breakfast request did not meet that standard. On the other hand, Deady declined to find the crew "wholly without fault." The "general rule" onboard ship was that a "seaman must obey what his superiors command." The order to refurl the sail had not been sufficiently "unreasonable or oppressive" to justify disobedience, so the crew's breakfast request cost each seaman a month's wages.

Deady sensibly refused, however, to enforce a stipulation in the Almatia's employment articles that even a single disobedient act forfeited all wages. Such a term was in "derogation of the general rights of seamen as established by the maritime law," and would be enforced only if "fully and fairly explained" and accompanied by appropriately higher wages.

Despite Judge Deady's generally protective attitude toward seamen asserting wage claims, in The T.F. Oakes (1888),[54] he ruled emphatically against a crew he believed guilty of "premeditated and persistent shirking and slighting of duty." A letter from the Coast Seamen's Union office in San Francisco had even congratulated the crew on their misconduct and suggested ways to continue and extend it. Thus, the captain's discharge of the crew at Acapulco had been fully justified, and they were entitled to no wages beyond those already paid.

Deady explained why he had taken unusual "pains and time" with the case:

> [T]he whole trouble grows out of the methods and purposes of the Seamen's Union of San Francisco. It appears to be organized for the purpose of controlling the conduct and employment of seamen on this coast, to the end that ships shall be navigated in the interest and

*at the pleasure of the forecastle, without any reference to the rights or interests of owners.*

That was an "anarchical" idea, and the law would "not tolerate such conduct." Deady's sympathy for the plight of individual seamen plainly did not extend to those who followed union orders to shirk or slight their customary duties.

## Personal Injury and Wrongful Death

The final category of admiralty disputes in early Oregon federal court consisted of claims for personal injury or wrongful death. Not surprisingly, Judge Deady inclined once again toward compensating both seamen and passengers.

In *Hanson v. Fowle* (1871),[55] the second mate sued both captain and first mate for a serious, unprovoked beating by the first mate. Ruling against both defendants, Deady quoted extensively from yet another Justice Story admiralty opinion, this one holding a captain who failed to protect his seamen equally liable with an actual assailant.[56]

Nor would Deady enforce against the second mate a receipt he had signed for wages received in satisfaction of "all demands and dues against the brig *Madawaska*, her officers, captain and owners." The word "demands," he explained, generally connoted only contract claims, not tort claims for personal injury. Moreover, because the sum paid had represented only wages admittedly due, the mate had received nothing for relinquishing his tort claim. And finally, there was again the matter of unequal bargaining power. Because the master and men dealt upon an "unequal footing," the law "very properly" looked with "distrust and suspicion" upon any such receipt as the one the seaman had signed. So the second mate recovered $360 for earnings lost due to his permanently damaged arm; $500 for pain and suffering, including the captain's "heartless neglect"; and $200 for attorney fees.

Four years later, in *The Oriflamme* (1875),[57] Deady awarded a similar amount to a *passenger* for injuries sustained when freight broke loose in the steerage room. Quoting a nationally renowned treatise on railroad law, he described how the law "very wisely" exacted from a passenger carrier the "utmost care and skill which prudent men are accustomed to use under similar circumstances."

A later case, *Holmes v. Oregon & Calif. Ry. Co.* (1880),[58] raised further difficult questions about the relation of federal admiralty jurisdiction to state substantive law. A passenger had drowned by falling off the railway's boat, and when his heir sued, the railway defended by contending that (1) federal admiralty law itself did not authorize a suit by heirs for an injury-related death, and (2) an 1862 Oregon *state* statute that did authorize such a suit did so only in a state-court action, not a federal admiralty suit.

Judge Deady disliked conceding even the first point. In his view, the lack of a right to sue in admiralty for "wrongful death" was neither "founded in reason" nor "consonant with justice." In a long dictum, he reviewed the history of wrongful-death actions under English common law; described Lord Campbell's Act in 1846, which established such an action; and noted that most American states (including Oregon) had since followed Parliament's "illustrious example." He also suggested that because civil law from the European continent historically had permitted wrongful death claims, an American federal admiralty court, "not governed by rules of the [English] common law," perhaps could entertain one on its own authority.

In any event, the drowned passenger's heir could certainly recover damages in federal court under the *Oregon* statute. That statute provided the "right" to sue for wrongful death, which, like other rights, "may be enforced in the proper national court."

The fact that the Oregon statute literally authorized only a wrongful-death "action at law" (and not in admiralty) did not bar the heir's suit. A long line of authority established that a "right" conferred by state statute was distinct from the "remedy" and could be enforced in federal admiralty court as well as the state's own "law" courts.

Having established the heir's right to sue in his court, Deady proceeded to construe evidence concerning fault favorably to the decedent. It was "too plain for argument" that his drowning had resulted from the boat personnel's "wrongful omission" and "negligence." Deady discounted evidence that the drowned man had been intoxicated and had failed to heed a warning, placing the burden of establishing such contributory negligence on the defendant:

> I admit the authorities are in hopeless conflict upon this question, but in my judgment any other rule than this violates all the analogies of the law, and is practically illogical and unjust.

The same year, however, in *The Chandos* (1880),[59] Deady uncharacteristically reduced an injured seaman's claim because the seaman's own negligence had contributed to his injury. On a dark and stormy night, a mate had ordered the seaman aloft to adjust the rigging. The crane-line, on which he sat to make the adjustment, severed, and the seaman fell 30 feet to the deck. Two months later, the ship arrived at Baker's Bay on the Columbia, where it remained ten more days before finally taking the seaman to a Portland hospital.

For the injury itself, Deady declined to award damages. A crane-line was an "insecure footing." It was "not primarily a foot-rope," and sitting on it during a storm was negligent. However, he did award the seaman $250 for improper care following his injuries. It was "well-settled law" that an injured seaman was entitled to reasonable care at the ship's expense. Thus, the captain's two months of virtual neglect, compounded by the needless ten-day delay at Baker Bay, constituted a "manifest neglect of duty" designed simply to avoid the expense of proper care.

Finally, in two important later rulings, Judge Deady essentially changed his mind about crane lines and, indeed, about whether a seaman's own contributory negligence should *ever* bar his recovery of damages for personal injury. The facts of *The Noddleburn* (1886)[60] were very similar to those in *The Chandos*. A mate had ordered a seaman aloft to adjust rigging. The seaman had necessarily stood for a short time on the crane-line, which—being frayed at another point—gave way. He fell to the deck, severely breaking a leg and dislocating an ankle. Both the captain and the mate had known about the frayed crane-line and, thereafter, had exhibited the usual officer cruelty and neglect toward the injured seaman.

On those facts, Deady both distinguished his earlier *Chandos* ruling and acknowledged his own "further acquaintance with the subject." In *Chandos* the "heavy" seaman had stood on the line "with all his weight" while using both hands at night to loose a stop. The *Noddleburn* seaman, by contrast, was lighter, had gone aloft during daylight, and had sensibly grasped the shroud with one hand while trying to adjust the staysail sheet.

More fundamentally, testimony from several witnesses suggested that while the crane-line was "not primarily a foot-rope," it occasionally "might be, and was, so used," even by careful seamen. Deady's earlier description of its purpose had been "somewhat narrower than the fact as known and practiced by seamen." Therefore, the injured seaman had not been contributorily negligent; rather, his injuries had resulted from the captain and mate's "willful negligence and wanton indifference," for which Deady awarded the seaman $1,570.

Then two years later, in *Olsen v. Flavel* (1888),[61] Deady issued his most pro-seaman ruling of all. Seamen's "limbs and lives," he reminded his readers, were in the "care and keeping of the superior skill and intelligence of the master."

Therefore, while "contributory negligence" might bar a non-admiralty common-law action for personal injury, a "better rule" should prevail in admiralty. Where both parties were at fault, admiralty courts could "apportion the damages or give or withhold them…according to principles of equity and justice." Counsel in earlier cases had not raised the apportionment issue, but now that it was before him in *Olsen*, Deady felt "justified…to follow the leaning of my own judgment, and hold that contributory negligence is not a bar to a suit in admiralty." It was simply not "just" to "leave a seaman to suffer without redress all the consequences of an injury caused by the fault of his employers as well as his own."

Thus, in a wide variety of admiralty decisions spanning nearly three decades, Judge Deady offered to merchants, passengers, and seamen alike substantial legal protection against perils of the sea. Feeling less bound than in land-title disputes by technicalities of the common law, Deady exhibited in his admiralty jurisprudence both greater sensitivity to the equities of particular cases and greater judicial creativity in crafting decisions to reflect those equities. He interpreted federal admiralty jurisdiction expansively in order to provide an appropriate legal forum to deserving claimants. He ruled repeatedly in favor of shippers whose goods had been lost or damaged at sea, giving little weight to the liability disclaimers that carriers routinely inserted into their bills of lading. He consistently awarded withheld wages to seamen, except when the seamen had engaged in deliberate, union-inspired misconduct. And he was especially sympathetic toward both passenger and seamen victims of personal injury, discounting not only the self-serving testimony of ships' officers but, by 1888, even the common-law doctrine of contributory negligence.

# FEDERAL LAW AND THE GROWTH OF INDUSTRIAL ENTERPRISE IN EARLY OREGON

At Oregon's 1857 constitutional convention, delegate Matthew Deady declared himself opposed to state-chartered corporations because he did not wish to encourage a "fungous growth of speculators." Deady preferred Oregon's agricultural, egalitarian way of life, "breathing the pure air" with the "canopy of heaven for a ventilator," to the fate of those "millions of poor human beings degraded into…mere servants of machinery," seething in "misery and crime from the age of puberty to the grave."[62]

Like others of his generation, however, Deady eventually accepted industrial enterprise as inevitable, perhaps even desirable, and in 1862 he himself drafted Oregon's landmark general-incorporation statute.[63] Then during the next three decades, as federal district judge, he heard and determined a great many enterprise-related disputes. The three principal categories of such disputes reaching the early Oregon federal court raised (1) "internal" issues of corporate organization, authority, and operations; (2) challenges to federal, state, or local laws seeking to promote or regulate enterprise; or (3) claims brought against enterprise by its victims. In all three categories, Judge Deady combined a detailed technical understanding of corporate law with a determination to protect Oregon investors, creditors, workers, and competitors against any "fungous growth of speculators."

## Early Oregon Corporation Law

In *Wallamet Falls Canal & Lock Co. v. Kittridge* (1877),[64] the plaintiff firm had received a $200,000 state grant to subsidize canal construction around the falls at Oregon City, then had hired a second firm to help with the work.[65] When the second firm failed to perform and defaulted on its $30,000 performance bond, the plaintiff sued bond surety Jonathan Kittridge.

Kittridge's first defense was that because the plaintiff's shareholders had voted to dissolve the firm, it had ceased to exist and so could not continue the action against him. Judge Deady disagreed, however, for under Oregon law only the directors could dissolve a corporation. True, exercise of that power by directors had first to be "authorized by the stockholders," but such authorization itself did not result in dissolution.

Kittridge urged next that because the plaintiff firm had ceased *conducting business*, it had ceased to exist. The Oregon corporations statute did provide that if a firm "shall…neglect and cease" its business for six months its corporate powers "shall also cease." However, decisions elsewhere had established that no party could enforce or take advantage of any such cessation except the "state which created or authorized the corporation." So surety Kittridge had to pay.

A second case, *Corbett v. Woodward* (1879),[66] raised issues concerning a corporate director's fiduciary duties to the firm. At a time when Oregon Iron Works was insolvent, it had borrowed $20,000 from First National Bank to pay certain debts, including a $2,000 promissory note which director Bernard Goldsmith had indorsed. Goldsmith, who received another $1,000 for arranging the loan, also had guaranteed its repayment. Then, to secure Goldsmith against loss as the guarantor, the firm had granted him a realty mortgage, which he later assigned to Elijah Corbett.[67]

The first issue in Corbett's suit to enforce the mortgage was whether it had been duly authorized at a meeting attended by only two of three Iron Works directors, Goldsmith himself and Edwin Russell. The corporations statute did permit director majority decisions, however; and because the third director, John McCracken, had been ill at the time, there seemed little reason to conclude that Goldsmith and Russell had deliberately excluded him from the meeting.

However, Goldsmith had certainly "secured an advantage to himself" by the mortgage, one which an equity court should not enforce. A corporate director was a "trustee" of the firm's property for its creditors and shareholders, and it was "contrary to the first principles of equity" to "deal with such property for his own advantage and to their injury." Thus, $3,000 of the mortgage (the $2,000 note plus the $1,000 commission) was unenforceable.[68]

Deady explained that vastly increased corporate dominance of the American marketplace made it "necessary" that the "salutary rules enforced by courts of equity in other cases of fiduciary relation" be "rigidly applied to the numerous and important trusts held by the managers of these organizations." Particularly in insolvency cases, there was "every reason to exact the most scrupulous conduct at the hands of their directors when dealing with the trust property."

The 1882 decision in *Faull v. Alaska Gold & Silver Mining Co.*[69] illustrates another recurring issue in early Oregon corporation law, the liability of past and present shareholders for corporate debts. The state constitution generally limited such liability to any unpaid balance of the original subscription price of a shareholder's stock.[70]

John Faull had recovered a judgment against the defendant mining corporation and, seeking to collect it, had garnished one F. B. Harrington, owner of partially unpaid-for shares. Harrington's attorney cited an Oregon Supreme Court ruling that such shareholder liability could be enforced only in an equity suit against *all* shareholders.[71] Deady declined to interpret the liability that narrowly, however, ruling that garnishment as a means of collecting on a judgment furnished an "additional remedy in certain cases."

The issue then became whether the unpaid share price was truly a "debt" due from shareholder Harrington to the corporation, and therefore subject to garnishment. Quoting from the corporations statute, Deady explained that it was, that a sale of stock both transferred all the seller's rights *and* subjected the buyer to payment of "any unpaid balance, due or to become due on such stock."

Judge Deady's most extensive corporation-law opinion came in *Oregonian Ry. Co. v. Oregon Ry. & Nav. Co.* (1884).[72] The Oregonian Railway had leased its narrow-gauge line to Oregon Railway & Navigation Co., which promptly failed to pay the $68,000 due in May 1884. OR&N's first defense was to deny Oregonian Railway's corporate existence. However, Oregonian Railway had properly organized under England's 1862 Companies Act and thus had a perfect right to do business in Oregon.[73] Moreover, an 1880 Oregon statute granting it various rights-of-way over state land was an express legislative recognition of its existence.

Defendant OR&N next denied its *own* power to lease the track, citing the corporations-act ban against navigation firms purchasing or leasing railroads.[74] However, Deady responded, OR&N's charter expressly granted it power to lease railroads, so that defense hardly commended itself to a "sense of justice"; moreover, in any event, the legislature had repealed the ban in 1878. Thus, neither Oregonian Railway nor OR&N had exceeded its lawful powers, and the latter owed the former $68,000.

Finally, in *Powell v. Oregonian Ry. Co.* (1888),[75] Judge Deady again held a shareholder liable for a corporate debt. The plaintiff Powell had recovered a $5,300 judgment against his lessee, the Dayton, Sheridan & Grand Ronde Railway, for negligently allowing the plaintiff's warehouse to be washed away by high water. He then sued in federal court to collect that judgment from the Oregonian Railway Company, holder of 1,000 shares of Dayton, Sheridan stock for which original subscriber Joseph Gaston had never paid.

Oregonian Railway contended that because the plaintiff's original claim against Dayton, Sheridan had been for an unspecified amount, it was not a corporate "indebtedness" within the statute defining shareholder responsibility. Deady concluded otherwise, however. Once the unliquidated claim became a judgment against Dayton, Sheridan for a sum certain, it was indeed a "debt" within the shareholder-liability statute, and Oregonian Railway was liable for it to the extent of any unpaid subscription price for its shares. Thus, three decades after his state constitutional convention remarks, Judge Deady still seemed disinclined to protect any "fungous growth of speculators."[76]

## Government and Enterprise in Federal District Court

Early Oregonians were cautious toward large-scale enterprise. Most sought to balance their conflicting aspirations of community and individualism by encouraging enterprise only in ways generally consistent with other public and private values. They strongly opposed the use of public money to subsidize private ventures, and—by a constitutional requirement that taxation be "uniform and equal"—precluded many of the enterprise-related tax exemptions so common elsewhere. Even the state's early commercial elite retained dominantly preindustrial aspirations, preferring their traditional merchant and banker roles to the conflict and risk often attending a major industrial undertaking.

Relations between government and enterprise in early Oregon were quite distant on the regulatory side as well. Indeed, the state attempted no significant regulatory initiative until the railroad-rate legislation of 1885. As a result, most government-and-enterprise disputes reaching Matthew Deady's early federal court were comparatively tame.

**Regulating "Foreign" Corporations.** In 1864 the Oregon Legislature directed that every out-of-state corporation or association intending to engage in "insurance, banking, brokerage, exchange or express" business within the state post a $50,000 bond and register an agent for service of process.[77] In *In re C. B. Comstock & Co.* (1874),[78] a bankruptcy trustee contended that the Bank of British Columbia's non-compliance with that act rendered its loan to the bankrupt Comstock & Co. "illegal and void." Reviewing an exhaustive list of authorities, Judge Deady agreed.

The registration requirement itself was plainly valid. The Supreme Court had held repeatedly that a state could either "exclude the foreign corporation entirely" or "exact such security...as...will best promote the public interest."[79] The only difficult question was whether the bank's non-compliance rendered the transaction entirely void. Seeking the "intention of the Legislature as far as practicable," Deady concluded that it did. The act's language, requiring that a corporation "must" register "before" entering the state, was "certainly mandatory in form." And its purpose, to "secure to the people of the State the right to sue the foreign corporation in the courts of the State," could only be accomplished by declaring all business done by noncomplying firms "illegal and void."

Three years later, however, in *Oregon & Washington T. & I. Co. v. Rathbun* (1877),[80] Deady declined to apply the statute to an unregistered Scottish lender. The state constitution required that every statute "embrace but one subject," which subject was to be "expressed in the title." The foreign-corporation statute's title was "An Act to Regulate and Tax Foreign Insurance, Banking, Express and Exchange Corporations…." Therefore, although its *text* seemed to require every foreign corporation to register before doing business in the state, its *title* (together with the constitution) restricted lawful application of it to "insurance, banking, express, and exchange corporations."[81] And because the plaintiff lent only "its own money, consisting of its capital stock contributed by its share-holders," it was not a "banking" corporation and could collect its loan despite having failed to comply with the statute.[82]

The following year, in *Semple v. Bank of British Columbia* (1878),[83] Deady again strongly endorsed the registration requirement for genuine foreign banking corporations. The Bank of British Columbia had sued in state court to foreclose a mortgage securing an unpaid debt and, follow-ing a judgment in its favor, had bought the property at foreclosure sale. Debtor Ruth Semple then asked the federal court to declare that the bank's failure to register rendered her note and mortgage to it "illegal and void." Citing both *Comstock* and a later Oregon Supreme Court deci-sion,[84] Deady agreed.

The bank's attorney had apparently criticized *Comstock* and similar rulings as "harsh" and prejudicial to the "large foreign capital" in the state. Deady responded to that criticism, as he often did, with a lecture of his own. He could see "no reason why this plain and wholesome statute should be refined and construed out of existence." A foreign corporation doing business in Oregon in "deliberate defiance of the law" had to "take the consequences of such illegal conduct" and hardly could complain "either of the harshness of the law or its enforcement."[85]

The final and most colorful case in this line was *Northwestern Mutual Life Ins. Co. v. Elliott* (1880).[86] Moses Elliott had insured his own life for $8,000, naming his father Jeremiah as beneficiary. Eight months later, Jeremiah claimed that Moses had drowned and collected the $8,000. Then eight *years* later, having discovered Moses still living on the family farm under an assumed name, the company sued Jeremiah for restitu-tion. Jeremiah contended, citing *Comstock* and *Semple*, that because the plaintiff foreign corporation had not registered an Oregon agent on whom legal process could be served, the policy itself was "null and void"; and, further, any alleged "implied contract" to return money improperly received was so closely connected with the "illegal" insurance contract that it too was "illegal and void."

The plaintiff's first rejoinder was that the insurance contract had been entered into in Wisconsin, not Oregon. Moses had submitted his application to the plaintiff's Portland agent, who forwarded it to the Milwaukie home office for signature, then returned it to Moses and collected the first premium. Judge Deady disagreed with the plaintiff's reasoning, however. The policy stated that it did not take effect until a premium "shall be actually paid"; therefore, the "final act...which made the transaction a contract" had definitely taken place in Portland.

That issue mattered little, however, for the company was suing not on the insurance contract itself but in restitution for fraud. The "tainted implied contract" defense was simply unpersuasive. If Jeremiah Elliott had *robbed* Northwestern Mutual's Portland agent, he could have "with as good grace defend[ed] an action to recover the stolen property on the ground that the plaintiff was not authorized to do business in this state."

Defendant Elliott's final contention was that because the plaintiff corporation had not qualified to do business in Oregon, it could not sue in Oregon's federal district court. Deady answered emphatically, however, that no state could deny citizens of other states access to its "national court," and Oregon's foreign-corporation statute did not even purport to do so.

**Unlawful Public Assistance to Enterprise.** In 1868 the Portland City Council, lured by the prospect of a rail link to San Francisco, voted to (1) guarantee $350,000 worth of Oregon Central Railroad bonds, (2) issue interest coupons for them, and (3) impose a property tax to help finance them. Property owners Henry and Theresa Coulson sued to have that ordinance declared unlawful, citing both a state constitutional prohibition against cities lending their credit to private corporations and a Portland city charter prohibition against public debt exceeding $50,000.[87]

The first issue in *Coulson v. City of Portland* (1868)[88] was whether federal equity jurisdiction existed to hear such a suit. The plaintiffs urged that it did because the suit would prevent (1) a cloud on their title, (2) a violation of municipal law, and (3) a series of repetitive, multiple suits by different taxpayers. Judge Deady chose the third as the basis for sustaining his court's equity jurisdiction. Preventing repetitive, multiple lawsuits was the "acknowledged head of equity jurisdiction." Because the city ordinance in question provided for 20 annual tax levies to pay the bond coupons, there was unquestionably a threat of multiple lawsuits. Therefore, a federal equity court did have power to consider the ordinance's legality and, if it were illegal, to enjoin its implementation.

Deady then proceeded to hold the ordinance "illegal and void." It plainly violated the city charter, which prohibited city debt exceeding $50,000. A California ruling that such an ordinance created no debt because it simultaneously enacted a corresponding tax was a "proposition in legal metaphysics" beyond Deady's comprehension. He praised Oregon's constitution and laws prohibiting public debt as laudable efforts to prevent mortgaging the "present and future property and labor of the country,…for building railways and the like, for the benefit primarily of a few individuals." The Coulsons received their requested injunction.

**Exclusive Textbook Contracts.** A decade later, in *Bancroft v. Thayer* (1879),[89] publishers A. L. and Hubert H. Bancroft challenged the state's right to repudiate an allegedly exclusive textbook contract. The State Board of Education, in both 1873 and 1877, had selected six Bancroft "Pacific Coast Series" books for use in the state's public schools. Oregon law then provided that books thus selected would be the "authorized" public-school texts for the next four years. In 1878, however, the legislature amended the textbook law, authorizing new book selections at any time for "good and sufficient cause." The following spring the board proposed to replace the Pacific Coast Series, and the Bancrofts sued to enjoin.

Once again the defendant denied that a federal court had power even to hear the case, this time citing the Eleventh-Amendment ban against suing a state. But Deady, as usual, disagreed with that defense, pointing out that the Supreme Court had held half a century earlier that the Eleventh Amendment prohibited only suits against the state *itself*, not those against its officials.[90]

The board's more serious contentions related to the underlying legal merits of the case. It urged that (1) the power to regulate common schools was within the state's inalienable police power; (2) even the original statute did not authorize book contracts for a definite term; and (3) in any event, the board's 1877 contract with the Bancrofts was not for such a term.

Citing two landmark treatises, Blackstone's *Commentaries* and

Cooley's *Constitutional Limitations,* Judge Deady described the nature of
the state police power:

> The term "police power of a state" is a convenient and comprehensive
> expression used to signify those powers by means of which it not only
> preserves public order and prevents crime, but also promotes and
> secures good manners in the intercourse between its citizens, and
> thereby prevents a conflict of rights.[91]

It was incorrect that a state could not "barter away the police power" by
making a long-term exclusive book contract. The British Parliament and
American legislatures had granted such exclusive privileges "from time
immemorial," and their power to do so had "never been questioned or
denied." If the state board in fact had lawfully entered into a four-year
contract, both "good faith" and the contract clause of the federal constitution required that it be performed.[92]

After "careful consideration," however, Deady could find no authority
even in the original legislation for such a contract. True, the board had
signed an apparently exclusive agreement with the Bancrofts extending
until October 1881, but no such agreement could be enforced against the
state unless the officials who signed it had acted manifestly within the
scope of their authority. Therefore, because the state board had exceeded
its statutory authority, the four-year contract was unenforceable, and the
Bancrofts were entitled to no relief.

**Federal Roadbuilding Subsidies.** A final important confrontation
between government and enterprise in early Oregon related to large federal land grants to finance construction of "military wagon roads."
Between 1864 and 1872, the federal government made five such grants
totaling nearly 2.5 million acres. One road ran eastward from The Dalles
to Fort Boise, two extended from the Willamette Valley over the
Cascades to Idaho, and two connected the Willamette and Umpqua val-
leys with the coast. In each case, Congress authorized the state to select
the grantee/contractor, furnish construction requirements, and perform all inspections.[93]

The grantees of this federal largesse built decidedly substandard
roads. The 330-mile road from The Dalles, for example, took only 63
days to complete, with most "construction" consisting simply of "driving an oxcart over the county while two men trudged behind with
shovels on their shoulders." Moreover, because a grantee could claim
land on both sides of whatever road it built, the route typically selected

was "about as crooked as the track of the ancient peoples through the wilderness"; this enabled the company to "gobble up all the available lands of that region."[94]

Beginning in the late 1870s, settler complaints about construction failures and real-estate hoarding became widespread. Eventually, Congress directed the attorney general to seek judicial recovery of the land grants, and the resulting federal litigation, both in Oregon and in the Supreme Court, was extensive.

The first case was *United States v. Dalles Military Road Co.* (1889),[95] in which the government sought to recapture one land grant for failure to comply with appropriate construction standards. Circuit Judge Lorenzo Sawyer ruled, however, that no such standards even applied. Neither the 1867 federal act authorizing the road nor the 1868 state act designating the grantee set forth roadbuilding standards, and Oregon's 1862 corporations act, which *did*, was not "part of the contract."

The government also alleged that the grantee had not adequately *maintained* the road after completion. But again Sawyer could find nothing in either statute requiring such maintenance. He declined to follow an 1879 Oregon Supreme Court decision awarding damages to a private mail carrier for poor maintenance.[96] That ruling, he believed, had been based on entirely different (i.e., private) rights and obligations.

Sawyer then sustained three further defenses. First, Congress had delegated to Oregon Governor George L. Woods authority to certify proper completion, so in the absence of fraud, the government could not challenge the validity of his 1869 certificate accepting the road. Second, purchaser Edward Martin, having placed "confidence in the truth of the said certificate," and in Congress's 1873 authorization of land patents, had purchased the disputed land for $125,000 without notice of any construction or maintenance failures. Therefore, he was a bona fide purchaser for value, and the government's contention that Martin himself should have inspected the road was "preposterous." Finally, because 15 years had elapsed since Congress's 1874 direction to issue the land patents, the government's suit was "stale" and "inequitable."

In May 1890, Judge Deady reached the same result in a companion case, *United States v. Wallamet Valley & Cascade Mountain Wagon Road Co.*[97]

The following year, however, the Supreme Court reversed both Sawyer's and Deady's judgments, ordering that the government at least be allowed to reply. In *United States v. Dalles Military Road Company*

(1891),[98] Justice Blatchford expressed the Court's view that Congress had intended a "full legal investigation of the facts" and that the "important interests involved" should not be "determined upon the untested allegations of the defendants."[99]

On remand, the trial court[100] ruled again for the landowners, excluding all testimony relating to road quality. Again it concluded that the governor's certificates had been "truthfully made, without fraud or misrepresentation," and that the purchasers had acted "in good faith, for valuable consideration, and without notice of any fraud or misrepresentation." On appeal to the new Ninth Circuit Court of Appeals,[101] a divided panel affirmed that ruling.

Other cases met similar fates on remand,[102] and eventually they all reappeared before the United States Supreme Court. In the 1893 decision *United States v. California & Oregon Land Co.*,[103] the Supreme Court affirmed all lower-court decrees in favor of landowners against the government. Thus ended a rather sorry and not untypical episode of early Far-West government indifference toward, and enterprise disdain for, the public interest.

## Protecting the Victims of Enterprise

As the nineteenth century drew toward a close, Oregon workers, passengers, and neighboring landowners began to bring more and more enterprise-related injury claims to federal court. Generally, they received a sympathetic reception.

In *McCune v. Northern Pac. Ry. Co.* (1884),[104] for example, the plaintiff bridge worker had fallen from a defective scaffold and permanently disabled his left arm. Following a jury verdict for the plaintiff against the defendant railway, Judge Deady denied the railway's motion for a new trial, expressing his own agreement that it should indeed have provided a more secure scaffold.

Deady's most notable personal-injury decision was *Gilmore v. Northern Pac. Ry. Co.* (1884),[105] in which he sustained a worker's recovery by refusing to apply the infamous fellow-servant rule (prohibiting a worker from suing his employer for a co-worker's negligent acts). The plaintiff had been a railroad-construction laborer in Montana, where occasionally it became necessary to thaw black powder for use as an explosive. The plaintiff's foreman had repeatedly ordered the thawing done over an open fire rather than in the reinforced kettle provided, and one day the powder exploded, killing the foreman and severely injuring the plaintiff laborer.

The railroad's principal defense was that the negligent foreman had been the plaintiff's "fellow servant," so under many nineteenth-century English and American authorities the plaintiff had, by implication at least, assumed all risk of the foreman's negligence.[106] Judge Deady instructed the jury that if the foreman and plaintiff had been "both employed in the same gang, in a common employment or service, under the same or a common boss or superintendent," they were indeed fellow servants, and the plaintiff could not recover. However, if the crew's work had been under the foreman's "practical direction and control," then the foreman instead had "represented the company."

Following a $4,500 jury verdict for the plaintiff, Deady denied the railroad's new-trial motion. He described how the fellow-servant rule had arisen in England in 1837 and then in America the following decade. He also noted that industrialization often substituted "invisible masters and employers" for the "visible ones of former times," and in such circumstances the fellow-servant rule had often resulted in "hardship and injustice." Therefore, the modern "tendency" was toward "modification and limitation of the rule" in order to place upon an employer a "due and just share of responsibility for the lives and limbs of the persons in its employ." The Supreme Court, for example, had "materially limited" and "sharply questioned" the rule, and several states had "much relaxed" it. In *Gilmore*, Deady concluded, the foreman's order to thaw powder over an open fire had subjected the plaintiff to a "serious danger not within the scope of his employment" and the fellow-servant rule should not bar his recovery of damages.

Later the same year, in *Heinrich v. Pullman Palace Car Co.* (1884),[107] a Pullman-car passenger sued for damages sustained when the defendant's porter accidentally shot him in the leg. Pullman's defense was that the porter had violated a company rule by accepting the gun from another passenger for storage.

After reviewing the authorities, however, including Justice Joseph Story's landmark Agency treatise, Deady concluded that an employer was indeed liable for its employee's negligence even though it had prohibited the harmful act. The issue was whether the employee had committed the act "in the course of his employment," an issue that would be determined from evidence produced later at trial.[108]

The next two "victim" cases involved not personal injury but threatened economic injury from bridges across the Willamette River at Portland. Deady reluctantly approved construction of one such bridge, then eloquently enjoined construction of the second.

In *Hughes v. Northern Pac. Ry. Co.* (1883),[109] an owner of wharves located just upstream from a planned bridge sued to enjoin the "great and lasting obstruction" to river navigation it would cause. The first issue, inevitably, was whether federal jurisdiction existed. Deady answered, as he often did, in the affirmative, explaining that because the suit arose under federal statutes creating and extending the Northern Pacific, jurisdiction plainly existed.[110]

The principal substantive question was whether Congress had authorized the Northern Pacific to build the planned bridge. The railway contended that such authority was implicit in federal statutes authorizing it to construct a main line west from St. Paul and eventually down the Columbia to Portland, including "necessary…bridges." Deady began his analysis by reiterating the familiar principle that such federal statutes constituted a "public grant," which had no effect beyond what they "plainly expressed, or clearly implied." Any "material doubt or ambiguity" would be resolved against the company in favor of the public.

Still, Deady's "deliberate conclusion," reached "not…without hesitation," was that Congress had indeed authorized a bridge across the Willamette. The only practical route from St. Paul to Portland crossed the river at that point, and the express reference to "necessary…bridges" could hardly be interpreted any other way.

So the ultimate issue became whether the particular bridge proposed was permissible. Regrettably, Congress had not specified the "site and character of the proposed bridge," so Deady could but "presume" that it had authorized only a bridge that would not unduly "impair the usefulness of said river for navigation." Northern Pacific's plans called for a 174-foot clear channel on each side of its central pier, a plan that compared favorably with bridges Congress had authorized elsewhere. It also would interfere less with navigation than an earlier bridge (never built) which Congress had authorized at exactly the same location. Therefore, landowner Hughes did not receive his requested injunction.

Judge Deady's opinion in *Hatch v. Wallamet Iron Bridge Co.* (1881)[111] is one of the most eloquent, yet ultimately unsuccessful he ever wrote. Three years earlier, the Oregon Legislature had authorized a bridge across the Willamette from Morrison Street on the west to N Street on the east. The statute required only that the bridge not "injuriously impede and obstruct the free navigation of said river." Thereafter, Willamette Iron

Bridge Company began building a drawbridge designed to leave a 100-foot draw on each side of the central pier.

Six months later, an owner of wharves and warehouses 600 feet above the bridge site joined with the owner of a federally licensed steamboat to seek a federal-court injunction against further construction. The bridge would constitute a "serious and unlawful obstruction to the navigation of the river," they contended, and Judge Deady agreed.

Federal jurisdiction existed because once again the plaintiffs' suit raised a "federal question." They alleged that the bridge would violate both (1) a federal steamboat-licensing statute and (2) the 1859 federal act admitting Oregon to the Union, which stipulated that the state's navigable waters remain "common highways and forever free."

Deady explained that although a state's police power allowed it to authorize a bridge over navigable water, Congress—by virtue of its Article I commerce power—had a "practical veto." If Congress did not exercise that veto, a federal court could not intervene; however, if the proposed bridge conflicted with either of the federal statutes invoked, it was "so far unlawful" and a "nuisance" that could be "prevented or abated."

The steamboat licensing statute, fairly construed, did not prohibit construction of the bridge. The Supreme Court had always been "careful not to declare a conflict between state and federal legislation on this subject upon mere implication," and there was no "necessary conflict" between the federal and state laws. Thus, both "authority" and "prudential reason" suggested that a federal steamboat license was merely a license to navigate "so far as [the river] may be navigable."[112]

The statehood act, however, was a different matter. The "common highways and forever free" language, taken from the 1787 Northwest Ordinance, related directly to navigability of the state's waterways. Indeed, the sole purpose of that language had been to preserve those waters for the "free use of all the citizens of the United States as common highways." The Supreme Court had repeatedly interpreted similar language in interstate compacts to preclude state obstruction of navigable waters, and, indeed, it was "self-evident" that a river could not be a "common highway, forever free" if a state had unreviewable power to obstruct it.

So, again, the ultimate question was whether any conflict actually existed between the particular state and federal statutes. In deciding, Deady explained, a court should consider carefully the "character and relative importance of the river and the commerce dependent thereon, and the character and need of the bridge and the commerce dependent upon it."

Deady then described in forceful language the importance of the Willamette River to all Oregonians. The "commerce of Oregon, both domestic and foreign," was largely dependent upon [its] free navigation." It was the "harbor of Portland," the "emporium and financial center of the Northwest," where the "valuable products of the country are gathered from far and near and stored for market and exportation, and the imports from sister states and foreign countries are received and distributed throughout the interior." By contrast, the proposed bridge would serve merely as a "more convenient" means of river crossing for the "small population that live in East Portland and the neighboring villages," a mere "drop in the bucket" compared to the statewide interests that the bridge would inconvenience or injure.

He then reviewed a long series of federal statutes authorizing bridges across the Mississippi, Missouri, and Ohio Rivers. In many, Congress had required a clear opening of 160 feet on each side of the central pier. Moreover, in 1874 Congress had authorized the Oregon & California Railway to bridge the Willamette at Portland (a bridge never built) and had specifically required that the central draws be not less than 150 feet.

Therefore, Deady had "no doubt" that the proposed bridge would constitute an unlawful "obstruction to the navigation of the Wallamet," one that would prevent it being a "free and common highway, to the citizens of the United States." Virtually all the area's river pilots had testified that the proposed draw was too narrow, as had the United States district engineer.

The following month, Circuit Judge Sawyer arrived in Portland to participate in the final decision. Following further testimony, Deady reiterated his view that the proposed bridge would be a "nuisance" and a "serious impediment" to navigation. Ninety percent of American exports produced west of the Rocky Mountains and north of the 42nd parallel arrived at Portland for shipment, and any bridge which materially restricted or impeded free use of the harbor would "destroy the town and injure the commerce of the country."

Sawyer fully concurred and had "very little to add" to his colleague's remarks. He cited and discussed the Supreme Court's landmark *Wheeling Bridge* decision in which, under apparently similar circumstances, the Court had enjoined any obstruction to navigation on the Ohio River.[113]

Six years later, however, the Supreme Court unanimously reversed

Deady and Sawyer's decision.[114] In its view, the proposed bridge did not violate the 1859 act admitting Oregon to the Union. That act, like the 1787 Northwest Ordinance from which it was taken, referred not to "physical obstructions" to navigation but "political regulations which would hamper the freedom of commerce." Therefore, the plaintiffs' suit did not "arise under the Constitution or laws of the United States," and the federal court lacked jurisdiction even to consider it.

Further, the court distinguished its own *Wheeling Bridge* decision. There, a Virginia-authorized bridge had constituted a "nuisance" because it had "injuriously affected a supra-riparian State [Pennsylvania] bordering on the river." The Willamette River, however, was wholly within Oregon, so the Portland bridge raised no such question of interstate fairness.[115] Thus was born Portland's Morrison Street Bridge.

In summary, Matthew Deady's decisions relating in some way to the growth of industrial enterprise in early Oregon illustrate several important themes in his jurisprudence. As the author of his state's 1862 general incorporation statute, Judge Deady was uniquely knowledgeable about the technicalities of corporate organization, authority, and operations. He generally applied those technicalities, however, with a healthy measure of common sense. For example, he excused a director's absence at a board meeting, but insisted repeatedly that directors violate no fiduciary duty to the firm. He believed there was "every reason" to exact the "most scrupulous conduct" possible from corporate officers and directors.

The same theme of insider responsibility appears also in Judge Deady's decisions imposing liability on shareholders for unpaid corporate debts. Considerably more willing than his state-court counterparts to impose such liability, he routinely rejected the technical, semantic defenses by which shareholders typically sought to avoid it.

More broadly, Judge Deady continued to recognize on the bench, as he had recognized at the 1857 constitutional convention, that the growth of industrial enterprise inevitably threatens other important public and private values. He therefore enforced with enthusiasm the "plain and wholesome" state law regulating foreign corporations, struck down the Portland city council's effort to subsidize a private railroad with public funds, and declined to interpret a state public-school statute as authorizing longterm exclusive textbook contracts. On the other hand, in one of his most inexplicable series of decisions, both he and Circuit Judge Sawyer turned essentially deaf ears toward government efforts to reclaim land granted for wagon-road construction.

In a third series of enterprise-related decisions, those interpreting the legal rights of its most immediate "victims," Judge Deady adopted again the largely protective posture he favored in many of his admiralty decisions. He construed broadly an employer's liability for employee negligence, refusing most notably to apply the unjust fellow-servant rule. Deady also wrote an opinion eloquently invoking the public interest in an unsuccessful effort to halt construction of a bridge across the Willamette River.

Thus, in enterprise-related disputes as in admiralty disputes, the early Oregon federal court generally provided to Oregonians a forum for the airing of grievances free from economic or political favor. Judge Deady could not fairly be called hostile to enterprise, but he certainly did not intend to allow it to avoid its legal or moral imperatives as he understood them.

# THE FEDERAL JUDICIAL RESPONSE TO RACISM IN EARLY OREGON

A persistent theme of American history has been the effort by white majorities to exclude or persecute other races. Even in nineteenth-century Oregon, settled largely by antislavery whites, with very small non-Indian minority populations until nearly 1880, an early and frequent concern was to exclude as many non-whites as possible and to deprive those who did remain of any meaningful participation in community life. The state constitution excluded black settlers; the legislature repeatedly mandated various forms of racial discrimination; prominent political and religious leaders set shameful examples of racial demagoguery and harassment; and even the state judiciary exhibited an occasional "blatant disregard for court procedure"[116] in minority-related cases.

Federal District Judge Matthew Deady was an important exception to that general pattern. For nearly two decades beginning in 1876, he wrote and published a remarkable series of decisions championing the rights and sensibilities of Oregon's immigrant Chinese and, by extension, other minority populations. Read together, those decisions recall a memorable example of federal judicial intervention against nineteenth-century American racism.

## Early Oregon Race Relations

By 1843, when 100 or so settlers met on the Champoeg plain to adopt Oregon's first Organic Act, race had become a paramount public issue throughout America. The rise of organized abolitionism the prior decade had contributed to vastly increased racial awareness and tension in all regions. The Supreme Court had recently upheld the federal Fugitive Slave Law; Congress was operating under a self-imposed "gag rule" prohibiting consideration of the many abolitionist petitions being directed to it; and bitter divisions over annexation of Texas as a slave state would soon erupt in the 1844 presidential election.[117]

Many early Oregon settlers arrived from "border" regions like Kentucky or Missouri, and the racial attitudes they brought west reflected the tensions existing there. Most opposed slavery, but opposed association with free blacks even more.[118] Thus, their 1843 Organic Act restricted political rights to "free male descendant[s] of a white man," and their first legislature excluded blacks and mulattoes from Oregon altogether. Further legislation the following decade reaffirmed and extended those restrictions and exclusions.[119]

Delegates to the 1857 state constitutional convention sidestepped the issues of slavery and free-black residence by submitting them to the voters separately from the proposed constitution. They did, however, include several other sections making clear their own preference for an all-white state. For example, they once again restricted suffrage to white males and prohibited nearly all Chinese from owning real estate or working a mining claim. In November 1857 Oregon voters approved the proposed constitution 7,193 to 3,125, disapproved slavery 7,725 to 2,645, and overwhelmingly prohibited residence by free blacks 8,640 to 1,081.[120]

Soon after the Civil War, Oregon nativists redirected their energies away from the state's tiny black population toward a more promising target, its growing number of Chinese miners and laborers. By 1870 industrialization was reaching Oregon, with large railroad, timber, textile, and canning firms beginning to emerge. The employer's desire for cheap labor began to conflict with the worker's need for an adequate wage, and the Chinese, lured to America with promises of industrial employment, became beleaguered scapegoats in the resulting bitter clashes.[121]

Working-class whites, fearful of losing their jobs, typically directed their anger and violence not against the industrialists hiring the Chinese, but against the Chinese laborers themselves. Governor Lafayette Grover in 1870 joined other politicians sounding a "note of warning against

Mongolian labor," and scattered protests and violence against Chinese laborers and shopkeepers continued throughout the next decade.[122] By 1880 anti-Chinese sentiment in Oregon was widespread and powerful. The state's Chinese population had tripled the prior decade, to nearly 10,000, just as a nationwide depression brought extensive, prolonged unemployment to the region.

In the winter of 1885-86, racial tension exploded into serious violence throughout the Far West. In September, white miners at Rock Springs, Wyoming killed 28 Chinese, wounded 15, and drove away the remainder. The following February, anti-Chinese riots in Tacoma and Seattle became so severe that the territorial governor had to declare martial law.

Similar, though less severe, violence soon followed in Portland. In late January a series of mass meetings raised white antipathy toward Chinese to new levels. During the next month, armed masked men drove 180 Chinese woodcutters from Albina, expelled 125 more from Mt. Tabor, raided a colony of Chinese truck gardeners at Guild's Lake, and tried to blow up a downtown Portland wash house. Thereafter, such sporadic violence against Chinese gradually subsided, as the economy began to improve and Portland's law-and-order elite slowly reasserted its dominance. Although many Chinese departed Portland that troubled winter and spring, a sizable number remained crowded into an area along Second Street, venturing forth occasionally to do odd jobs or work in nearby canneries and truck gardens.[123]

## Federal-Court Policing of
## Local Discrimination and Lawlessness

One particularly notable series of Chinese-rights case tried in Judge Deady's federal court were those in which Chinese sought protection against discriminatory state or local laws or, in one instance, against mob violence.[124] In every such case, Deady scrutinized the relevant legislation strictly to determine whether it had been lawfully enacted and whether it violated the federal constitution or laws. He also departed frequently in such cases from his customary formality on the bench to express deep personal sympathy for the plight of immigrant Chinese and strong distaste for both the politicians who "demagogued" about them and the "sandlot" whites who harassed them.

**Chinese Employment on Public Works.** In 1878 the Oregon Legislature made it unlawful to employ Chinese laborers on "any public works or public improvement of any character, except as a punishment for crime." Violation would render any contract for such work "null and void."[125]

The following summer the city of Portland sued in state court to enjoin violations of both the statute and city contracts containing its prohibition. The defendant contractors responded by suing in *federal* court to enjoin the state-court suits, contending that (1) the statute violated an 1868 treaty between the United States and China granting China "most favored nation" trade and immigration rights;[126] (2) it also violated the statutory rights of city taxpayers (including the contractors) to have public contracts awarded to the lowest responsible bidders; and (3) it interfered with legitimate expectations under existing contracts that had been bid assuming employment of Chinese labor.

Judge Deady began his celebrated opinion in *Baker v. City of Portland* (1879)[127] by lecturing the Oregon Legislature about honor and explaining why its statute did violate the Burlingame Treaty:

*An honorable man keeps his word under all circumstances, and an honorable nation abides by its treaty obligations, even to its own dis-*

*In a series of cases concerning the rights of Chinese immigrants, including their right to work in Oregon, Judge Deady carefully reviewed state and local laws to determine whether they violated the federal constitution or laws. He also frequently expressed his sympathy for the Chinese and his dislike of those who harassed them. (Oregon Historical Society Negative #50082)*

*advantage....[The Burlingame Treaty] recognizes the right of Chinese to change their home and...guarantees to them all the privileges and immunities that may be enjoyed here by the citizens or subjects of any nation.*

It would be "difficult to conceive a grosser case" of treaty violation, he continued, than to "invite Chinese to become permanent residents...and then to deliberately prevent them from earning a living." That inspirational lecture turned out to be mere dictum, however, for ultimately Deady sustained the city's demurrer on the ground of party misjoinder: the contractors had no "common interest in the subject or object of the suit," so could not sue together.[128]

*Baker* was one of Deady's most widely noted decisions. The *Oregonian* praised his "common sense view" of the statute: "[T]hough the demurrer...was sustained on other grounds, there comes with it the announcement of a principle which is fatal to the attempt to prohibit the employment of Chinese." At least six national legal periodicals reprinted the opinion, and even the celebrated author and jurist Thomas Cooley sent a congratulatory note:

*"My dear sir, I have read with much interest your opinion in* Baker v. Portland, *and I need hardly say I am pleased with it, since it has been received with such general favor and satisfaction."* [129]

Two weeks later, however, state judge Charles Bellinger (who 14 years later would succeed Deady as federal district judge) granted the city its requested state-court injunctions. He also expressed disagreement with Deady's conclusion that the state statute was invalid: "The case of *Baker vs. The City of Portland* is in point," he wrote, "but I cannot admit the correctness of its conclusions." Moreover, the city and contractors had agreed by *contract* that no Chinese would be employed, so "upon this ground the injunction in these cases should be granted whether the State law is void or not."[130]

Two weeks later, Supreme Court Justice Field affirmed Deady's misjoinder ruling. Deady himself took that opportunity to add a long footnote reminding Judge Bellinger that the state, "being a member of the Union,...may be restricted in the exercise of [the police power] by the [federal] Constitution, laws or treaties." The Burlingame Treaty, he repeated, guaranteed to Chinese the "same privileges and immunities as the subjects of Great Britain, Germany and France," and a state could not, without violating that treaty, deny Chinese aliens "the privilege of laboring for a living in a field where it permits all other aliens to be employed."

He ended with a typical flourish:

> [T]he anti-Chinese legislation of the Pacific Coast is but a poorly disguised attempt on the part of the state to evade and set aside the treaty with China, and thereby nullify an act of the national government. Between this and the firing on Fort Sumter, by South Carolina, there is the difference of the direct and indirect—and nothing more. [131]

The final episode in *Baker* was the contractors' appeal of Judge Bellinger's decision to the Oregon Supreme Court. Undoubtedly having in mind Judge Deady's strong attack on the statute, that court exercised its discretion to withhold relief when a plaintiff cannot demonstrate likelihood of irreparable injury. Because the city had no economic interest in who performed the work, the court declined to "interfere by injunction," a decision that rendered unnecessary any inquiry by it into whether the state law violated the treaty with China.[132]

**Chinese Liability for Public Road Assessments.** From the earliest days of Oregon's provisional government, able-bodied males were required to work annually on public roads and highways. The supervisor of each road district was to recruit needed labor first from owners of taxable property within the district, one day's work for each $1,000 assessed value, and second from men aged 21 to 50 "residing within his road district," two days work each. Recruits could pay $2 per day in lieu of working.[133]

The supervisor was to notify each recruit "personally or by writing, left at his usual place of abode," and anyone neglecting such notice became liable for the "amount of his road tax in money." The supervisor was then to collect that tax, together with "twenty per centum thereon," by levy and sale of the delinquent's property if necessary. Another statute, passed in 1866 to facilitate tax collection generally, permitted tax collectors to garnish assets of anyone indebted to a delinquent taxpayer; it also directed road supervisors to turn over delinquency statements to the sheriff, who was to collect them, together with a "sum equal to one fourth part of the delinquent tax" for his services.[134]

In early 1882 the Oregon Railway and Navigation Company hired nearly 1,500 migrant Chinese laborers to work on its new line eastward from Portland along the Columbia River. The local road supervisor promptly listed 1,449 of those laborers by number, declared them liable for road duty, notified them in some unknown way, and delivered a delinquency statement to the sheriff. The sheriff then immediately garnished the several Chinese firms that had supplied the laborers, and also the railroad, for 1,449 times $6. In *On Yuen Hai Co. v. Ross* (1882),[135] the firms asked Judge Deady to restrain the supervisor and the sheriff from such garnishment.

In an elegant, understated opinion, Deady granted the requested injunction. He first questioned the procedure of the sheriff's immediate garnishment, calling it "very irregular if not illegal." Even assuming that the supervisor had duly assessed road work to 1,449 unnamed Chinese laborers and somehow had given them adequate notice, the garnishment was improper because the sheriff had not tried to collect any amounts due from the laborers themselves.

Second, Deady faulted the sheriff's arithmetic, noting that his demand was "in excess of the sum due." The road-work statute authorized a levying supervisor to collect a 20 percent penalty; and the 1866 garnishment act permitted a sheriff to collect an extra "one fourth part" of any delinquent tax, again apparently as a penalty. Deady reasoned sensibly that the two penalties were not cumulative. Assuming that the *second* applied, because the sheriff and not the supervisor had acted as collector, the total garnishment demand should have been only $5 per laborer. Even assuming that the two penalties *were* cumulative, the correct amount would still have been less than the $6 assessed.

Following that foray into the garnishment statute, Deady ascended to higher ground to conclude that in any event the road-work statute did not even apply to itinerant laborers:

> The provisions of the statute upon the subject are somewhat indefinite, but it is evident from what is provided and from the nature of the case that persons only transiently in the district are not within its purview or operation. The party must be "residing" within the district…; and the notice to labor, if not served on him personally, must be left at his usual place of "abode."

Residence implied "more than a temporary sojourn in a place," Deady reasoned, and because (1) road work was an annual duty and (2) the road district property tax was assessed on district property owned during the prior year, it was "but reasonable to conclude…that the statute contemplates that such residents shall have enjoyed the privilege of at least one year's inhabitancy of the district before the corresponding duty of working the road begins."

Finally, Deady ended as he had begun in *Baker*, censuring those responsible for racist official action directed at Chinese aliens and concluding with an appeal to "natural justice":

> *[I]f these laborers had been European instead of Asiatic foreigners, it is not probable that anyone would have thought of attempting to make them work the roads.…The statute makes no discrimination in this matter between Chinese and other foreigners, and it is not only contrary to the treaty with China, but to the dictates of natural justice, that any should be made in the administration of it.*

**Gambling, Laundries, and Opium.** A troublesome issue in nineteenth-century American politics was the appropriate division of power between state and local governments. By 1872, when John Dillon published his landmark treatise on municipal corporations, American lawyers generally agreed with the doctrines he expressed: (1) cities were mere "public corporations" subject entirely to state control and restricted to "public" functions; and (2) city charters were to be construed narrowly, with all reasonable doubts regarding city authority resolved against its existence.[136] The latter doctrine became widely known as "Dillon's Rule," and became the primary doctrinal basis for Judge Deady's next three Chinese-rights decisions.

In *In re Lee Tong* (1883),[137] Judge Deady invoked Dillon's Rule to free a Chinese petitioner accused in police court of violating a Portland gambling ordinance. It was at that time a misdemeanor throughout the state to participate in "any…game played with cards, dice, or any other device." In addition, the Portland city charter authorized the *city* to "*suppress* bawdy houses, gaming and gambling houses, places kept for smoking opium and opium smoking" and also to "*punish* inmates of bawdy houses, houses of ill-fame, keepers of places kept for smoking opium and opium-smokers." Invoking the "gaming and gambling" houses authority, the city council in 1883 prohibited a long list of games (including the Chinese game of tantan) and provided a jail term or fine for each violation.[138] Arrested and held in custody for violating that ordinance by playing tantan, Lee Tong petitioned for a federal writ of habeas corpus.

Deady began his opinion granting the writ by reaffirming federal-court authority to discharge a prisoner in custody "in violation of the constitution, or of a law or treaty of the United States."[139] Then, on the merits of the case, he accepted Lee Tong's argument that the ordinance language being applied to him was invalid because it went beyond the city's charter authority to "suppress" gaming by attempting to "punish" it as well. The city had charter authority only to "suppress" gaming, not to "punish" it. It could enforce the existing *state* gaming law, but not enact and enforce its own. Therefore, the proceedings against Lee Tong were "void"; he was being held without "due process of law," and he was "entitled to the writ of habeas corpus for his deliverance."

Two years later, Deady reached a similar result in a case involving alleged violation of city laundry regulations. In December 1884, under charter authority granted to "control and regulate public laundries," the Portland City Council had passed an ordinance purporting to "license and regulate" them. It required each proprietor to keep records of clothes received and returned, keep the premises in sanitary condition, and pay a $5 quarterly license fee.

Six weeks later, a Portland police court convicted washhouse proprietor Wan Yin of failing to pay the license fee and sentenced him to seven days in jail or a $15 fine. He promptly sought a habeas corpus writ from Judge Deady, urging principally that the ordinance was invalid because the five-dollar-per-quarter fee was neither a regulation nor a license fee, but instead an "onerous tax."

In *In Re Wan Yin* (1885),[140] Deady agreed. While the power to *license* might legitimately be inferred from charter authority to regulate, the power to *tax* could not be. A municipal corporation had "no authority to impose a tax, otherwise than in pursuance of an express grant of power to that effect, or a clear and necessary implication from an express grant…." After again reviewing treatises by John Dillon and Thomas Cooley, and decisions from Michigan, Indiana, Massachusetts, and Iowa, Deady concluded it was "apparent" that the so-called "license fee" was "far beyond" any corresponding city expense and was "in effect a tax, and was so intended."

Nor was the ordinance saved by city charter authority to tax "offensive trades and occupations." Such a "general welfare" clause could not be "construed as applicable to any subject [like washhouses] that is elsewhere otherwise specifically provided for." Deady also reminded his readers that washing clothes was a "useful and inoffensive occupation," and the fact that Chinese performed most of it in Portland might excite "race prejudice" but did not make it "offensive" to the senses.

Deady concluded his *Wan Yin* opinion with an outspoken defense of federal habeas corpus jurisdiction. At both the 1883 and 1884 American Bar Association meetings, state court judges had attacked supposed "abuses" of such jurisdiction, particularly by the "lowest class" of federal judges who had "unlocked the penitentiaries of the states." One 1884 speaker had even referred specifically to one of Deady's decisions as a "fla-grant" such instance.[141] Deady, as usual, declined to turn the other cheek:

> The case of Lee Tong is referred to in the discussion of "Habeas
> Corpus," at the meeting of the American Bar Association for 1884, as
> a "flagrant" one—whatever that may mean....But beyond this
> ornate epithet,...it is not denied that the jurisdiction is conferred,
> and therefore no "federal judge," however "low" he may be in the
> judicial hierarchy, can decline to exercise it when a case is brought
> before him.

Moreover, such jurisdiction was necessary if the Fourteenth Amendment was not to become a "dead letter":

> But if the jurisdiction to discharge a person from imprisonment, who
> is deprived of his liberty without due process of law by a state, was not
> conferred upon the district and circuit judges, this provision of the
> fourteenth amendment, that was plainly intended as a bulwark
> against local oppression and tyranny, as well "up North" as "down
> South," would be a dead letter. The supreme court is too far away,
> and the way there is too expensive, to furnish relief in the great
> majority of cases.

By early 1886 Judge Deady had become thoroughly irritated with Portland's escalating white hostility toward the Chinese. Increasingly, he viewed the conflict as one between a shiftless "mob" on the one hand and public-spirited "citizens" on the other.[142] In February, he issued his most outspoken decision yet on the subject.

The 1882 version of the Portland city charter had granted the city broad power to "suppress...opium smoking" and to "punish...opium smokers." An 1883 ordinance implementing that power declared it a mis-demeanor to "smoke opium in any house or place" or "be in any house or place where opium is being smoked, without any lawful business." In 1885, however, the legislature responded to Deady's *Lee Tong* decision by amending the city's authority over gambling, prostitution, and opium use in a way that, inadvertently, seemed to *narrow* its power over the lat-ter: The city thereafter could "*prevent and suppress* opium smoking and houses or places kept therefor" and "*punish* any keeper of such house or place or person who smokes therein or who frequents the same."

In December 1885 the Portland police arrested Ah Lit for smoking opium in a private home, alleging a violation of the 1883 ordinance. Convicted in police court, fined $15, and imprisoned for seven days, Ah Lit sought a federal writ of habeas corpus.

In *Ex Parte Ah Lit* (1886),[143] Deady once again read the city charter narrowly, declared the ordinance beyond the council's power, and freed the petitioner. The charter did not authorize the council to punish a person for "smoking opium in his own house," or anywhere else other than "in a house or place kept for that purpose—what is known, I suppose, in police jargon, as an 'opium joint.'" Ah Lit had been "charged with and convicted of smoking opium in a private house," which, under the city's amended charter authority, was "not a crime."

A central, revealing passage of Deady's *Ah Lit* opinion was his accusation of hypocrisy against Portland whites who sought to suppress Chinese opium use while indulging in their own vices, tobacco and liquor. After asserting that the "abuse, if not the common use" of those two substances was far more injurious to the "health, peace, and morals of society" than the use of opium, he recalled the parable of the Puritan and the Bear:

> Indeed, it is well understood that this legislation, however right in the abstract, is not so much the result of a desire on our part to reform the "Heathen Chinee" as to annoy him. In short, it is the old story of the Puritan and the bear. His opposition to the practice of "baiting" the beast was not because of the pain it gave Bruin, but the pleasure it gave the parties engaged in it.

**Criminal Liability of Anti-Chinese Conspirators.** As white hostility toward Chinese turned more frequently violent in 1886, West Coast federal prosecutors and judges searched for a legal theory to help control it. Deady's contribution to that search was a stirring March 23, 1886 charge to the federal grand jury in Portland, which he also prepared for publication in the *Oregonian*.[144] As the dramatic centerpiece of Deady's effort to assist Chinese victims of white racism in Portland, his morality tale delivered from the bench on that occasion merits extensive quotation. He began with an historical parallel:

> An evil spirit is abroad in this land,—not only here, but everywhere. It tramples down the law of the country and fosters riot and anarchy. Now it is riding on the back of labor, and the foolish Issachar couches down to the burden and becomes its servant....Nothing like it has afflicted the world since the Middle Ages, when the lawless barons and their brutal followers desolated Europe with their private wars and predatory raids.

He then reviewed the recent events in Oregon:

> Lately, this spirit has been manifesting itself in Oregon, by assaulting,

*robbing, and driving out the helpless Chinese who are engaged*
*among us at lawful labor for an honest living.*

*. . . .*

*It is commonly known that during the past few weeks gangs of*
*masked men have, in the night-time, entered the houses and camps*
*of peaceful Chinese residents, engaged in useful labor at various*
*points in this vicinity, and, by serious intimidation and threats of*
*personal violence, have compelled them to leave their homes and*
*work, and come to Portland.*

Finally, Deady proceeded to the difficult legal question, whether such
"brutal and inhuman conduct" violated any federal statute. The answer
was important because the widespread "illusion" that each *state* would
protect persons living within it had been dispelled; by then it was clear
that "unless the general government furnishes the Chinese on this coast
with protection, their treaty rights may be violated with impunity."

Conceding that the matter was "not free from doubt," Deady concluded that federal Revised Statutes § 5336 did furnish a basis for prosecution. Originally a Civil War antisedition act, it applied when

*two or more persons within any State or Territory conspire together*
*to overthrow, or to put down, or to destroy by force the government of*
*the United States…or by force to prevent, hinder or delay the execu-*
*tion of any law of the United States.*[145]

Unlike certain other possibly relevant statutes, there was "no doubt" of
section 5336's constitutionality. The only question was whether it
applied to harassment and intimidation of Chinese, and Deady concluded that it did:

*The attempt to drive the Chinese out of the country, or to maltreat or*
*intimidate them with a view of constraining them to depart, is* prima
facie *an attempt to prevent and hinder the execution, operation, or*
*fulfillment of a law of the United States, namely, the treaties with*
*China of 1868 and 1880; and a conspiracy or agreement of two or*
*more persons to engage in such conduct may, for that reason, be well*
*characterized as a seditious and treasonable conspiracy against the*
*authority and laws of the United States.*

The grand jury responded by indicting 13 persons.

The following year, in a similar case from California, the Supreme
Court expressed disagreement with Deady's interpretation of section
5336.[146] By then, however, the worst of Portland's anti-Chinese agitation
and violence had subsided. Although many persons contributed to that

restoration of relative calm, Judge Deady's dramatic, well-publicized grand jury charge at the height of the violence unquestionably played an important part. His appeals to history, to morality, and ultimately to federal law helped rally responsible public opinion and minimize Portland's contribution to the shameful events of early 1886.

# CONCLUSION

Matthew Deady died in March 1893, after nearly 34 years as federal district judge for the District of Oregon. His record of achievement and public service in that position may never be equalled. As Oregon's first federal judge, and its only federal judge for 34 years, Deady personified to a remarkable degree the civilizing force of federal law in the early Far West. He also contributed to both his courtroom and his community a dignified personal example of respect for law and concern for the underprivileged.

Judge Deady's public land law decisions illustrate, in part, the centrality in American law of tradition, continuity, and rule of law. In rulings affecting ownership of land, the common law's most esteemed form of property, Deady frequently applied ancient conveyancing principles in a relatively formalistic decisionmaking style. Regrettably in some cases, the results he reached tended to favor holders of formal legal title rather than persons with more equitable claims arising from good-faith purchase and improvement of the land.

Deady's response to cases not involving land, however, was generally quite different. In both admiralty and enterprise-related disputes, he typically interpreted the disputed facts or law favorably to parties he perceived as disadvantaged in the underlying transaction: seamen, cargo owners, passengers, unsecured creditors, laborers, or adjoining landowners. Moreover, except in the federal road-subsidy litigation so tainted by long government delays, he consistently promoted *public* values and interests rather than those of private capital. His decisions in these areas reflect clearly his abiding concern for substantive justice rather than merely formal justice.

Nowhere was this concern more apparent than in Judge Deady's Chinese-rights opinions. Although one can also detect in those opinions a certain aristocratic disdain for the working-class politics of his day, their principal theme both a century ago and today is one of compassion and human solidarity. Deady's repeated outspoken defenses of the rights and lives of embattled Chinese immigrants provide yet another dramatic illustration of the importance to early Oregon of federal law, the United States District Court, and Judge Matthew Paul Deady himself.

# NOTES

1. Minute Book, United States District Court for the District of Oregon 3 (Sept. 12, 1859 entry). In late 1859 Judge Deady journeyed to Washington, D.C. to persuade Congress to relocate the court in Portland, where the "bulk of the business peculiar to his court" likely would arise. H. Bancroft, *Chronicles of the Builders of the Commonwealth* 620 (1890).

2. *Id.* at 604-05. There exists relatively little information about Deady's early life. Currently the three best sources are (1) Malcolm Clark, Jr.'s able Introduction to Deady's 1871-1892 diary, *Pharisee Among Philistines* (1975); (2) P. Overmeyer, The Oregon Justinian (1939) (Ph.D. diss., Univ. of Minn.); and (3) a shamelessly reverent 75-page "biography" in H. Bancroft, *supra* note 1, which Deady himself wrote.

3. The nature of the disagreement remains a mystery, but, in any event, father and son never reconciled. Learning of Daniel's death in 1878, Matthew, by then with three sons of his own, confided to his diary:

> *The news makes me feel sad. It is a great pity that father and son should become estranged from one another....Poor old man, how I have tried to get upon the good side of him during the last 20 years and condone our early disagreements and misunderstandings, but to no avail.*

Clark, supra note 2, at 259.

4. H. Bancroft, *supra* note 1, at 606-09.

5. Deady likely would have affirmed the common jest among early Oregonians that at Pacific Springs on the overland trail a sign pointed the way "To Oregon" while a chunk of ore marked the trail to California, and that all travelers who could read turned northward. See J. Unruh, Jr., *The Plains Across* 93 (1979).

6. See 1851 Statutes of a General Nature Passed by the Legislative Assembly of the Territory of Oregon; Beardsley, *Code Making in Early Oregon*, 23 Or. L. Rev. 22 (1943). On early Oregon politics, see R. Johannsen, *Frontier Politics on the Eve of the Civil War* (1955); W. Woodward, *The Rise and Early History of Political Parties in Oregon 1843-1866* (1913).

7. For the furor following Pierce's misnaming of "Mordecai P. Deady" to the territorial court, see *supra* chapter 2. For an account of Deady's prominent role at the constitutional convention, see C. Carey, *The Oregon Constitution* (1926). Deady himself claimed later that the District Court judgeship was "literally forced upon" him by Joseph Lane and others who wished to eliminate a formidable rival for the United States Senate. See H. Bancroft, *supra* note 1, at 620.

8. M. Deady, Law and Lawyers: A Lecture Delivered Before the Portland Law Ass'n (1866). See also M. Deady, Address to the Third Annual Reunion of the

Oregon Pioneer Association (1875); H. Bancroft, *supra* note 1, at 629.

9. On federal public land law generally, see P. Gates, *History of Public Land Law Development* (1968); *The Public Lands: Studies in the History of the Public Domain* (V. Carstensen ed. 1963). On the symbolic importance of western land in American history, see H. Smith, *Virgin Land: The American West as Symbol and Myth* (1950); F. Turner, *The Frontier in American History* (1920).

10. See, e.g., *Wythe v. Smith*, 30 F. Cas. 771 (1876); *Wythe v. City of Salem*, 30 F. Cas. 770 (1876); *Dalles City v. Missionary Society*, 6 F. 356, *aff'd*, 107 U.S. 336 (1883); *McConnaughey v. Pennoyer*, 43 F. 196, *aff'd*, 43 F. 339, *aff'd*, 140 U.S. 1 (1890); *United States v. Willamette Valley & Cascade Mountain Wagon Road Co.*, 42 F. 351, *aff'd*, 140 U.S. 599 (1891).

11. 9 Stat. 496 (1850). See generally H. Head, The Oregon Donation Acts: Background, Development and Application (1969) (M.A. thesis, Univ. of Oregon); Bergquist, *The Oregon Donation Act and the National Land Policy*, 58 Or. Hist. Q. 17 (1957).

12. Standard sources on early Portland include H. Scott, *History of Portland, Oregon* (1890); J. Gaston, *Portland, Oregon: Its History and Builders* (1911); E. Snyder, *Early Portland: Stump-Town Triumphant* (1970).

13. For the similar schoolhouse litigation, see *Chapman v. School District No. 1*, 5 F. Cas. 483 (1865).

14. *Parrish v. Stevens*, 1 Or. 59, 70 (1853).

15. 15 F. Cas. 1030 (1861).

16. *Oregonian* editor Harvey Scott, for example, lamented that Portlanders had taken "no wise steps to secure their rights." The city council's actions regarding the levee had been "peculiar and contradictory," particularly its 1852 adoption of a map containing no reference to any alleged dedication. By that act alone the councilors had "signed away whatever right they had to the levee." H. Scott, *supra* note 12, at 134; see also J. Gaston, *supra* note 12, at 225-26.

17. Judge Deady himself made several diary references to that effect, the last as late as 1883, when he wrote wearily, "I have one more of the old Lownsdale cases, and then I am done after 15 years."

18. H. Scott, *supra* note 12, at 125.

19. *Fields v. Squires*, 9 F. Cas. 29 (1868).

20. In 1864 Nancy's two Gillihan children had obtained a state-court decree partitioning her 90 acres three-fifths to William Gillihan, Jr. and Millard and Ruth Lownsdale and two-fifths to Daniel (his own fifth and Isabella Gillihan's fifth, which he had purchased). Still, Deady conceptualized the later federal grant to Daniel of land within his partitioned share (including the Fields land) as passing three-fifths through William, Millard, and Ruth.

21. Purchaser Fields tried one more argument, similar to the city's in the levee litigation. He contended that Daniel Lownsdale's repeated oral statements that he would convey full title upon receiving it, together with his and the heirs' long acquiescence in Fields's possession, barred the heirs' claim. But Deady again was unreceptive:

> *This is a question of title-ownership of the soil, and not a mere easement or privilege. Titles would not be worth the paper upon which they are written, if*

*they could be called in question or destroyed in this way—by the proof of state parol declarations inconsistent with or in opposition to them.*

9 F. Cas. at 41. For five related decisions by Deady during the next two years, on similar but not identical facts, see *Lamb v. Starr*, 14 F. Cas. 1024 (1868); *Lamb v. Carter*, 14 F. Cas. 991 (1870); *Lamb v. Burbank*, 14 F. Cas. 989 (1870); *Lamb v. Kamm*, 14 F. Cas. 1014 (1870); *Lamb v. Wakefield*, 14 F. Cas. 1040 (1870). Together, the five seem somewhat erratic in both result and tone, as Deady appeared to waver between construing the various old deeds narrowly to favor the heirs (e.g., *Wakefield*) and broadly to favor the purchasers (e.g., *Carter*).

22. *Davenport v. Lamb*, 80 U.S. (13 Wall.) 418 (1871).

23. In 1869 Congress created circuit judgeships to assist Supreme Court justices with their circuit duties. 16 Stat. 44 (1869); see generally F. Frankfurter & J. Landis, *The Business of the Supreme Court* (1927). Judge Deady was the early frontrunner for the Ninth Circuit appointment. Justice Stephen Field strongly supported his candidacy, lobbying senators and organizing support within the San Francisco bar. Eventually, however, Judge Lorenzo Sawyer of the California Supreme Court received the appointment.

24. *Lamb v. Davenport*, 14 F. Cas. 996, 1001 (1872).

25. *Lamb v. Davenport*, 85 U.S. (18 Wall.) 307, 315 (1873).

26. *Starr v. Stark*, 2 Or. 185 (1865).

27. *Stark v. Starr*, 73 U.S. (6 Wall.) 402, 410 (1868). As Judge Deady had ruled in *Lownsdale v. City of Portland, supra*, the Townsite Act did not apply to Oregon until well after the settlement of Portland. Therefore, Justice Field reasoned, the city's patent was invalid; the Starrs' legal title was defective so not a "claim of right"; and the Starrs were not "in possession" and hence were unable to challenge Stark's patent. That rationale rendered "unnecessary" any inquiry into Stark's own "original settlement and residence."

28. *Stark v. Starr*, 22 F. Cas. 1084 (1870).

29. *Starr v. Stark*, 22 F. Cas. 1113 (1870).

30. *Starr v. Stark*, 22 F. Cas. 1116 (1874).

31. *Stark v. Starr*, 94 U.S. 477 (1875).

32. See P. Merriam, Portland, Oregon, 1840-1890: A Social and Economic History 228-95 (1971) (Ph.D. dissertation, Univ. of Oregon); A. Throckmorton, *Oregon Argonauts: Merchant Adventurers on the Western Frontier* 53-55, 107-110 (1961); 1 J. Gaston, *Portland Oregon: Its History and Builders* 109-125 (1911).

33. 1 Stat. 76-77 (1789); see also U.S. Const. art. III, sec. 2; see generally Putnam, *How the Federal Courts Were Given Admiralty Jurisdiction*, 10 Corn. L.Q. 460 (1925).

34. *American Ins. Co. v. Canter*, 26 U.S. (1 Pet.) 511, 545-46 (1828).

35. See E. Benedict, *The American Admiralty: Its Jurisdiction and Practice* 146-176 (1850); R. Newmyer, *Supreme Court Justice Joseph Story: Statesman of the Old Republic* 104-24, 207-08 (1985).

36. 3 F. Cas. 279 (1874).

37. *The Noddleburn*, 28 F. 855, 857 (1886).

38. 8 F. Cas. 491 (1875).

39. See *Roach v. Chapman*, 63 U.S. (22 How.) 129 (1859); *People's Ferryboat v. Beers*, 61 U.S. (20 How.) 393 (1857).

40. 39 F. 807 (1889).

41. 39 F. at 815. For other admiralty jurisdiction decisions, see *The Hermine*, 12 F. Cas. 24 (1874); *The Steamship Idaho*, 29 F. 187 (1886).

42. A similar issue litigated frequently in Deady's court concerned the appropriate relations between federal and state *substantive* law. The issue arose most commonly in suits by bar pilots or river pilots to recover the statutory pilotage fees that state law granted them for a vessel's improper refusal of their services. Deady inclined strongly toward federal rather than state law here as well, partly to counteract the local monopoly that state "regulatory" law tended to promote. See, e.g., *The Panama*, 18 F. Cas. 1068 (1861); *The George S. Wright*, 10 F. Cas. 224 (1869); *The Glenearne*, 7 F. 604 (1881); *The Glaramara*, 10 F. 678 (1882); *The Whistler*, 13 F. 295 (1882).

43. See generally T. Parson, *A Treatise on Maritime Law* (1859); A. Conklin, *The Admiralty Jurisdiction, Law and Practice of the Courts of the United States* (1848). In the event of loss or damage, the owner of the goods had lien rights against the vessel to assist recovery. The shipowner *also* had lien rights, against the goods for any unpaid transportation charges. Thus the maxim, "The ship is bound to the merchandise, and the merchandise to the ship."

44. 21 F. Cas. 1040 (1861).

45. See *New Jersey S.S. Nav. Co. v. M. Bank*, 47 U.S. (6 How.) 344 (1848).

46. 13 F. Cas. 547 (1864).

47. See *The Oregon*, 18 F. Cas. 760 (1866) (delivery of household furniture and apparel to wharf, at the carrier's direction, constituted delivery to carrier itself); *The Live Yankee*, 15 F. Cas. 656 (1868) (burden of proof on carrier to demonstrate lack of responsibility for damage to wine casks); *The Oriflamme*, 18 F. Cas. 810 (1870) (where carrier failed to establish cause of whiskey-shipment loss, court would "presume" want of ordinary skill on its part).

48. *The California*, 4 F. Cas. 1058 (1871).

49. For later rulings favoring cargo owners, see *The Blenheim*, 3 F. Cas. 696 (1878); *The Nith*, 36 F. 86 (1888).

50. 28 F. Cas. 1367 (1862).

51. See also *The Pioneer*, 19 F. Cas. 711 (1864).

52. 1 F. Cas. 535 (1868).

53. *The Mentor*, 19 F. Cas. 15 (1825).

54. 36 F. 442 (1888).

55. 11 F. Cas. 469 (1871).

56. See *Thomas v. Lane*, 23 F. 957 (1813).

57. 18 F. Cas. 812 (1875).

58. 5 F. 75 (1880).

59. 4 F. 645 (1880).

60. 28 F. 885 (1886).

61. 34 F. 477 (1888).

62. C. Carey, *supra* note 7, at 248-49 (1926). Deady's view was partly political as well, for in manufacturing countries, he explained, "power, political and otherwise," was "in the hands of capitalists." *Id.*

63. 1862 Or. Laws 3-15. For Deady's own account of the statute and its impor-

tance, see H. Bancroft, *supra* note 1, at 621.

64. 29 F. Cas. 85 (1877). Throughout his career, Deady insisted on spelling the state's largest internal river "Wallamet," an "Indian word and the true and original name of the river." Apart from historical accuracy, he contended, there was simply "no comparison in point of strength, dignity or euphony." Letter to *The Oregonian,* Oct. 15, 1874, at 1, col. 2.

65. Generally, the Oregon constitution prohibited such public subsidies for private enterprise. Or. Const. art. XI, secs. 6-10. Canal proponents, however, convinced the legislature that that prohibition did not apply to federal "internal improvement funds," i.e., funds which Congress granted to the state from sales of public land within its borders. See generally 11 Stat. 383 (1859); Young, *The Financial History of Oregon,* 12 Or. Hist. Q. 110 (1911).

66. 6 F. Cas. 531 (1879).

67. Goldsmith was a prominent early Oregon entrepreneur with interests in retailing, transportation, and banking. He served as Portland's mayor for two years (1869-71) and hired Deady occasionally for legal advice. See S. Lowenstein, *The Jews of Oregon* 17-21 (1987); Clark, *supra* note 2, at 10-11.

68. The question whether such "illegal consideration" invalidated the *entire* mortgage was "not free from doubt." Deady concluded, however, that the "better rule" was "where the illegal consideration is clearly separable from the legal, that the contract is good for the latter, and only void as to the residue." 6 F. Cas. at 420.

69. 14 F. 657 (1882).

70. See Or. Const. art. XI, sec. 3; 1862 Or. Laws 6; see generally C. Carey, *supra* note 73, at 232-65.

71. *Ladd & Bush v. Cartwright,* 7 Or. 329 (1879).

72. 22 F. 245 (1884). Oregonian Railway was a successor firm to Dayton, Sheridan & Grand Ronde Railway, which pioneered inexpensive narrow-gauge rail lines in the Willamette Valley. See Scott, *History of the Narrow Gauge Railroad in the Willamette Valley,* 20 Or. Hist. Q. 141 (1919). For an early Oregon Supreme Court decision recounting the firm's financial difficulties, see *Branson v. Oregonian Ry. Co.,* 10 Or. 289 (1882).

73. An 1878 Oregon statute granted foreign railroad corporations the same rights as their domestic counterparts, thus insuring, in Deady's words, that there be "no mystery or monopoly in the railway business in Oregon." *Oregonian Ry. Co. v. Oregon Ry. & Nav. Co.,* 23 F. 232, 238 (1885).

74. Deady explained that "interested parties" had inserted into his 1862 corporations statute the ban against navigation firms acquiring railroads. By it they sought to prohibit the powerful Oregon Steam Navigation Company from gaining control of key portage railways along the Columbia River.

75. 36 F. 726 (1888).

76. During the same period, the Oregon Supreme Court was considerably more receptive to shareholder defenses against creditor claims. See, e.g., *Ladd & Bush v. Cartwright,* 7 Or. 329 (1879); *Hodges & Wilson v. Silver Hill Mining Co.,* 9 Or. 200 (1881); see generally Mooney & Moser, *Government and Enterprise in Early Oregon,* 70 Or. L. Rev. 257 (1991).

77. 1845-1864 Or. Laws 745-47. Acting for a noncomplying firm was a misde-

meanor punishable by a fine and jail term.

78. 6 F. Cas. 244 (1874).

79. *Id.* at 245; see *Bank of Augusta v. Earle*, 38 U.S. (13 Pet.) 538 (1839); *Paul v. Virginia*, 75 U.S. (8 Wall.) 168 (1868).

80. 18 F. Cas. 764 (1877).

81. See Or. Const. art. IV, sec. 20; 1845-1864 Or. Laws 745. The inconsistency between title and text apparently arose from a legislative "oversight" when combining two related bills. 18 F. Cas. at 766.

82. Deady concluded by expressing trust that it was "not necessary to apologize for holding this act of the legislature partially void." In doing so he was merely upholding and obeying "that supreme law—the constitution—to which both courts and legislatures are bound to conform their conduct."

83. 21 F. Cas. 1063 (1878).

84. *Bank of British Columbia v. Page*, 6 Or. 431 (1877).

85. 21 F. Cas. at 1064. The most interesting legal issue in *Semple* was whether the state-court decree was *res judicata*, precluding any inquiry into the registration requirement. Deady concluded that while it was *res judicata* with respect to the foreclosure decree, it was *not* with respect to the bank's foreclosure purchase of the land. That latter act by the unregistered bank was void, and thus title remained in the mortgagor Semple.

86. 5 F. 225 (1880).

87. See Or. Const. art. XI, sec. 9; 1864 Or. Special Laws 27.

88. 6 F. Cas. 629 (1868).

89. 2 F. Cas. 580 (1879).

90. See *Osborn v. Bank of the United States*, 22 U.S. (9 Wheat.) 738 (1824).

91. 2 F. Cas. at 581; see 4 W. Blackstone, *Commentaries* *162; T. Cooley, *Constitutional Limitations* *572.

92. U.S. Const. art. I, sec. 10 provides that no state may enact a law "impairing the obligation of contract."

93. For full accounts of both the legislation and the roads built, see C. Amundson, History of the Willamette Valley and Cascade Mountain Wagon Road Company (1942) (M.A. thesis, Univ. of Oregon); H. Bruce, A History of the Oregon Central Military Wagon Road Company (1936) (M.A. thesis, Univ. of Oregon).

94. H. Bruce, *supra* note 93, at 65-66; 3 H. Scott, *History of the Oregon Country* 98 (1924).

95. 40 F. 114 (1889).

96. See *Schutz v. Dalles Military Road Co.*, 7 Or. 259 (1879).

97. 42 F. 351 (1890).

98. 140 U.S. 599 (1891).

99. *Id.* at 631-32. Nor did the Court agree that the government's claims were stale. Such a ruling would suggest that "Congress deliberately directed suit to be brought upon a stale claim." Besides, the laches (staleness) defense was unavailable against the government.

100. Because the trial court's remand decision is unrecorded, one cannot tell whether Judge Sawyer or Judge Deady presided. The later Court of Appeals decision, *infra* note 101, describes it only briefly.

101. *United States v. California & Oregon Land Co.*, 49 F. 496 (1892). In March 1891 Congress enacted the Circuit Court of Appeals Act, abolishing appellate jurisdiction of existing circuit courts, establishing nine circuit courts of appeals, and adding a second circuit judge to each. See generally F. Frankfurter & J. Landis, *supra* note 23, at 93-102. In September 1891 Circuit Judge Lorenzo Sawyer died and President Harrison nominated Judge Deady to succeed him. Deady's advancing age and poor health prevented him from accepting, but he did serve as acting circuit judge in both January and April 1892.

102. See, e.g., *United States v. Dalles Military Road Co.*, 51 F. 629 (1892); *United States v. Wallamet Valley & Cascade Mountain Wagon Road Co.*, 54 F. 807 (1892).

103. 148 U.S. 31 (1893).

104. 18 F. 875 (1884).

105. 18 F. 866 (1884).

106. The leading American authority establishing the fellow-servant rule was *Farwell v. Boston & Worcester R.R. Co.*, 4 Metc. 49 (Mass. 1842). See generally L. Levy, *The Law of the Commonwealth and Chief Justice Shaw* (1957).

107. 20 F. 100 (1884).

108. For a decision holding a telegraph company liable for a negligent transmission error despite an exculpatory clause in its standard-form agreement, see *Abraham v. Western Union Telegraph Co.*, 23 F. 315 (1885) (it would have been "contrary to public policy" to allow the company to "limit [its] liability for negligence").

109. 18 F. 106 (1883).

110. Congress created "federal-question" jurisdiction in 1875, principally so that federal courts could protect the rights of recently emancipated blacks in the South. 18 Stat. 470 (1875). See F. Frankfurter & J. Landis, *supra* note 23, at 56-85; C. Wright, *The Law of Federal Courts* 90-126 (1983).

111. 6 F. 326 (1881).

112. *Id.* at 332. The Supreme Court had held repeatedly that various federal enrollment and license statutes for travel upon navigable waters were "not sufficient to warrant the inference that Congress thereby intended to limit the right of the states to dam or otherwise obstruct the navigation of said waters." See, e.g., *Willson v. Blackbird Creek Marsh Co.*, 27 U.S. (2 Pet.) 245 (1829); *The Passaic Bridges*, 70 U.S. (3 Wall.) 782 (1865).

113. *State of Pennsylvania v. Wheeling & Belmont Bridge Co.*, 54 U.S. (13 How.) 518. See also *Wallamet Iron Bridge Co. v. Hatch*, 19 F. 347 (1884) (application for bill of review denied).

114. *Willamette Iron Bridge Co. v. Hatch*, 125 U.S. 1 (1887).

115. Deady rarely could resist commenting on views contrary to his own, even (or perhaps particularly) when expressed by the Supreme Court. After the Court had previewed its *Hatch* reversal by similar reasoning in *Cardwell v. American River Bridge Co.*, 113 U.S. 205 (1885), he "respectfully" suggested that the Court's "open to all without preference to any" interpretation of the statehood act meant in practice "open to all or *to none,* as the state may judge expedient." *Scheerer v. Columbia St. Bridge Co.*, 27 F. 172, 174 (1886).

116. Wunder, *The Chinese and the Courts in the Pacific Northwest: Justice*

*Denied?*, 52 Pac. Hist. Rev. 191, 196 (1983); see generally E. McLagan, *A Peculiar Paradise: A History of Blacks in Oregon*, 1788-1950 (1980).

117. See *Prigg v. Pennsylvania*; see generally D. Fehrenbacher, *The Dred Scott Case* (1978); D. Dumond, *Antislavery Origins of the Civil War* (1939).

118. Jesse Applegate, a leader of the 1843 migration, recalled later that many of his companions had "hated slavery," but a "much larger number of them hated *free negroes* worse even than slaves." J. Applegate, Views of Oregon History 74 (1878) (unpublished manuscript, Univ. of Oregon).

119. See generally E. McLagan, *supra* note 116; Richard, *Unwelcome Settlers: Black and Mulatto Oregon Pioneers*, 84 Or. Hist. Q. 29, 173 (1983).

120. See E. McLagan, *supra* note 116; C. Carey, *supra* note 62, at 22, 318-19, 359-62 (1926). The 1860s were a relatively quiet decade in Oregon race relations, although the legislature continued its occasional harassment of minorities by directing, for example, poll taxes and interracial marriage bans against them. In 1865 the legislature did ratify the Thirteenth Amendment, and the next year the Fourteenth, but in 1868 it voted nearly unanimously to rescind the latter vote, and two years later it refused to ratify the Fifteenth Amendment.

121. See generally V. Currier, The Chinese Web in Oregon History (M.A. Thesis, Univ. of Oregon).

122. The most spectacular single incident was an August 1873 fire, widely believed set by anti-Chinese ruffians, which consumed 20 blocks of downtown Portland. See generally V. Currier, *supra* note 121; Clark, *The Bigot Disclosed: 90 Years of Nativism*, 75 Or. Hist. Q. 109 (1974).

123. *Id.*; see also P. Maddux, *City on the Willamette* 80-83 (1952).

124. The other principal series of Chinese-rights cases in early Oregon federal court were those involving the 1882, 1884, and 1888 federal Exclusion Acts restricting further immigration of Chinese laborers. See, e.g., In *re George Moncan*, 14 F. 44 (1882); In *re Ho King*, 14 F. 724 (1883); *Ex parte Chin King*, 35 F. 354 (1888); In *re Yung Sing Hee*, 36 F. 437 (1888); In *re Chung Toy Ho*, 42 F. 398 (1890).

125. 1878 Or. Laws 9.

126. In 1868 the United States and China entered into a treaty to increase mutual trade and understanding. Commonly called the Burlingame Treaty, it provided for appointment of consuls, guaranteed free migration and religious tolerance, and granted to citizens or subjects of each nation living in the other "the same privileges, immunities, and exemptions in respect to travel or residence" as the host country granted to citizens or subjects of its "most favored nation." See 16 Stat. 739 (1868).

127. 2 F. Cas. 472 (1879).

128. For a similar decision, in which Deady criticized discriminatory federal and state mining laws but felt he could not rule in favor of the Chinese defendants without "disregarding the plain letter and purpose of the law," see *Chapman v. Toy Long*, 5 F. Cas. 497 (1876).

129. *Oregonian*, July 22, 1879; e.g., 11 Chi. Leg. News 375, 3 Pac. Coast L.J. 469; letter from Thomas Cooley to Deady (Nov. 28, 1879).

130. *Oregonian*, Aug. 6, 1879.

131. 2 F. Cas. at 475.

132. *City of Portland v. Baker*, 8 Or. 356, 357-58 (1880).

133. 1843-1872 Or. Laws 726-28.

134. *Id.* at 769-70.

135. 14 F. 338 (1882).

136. J. Dillon, *Commentaries on the Law of Municipal Corporations* 17-18, 28-31, 70-85, 101-05; see generally Frug, *The City as a Legal Concept*, 93 Harv. L. Rev. 1059 (1980).

137. 18 F. 253 (1883).

138. 1864 Or. Laws 10; 1880 Or. Laws 100; 1882 Or. Laws 151 (emphasis added); 1876 Or. Laws 39 (emphasis added); Portland Ordinance 3,911 (Aug. 24, 1883).

139. 14 Stat. 385 (1867). The scope of federal habeas corpus power became a central issue in late nineteeth-century American federalism debates. In the Far West, the principal substantive issue underlying those debates was federal-court protection of Chinese rights. For early judicial interpretations of the broad postwar grant of federal habeas power, see *In re Tiburcio Parrott*, 1 F. 481 (1880) (Hoffman and Sawyer, JJ.); *In re Ah Lee*, 5 F. 899 (1880) (Deady, J.).

140. 22 F. 701 (1885).

141. Reports of the Sixth and Seventh Annual Meetings of the American Bar Association 243-67 (1883); 13-44 (1884). For two decades a common complaint against federal habeas corpus power was that in 1868 Congress had repealed much of the Supreme Court's appellate jurisdiction over it. See 14 Stat. 385 (1867); 15 Stat. 44 (1868); *Ex parte McCardle*, 74 U.S. 506 (1869). Congress finally restored that jurisdiction in 1885. 23 Stat. 437 (1885); see generally W. Duker, *A Constitutional History of Habeas Corpus* 181-224 (1980).

142. Pharisee, *supra* note 2, at 490.

143. 26 F. 512 (1886).

144. *In re Impaneling and Instructing the Grand Jury*, 26 F. 749 (1886).

145. 17 Stat. 13 (1871); see generally Gressman, *The Unhappy History of Civil Rights Legislation*, 50 Mich. L. Rev. 1323 (1952).

146. See *Baldwin v. Franks*, 120 U.S. 678 (1887).

CHAPTER 3

∾

# YEARS OF GROWTH
# 1893–1927

## BY TODD A. PETERSON AND JACK G. COLLINS

*"Hear ye, hear ye, hear ye! The honorable district court of the
United States of the District of Oregon is now in session
pursuant to adjournment."*[1]

In the 34 years between 1893 and 1927, the U.S. District Court for
Oregon addressed a diverse range of colorful cases that bridged the
nineteenth and twentieth centuries and mirrored a nation in transition.

The year 1893 marked a watershed period of change. In contrast to
the cyclical fluctuations that characterized previous years,[2] a phenome-
non known as the "Panic" now twisted Oregon's economy. For the district court it was a pivotal year, too. With President Cleveland's appointment of Portland attorney Charles B. Bellinger, another besides Matthew
P. Deady presided in the old federal building for the first time in 34 years.

On March 6, 1893, Deady opened the new term but fell ill a week later,
before lapsing into an irreversible coma. The end came March 24, with
Deady's family gathered about. Roused momentarily, writes historian
Malcolm Clark, Deady

> ...asked for a drink of water. A little dribbled onto his wrist and he
> flicked it away irritably before sinking back on the pillows. Dr.
> Strong, who was in attendance, leaned over the bed and asked if there
> was anything more he wished to say. "Nothing," the old man mur-
> mured wearily. "Nothing."[3]

After his death, many of the cases before the district court involved
recently enacted progressive reform legislation. Such laws as the Interstate
Commerce Act, the Sherman Antitrust Act, the Forest Reserve Act of
1891, and others expanded the court's federal jurisdiction into new direc-

tions. With recent expansion of the railroad industry during this period, conservatives were determined to fight these laws in the courts rather than acquiesce in the rule of the majority. The result was a series of cases concerned with interpretation and application of the new federal laws.

Through the early 1900s, corporate influence would continue to lose ground in the face of an increased public desire for regulatory control. In particular, new pure food and drug laws, labor reform, and a rush of other progressive reforms were evidence that the court was leaving the old century and entering the next, with new and broader segments of society now affected by its rulings.

This was a time when world war, labor strife, and a cacophony of fringe groups—including Socialists, Wobblies, and the Ku Klux Klan—pitted individual against societal interests. The trend continued until the mid-1920s, when a late-nineteenth-century premise of liberalism came full circle with the landmark decision of *Pierce v. Society of Sisters.*

# JUDGE BELLINGER

Charles Byron Bellinger was born in Maquon, Illinois, on November 21, 1839, and at eight years of age emigrated with his family to Oregon. After a "common-school" education and two years at Willamette University, Bellinger read law in the Salem office of B. F. Bonham—later U.S. consul in Calcutta. After being admitted to the bar in September 1863, he opened a practice with future Portland U.S. Attorney J. C. Cartwright.[4]

Bellinger tired of law and became editor of *The Arena*—an "Oregon-style" Democratic tabloid of biting commentary and satire. It was said Bellinger wielded a pen dipped in vitriol, while being suave and courteous.[5]

With his health in decline, Bellinger entered the mercantile business in 1866. A stint in the legislature representing Benton County followed in 1868, and the following year he moved to Albany to resume his law practice but changed plans and re-entered publishing, now as editor of the *Albany Democrat.*[6]

Bellinger relocated to Portland in 1870 and founded the *Portland News*, known later as the *Portland Telegram*. He served with the Oregon Militia in 1873 during the Modoc War, fought in the Battle of the Lava Beds, and was appointed clerk for the Oregon Supreme Court in 1874.[7]

In the fall of 1878 Bellinger assumed a vacancy on the Oregon Circuit Court, created after a judicial reorganization. He became Democratic nominee for the post in 1880 and lost in the general election, though he carried between 1,100 and 1,200 votes.

He resumed the practice of law with Portland attorney John N. Gearin and was partner with the pre-eminent law firm of Dolph, Bellinger, Mallory, and Simon from 1880 to 1893. During this period he broke from the Democratic party, becoming an Independent when its standard bearer, William J. Bryan, heralded free silver.

As a protégé of Salem banker Asahel Bush—who had the ear of President Cleveland—and with support from former law partner (and now Senator) Joseph N. Dolph, Bellinger was appointed and took the oath as the second federal judge for Oregon on May 1, 1893, following Judge Matthew Deady's death.[8]

In 1898 Bellinger and William W. Cotton published the *Annotated Laws of Oregon*—the "B & C." It was said that the care and labor Bellinger put into the "B & C" hastened the breakdown that resulted in his death on May 9, 1905 during the trial of U.S. Surveyor General Henry Meldrum, charged with forging survey applications.[9]

Bellinger's body was cremated, for he believed cremation to be a practice of "great benefit to every large community."

∾

# JUDGE BELLINGER AND THE 1903-1910 LAND-FRAUD TRIALS

Between 1903 and 1910 the district court presided over the most far-reaching and sensational series of trials in its history—the Oregon "land-fraud trials." Before they ended, an incumbent U.S. senator, a defrocked U.S. attorney, and a cast of other colorful characters were convicted of bribery and conspiracy to defraud the federal government of its public lands. Spurred by a tenacious special prosecutor and a special federal grand jury, which it was said would "crucify Christ," the Oregon land-fraud trials became the impetus to reform twentieth-century public-land policy.

## Setting the Stage

In 1893 historian Frederick Jackson Turner wrote that America's frontier was "no more."[10] As the rallying cry "Manifest Destiny" slowly faded from the national conscience, eastern progressives lobbied to establish federal public land reserves in the West. Recognizing the possibility that western lands might forever be changed in the absence of federal intervention, Congress passed legislation in 1891 that authorized the president to "set apart and reserve" in any state or territory "public lands wholly or in part covered with timber or undergrowth."[11] Carrying the Congressional mandate further, the Harrison administration set aside 13,053,440 acres nationwide, and in September 1893 President Cleveland created the Ashland and Cascade Range Forest Reserves—virtually cutting a continuous swath across Oregon.

To manage the new reserves, Congress created the Forestry Bureau in 1891. That bureau undertook a geological survey to inventory Oregon's forests. It identified species, estimated board feet, and inspected the condition of virgin trees. The data confirmed tremendous resources. The first case involving reserve lands arose in 1893 before the new federal judge, Charles Bellinger. Like today's environmental conflicts, it pitted two competing parties with differing economic interests in federal court.

For years sheep had roamed into Oregon's timbered highlands and had continued to do so without restraint, even after the reserves were created—largely because there was no documentation to show that the *sheep* were damaging the reserves. In addition, great bitterness had existed since the 1880s between cattlemen and sheepmen, and further conflicts with timber interests loomed as public domain lands became scarcer with the establishment of each federal reserve.[12] Finally, although the power of the state grange movement (officially the Patrons of Husbandry) had subsided, that movement remained a potent force, making a clash seem likely.[13]

Evidence to support a test case concerning the sheep came from Gifford Pinchot, Theodore Roosevelt's new chief of the Forestry Bureau. Pinchot documented and observed a mother ewe trail back from a winter rangeland area and peel the resinous bark from a sapling lodgepole pine.[14] That evidence was provided to the Portland U.S. Attorney's Office.

Then, in what proved the first challenge to the executive order that had established the reserves, two sheep "barons," J. H. Sherar and Phil Brogan, faced trespassing allegations in the district court for leading several flocks of sheep on reserve lands. Because of the absence of a clean statute regulating what had been charged, Judge Bellinger dismissed both cases but issued an injunction that ordered the parties, in words of the order, "under pains and penalties" to desist from the trespassing and herding of sheep onto reserve lands.[15]

*Steven A. D. (S.A.D.) Puter, a lumber assessor, was one of the ringleaders of a scheme to obtain forest-reserve land through fraudulent homestead claims. While in jail, he worked on* Looters of the Public Domain, *his account of the land-fraud trials. (Oregon Historical Society Negative #087772)*

In 1897, with conservation sentiment garnering more acceptance, Congress passed further legislation, the Forest Lieu Exchange Act, which established additional timber reservations on the national domain[16] and allowed bona fide settlers within the reserves to deed their land to the federal government and select other, often more valuable, land in "lieu thereof." Landowners who pursued a "landswap" submitted affidavits to their local land offices, proving that they had settled the land, had lived on their claims prior to the act, and had built dwellings and made improvements.

In 1900 a three-man Portland syndicate began undercutting this enlightened piece of legislation by preparing a series of fraudulent homestead claims in collusion with officials in several state land offices—principally in Roseburg, Eugene, and Oregon City. Heading the ring were lumber assessor Steven A. D. (S.A.D.) Puter, a former Portland U.S. attorney and state senator, Franklin P. Mays, and minor timber speculator Horace G. McKinley.[17]

## The "24-1" Deal

In October 1903 U.S. Attorney John H. Hall secured a string of indictments from a Portland federal grand jury, based on information from a federal investigation into California's "Benson-Hyde" fraud "combine" scheme and the practices of the U.S. land office in Oregon. The Oregon investigation was carried out by two Secret Service agents under command of William J. Burns. Those charged were Puter, McKinley, reserve attorney Dan "Lookout" Tarpley, and several others accused of colluding with Eugene Land Commissioner Marie L. Ware to prepare fraudulent homestead claims.[18] By bribing both settlers and land-office employees, the ring had obtained affidavits and deeds for nonexistent settlers throughout Lane County in the newly created Cascade Forest Reserve (Township 24 south range 1 east of the Willamette Meridian). These fictitious entrymen or "strawmen" had held the lands and—under terms of the act—exchanged them later for more valuable lands, subsequently transferring them to the "syndicate."[19]

Before convening the grand jury, Judge Bellinger examined the fraudulent affidavits and summoned Ware to Portland. After the meeting, it was "mutually decided" she would remove herself from office.[20] Bellinger also removed three clerks from the Eugene land office after it was disclosed that the syndicate had paid $100 for each bogus claim filed in that office.[21] The court set the trial for December 14 and in the interim, following the recommendation of Attorney General Knox and Interior

Secretary Ethan A. Hitchcock (both of whom supervised the prosecution from Washington), a special assistant U.S. Attorney was appointed to "assist" Hall in the "24-1."

That individual was Francis J. Heney of San Francisco, a shrewd, colorful, and tenacious lawyer who was considered one of the best in the nation and certainly the most formidable on public-land law. Heney became, in the words of "S.A.D." Puter, a "veritable cyclone."[22] He took charge of the prosecution and, suspecting Hall of selecting a weak case in hopes of an acquittal, executed a startling coup by substituting, for the "24-1," another case—the famous "11-7" (in Puter's words a much "rawer" deal). Before it was over, the "11-7" became the conduit that would expose the full extent of the fraud.

## The "11-7" Trial

Involving essentially the same three-man syndicate as the "24-1," the November 1904 "11-7" trial concerned homestead lands adjacent to the Marion Fork of the Santiam River.[23] However, at Heney's request, Judge Bellinger dropped Marie Ware from the indictment since she was not involved directly in the "11-7" transaction.[24]

With a resonant voice and magnificent vocabulary, as reported daily in *The Oregonian*, Heney set to work. For several days he laid the groundwork for the conspiracy charge by establishing that Puter and Emma Watson, also charged as one of the group's bogus entrymen, had lived together and traveled under aliases in order to defraud the government. Other members of the syndicate, except Franklin P. Mays—still a confidant of Hall—were then easily implicated.[25] According to Puter, the climax of the trial came when Robert Montague, a timber guide who had escorted one of Burns' agents investigating the case, testified in a nervous, highly agitated manner, becoming almost hysterical as he described how he had become involved, tried to quit, and eventually been exposed.[26]

Heney also attempted to subpoena Oregon's four-term popular senator, John H. Mitchell, to testify concerning his relationship with the Washington land office, but Mitchell refused, implicitly asserting senatorial privilege.[27]

The defendants presented no witnesses but were advised by celebrated handwriting expert Professor F. J. Toland who, it was said, never failed to secure a verdict in favor of his clients.[28]

In December 1904 the jury found the group guilty of conspiracy to defraud the government, but the court delayed sentencing in order to permit the defendants to testify in the trials expected to follow.[29] In the interim, however, several members of the ring absconded. Puter went to Boston, where he escaped at gunpoint from the agent named Burns, only later to be recaptured in California attempting to meet with Heney. McKinley fled to Chicago, married Marie Ware of the "24-1" case, and went to Manchuria, accompanied—according to reports of the day—by the notorious belly dancer "Little Egypt."

After a 30,000 mile chase, U.S. Deputy Marshall J. F. "Jack" Kerrigan later returned McKinley to Portland for sentencing. In July 1906 the court imposed a $7,500 fine and sentenced Puter to two years in the Multnomah County jail where, guarded by H. P. "Dad" Hunter, he worked (with Horace Stevens) on his account of the land-fraud trials— *Looters of the Public Domain.*

### *United States v. Mitchell*

The "11-7" trial did not mark the end of the land-fraud trials. In reality, it was a harbinger of greater trials to come. Styling himself the "land-fraud king," Puter testified before an awe-struck grand jury in October 1904 on the full extent of the fraud. He described how Oregon Senator John H. Mitchell had accepted two $1,000 bills to "influence" Oregon Congressman Binger Hermann, commissioner of the General Land Office in Washington, to process the fraudulent claims in the "11-7" deal.[30] This time Mitchell wasted no time and returned to Portland to testify before the grand jury.[31]

A storm of sympathy supporting Oregon's senior senator swept the state after he and Hermann were indicted in February 1905. Mitchell— certainly the most colorful and controversial figure in Oregon politics—denounced the prosecution, asserting it was based on revenge and politics. Senator Charles W. Fulton called the indictment "a foul charge—and as false as foul." The Oregon legislature also acted, giving Mitchell a vote of confidence in February 1905.[32]

In April of that year, Mitchell tried to set the indictment aside, alleging that Heney had vindictively charged him and had improperly swayed the grand jury.[33] Bellinger dismissed these claims, stating that it was "natural" for a defendant's feelings and interest to create an opinion that the prosecution had acted unfavorably. Bellinger wrote, in this his final opinion, that Heney may have "greatly influenced" the grand jury, but something tangible beyond conclusions and opinions is required before the court would interfere with the indictment.[34]

*Charles Byron Bellinger*

*Horace G. McKinley*

*Dan "Lookout" Tarpley*

*John H. Mitchell*

*The land-fraud trials, presided over by The Honorable Charles Byron Bellinger, were full of drama. One syndicate member, Horace G. McKinley, fled to Manchuria with a notorious belly dancer named Little Egypt and was caught only after a 30,000-mile chase. Forest-reserve attorney Dan "Lookout" Tarpley and several others were charged and accused of colluding with the Eugene land commissioner to prepare fraudulent homestead claims. Another central figure, Oregon's popular four-term senator John H. Mitchell, was barred from office after being found guilty. (Oregon Historical Society Negatives #CN21178, #ORHI87773, #ORHI87771, and #ORHI26849)*

The grand jury and Heney did not stop after snaring Mitchell and Hermann. Between December 1904 and April 1905 the grand jury poured out indictments,[35] and Oregon was in a near state of siege as indictments, accusations, and countercharges were played out. Franklin P. Mays—an early participant in the original "24-1" syndicate—was charged along with dismissed U.S. Attorney Hall.[36]

The Mitchell trial was nothing short of spectacular. In a hot and cramped courtroom, District Judge John J. DeHaven of San Francisco, who presided temporarily on the district court after Bellinger's death in May, realized the case was unprecedented. Portland's major political and social movers were daily spectators.

With the assistance of a brilliant young future U.S. attorney, William C. Bristol, Heney quickly discredited a 1901 letter from Mitchell to the Washington General Land Office, a letter that appeared at first to exculpate the senator. By showing that the watermark on the stationery was different from that used by the senator's law office in 1901, Heney and Bristol proved that the letter was actually drawn and signed in 1904. Mitchell's attorney, ex-United States Senator John M. Thurston of Nebraska, then switched tactics, stating that Mitchell did receive money, but was unaware of its source, like "manna in the wilderness."[37] Finally in July 1905, after deliberating nearly eight hours, the jury found the senator guilty as charged.[38]

Mitchell, shocked at the verdict, broke down in court. He became, according to reports, "…old, broken in body and mind."[39] The court sentenced him to six months in jail and imposed a $1,000 fine.[40] Mitchell became a pariah, barred from office on the order of the court, never seeming to accept the verdict, and stating once to his secretary, "All I ever got was some little checks."[41] Mitchell appealed to the U.S. Supreme Court in 1906 and argued that the sentence, a misdemeanor, was illegal because Article I section 6 of the Constitution permitted interfering with a senator's duties only when that individual has been charged with a felony.[42] Mitchell never saw the inside of a jail cell and after he died, in December 1905 following a tooth extraction, the Supreme Court denied review.[43]

The land-fraud trials continued insatiably through 1910. Considered the most bitter, the Blue Mountain Forest Reserve conspiracy was a scheme to fraudulently obtain title to vacant "school lands" in central and eastern Oregon through the Salem state land office.[44] In February 1905 Heney indicted state Senators George Sorenson and Willard Jones, along with former U.S. Attorney Franklin P. Mays and U.S. Congressman John

N. Williamson, for influencing Mitchell and Hermann to withdraw lands from the reserve when the introduction of railroads into eastern Oregon caused land values to skyrocket. Mays was convicted in 1907, sentenced to four months imprisonment, and ordered to pay a fine of $10,000.[45]

The leading "school-land" operator, however, was F. A. Hyde, who between 1898 and 1902 defrauded Oregon of 47,000 acres of school lands that he acquired for $1.25 per acre under the state's Admission Act (which granted, to the state, sections numbered 16 and 36 in public lands for use of schools).[46] In 1910 the Interior Department began adverse proceedings against the Hyde forest lieu selections. These proceedings were suspended in 1912 so that Oregon could initiate its suits against Hyde in 1913, suits that involved 29,078.74 acres of school-lands.[47]

John H. Hall, removed earlier from office by Attorney General Moody, was indicted in February 1905 along with Mays and Sorenson for conspiring to defraud the government of its public lands and for instituting a civil, as opposed to criminal, prosecution against Butte Creek Land, Livestock, and Lumber Company of Fossil concerning fraudulent homestead claims and illegal fencing of reserve lands in Wheeler County.[48] After Hall's trial, the court sentenced him in 1909 to 60 days in the Multnomah County Jail and imposed a $1,000 fine.[49]

President Taft would later pardon Mays and Hall, after a federal investigation into the trials revealed that agent William J. Burns, who closely worked with Heney, received advance lists of the veniremen and improperly pressured and cajoled those selected for the jury.[50]

Due to a holdout juror, Congressman Binger Hermann (ex-land commissioner in Washington) was never convicted for his role in passing information between Senator Mitchell and the Puter ring. When Judge Charles E. Wolverton, Bellinger's successor on the bench, questioned the jurors on the possibility of reaching a verdict, juror Selkirk (as described in the reports of the day) passed a note stating that he had a "conscientious conviction" in the case. *United States v. Binger Hermann* was dismissed and Oregonians later re-elected Hermann to Congress.[51]

In retrospect, the Oregon land-fraud trials exposed the ugliness of Oregon politics and the inherent weakness of nineteenth-century public-land law. The scramble for resources—timber, mineral, and grazing lands—in the 1890s and the trials had set a new course. Between 1904 and 1906 Theodore Roosevelt created ten new reserves in Oregon. The revelations of fraud also signaled change. Those convicted—Mitchell, Hall, and the others—were victims of their times, unable to comprehend a basic notion of the public trust. The trials publicized this conflict between new and old attitudes on a national scale, but they also gave rise to a new environmental ethic. President Theodore Roosevelt and Gifford Pinchot capitalized on this sentiment and moved conservation onto the American agenda.

～

# THE MEN WHO FOLLOWED JUDGE BELLINGER ON THE BENCH

## The "Judge" Who Never Was

For two months following Judge Bellinger's May 1905 death, aspirants scrambled to fill the court vacancy. Oregon junior Senator Charles W. Fulton and Special Prosecutor Francis J. Heney, now also acting Portland U.S. attorney, were instrumental in the nominating process, and with the "land-fraud" trials in progress, interest intensified. District Judge John J. DeHaven of San Francisco and Portland's U.S. Circuit Court of Appeals Judge William B. Gilbert presided in the interim.

By 1905 railroads were a force in Oregon politics and society, with Harriman & Hill controlling the two leading networks that linked the state—the O.R.& N. and the Southern Pacific. Senator Fulton, who headed Southern Pacific's legal department, recommended William Wick Cotton to U.S. Attorney General Moody for the nomination. Were Cotton, chief counsel of the O.R.& N., to accept the nomination, Fulton likely would have headed a consolidated legal department for Harriman & Hill.[51]

Cotton, a native Iowan, came to Portland in 1889 from Nebraska to continue as counsel for the Union Pacific, which later was absorbed into the Harriman syndicate. Cotton also practiced with Cox, Cotton, Teal and Minor from 1889 to 1904 and appeared often in railway litigation before the district court. Joseph Gaston writes in *Portland—Its History and Builders* that Cotton had a knowledge of law possessed only by those who burned the "midnight oil" in a quest for points and authorities of law.[52]

With litigation over railroad rates on the rise and New York Harriman officials urging him to decline, Cotton may have sensed potential conflicts of interest and consequently wavered for two months before firmly accepting Fulton's recommendation.[53] Financial considerations may also have played a role in his recalcitrance. As counsel for the O.R.& N., Cotton received $1,200 monthly, while federal judges were paid $500.[54]

Cotton accepted the nomination and was commissioned June 17, 1905.[55] Portland's legal community feted and toasted "Judge" Cotton with a grand banquet, but he never was administered the oath of office. Portland historian E. Kimbark MacColl writes that Francis J. Heney, whose influence with Washington was at its peak with the "land-fraud" trials in full swing, "forced" President Theodore Roosevelt to withdraw his support.[56] Cotton met the president at Oyster Bay on July 26, 1905 and resigned his commission.[57] Though referred to in later years and in the *Federal Reporter* as "Judge" Cotton, he never in fact was a judge.[58]

In 1906 Theodore Roosevelt appointed Oregon Supreme Court Chief Justice Charles E. Wolverton to the U. S. District Court for Oregon and in 1909 his colleague on the Oregon court, Robert S. Bean, joined him when Congress allotted an additional judgeship.

*Following Judge Bellinger's death in 1905, Theodore Roosevelt nominated William W. Cotton to the district court bench. Later, Roosevelt withdrew his support at the urging of Francis J. Heney, a shrewd, tenacious lawyer who led the prosecution during the land-fraud trials. Although Cotton never served, he was later referred to as "Judge" Cotton. (Oregon Historical Society Negative #ORHI087768)*

## Charles Edwin Wolverton

Charles E. Wolverton was born on May 16, 1851, in a small log cabin ten miles from present-day Burlington, Iowa. Two years later the Wolvertons made a five-month trek west, ending their journey on the old Barlow Road near Oregon City.

After eight years of study at a "stump school" near the Wolverton's Monmouth homestead, Charles Wolverton entered Christian College in 1868 and received his B.S. degree in 1871 and his B.A. the following year, graduating as class valedictorian. Among his classmates were future Oregon Senator William D. Fenton and future District Court Judge Robert S. Bean.[59] At college, Wolverton attended court sessions in The

*Charles Edwin Wolverton served on the district court bench from 1905 to 1926, after two terms as an Oregon Supreme Court judge. (Oregon Historical Society Negative #CN021178)*

*Robert Sharp Bean was a district and circuit court judge, Oregon Supreme Court justice, and senior U.S. Court of Appeals judge. (Oregon Historical Society Negative #CN000171)*

Dalles and became impressed with the oratory of attorney Nehemiah L. Butler. Near the end of Wolverton's legal career, the *Oregon Journal*'s "On the Scene" columnist Fred Lockley asked the judge how he had decided to pursue the law. Wolverton replied that when he and his father were plowing a field, he gave his horse a rest, stepped across to where his father was working, and told him he had just decided to enter the legal profession.[60] Wolverton continued working his father's thresher to earn tuition money and entered the University of Kentucky Law School, to graduate with his brother, Bruce Wolverton, in a class of nine in 1874.

Wolverton returned to Oregon and practiced law in Albany through 1894. Later he reminisced that in his first and unsuccessful case, the judge had sentenced Wolverton's client (who had stolen a horse and saddle) to three years imprisonment so that the client could "distinguish his own and some other man's horseflesh." From 1876 to 1878 Wolverton was justice of the peace in Albany.[61]

Wolverton served as delegate to many state political gatherings and was a delegate-at-large for the 1892 Minneapolis Republican National Convention. His only political loss occurred in 1884 against future Oregon Governor George Chamberlain in a contest for district attorney.

Wolverton was elected to the Oregon Supreme Court in 1894 and re-elected in 1900. On November 21, 1905, following Judge Bellinger's death, President Theodore Roosevelt nominated Wolverton to become the third federal district court judge for Oregon.[62] Between 1912 and 1925 he also lectured at the Northwestern College of Law in Portland.[63]

Wolverton died from a heart attack during a visit to Gearhart, Oregon, on September 21, 1926, with his wife, the former Clara Ellen Price. His interests included hunting and trout and salmon fishing on the McKenzie and Rogue Rivers.

## Robert Sharp Bean

The Portland *Oregonian* reported once that the "central feature" distinguishing Judge Bean was an "unassuming simplicity and integrity, augmented with a penetrating legal mind."[64] It also wrote that when Bean began smoking a cigar, he had taken an "unprecedented plunge into liberalism."[65]

Bean was a native Oregonian, born on a Yamhill County farm on November 28, 1854. He received his B.S. degree in 1873 from Monmouth's Christian College and afterward worked in a dry goods store in Junction City, learned carpentry, and studied law with Eugene state circuit Judge John M. Thompson. Admitted to the state bar in 1876, Bean formed a partnership with Thompson and then graduated from the first class of the University of Oregon School of Law in 1878.[66]

At age 27, during a raucous 1882 state Republican convention, Bean was nominated for the Eugene judgeship held previously by Thompson. Later, during a 1924 state bar association tribute to Judges Wolverton and Bean, Judge Bean stated that after conventioneers had begun leaving the hall, its chairman took the floor, noted that no one had been nominated, and asked whose name should be placed in nomination for judge. Those listening replied, "Any damn fool will do!" and the chairman asked, "How will Bean satisfy you?"[67]

Robert Bean presided as circuit judge from 1886 to 1890, when he was elected to the Oregon Supreme Court. Bean's circuit covered five counties in southwestern Oregon, almost 16,000 square miles. Bean once remarked:

*Lawyers? There were real lawyers in those days. None of this modern business of having a clerk look up the law for you and coming into court without the slightest knowledge of what was going on. When an attorney got a case in those days he usually had several months to prepare it before the judge came around, and when the judge did arrive, the attorney knew his case.*[68]

Bean sat on the Oregon Supreme Court, serving as chief justice for three terms, until he resigned on Saturday, May 1, 1909, to accept nomination by President Taft to the federal district court. Bean became senior district judge for the U.S. Court of Appeals and served as a judge for 49 years, with the exception of the Sunday after his resignation from the Oregon Supreme Court.[69]

Bean died in his Portland home on January 7, 1931, surrounded by his two sons Ormond and Robert Jr., and his wife, Ina C. Bean, and was buried in Riverview Cemetery.

In 1943 U.S. District Judge James A. Fee delivered an address at ceremonies in St. John's to launch a World War II Liberty ship named *The Robert S. Bean.*

# A QUESTION OF CITIZENSHIP[70]

Throughout the 1890s Asian-American immigrants and aliens in the U.S. continued to face subtle tones of racism and prejudice. During that period, Congress extended The Chinese Exclusion and Expulsion Immigration acts, China was torn by social strife, and the Sino-Japanese War caused many Asians to emigrate. By 1900 the Pacific Northwest was a major demarcation point, with Portland having the second largest Chinese community in the nation.[71]

One of the more repressive in a series of immigration acts of the period was the Immigration Act of 1882, which had the effect of suspending the immigration of Chinese laborers for ten years and deporting immigrants who lacked proper documentation or proof of residence, even though they were already settled in America.[72] Other acts followed, including the 1892 Geary Act, which permitted an immigrant to avoid expulsion, but only upon testimony of at least "one credible white witness."[73]

Eventually, in 1911, Congress conferred full appellate jurisdiction to the federal courts over judgments and orders of the U.S. commissioners in individual cases arising under these laws.

With the annexation of the Kingdom of Hawaii in 1898, Chinese and Japanese residents were eligible to become citizens. This event inspired Japanese residents of the continental United States to seek citizenship, some successfully. However, in 1922 the U.S. Supreme Court in *Ozawa v. United States* put an end to Japanese efforts to acquire citizenship until 1952.[74]

Questions of Asian citizenship did not die with the *Ozawa* case, however. In the 1920s the case of an Indian logger in the district court of Oregon drew national attention. Bhagat Singh Thind was born December 5, 1892, in Amritsar, India, emigrated from Manila, then an American possession, May 28, 1913, aboard the vessel *Minnesota*, and arrived in Seattle July 4, 1913. As a married soldier at Camp Lewis, Washington, he petitioned for citizenship on July 22, 1918, obtained two officers as witnesses on September 29, and, appearing in full uniform in the court of Judge Edward E. Cushman, filed his application with the clerk of the U.S. District Court, Western District of Washington (Tacoma), on December 2, 1918. He foreswore allegiance to George V, king of Great Britain and Ireland, on December 9 and was admitted to U.S. citizenship, which lasted four days. On December 13 his petition was denied by Naturalization Examiner Edwin R. Stevens, whose decision was affirmed by the court on the grounds that "petitioner is not prepared to prove that he is a free white person."[75] The June optimism expressed by the Camp Lewis *Trench and Camp* headline "Army Aliens Will Soon Be Citizens" was a bit tarnished, but the undaunted Indian persevered.[76]

In September 1920, Bhagat Singh Thind again applied for United States citizenship, this time in the U.S. district court of Oregon. His petition was bound with copies of other papers placing him in 1917 at the Hammond Lumber Company in Astoria, Oregon, in the company of Hindu radicals opposed to British rule in India. Their 1919 correspondence with another group of Hindus in San Francisco had been intercepted by Military Intelligence and forwarded to the Department of Justice. A cover letter indicated American and British interest in Hindu revolutionaries dating back to the San Francisco conspiracy trial of 1917-18.[77]

In reviewing the case for naturalization, Judge Charles E. Wolverton filed a memo outlining Bhagat Singh Thind's military service, including an honorable discharge.[78] The judge noted Thind's connection to the San Francisco defendants, including Thind's visitations to the Hindu prisoners in Portland and at McNeil Island penitentiary in Washington, but he accepted the man's disavowal of armed revolution in India or the United States based on the testimony of disinterested witnesses. Judge Wolverton passed over ethnological discussions as to whether or not a "high class

Hindu" from Punjab was a white person and took note of a series of precedent cases, including *In re Halladjian,* a 1909 Boston federal case in favor of Armenians becoming citizens. The judge took care to differentiate between congressional intentions on immigration and naturalization. He thought Indians entering legally before 1917 could be naturalized after the Asian immigration gates had closed.[79]

Acting on Judge Wolverton's opinion, the U.S. District Court for Oregon issued citizenship certificate #1076958 on November 18, 1920. On January 7, 1921, the U.S. attorney for Oregon took a deposition from INS Naturalization Examiner V. W. Tomlinson and filed a complaint the next day, thus starting a train of events that would not end until June 26, 1926, when Thind's certificate would be rescinded. In the meantime, his case was certified by the Ninth Circuit Court of Appeals directly to the U.S. Supreme Court.[80]

In arguing before the Supreme Court, Thind's attorneys based most of their case on ethnology, philology, and history. The court demolished their argument, beginning with a reference to *Ozawa v. United States,* in which it avoided discussing groups to be excluded from citizenship in favor of those considered "white" in common language at the time naturalization laws were passed. Applying the lessons of the *Ozawa* case to *Thind,* Justice Sutherland dispensed with questions of ancient history, remote ancestry, and divergent public and scholarly opinions on the meaning of such terms as "Aryan" and "Caucasian." He was content that the frame of reference in 1790 was naturalization of northwestern Europeans and with the passage of time, dark-eyed and swarthy eastern, southern, and middle Europeans, but not Asians. As evidence that Congress had not changed its mind in the twentieth century, Justice Sutherland cited the Act of February 5, 1917, which excluded Indian immigrants from entering the United States. "It is not likely," he said, "that Congress would be willing to accept as citizens a class of persons whom it rejects as immigrants."[81] Having disposed of the heart of the case, Justice Sutherland refused to discuss conflicting statutes. Thind expressed bitter disappointment with the decision. As a graduate of Punjab University, he had attended the University of California and wished to enter the legal profession. Now he could not.

Editorial opinion in the Portland *Oregonian* viewed the decision as a necessary separation of Asiatics and Caucasians in both America and India. Undeterred, Thind did not publicly concede his case until December 28, 1925. Two days later, immigration officials warned Indians that their citizenship papers were no longer recognized at American ports of entry, in case any were tempted to travel to India and return.[82]

Bhagat Singh Thind disappears from our view after this incident, but questions of Asian citizenship did not abate. The *Thind* decision threatened to upset *In re Halladjian* (Boston, 1909) and denaturalize over 10,000 Armenian-Americans from New York to California, thereby affecting their ability to own land or practice law.

In 1906, Tatos Osgihan Cartozian arrived in New York City. He lived in New England for four years, joining his brother Aram in Portland, Oregon, about 1910. He declared his intention to become a citizen on December 15, 1917, and filed his petition January 20, 1923. Aram was naturalized in the U.S. district court in Spokane in 1920. Tatos and Aram's older brother Hovsep had been previously naturalized in the U.S. District Court for Oregon without incident.[83] Following the report of the *Thind* case in February 1923, Oregon District Court Judge Bean expressed doubt about naturalizing Armenians, but admitted Tatos to citizenship on May 17 anyway because denial gave him no recourse and admission allowed the federal government to appeal. By September the secretary of labor had decided to test the Cartozian case in the federal courts.[84] This time the defendant was not a wage earner but a member of the Portland business establishment, and the target group was not isolated Asiatics but established eastern European Christians. By the end of the year, the case produced a shock wave in Armenian communities across the United States that culminated in the formation of a national committee.

In May 1924 the case came to trial under Judge Wolverton. Cartozian's attorneys came directly to the point: Was their client a white man? From the *Ozawa* and *Thind* cases, they noted Justice Sutherland's requirement of a racial test based not on color but on who had been assimilated into white society at the time immigration laws had been enacted. As of the 1920 census there were 52,840 persons of Armenian birth or parentage in the United States, of whom 10,574 were naturalized American citizens.

Cartozian's attorneys stressed the nationwide scope of denaturalization proceedings, should their client lose his case. In the largest group of Armenians (New York City), nine lawyers would thus be disbarred; in the second largest group (San Joaquin Valley, California), Armenians would lose ownership of lands acquired after May 19, 1913. In Oregon and Washington, similar losses would occur based on 1923 alien land laws.

Returning to the definition of race, the attorneys again cited Justice Sutherland's opinion in the *Ozawa* case requiring citizens to be accepted as Caucasians by their peers and offered the depositions of three world-renowned scholars that Armenians were Caucasians. In addition, Cartozian's attorneys cited the same official documents Justice Sutherland had used in the *Thind* case, this time to establish the affinities of the Armenian language to Europe rather than Asia. They also used the Sutherland opinion to point out that in 1917 Congress had not placed Armenia in the "Exclusion Zone" that prohibited Asiatics like Thind from immigrating. The final argument for the defense was that Armenians intermarried with host populations throughout the world and assimilated very quickly.[85]

The U.S. attorney for Oregon argued that Armenians had been inhabitants of Asia for 700 to 800 years and were considered Asiatics in the popular mind and in official, as opposed to scholarly, reports. Because Judge Wolverton was temporarily assigned to a New York district court, his decision was delayed for some time. Finally, on July 27, 1925, he dismissed the government's bill of complaint. The public remained in suspense as late as July 20, 1926, when a new U.S. attorney for Oregon reported to a correspondent that though his office had requested an appeal, it had been denied. Without fanfare, Tatos Cartozian finally retained his citizenship. In 1942 he retired to California, where he died in 1953.[86]

The episodes of Thind's and Cartozian's fights for citizenship remind us that our records reveal a different America and therefore serve as a benchmark of change in our society.

# THE OREGON AND CALIFORNIA RAILROAD LAND GRANTS

Between 1908 and 1925 the district court grappled with an illusory, though well-intentioned, piece of federal legislation that pitted some of the most powerful interests in Oregon in a protracted period of litigation.

In 1850 the U.S. government began providing land grants from the public domain to serve as incentives to develop canals and wagon roads. Western entrepreneurs, bent on tapping the frontier's riches and opportunities, eagerly applied and used additional grants as credit or to raise necessary capital.

146

By 1866 railroad was king, with the golden spike at Promontory Point, Utah, linking the nation with a rail network achieved through the land-grant system. After 1869 Congress inserted "homestead clauses" in new grants, requiring land grantees to sell their excess grant lands, over 160 acres, to legitimate settlers for $2.50 an acre.

Because of the Northwest's isolation, Oregon's rail system was not completed, and two corporations, each called the "Oregon and Central Railroad Company," competed for a grant from Congress. The story of their rivalry cannot be told here. Suffice it to say that railroad building in Oregon was fraught with financial difficulties, mismanagement, and construction delays.

The railroad's financial mismanagement and abuses incensed the public, a fact the populist movement capitalized on, pressuring Congress to pass the General Forfeiture Act in March 1889.[87] Under the act, sections opposite unfinished portions of grant lands reverted to the public domain. As a result, nationally, a pattern of grant, failure, and then forfeiture restored nearly 35 million acres to the public domain.[88]

Following successful forfeiture suits in other states, the 1907 Oregon State Legislative Assembly passed a resolution asking Congress to forfeit the entire "O&C" grant.[89] At the time, Oregon's population was rapidly growing and demand for accessible land was acute. Harriman and Hill controlled all Oregon railroads, including the Southern Pacific, and continued holding grant lands adjacent to its lines. Those lands contained the largest stands of marketable timber in the nation and were to be marketed under terms of the Forfeiture Act. Harriman realized this and discouraged sales by not pressing for patents.

U.S. Attorney General George Wickersham reviewed Oregon's resolution and, after a year-long investigation, reported that Harriman and Hill was ignoring the "homestead clause" when disposing of O&C-based tracts. Congress responded and authorized an equity suit in the United States district court.[90]

Federal authorities filed suit in September 1908 against the Oregon and California Railroad, the Southern Pacific, and the Union Trust Company, asking that the court forfeit by decree all unsold grant lands, permit settlers to purchase them, or impose a mandatory injunction requiring that grant lands be sold pursuant to the homestead clause.

Outright forfeiture might have enabled Congress to establish additional forest reserves from the grant lands, most of which were heavily timbered or rough and mountainous. Under the act, they would be sold for $2.50 an acre—making land speculation of the Puter land-fraud variety a possibility.

In its petition the government reasoned that the 1869 homestead clause was a "condition subsequent," requiring completion of the "O&C" within a specified period, and argued that it should be forfeited, since the remaining grant lands were unsuited for their designated use. The railroads, represented by future Oregon Congressman A. W. Lafferty, argued that the 1869 Homestead Act was not retroactive since the railroad was a grantee under the original 1866 act. Judge Wolverton took the case under advisement, and in February 1909 settlers who had received post-1869 land grants filed 45 additional suits against the railroads, followed eventually by 6,000 more.

In 1911 Wolverton overruled the railroad's demurrer to the cross-complaints filed and wrote that the O&C had "assented" to terms of the 1869 amendment since it had taken the grants.[91] He continued that the government would never be a party to "such an idle ceremony," as a directive, restrictive, unenforceable covenant, and held—despite an absence of the usual conditional language—that the 1869 clause was a "condition subsequent."[92] Wolverton decreed a forfeiture in 1914, prompting the O&C to appeal directly to the U.S. Supreme Court.

After reviewing 17 volumes of records, Supreme Court Justice Joseph McKenna found that the forfeiture ordered by Wolverton was proper but held that since Congress had failed to allow forfeiture on the breach of a condition, the 1869 amendment was not a condition subsequent.[93] Justice McKenna denied the O&C's argument that the Homestead Act was unenforceable and stopped the sale of grant lands until Congress protected forested lands and profits due the O&C.

In 1916 Congress passed the Revestment Act (the Chamberlain-Ferris Act), which provided that all grant lands not sold as of July 1913 and in actual use by the railroads "revested" to the national domain.[94] Revested land was classified as power sites, timberland, or agricultural land suitable for settling.[95]

Through 1917 the Southern Pacific Railroad stalled and ignored terms of the act, as the remaining timbered grant lands—still priced at $2.50 an acre—increased in value. The O&C appealed Wolverton's remand decree directly to the U.S. Supreme Court and challenged the Chamberlain-Ferris Act. Justice McKenna upheld Wolverton's decree on the basis that revestment did not infringe the vested rights belonging to the O&C as long as they received the full value of the grants.[96]

Litigation over the remand decree continued through 1925, when special Assistant U.S. Attorney S. W. Williams sought an "accounting" in the district court following the Supreme Court's decree that revestment encompass the "full value" of lands at the time the land grants were made. After adjusting and reviewing the entire record, Wolverton determined that 3,539,583.37 acres, valued at $8,848,958.43 should revert to the national domain; the O&C would recoup $1,723,470.54 and the lien holders $2,354,007.81.[97]

After nearly a decade of litigation, the Oregon and California land-grant suits seemingly ended (though to this day, revestment claims are received by the U.S. District Court clerk's office). The court returned— though not exactly in the manner it wished—a natural resource that had developed the Oregon transportation system. In turn, communities along that network expanded: the city of Bend prospered in central Oregon along the Oregon Central line, while Halfway, Unity, Richland, Imnaha, and Troy rose in northeastern Oregon. In one sense, the problems of Oregon's early railroads provided the impetus necessary to redistribute public lands, making those communities a reality.

∾

# THE PROGRESSIVE CHALLENGE

By 1910 Oregon no longer was a frontier outpost of the mid-nineteenth century. According to a contemporary account the population of Portland was 207,214.[98] Portland was a thriving, bustling city. Increasingly, the regulatory nature of progressive reforms led to litigation before the district court on almost every imaginable subject, from licensing billiard halls in Marshfield, Oregon,[99] to reviewing a petition by thousands of Oregon residents to enjoin the secretary of state from registering the now-ubiquitous automobile in 1926.[100] This was the muckraking era and popular magazines carried to the public stark tales of food and other consumer evils.

In the years preceding this period the common law doctrine of *caveat emptor*, or "let the buyer beware," had done little to control the largely unregulated marketplace. For example, in 1898 the N.K. Fairbank Company sued the Luckel, King, & Cake Company in the district court on grounds that Luckel's "Gold Drop" washing powder infringed its trademark. Without benefit of regulatory legislation for guidance, Judge Bellinger acted personally to inspect both products. In finding that there was not an infringement, the Judge wrote "the style of the letters used, arrangements of the words and designs of the respective labels [were] totally dissimilar."[101]

## Pure Food and Drugs

The hallmark of progressive reform legislation during this period was the Pure Food & Drug Act of 1906.[102] Since 1879, over 190 food bills had been introduced in Congress, but only publication of Upton Sinclair's *The Jungle*, plus the leadership of its sponsor, Dr. Harvey W. Wiley, made food and drug protection a function of the federal government. State officials were the first proponents of a federal law, and recognized the weaknesses and problems of controls prior to the federal law.

Early in the debate over Food & Drug, Oregon Dairy and Food Commissioner J.D. Mickle was on the defensive in district court for threatening to bar the sale of Crescent Baking Powder, manufactured in Washington State and sold in Oregon.[103] Testimony in the case revealed that its baking powder contained "egg albumen," which Crescent claimed was a natural derivative used to maintain leavening properties. Judge Wolverton agreed. Persuaded by an affidavit from the federal law's sponsor, Dr. Wiley, the judge wrote it would be "sticking in the bark" to hold that Crescent violated state law, and finding that "the substance" was wholesome and nutritious," the judge ordered the commissioner to withdraw the ruling.[104]

After the federal law became effective in June 1907, the federal Bureau of Chemistry was charged with its enforcement. The bureau was a research organization and previously had had limited expertise in regulatory enforcement. The remoteness of the nearest field laboratory, in San Francisco, added to enforcement difficulties until a testing site opened in Portland in late 1908.[105]

Conditions in the Oregon food and drug trade were not as poor as those in other regions. In the early years, product seizures and criminal prosecutions were primarily used to enforce the act; only in 1938 was federal injunctive power against future violations added to these legal remedies.[106]

A case that illustrates the early federal prosecutions is a 1914 one in which U.S. Attorney Everett A. Johnson sought to have the court condemn 200 cases of tomato catsup as adulterated.[107] The act prohibited the interstate shipment of adulterated food that "consist[ed] in whole or part of filthy, decomposed, or putrid animal or vegetable substance".

*Progressive reform legislation led to several district court cases during this*
*period. Some involved unsanitary conditions in Oregon salmon canneries.*
(Oregon Historical Society Negative #ORHI45709)

Testimony in the case showed that the tomatoes were transported to
the factory in car loads and, with minimal inspection, emptied into 150-
gallon vats of water for washing. Johnson alleged the water was only
changed daily, a practice that, according to his research, resulted in a sam-
ple containing bacteria, yeast, and mold from 350 million to 1 billion bacteria and spores per cubic centimeter.

In deciding another case concerning progressive reform legislation,
Judge Bean condemned the catsup and, revealing his mid-nineteenth
century market philosophy, noted that better production methods were
in "vogue" than the testimony revealed and wrote that it was not "surprising" that the food sorters, who were paid by the piece, were indifferent
and careless because they were not given incentives to remove decayed
portions.[108]

In subsequent years, food and drug prosecutions continued to reflect
the makeup of the Pacific Northwest's food and export products. During
the 1920s a young microbiologist with the Bureau of Chemistry visited
Oregon salmon canneries. There he discovered that many canneries were

packing fish in "deplorable quality from the standpoint of decomposition."[109] As a result, there occurred large seizures and many criminal prosecutions in the district court. Other cases involved the export of apples and pears, and later agreements between federal and state science authorities reduced the number of legal actions necessary. Future changes in the food and drug laws reached a high point with the creation of the Food, Drug, and Insecticide Administration in 1931. The federal role in consumer protection has continued and still reflects the progressive era's desire for a safer, cleaner, and better environment for the public.

## White Slavery

Progressive reformers also pressured Congress in June 1910 to pass the White Slave Traffic Act. As one of the earliest pieces of federal legislation to penalize interstate crime, the Mann Act, as it was soon called, made it a federal offense to transport or cause to be transported in interstate or foreign commerce "any woman or girl for the purpose of prostitution or debauchery, or for any other immoral purpose."[110] Progressives so named the act because they believed there existed a serious and widespread problem: taking young women for commercial exploitation and holding them captive with threats to their lives.

Although the Mann Act was based on Congress's power to regulate commerce, it was not intended to address prostitution and vice on the state level.[111] Rather, its purpose was to prevent promoters of prostitution from transporting women for immoral purposes over interstate lines and to end what progressives saw as a nationwide organization of vice rings.[112]

Nonetheless, local conditions and public sentiment played a large role in early enforcement of the Mann Act. In August 1911 Portland's city council authorized Mayor A.G. Rushlight to create a 15-member city vice commission. Democratic reform governor Oswald West launched anti-vice campaigns in Huntington and Redmond. At the time, energetic Assistant U.S. Attorney Walter H. Evans was leading a vigorous and successful federal effort against white slavery. Evans' success led Governor West to appoint him as a special prosecutor in what soon would become a regional campaign against vice.[113]

Shortly after its enactment, the Mann Act's constitutionality was challenged in the district court, where David Westman was indicted on nine counts under the act for transporting Carrie Bledsoe and Myrtle Westman for what was described only as "immoral purposes" across the

Oregon border. J.M. Long, Westman's counsel, argued to Judge Wolverton that transporting persons from one state into another was not a "proper subject" of commerce and, therefore, Congress was without power to enact the white-slavery legislation. In a short opinion, Wolverton overruled Long's argument and wrote that the act was aimed at transporting such persons from one state into another for "evil, immoral, and pernicious purposes."[114] In finding that transportation of passengers was a part of commerce, Wolverton asked, "But can there be any further doubt that the subject of legislation is one of interstate commerce?"[115]

Wolverton presided over many of the white slavery prosecutions and routinely imposed long sentences. Reflecting the sensational manner in which the reading public received these cases, one editorialist commented: "Our only regret is that he (Wolverton) did not see his way to make them [the sentences] longer. In a civilized and Christian country 'white slavery' cannot be tolerated."[116]

By March 1912 there were 25 convictions of "white slavers" in the federal court.[117] Although a state vice law had existed since February 1911, there were no active state prosecutions.

Contrasting the state and federal efforts, one newspaper editorialist called for the "gray wolves of society" to be hunted out of the city of Portland and asked, "Why is there not equal activity by the state in prosecuting this infamous traffic? Why is the United States more effective in punishing the destroyers of womanhood?"

Despite the efficiency of early Mann Act prosecutions, the act's enforcement was not without cost in this heated and acrimonious climate. In November 1914 the Portland office of the U.S. Immigration Department summarily deported two Chinese women, described in grossly sensationalized reports as "slave girls," on the grounds that they were in Oregon for "immoral purposes" as defined under the act.[118] Despite being free on bonds of $4,000 and supported by wealthy and influential members of Portland's Chinese community, the women were deported without any post-trial hearing. Although writs of habeas corpus were then in preparation and one was in fact delivered, acting immigration chief R. P. Bonham could only offer the meager explanation of following advice of the Department of Justice.[119] With the women outside American jurisdiction, the court, under the then existing Chinese Expulsion Act, was without power to remedy what had transpired.

One of the more publicized vice rings, illustrative of the climate surrounding the federal effort, surfaced in June 1923, when Portlander Lawrence F. Capri was charged with two counts under the act. In reports of the day, Capri was described as a "typical sheik" with patent-leather hair, peon pants, exaggerated clothes, and sideburns.[120] A federal investigation disclosed that Capri had become acquainted with a 17-year-old female at a dance hall, won her confidence, and then married her shortly before leaving Portland for Aberdeen, Idaho. Working in conjunction with Aberdeen authorities, federal agents discovered what reports described as a "notorious den," comprised of numerous other recently betrothed brides.

At the time, the Mann Act was enforced only against men who violated its provisions. Capri and another Portlander named Cecil Gorin were arrested and appeared before Judge Bean. To forgo a public trial, Capri pled guilty to the two charges and made no attempt to deny responsibility. In finding that "aggravated features" to the case merited a severe punishment, Bean, reports say, bellowed, "Two years in Leavenworth Prison."[121] Capri, who was reported to have maintained an "indifferent air" throughout the trial, broke down and wept when confronted by his mother and young sisters outside the courtroom.

Despite Congress's clear intention that the Mann Act was to be invoked in cases of commercial vice, the court in Oregon, along with those in other federal districts, continued to convict defendants under the law where there was seemingly little evidence that the women involved were actual prostitutes or were being subjected to involuntary servitude. As public sentiment changed, however, white slavery prosecutions declined. In retrospect, the courts had relied on one conventional view of immorality to become for a time a censor of sexual morality. Although rarely enforced, the Mann Act with minor changes remains today codified in federal law.[122]

## World War I Patriotism

By the spring of 1918, the city of Portland was in a patriotic frenzy. Citizen leaders erected the Liberty Temple, and the Third Liberty Loan Drive led a nationwide effort to raise $3 billion for the war effort. So strong did patriotic sentiment run that when Assistant Portland Librarian Miss M. Louise Hunt refused to buy war bonds, the fact was reported in an *Oregonian* headline. And although Portland U.S. Attorney Bert E. Haney declined to charge Hunt because no existing law could force her to

purchase Liberty Bonds, he stated that "[with] such unloyal and unpatri-
otic tendencies...the woman in question should not be permitted to hold
a public office."[123]

**The IWW and the Heyday of Oregon Socialists.** In this climate of opinion, Congress passed the Espionage and Sedition Acts, which penalized
speaking, printing, or "otherwise expressing contempt" for the government, Constitution, flag, or uniform of the armed services.[124] Oregon was
spared the anti-conscription riots common in other states, but dis-
senters—including Socialists and Wobblies—became identified with
pro-Germanism.

Led by Chicagoan William F. "Big Bill" Haywood, the Industrial
Workers of the World (Wobblies) proclaimed "industrial unionism," a
philosophy of worker ownership and economic redistribution. Oregon
Wobblies were aligned with Socialists, who at the time were the third
largest party in Oregon and often received 15 to 25 percent of the popular
vote.[125] When prosecuted, Wobblies and Socialists courted publicity but
raised important questions concerning the freedoms available in a war-
time democracy.

*U.S. v. Floyd Ramp.* In January 1918 Roseburg Socialist and self-professed
"agitator" Floyd Ramp was charged with violating the Espionage Act.
According to Ramp, a year earlier in a train station filled with army
recruits, he had asked a group of soldiers who blocked his way whether
they knew what they were fighting for, had bellowed that it was for "John
D.'s Money," and had been arrested.[126]

Despite having failed the Oregon state bar exam, Ramp (a law school
graduate) had acted as his own counsel and created what the Portland
*Oregonian* called a "spectacular," but unsuccessful defense. During his
trial before Judge Wolverton, the number of spectators grew so large that
the trial had to be moved to the Federal Building's larger courtroom.
During voir dire, Ramp tested Judge Wolverton's patience by inquiring
about the venire's attitude toward the Irish Rebellion.

The "amateur attorney," reported the Portland *Oregonian*, was
silenced when the judge stated, "I'll hear no argument on that point!"[127]
When Ramp argued that free speech had justified his statement to the soldiers, Wolverton instructed the jurors:

> *A citizen is entitled to fairly criticize men and measures; that is men
> in public office whether high or low degree...but not when this criti-*

155

*cism extends by willful intent to the incitement of disorder or riot or the infraction of the laws of the land....*[128]

After deliberating 45 minutes, the jury found Ramp guilty of using seditious speech to cause "insubordination, disloyalty, and mutiny among the military forces."[129] At sentencing, Ramp asked to be "banished to Siberia" and Wolverton responded that he had not been prosecuted for being a Socialist but for interfering with the nation's "military efficiency" in war time.

Ramp served only two years of his sentence (at McNeil Island federal prison) and was fined $500.[130] However, the experience seemed to have had no effect on the Roseburg "agitator," who 54 years later, at age 94, was distributing Socialist literature on the University of Oregon campus.

***United States v. Equi.*** In November 1918 Dr. Marie Equi, later to be known as the "Queen of the Bolsheviks" and "the stormy petrel from the Northwest," was tried for sedition under the Espionage Act.

During a 1916 war preparedness parade, Dr. Equi—having borrowed a lineman's spurs and evaded police—climbed a telephone pole to unfurl a banner that read, "Down with the Imperialist war!" She later refused to kiss an American flag pushed upon her by the surrounding mob and stated at the time, "she did not want to choke on it."[131] Dr. Equi was stating that she and the Industrial Workers of the World (IWW)

> *...were not fighting for the flag containing the red, white, and blue, not the British flag, nor a flag of any country, but that fellow workers and the IWW stood for the industrial flag, the red banner that stood for the blood of the industrial workers.*[132]

Representing Equi in district court were W. D. Fenton and Socialist counsel George Vandeveer, who argued that Equi had operated within the existing political framework and that her "agitation" had the approval of President Wilson, who they quoted as previously having stated that the United States was a "foster child of special interests."[133] Equi stated that her "fight wasn't against the American flag nor the system of government," but that she was opposed to "conditions."[134]

On November 22, in a crowded courtroom, the jury found Equi guilty on all eight of the counts charged. Afterward, reported the Portland *Oregonian*, Equi said she had been "hounded for the past five years" and asked,

> *Why didn't they arrest the men who were wearing iron rings and took them off....What do I mean by an iron ring? Men friendly to Germany before we entered the war were wearing them....*[135]

Later it was reported that Equi became the center of a crowd, which she addressed in an "excited, vehement manner, with an occasional emphatic 'damn.'"[136]

The following December, Judge Bean imposed a fine of $500 and sentenced Equi, who came to court leading a small child, to three years imprisonment in San Quentin. Bean stated that there were "two classes of citizens" in the country—"those who supported the government in the prosecution of the war and those who did not. All the government asked was that those who did not would keep quiet and not embarrass the government in its conduct of the war."[137]

Later, when Equi was represented by C. E. S. Wood before the Ninth Circuit Court of Appeals, that court affirmed her conviction and found that on the basis of national sovereignty, the federal government could prohibit "certain acts" that directly interfered with the war effort and the raising of an army.[138]

Today the actions of Marie Equi and Floyd Ramp might not satisfy the "clear and present danger" test articulated by U.S. Supreme Court Justice Oliver W. Holmes in *Schenk v. United States*,[139] but in 1918 America led an international crusade for democracy. Later, Justice Holmes would give "poor and puny anonymities" of dissent more protection.[140]

Marie Equi served one year in San Quentin before her sentence was commuted by President Wilson. She died in Portland in 1952, almost forgotten except by a few close friends.[141]

~

# FORTUNES OF LABOR—
# THE 1922 STRIKE

Following the First World War, Oregon's economy stagnated and conservatism spread. Between 1917 and 1918 three major Oregon shipbuilding concerns and several smaller firms alone had launched 44 steel ships. In 1919 another 52 were launched, as the companies finished standing orders after the armistice.[142] Total employment for the shipyards had reached a peak of 28,000 in October 1918. By November 1919, however, Portland shipyards began to close and lay off workers. By 1920 fewer than 3,000 workers were employed in the shipyards.[143] Between 1919 and 1923 the cost of living in Oregon escalated and the question of a "living" wage arose.[144]

One of the most turbulent years in the history of Portland's water-front and its longshoremen was 1922. The 1922 strike would signal the end of craft unionism and clear the way for the emergence of industrial unionism.[145] The origins of the strike have been traced to 1919, when the shipbuilders' counter organization, the Waterfront Employers' Union, began to take measures to bust the fledgling unions. One of the clashes, described in published reports as "The Ambuscade," occurred in 1921 and required the court to invoke its injunctive power to quell the violent tensions that existed.

Despite the economic difficulties in Portland's shipyards, the Sailors Union of the Pacific, which had not received a wage increase since shortly after World War I, began picketing. This action led to strike-breaking measures by the state shipping board and Portland police and resulted in several violent incidents that led Judge Wolverton to temporarily restrain the picketing.[146] (Although striking in itself was not illegal, the threat of irreparable harm could cause a court to halt it.[147]) Wolverton made the injunction permanent in June, and four days later union leaders appeared to have ended the strike.[148]

Later that month, however, Sailors Union member Nestor Varrio led a group of members and battled with Portland police at the Linnton Shell Oil company docks where the *City of Reno*—a "scab" ship, according to Varrio—was moored. The Portland *Oregonian* reported that rifle shots were fired at plainclothes Portland police, who apparently were mistaken for the *Reno*'s crew, and that Varrio was killed. As a result, union members faced contempt charges for violating Wolverton's injunction.[149]

When the case came before the district court, Progressive William S. U'Ren represented the Sailors Union. With public sentiment favoring the strikers, who had been manacled while being led into the federal building, U'Ren persuaded Judge Wolverton to lower the bail that had been imposed. Ultimately, Judge Wolverton dismissed the conspiracy charges because it was unclear from testimony presented at the contempt hearing who was responsible in the confusion during the confrontation. Wolverton released all of the strikers except Olaf Pederson, who received a sentence of one year after he admitted discharging a weapon during the altercation.[150]

Despite the confusion over responsibility for the violence in the so-called Ambuscade, the Employers' Union was not entirely responsible for the strike. The longshoremen's unions were internally weak and during early picketing, non-union workers crossed the lines and went to work.[151]

Further, among the nonstrikers were Wobblies, which added to the tense situation and resulted in even greater bitterness.

In July 1922 the Sailors Union ordered members to return to the ship-yards, and the tension and outbreaks of labor strife ended. After the 1922 strike there were no powerful unions on Portland's waterfront or else-where on the West Coast. Although the court had stilled the violence, the rise of unionization would have to await the safeguards of the National Recovery Act of 1934.

❧

# ANTITRUST LEGISLATION

Between 1865 and 1910 the nation's industrial structure and traditional patterns of business were rapidly altered. Recent developments in corpo-rate business practices began to transform numerous small family busi-nesses into intricate networks of monopolies and oligopolies. Beginning in the 1880s public sentiment increasingly focused on the negative aspects of this economic change and looked to both government and the courts to fix what was wrong in the national economy.[152]

The word "trust" soon denoted more than a legal device to consoli-date several corporations. It became a progressive call for reform and sig-naled a debate over the direction of economic productivity and distribu-tion of wealth. With trusts now viewed as an intolerable evil, Congress passed the Sherman Antitrust Act in 1890.[153] Relying on simple judicial authority and common law theory to control the trusts, Congress intend-ed the law to protect consumers from unreasonable price increases and to guarantee that local markets remained open for small businesses.[154]

Although trusts in Oregon were modest in comparison with the large eastern trusts such as Standard Oil, early antitrust litigation in Oregon reflected the state's transformation from a regional and self-sustained agrarian outpost to an integrated, interstate market economy. For exam-ple, in February 1913 a Portland federal grand jury indicted 15 Front Street fruit and produce dealers for conspiracy and restraint of trade in violation of the Sherman Act.[155] The "Combine," as published reports described the group, was actually the Produce Merchants' Association of Portland, and was alleged to have, by agreement, increased prices when marketing produce. The effect, the indictment alleged, was to stifle com-petition. The association was said to have forced closing of the Columbia Fruit and Produce Company and the T. O'Malley Company due to the stress of competition.[156] To support its case before the grand jury, federal authorities granted immunity to J. W. Bunn, the association's secretary, who produced ledgers that proved the produce handled by the Merchants' Association had comprised 90 percent of the nuts, fruits, vegetables, and melons shipped into Portland from southern states and the Hawaiian Islands.[157]

Shortly after the indictments were made public, all 15 of those merchants charged entered guilty pleas before the court, thereby avoiding what likely would have been a highly publicized trial. Stating that he could not believe that the merchants deliberately conspired to restrain trade when the group was formed in 1902, Judge Bean announced that only fines, totaling $8,450, would be imposed. Although the Sherman Act permitted imprisonment for such offenses, the judge stated that the penalties imposed were appropriate after making a finding that the Merchants' Association was apprised of its effect on competitors and that the organization had only gradually changed from its original function as a credit association.[158]

On grounds that it did not want to discourage business, the Oregon Legislature had consistently refused to enact a state antitrust law to prevent the growth of intrastate trusts. However, the so-called "cash register trust," consisting of secret working agreements between railroad and telegraph companies, had in the 20 years preceding 1913 unofficially driven 150 manufacturers into bankruptcy and established a monopoly of 95 percent over the competitors that remained.[159] Given this fact, on February 14, 1913, U.S. Attorney General George W. Wickersham appointed Portland U.S. Attorney John McCourt to be a special assistant U.S. attorney in the western district of Washington to investigate the Bell Telephone Company for alleged violations of antitrust laws.[160] A petition under the 1890 Sherman Antitrust Act was filed July 24, 1913, in the district court against the American Telephone and Telegraph Company and 41 others, alleging that AT&T had acquired a monopoly of telephone business on the Pacific Coast by means of exclusive contracts.[161] During the trial, which was to cost approximately $10,000, AT&T and its subsidiaries voluntarily agreed to comply with the demands of the government, and a consent decree that affected nearly $2 million worth of physical property was entered March 26, 1914, by Judge Bean.[162] The consent decree perpetually enjoined further operation of the combination and cancelled the exclusive contracts. The Portland *Oregonian* reported that the decree represented an "unconditional surrender" by the "telephone trust," and Judge Bean stated, "It is believed that the public interest will be served by the adjustment of this controversy."[163] The decree was modified September 7, 1914, to permit consolidation of two telephone exchanges in Spokane, Washington, and on January 9, 1919, an order was entered to modify the decree to permit Pacific Telegraph & Telephone Company to acquire the Home Telephone Company. (A final order, entered October 20, 1922, permitted the same company to acquire the Northwestern Company.)

The subsequent orders to the 1914 decree allowed a measure of flexibility for the telegraph and telephone companies to adopt new technologies to the existing infrastructure. Within three decades a new focus in antitrust law would emerge. The question would not be whether the corporation had done wrong, but whether the organization was a monopoly and had become so purposefully.

❧

# THE NOBLE EXPERIMENT

Oregon's crusade to eradicate "ardent spirits" began early. Christian missionaries proselytized against demon rum in 1834, the Oregon Temperance Society was formed in 1836, and state temperance-union members marched against Portland saloons in 1873. Four years before passage of the National Prohibition Act, Oregon's 1916 "bone-dry" law prohibited importation of liquor.[164]

Under the federal "Volstead Act" the Bureau of Internal Revenue performed investigative functions and referred cases to local U.S. Attorney offices.[165] In Judge Bean's words, the prosecutions, "incumber[ed] the dockets of trial and appellate courts in which the parties clearly guilty of the Prohibition law endeavored to escape punishment."[166] The judge, who decided many prohibition cases, not only was a teetotaler but, it was said, "without ostentation or reproach would absent himself from any company in which liquor was served."[167] Enforcing the Prohibition Act proved difficult, though not impossible, in the Pacific Northwest, whose coastal environs facilitated smuggling across the Canadian border, where liquor remained legal.

In 1928 the court held that Coast Guard officers of the steamer *Algonquin* lawfully stopped the *Pescawha*, a Canadian registered schooner, and seized its $63,180 cargo of liquor off the Oregon-Washington coast pursuant to the Tariff Act of 1922.[168] (That act permitted authorities to pursue "escaping" vessels beyond the traditional 12-mile coastal limits.) Facts in the case showed that the *Pescawha* cleared the port of Vancouver, B.C., November 8 with a cargo of liquor destined ostensibly for a Canadian port. Instead, the vessel headed south and hovered off the Oregon-Washington coast, with the intention of delivering the liquor to smaller vessels from the shore. Later that month the *Pescawha* made contact off Oregon's coast with the gasoline schooner *Azalia*, to which part of the liquor was delivered. (The *Azalia's* crew was subsequently convicted.) The story concludes in February 1925, when the *Algonquin*, at the time cruising off Grays Harbor in search of the crew of the floundered *Caoba*, sighted the *Pescawha* 6.6 miles from the Washington shoreline. After a ten-mile pursuit, the *Algonquin's* crew boarded the *Pescawha* and found the ill-fated crew of the *Caoba*, together with a large quantity of liquor.

After the trial, Judge Bean wrote that the seizure of liquor and the *Pescawha* herself, appraised at $30,000, was lawful and fully within the 1922 Tariff Act. Section 581 of the act authorized the Coast Guard to board any vessel within four leagues of the coast and, in the event the vessel attempted to escape, to pursue it until apprehended. From the testimony at trial, Bean concluded, "It was a fair inference from the testimony that the *Pescawha*, when she recognized the *Algonquin*, attempted to escape by preceding to sea, and therefore the *Algonquin* was justified in pursuing and seizing her, even beyond the twelve-mile limit."[169]

That same year, federal authorities seized a cache of liquor from the British vessel *Westmoor*, all of which was "under seal" except a small quantity released to its captain for medicinal purposes. In Judge Bean's words, an acquaintance of the captain, James V. Mason, came aboard to "perhaps partake of his hospitality,…drank it to excess," and died subsequently from injuries received when falling down a stairway.[170] Mason's estate filed suit against owners of the *Westmoor*, which had also been seized, in order to recover damages for his death. Contending that the captain's "plying him" with liquor was unlawful, the estate argued that the owners, by default, were liable for Mason's death. The Volstead Act did allow a remedy for injuries sustained when others supplied or furnished liquor.[171] Judge Bean, however, refused to permit the estate to recover damages on its lien claim, because the Oregon Supreme Court, which had construed a similar state law, required that the injury be caused by the vessel, and not reflect damage that had occurred on board.

Defining an alcoholic beverage arose when the Phez Company, Portland manufacturer of the unfermented loganberry juice "Lo-ju," filed suit to recover $14,283.89 paid in federal taxes under the Revenue Act of 1918. The Revenue Act of 1917, under which the tax on Phez's Lo-ju was levied, provided that all unfermented grape juice, ginger ale, root beer, sarsaparilla, pop, mineral water…and other "soft drinks" should be taxed. Testimony in that case had showed that one gallon of the clarified loganberry juice was sweetened by adding 2¾ to 3 lbs. of sugar and then "superadding" 2 quarts of water to 1 quart of "said juice." Thus, the question before the court was whether Lo-ju was a soft drink. Although the U.S. Attorney's office conceded that pure loganberry juice with added sugar was not covered by the Revenue Act, it argued that adding water to Lo-ju before sale made it a taxable soft drink. Complicating the case further, a Mr. Sales, the government's expert witness, defined a soft drink as "a potable or drinkable nonintoxicating manufactured or compounded sweet beverage, served cold in bottles or in glasses.[172] Ruling for Lo-ju, Judge Bean wrote that while the phrase "soft drink" under the statute might be construed as a general term, the word should be interpreted with reference to the class of products with which soft drinks were associated. Therefore, because of its uniqueness Judge Bean found that "Lo-ju" was not a soft drink under section 628 of the act and it was not subject to the federal tax imposed.[173]

Section 26, title 2, of the Prohibition Act also required that after a defendant's conviction, any vehicle used to transport liquor must be forfeited.[174] In 1925 Judge Bean admitted evidence of liquor, seized from a defendant's automobile by Oregon State Police, and would not address the seizure's legality because only federal authorities were restrained by the Fourth Amendment.[175]

By 1926 and 1927 Oregon led western states in prohibition enforcement, with convictions numbering 183 and 229 respectively and fines (ranging from $1,000 to $10,000) equalling $89,087 in 1926 alone.[176]

Gradually, however, Americans became dissatisfied with Prohibition and repealed the Eighteenth Amendment in December 1933.

∾

# PIERCE v. SOCIETY OF SISTERS

The impetus behind the labor strife of the 1920s and Prohibition was the inability of society to manage post-war change. World War I had failed to

*In the early 1920s KKK leader Fred L. Gifford helped lead a successful effort to pass a state law to prohibit private and parochial schools. When the bill was challenged in district court, it was invalidated. (Oregon Historical Society Negative #ORHI087769)*

bring stability or assure continuity, as the world had hoped it would. Instead, the Bolshevik revolution seized Russia and Communist revolt erupted in Germany, while America became isolationist.

From 1921 to 1924 the Ku Klux Klan flourished in Oregon and, capitalizing on post-war disillusionment, became a force in state politics.[177] In 1922 the Oregon State Legislative Assembly passed the "Compulsory School Bill," which made parents criminally liable for not sending their children to public schools.[178] The School Bill, which originated as an initiative measure in the 1922 state election campaign, would have effectively abolished private and parochial schools in Oregon.[179]

Support for the bill began growing in 1916, led by Portland Masons who formed the Federation of Patriotic Societies. However, its most fervent supporter was the KKK, which owed its strong support in rural Oregon to Klan leader Fred L. Gifford and which used the bill to attack Roman Catholics (only eight percent of the state's population).[180] The Klan said parochial schools made Oregon youth "lackeys of Rome" and "The Scarlet Harlot of the Seven Hills."[181] Oregon Governor Ben Olcott signed the School Bill, stating at the time that it was aimed at "German and Bolshevik propaganda" and remained unsympathetic to the Klan. His opponent in the 1922 state gubernatorial election, Democratic State Senator Walter Pierce, had become aligned with the Klan because he supported the School Bill and advocated free public schools.[182] Pierce narrowly won the election and the School Bill passed by a lesser margin.

In the summer of 1923 the Society of Sisters, a Roman Catholic orphans' home, and Portland's Hill Military Academy challenged the School Bill in district court.[183] In 1910, amid concern that federal judges too frequently enjoined state legislation, Congress required that such petitions be made before a panel of three federal judges (one of whom was to be a federal circuit judge). Before District Court Judges Wolverton and Bean and federal Circuit Judge William S. Gilbert, both schools maintained that the School Bill deprived them and the parents of school children of the liberty and due process guaranteed in the Fourteenth Amendment.[184] Oregon Attorney General Isaac H. Van Winkle argued that the state had a "paramount right" to see parents raise their children according to minimum standards and guidelines, stating that were the bill not upheld, "the great centers of population in our country will be dotted with elementary schools which instead of being red on the outside will be red on the inside."[185]

Writing for the panel, Judge Wolverton enjoined the School Bill in March 1924 and stated that the "searching question" of whether to allow the law to become effective did not have to await the "consummation of threat and injury to obtain preventive relief."[186] Wolverton found that schools and parents of school children had constitutional rights protected by the Fourteenth Amendment and stated:

> It can scarcely be contended that complainants' right to carry on their schools whether parochial or private is not a property right, [or that] the right of parents and guardians to send their children to schools as they may desire, if not in conflict with lawful requirements, is not a privilege they inherently are entitled to enjoy.[187]

By invalidating the School Bill, Wolverton had permitted a private school to assert "substantive" due process rights of parents and children as third parties based on the "rational relationship" test established by U.S. Supreme Court in *Meyer v. Nebraska*.[188] Judge Wolverton stated,

> …unless there exists a reasonable relation between the character of the legislation and the policy to be served…property rights cannot be ruthlessly destroyed by wrongful enactment.[189]

Wolverton concluded that parochial and private schools had existed "almost from time immemorial" and "no state" had "ventured so far as to eliminate" such schools altogether.[190]

In August 1924 the U.S. Supreme Court reviewed the panel's decision directly and affirmed the injunction issued. Writing for the majority, Justice James C. McReynolds stated that the "inevitable practical result" of enforcing Oregon's law would be to destroy the plaintiffs' schools— "long regarded as useful and meritorious."[191] The Supreme Court found that the state of Oregon had alleged no beneficial social interest to monopolize primary education which, Justice McReynolds wrote, would abridge four interrelated classes: the schools, teachers, parents and guardians, and the children.[192]

*Pierce v. Society of Sisters* marked a turning point in defining the "liberty clause" of the Fourteenth Amendment. Prior to the case, the U.S. Supreme Court had used "substantive" due process to overturn narrow economically based legislation.[193] Nearly 50 years after Wolverton's decision, the Supreme Court, citing Pierce, would uphold the right of Amish parents to withdraw their children from public schools after the eighth grade.[194]

∾

# CONCLUSION

By 1927 the district court had come full circle from its precarious transition from the Deady years. These years of growth bridged two contrasting centuries when society and the court entered the modern era and world war, prohibition, and the various cords of social upheaval severed forever the innocence of the Oregon frontier.

∾

# NOTES

1. This modernization of an ancient Anglo-Saxon cry daily opened district court through the early 1900s. *Oregon Journal*, Nov. 28, 1937, at 5.
2. O. West, *Reminiscences and Anecdotes: Mostly About Politics*, 51 Or. Hist. Q. 95 (June 1950).
3. M. Clark, 2 *Pharisee Among Philistines*, 628 (1975).
4. Oregon Historical Society Scrapbook #9, at 55.
5. *Portrait and Biographical Record of Portland and Vicinity* 409 (1903).
6. O.H.S. Scrapbook, *supra* note 4.
7. *Id.*
8. *Id.*
9. J. Gaston, *Portland – Its History and Builders* 58 (1911).
10. 12 R. Athearn, *American Heritage History of the United States*, 995 (1971).
11. 26 Stat. 1095, 1103 (1891).
12. G. Dodds, *The American Northwest: A History of Oregon and Washington* 157 (1986).
13. J. Oliphant, *History of Livestock Industry*, 49 Or.Hist. Q. 3 (1948).
14. H. Langille, *Most Division 'R' Days – Reminiscences of the Stormy, Pioneering*

*Days of the Forest Reserves,* 57 Or. Hist. Q. 301 (1956).

    15. *Id.*

    16. Act. Cong., June 4, 1897, Ch. 2, 30 Stat. 36.

    17. J. Messing, *Public Lands, Politics and Progressives: The Oregon Land Fraud Trials, 1903 - 1910,* 35 Pac. H. Rev. 35 (1966).

    18. Case #2799, RG 118- NA.Pac.NW, CR 45; Records of the Portland U.S. Attorneys Office, National Archives - Pacific Northwest Region, Seattle, WA (hereafter cited as RG ___, NA-Pac.NW, CR ___).

    19. S. Puter and H. Stevens, *Looters of the Public Domain* (1908).

    20. *Id.* at 92.

    21. Bellinger to U.S. Atty. Hall, May 5, 1903, National Archives, D.O.J. Central Files 1903-6442.

    22. Puter and Stevens, *supra* note 19, at 140.

    23. Case #4735, RG 118, NA-Pac.NW.

    24. Puter and Stevens, *supra* note 19, at 177.

    25. *Oregonian,* Nov. 26, 27, 29; Dec. 1, 1904.

    26. Puter and Stevens, *supra* note 19, at 161.

    27. *Oregonian,* Nov. 28, 1937, at 10.

    28. Puter and Stevens, *supra* note 19, at 125.

    29. Case #4735, RG 118, NA-Pac.NW, CR at 1; *Oregonian,* Dec. 7, 1904.

    30. Case #2902, RG 118, NA-Pac.NW, CR 12.

    31. Messing, *supra* note 17, at 44-46.

    32. *Oregonian,* Nov. 28, 1937 at 10.

    33. *United States v. Mitchell,* 136 F. Cas. 896, 907 (C.C.D. Or. 1905).

    34. *Id.*

    35. See RG 118, NA-Pac.NW.

    36. Case #2887, RG 118, NA-Pac.NW.

    37. *Oregonian,* June 22, 1905, at 1.

    38. Case #2902, RG 118, NA-Pac.NW, CR 12.

    39. *Oregonian,* June 22, 1905.

    40. *Id.*

    41. *Oregonian,* June 27, 1905.

    42. *Oregonian, supra* note 37.

    43. 199 U.S. 616 (1905).

    44. Case #2918, RG 118, NA-Pac.NW, CR 20; *Oregonian,* Nov. 20, 1909, at 12.

    45. *Id.*

    46. Ch. 33, 11 Stat. 383, sec. 4 (1859)(now codified in 43 U.S.C. sec. 851 (1976)); *State of Oregon v. Hyde,* 88 Or. 1 (1918).

    47. See *State of Oregon v. Bureau of Land Mgt.,* 876 F. Supp. 1047 (D. Or. 1987), remanded 876 F. 2d 1419 (9th Cir. 1989)(Issue of patented lands left unresolved).

    48. Case #2937, RG 118, NA-Pac.NW, CR 21.

    49. *Oregonian,* Dec. 20, 1912, at 2.

    50. Case #2891, RG 118, NA-Pac.NW; *Oregonian,* Feb. 15, 1910, at 1, 14.

    51. *Oregonian,* July 27, 1905, at 10.

    52. Gaston, *supra* note 9.

    53. *Oregonian,* June 17, 1905, at 16.

54. *Oregonian,* July 28, 1905.

55. 137 F. 11 (1905).

56. K. MacColl, *The Shaping of a City* 297 (1976).

57. *Oregonian,* July 27, 1905, at 10.

58. 138 F.V., *supra* note 55.

59. *Oregon Journal,* May 16, 1923, at 1.

60. *Oregon Journal,* March 11, 1924, at 8.

61. *Id.*

62. *Oregonian,* May 17, 1924, at 6.

63. *Judges of the United States* 544 (1983).

64. *Oregonian,* Jan. 8, 1931, at 8.

65. *Id.*

66. R. Bean, autobiographical manuscript (O.H.S. Archives), Oct. 1929.

67. *Toasts to Judges Wolverton and Bean,* 4 Or. L. Rev. 69 (1924).

68. *Oregon Journal,* March 12, 1925, at 2.

69. C. Carey, *Robert Sharp Bean,* 32 Or. Hist. Q. 70 (1931).

70. This section was first published in *Prologue* – Quarterly of the National Archives, Fall 1989, and is included here by permission of its author, Phillip E. Lothyan.

71. Dodds, *supra* note 12, at 123.

72. See F. Riggs, *Pressures on Congress—A Study of the Repeal of Chinese Exclusion* (1950).

73. *Id.*

74. *Ozawa v. U.S.,* 260 U.S. 178 (1922).

75. Petition No. 5707 for Certificate of Naturalization No. 1150336, Vol. 23, U.S. District Court for the Western District of Washington (Tacoma), Records of District Courts of the United States, RG 21, NA-Pac.NW. Thind had experienced an earlier bureaucratic rebuff upon his entry into the United States. Immigration officials tried to turn back Thind and 75 of his fellows, but the courts blocked such actions; Portland *Oregonian,* Feb. 20, 1923.

76. Camp Lewis *Trench and Camp,* June 2, 1918, microfilm A6986, University of Washington Library. Thind was one of 5,199 aliens (29 nationalities) at Camp Lewis.

77. Hindus in Germany in 1915 began a conspiracy to ship arms to India that ultimately involved British and German intelligence services, led to a munitions ship seizure in Hoquiam, Washington, and culminated in a San Francisco trial on charges of violating U.S. neutrality laws. At the end of the trial, one of the defendants shot another defendant and was killed in turn by a U.S. marshal. A special list of Record Group 118 at the National Archives-Pacific Sierra Region in San Bruno, California, drafted by Hanna Regev in 1974, provides background information as well as descriptions of relevant records of the U.S. attorney in San Francisco. The court case is Criminal Case 6133 in the Southern Divison of the Northern District of California, First Division.

78. Bhagat Thind's documents included a reply to his inquiry on receiving a commission as an army pilot that officers must be naturalized citizens. Another letter designated him an acting sergeant.

79. 268 F. 683 (D. Or. L. 1920).

80. The legal chronology may be followed in *U.S. v. Bhagat Singh Thind*, Equity Case E-8547 (Judgment Roll No. 9341), U.S. District Court for the District of Oregon, RG 21, NA-Pac.NW.

81. 260 U.S. 178, 261 U.S. 204 (1923).

82. Portland *Oregonian*, Feb. 24, 1923, Mar. 2, 1923, Dec. 29, 1925, and Dec. 30, 1925.

83. *U.S. v. Cartozian*, Equity Case E-8668, U.S. District Court for the District of Oregon, RG 21, NA-Pac.NW.

84. John W. H. Crimm, assistant attorney general, to John S. Coke, U.S. attorney for Oregon, Sept. 28, 1923, Cartozian File, container 46412, Records of U.S. Attorneys and Marshals, RG 118, NA-Pac.NW; Portland *Oregonian*, July 28, 1925. Because of his doubts, Judge Bean required Tatos Cartozian to bring his wife, three sons, and a daughter to court to see what complexions they had. The family was described as olive-complexioned, well dressed, and prosperous, "an average American family." Portland *Oregonian*, May 18, 1923.

85. Cartozian File, defendant's brief, 1-28, RG 118, NA-Pac.NW.

86. Plans to appeal the case appeared in the Portland *Oregonian*, May 10, 1924. Portland *Oregonian*, July 28, 1925; George Neuner, U.S. attorney for Oregon, to S. C. Pandit, July 20, 1926, Cartozian File, RG 118, NA-Pac.NW. See also Judge Wolverton's decision in 6 F. 2d 919 (D. Or. 1925). The Department of Justice was still considering an appeal as late as October 2, 1925, but thereafter silence reigned: Portland *Oregonian*, Oct. 2, 1925; *Oregon Journal*, Feb. 26, 1953.

87. 25 Stat. 850 (1889).

88. G. Joseph, *The Oregon and California Railroad Land Grants: A History Lesson for the Urban-Renewal Program*, 41 Or. L. Rev. 97 (1962).

89. S. J. Mem. no. 3, Or. Laws 1907, p. 516.

90. 29 Stat. 42.

91. *U.S. v. Oregon & C.R. Co.*, 186 F. Cas. 861 (C.C.D. Or. 1911)(No. 3,340).

92. *Id.*

93. 238 U.S. 393 (1915).

94. 39 Stat. 218 (1916).

95. O&C Railroad Grant Lands Regulations, U.S. Land Office, Roseburg, Or (1917)(O.H.S.).

96. *Oregon & C.R.R. v. U.S.*, 243 U.S. 549 (1917).

97. *U.S. v. Or. & C.R. Co.*, 8 F. 2d 645 (C.C.D. Or. 1925).

98. U.S. Census Portland (1910).

99. *Ashland Electric Power & Light v. City of Ashland*, 217 F. 2d 158 (1914).

100. *Martine v. Kozer*, 11 F. 2d 645 (D. Or. 1926).

101. *N. K. Fairbank Co. v. Luckel, King, & Cake Co.*, 88 F. Cas. 694 (C.C.D. Or 1898).

102. Act. Cong., June 30, 1906, ch. 3915, 34 Stat. 768.

103. *Crescent MFG. Co. v. Mickle*, 216 F. 246 (1914).

104. *Id.*

105. The FDA in Seattle: The First Fifty Years (unpublished work; the authors wish to thank Alan Bennett of the FDA for providing this material).

106. Federal Food, Drug, and Cosmetic Act, 52 Stat. 1040 (1938).

107. *United States v. Two Hundred Cases of A.T. Catsup*, 211 F. 780, 781 (D. Or. 1914).

108. *Id.* at 782.

109. FDA in Seattle, *supra* note 105.

110. Ch. 395, 36 Stat. 825 (1910).

111. Beckman, *The White Slave Traffic Act*, 72 Geo. L.J. 1111, 1112 (1984).

112. H.R. Rep. No. 47, 61st Cong. 2d Sess. 1-2 (1909).

113. MacColl, *supra* note 56, at 404.

114. *United States v. Westman*, 182 F. Cas. 1017, 1018 (D. Or. 1910).

115. *Id.*

116. *Oregonian*, Nov. 24, 1910, at 10.

117. *Oregon Journal*, Mar. 15, 1912, at 8.

118. *Oregonian*, Jan. 13, 1914, at 2.

119. *Id.*

120. *Oregonian*, June 23, 1923, at 22.

121. *Id.*

122. 18 U.S.C. sec. 2421.

123. *Oregonian*, April 12, 1918, at 2; see also, A. Bartholomae, *A Conscientious Objector: Oregon, 1918*, 71 Or. Hist. Q. 213 (1970).

124. 40 Stat. 217 (1917).

125. *Oregonian*, "The Heyday of Oregon Socialists," Dec. 19, 1976 at NW Mag., 15.

126. *Oregonian*, Jan. 30, 1918, at 11.

127. *Oregonian*, Feb. 2, 1918, at 1, 2.

128. *Id.*

129. *Oregonian*, Feb. 20, 1918, at 6.

130. *Oregonian, supra* note 125.

131. *Oregon Journal*, Nov. 25, 1971, "Early Day Woman Doctor Made Mark With Radical Reforms" at NW Mag., 4.

132. *Equi v. United States*, 261 F. 53, 54 (9th Cir. 1919) cert. denied, 251 U.S. 560 (1920).

133. *Oregonian*, Nov. 20, 1918, at 18.

134. *Id.*

135. *Oregonian*, Nov. 22, 1918, at 12.

136. *Id.*

137. *Oregon Journal*, Dec. 31, 1918.

138. *Equi, supra* note 132.

139. 249 U.S. 47 (1919).

140. *Gitlow v. New York*, 268 U.S. 652, 673 (1925)(Holmes, J., dissenting).

141. *Oregon Journal, supra* note 131.

142. C. Abbott, *Portland—Planning, Politics, and Growth in a Twentieth-Century City* 74 (1983).

143. U.S. Bureau of the Census, Fourteenth Census of the United States: 1920, vol. 4.

144. H. Tobie, *Oregon Labor Disputes, 1919-1913: II; Government and Wages*, 48 Or. Hist. Q. 195 (1947).

145. W. Pilcher, *The Portland Longshoremen* 31 (1972).

146. *Oregon Labor Press*, May 10, 1921.

147. F. Frankfurter & Greene, *The Labor Injunction* (1921).

148. *Oregonian*, June 17, 1921.

149. *Oregonian*, June 22, 1921, at 20; June 23, at 4; June 29, at 4.

150. *Oregonian*, June 30, 1921.

151. Tobie, *supra* at 195.

152. F. Fox and R. Sullivan, *The Good and Bad Trust Dichotomy: A Short History of a Legal Idea*, 35 Antitrust Bulletin 57 (1990).

153. 26 Stat. 209 (1890).

154. R. Sherman, *The Regulation of Monopoly* (1930).

155. *Oregonian*, Feb. 6, 1913.

156. *Id.*

157. *Id.* at 3.

158. *Oregon Journal*, Feb. 6, 1913.

159. *Oregonian*, March 27, 1914, at 1.

160. *Id.*

161. Decree #6082, (NA-Pac.NW).

162. 1 D&J. 483.

163. *Oregonian*, *supra* note 159.

164. J. Kobler, *Ardent Spirits – The Rise and Fall of Prohibition* (1973).

165. 41 Stat. 305 (1919).

166. *Poetter v. United States*, 31 F. 2d 438 (9th Cir. 1929).

167. *Oregonian*, Jan. 8, 1931, at 8.

168. *The Pescawha*, 45 F. 2d 221, 222 (1928).

169. *Id.*

170. *The Westmoor*, 27 F. 2d 886 (1928).

171. 27 U.S.C. 1 (1919).

172. *Phez Co. v. United States*, 25 F. 2d 1011 (1928).

173. *Id.* at 1012.

174. 41 Stat. 305, *supra* note 165.

175. *United States v. Brown* F. 2d 630 (D. Or. 1925).

176. *Oregon Journal*, Dec. 7, 1927, at 11.

177. E. Toy, *The Ku Klux Klan in Tillamook, Oregon*, 53 Pac. N.W. Q. 60 (1962).

178. Oregon Compulsory Education Act, Or. Laws, section 5259 (1922).

179. J. Mooney, *Pierce v. Society of Sisters, Religion and Law in Twentieth Century Oregon*, U. of Oregon (unpublished) 1985.

180. Toy, *supra* note 177.

181. Dodds, *supra* note 12, at 218.

182. Mooney, *supra* note 179.

183. JR 16429 and 16428, RG 21, NA-Pac.NW.

184. *Society of Sisters of the Holy Name of Jesus and Mary v. Pierce*, 296 F. 928 (1924).

185. Mooney, *supra* note 179.

186. *Society of Sisters*, *supra* note 184, at 933.

187. *Id.*

188. 262 U.S. 390 (1923).

189. *Society of Sisters, supra* note 184, at 935.

190. *Society of Sisters, supra* note 184, at 937.

191. *Pierce v. Society of Sisters,* 268 U.S. 510 (1925).

192. *Id.* at 515.

193. See *Lockner v. New York,* 198 U.S. 45 (1905); *Adkins v. Children's Hospital,* 261 U.S. 525 (1923).

194. *Wisconsin v. Yoder,* 406 U.S. 205 (1972).

# CHAPTER 4

∾

# A TIME
# OF CHANGE
# 1927–1950

BY RANDALL B. KESTER

*T*he period 1927 to the 1950s brought major changes to
the U.S. District Court for Oregon. There were new
and additional judges, a new courthouse, a new method of procedure, repeal of the Eighteenth (Prohibition) Amendment,
and societal disruptions accompanying the Great Depression
and World War II. The Tillamook Burn and its successive
fires were a blow to the forest industry, but the completion of
Bonneville Dam in 1937 and McNary Dam in 1954 stimulated the growth of the aluminum and other industries.
Several court decisions of this period were destined to have far-
reaching effects.

In particular, decisions regarding the Federal Rules of Civil
Procedure set the pattern for a new approach to litigation; decisions regarding reorganization of a utility holding company laid
the foundation for public services that are still in operation; decisions regarding modes of transportation affected the economic
development of the region; and the impact of the war-time
Japanese exclusion cases was still being felt a half-century later.

173

∾

# COURT PERSONNEL

While the U.S. district judges occupy the most visible positions, the work of the court requires many more people—the clerk of the court and his staff, the U.S. marshal, the probation officer, the U.S. attorney's office and (later) the magistrates and public defender, to say nothing of the bailiffs, law clerks, court reporters, secretaries, and others. Their omission from this history in no way minimizes their importance. Brief biographies of the judges of this period follow, and more details with respect to Judge Solomon appear at the end of the next chapter.

## District Judges

For the first part of this period, there were two federal judges in Oregon, and in 1949 a third judge was added. Judge Robert S. Bean had taken office on May 3, 1909, and Judge John H. McNary on March 7, 1927. Judge Bean died on January 7, 1931, and to replace him President Hoover appointed Judge James Alger Fee, who took office on April 6, 1931. Judge McNary served until his death on October 25, 1936, and to replace him President Roosevelt appointed Judge Claude McColloch, who took office on September 24, 1937. On August 3, 1949, a third position was authorized, and Judge Gus J. Solomon was appointed by President Truman, taking office on November 14, 1949.

**Judge Fee.** Judge James Alger Fee came from Pendleton, where he had served as a circuit judge for Umatilla County from 1927 to 1931. He had been an officer in the first world war and maintained a stern atmosphere in his courtroom, which some attributed to his military experience. He has been described as a "martinet,"[1] as "formidable,"[2] and as "imposing."[3] Although his manner sometimes struck terror into the hearts of lawyers inexperienced in the Federal Court, he was a kindly person at heart and gentle when off the bench.

He served on the federal district court for 23 years, from 1931 to 1954, before his appointment to the Court of Appeals for the Ninth Circuit. He died on August 25, 1959.

**Judge McNary.** Judge John H. McNary was born in Marion County, Oregon, in 1867 and attended Willamette University in Salem. He read law in the office of George H. Burnett (later a justice of the Oregon

Supreme Court) and was admitted to the bar in 1894. He practiced law in Salem until he was appointed by President Coolidge to the U.S. District Court for Oregon. He took office on March 7, 1927 and served until his death on October 25, 1936.

**Judge McColloch.** Judge Claude McColloch likewise had eastern Oregon connections. Although he grew up in Portland, he practiced law in Baker with his father, then in Portland with former Governor Oswald West, and then in Klamath Falls until his appointment to the federal bench. He served on the federal court for 21 years and died on December 31, 1958.

During World War II, when the United States government was a frequent litigator, Judge McColloch developed a reputation of being "tough" on the government. Agencies such as the Office of Price Administration wanted to use their own attorneys, but Judge McColloch insisted that the government appear by the United States attorney, so it was sometimes necessary to have both the OPA attorney and an assistant U.S. attorney in court together. As will be shown later, the judge regarded the Emergency Price Control Act as unconstitutional and the OPA regulations and orders as invalid.

**Judge Solomon.** Judge Gus J. Solomon was born and raised in Portland and practiced law there for some 20 years before his appointment to the federal court. At the time of his death on February 17, 1987, he had served on the Oregon federal court longer than any other judge—over 37 years.

In Judge Solomon's law practice he had achieved prominence as an advocate for minorities and civil rights, at a time when such advocacy was not only unpopular but could be damaging to a lawyer's reputation. As a result, his nomination aroused some opposition. When it came before the Senate Judiciary Committee, he was accused of being a Communist, a charge he vigorously denied. His appointment was strongly supported by Senator Wayne Morse and several prominent Portland lawyers, and the committee approved his nomination, discounting the charge against him.[4] When he ascended to the bench, he vigorously applied those same moral convictions that had characterized his practice.[5] More information about Judge Solomon appears in Chapter 5.

## The Bankruptcy Court

Under the Bankruptcy Act of 1898, which remained substantially in effect until 1946, referees in bankruptcy were appointed by the U.S. dis-

John H. McNary

James Alger Fee

Claude McColloch

Estes Snedecor

*During the early years of the period covered by this chapter, three new judges served on the U.S. District Court for Oregon: John H. McNary (upper left), appointed in 1927; James Alger Fee (upper right), who took office in 1931, after Judge Robert S. Bean died; and Claude McColloch (lower left), who began serving in 1937 after Judge McNary's death. Another familiar federal-court figure of the period was Estes Snedecor (lower right), who was referee in bankruptcy for 33 years.* (Oregon Historical Society Negatives #ORHI87770, #ORHI77495, #CN013059, and #CN015056) trict courts for terms of two years, with compensation on a fee basis. The referees were officers of the courts, their actions were always subject to review by the judge, they performed both administrative and judicial functions, and they had no independent judicial authority.

In 1936 Judge Fee appointed Estes Snedecor as referee in bankruptcy. Judge Snedecor (as he was usually called, even before referees became judges) was born in Florida in 1887, graduated from the University of Alabama Law School, and practiced law in Portland from 1910 until his appointment as referee. He served as referee for 33 years, retired in 1969, and died in May 1974.

Judge Snedecor attained prominence as one of the outstanding bankruptcy experts in the country, but he is probably best remembered for his athletic prowess, attained despite the loss of one leg. As a result of childhood osteomyelitis, Snedecor's right leg was amputated, but that did not prevent him from engaging in tennis, rowing, swimming, golf, and mountain climbing. He even climbed Mt. Hood on crutches![6]

∾

# COURTHOUSES[7]

## New Building In 1933

From 1875 to 1933, the U.S. District Court for Oregon was housed in a building at S.W. Fifth and Morrison streets in Portland that was also a branch post office. The oldest United States courthouse in the Far West, and the second oldest federal courthouse west of the Mississippi River, the "Pioneer Courthouse," as it was later called, became a focal point for downtown Portland redevelopment.

In 1928 Congress authorized a new courthouse and made the first appropriation for the building of $500,000 toward a total estimated cost of $1.5 million, which was later revised to nearly $2 million. In 1930 the site survey was completed and the architect chosen. He was Morris H. Whitehouse, a well-known Portland architect who had designed many other outstanding local buildings.

In 1931 the design was completed, the site at 620 S.W. Main Street cleared, and the building contract let to the Murch Construction Company of St. Louis. Ninety-two percent of the contract money for labor and material went to Portland and Seattle area firms, providing an economic boost in depression times. Actual construction began in 1932, and the cornerstone-laying ceremony was held on August 23 of that year.

Use of the federal courtrooms began in September 1933, and on September 14 the Court of Appeals held a session with Judges William H. Sawtelle, Curtis D. Wilbur, and Francis A. Garrecht in attendance. On September 25 the U.S. district court held its first session in the new building, with Judges John H. McNary and James Alger Fee. The court of tax appeals also conducted a session on that day, with Judge C. Rogers Arundell, formerly a Portland lawyer, presiding.

The "new" building (still in use by the district court) is of steel and concrete construction, faced with sandstone from a quarry near Tacoma, Washington. (At the time it was built, Oregon's Senator Steiwer tried to get Oregon granite substituted for sandstone, but he was unsuccessful.) The hallways are trimmed in marble from Utah, bearing delicate threads of gold. Fortunately, the gold was too tightly compressed in the marble to permit it to be mined, so it was left intact.

When Congress made the appropriation for the new building, it specified that the old courthouse at Fifth and Morrison should be sold for not less than $1.75 million. However, during the Great Depression there was apparently no market for the building, and in 1939 Congress authorized it to be destroyed and the property cleared. World War II intervened, and the building was reactivated for military personnel. In the late fifties, the old courthouse was again placed on the auction block and was practically abandoned until 1968, when the court of appeals agreed to move into it if it was properly restored.

Due largely to the efforts of Judge John F. Kilkenny and the ability of Congresswoman Edith Green to obtain the necessary appropriations, Pioneer Courthouse was restored and rededicated in 1973. Later, both the old and the new buildings were placed on the Register of National Historic Landmarks.

As additional judges were added, the "new" courthouse itself became inadequate, requiring an additional courtroom to be added in 1957 and two more in 1985. With the remodelling, the use of the building as a branch post office was discontinued. The newly remodelled courthouse was dedicated on August 30, 1985, and on April 28, 1989, it was renamed the "Gus J. Solomon U.S. Courthouse."[8]

## Other Locations

Unlike some other federal district courts, which have "divisions," Oregon constitutes one judicial district.[9] Prior to 1950, court was authorized by statute to be held at Medford, Klamath Falls, Pendleton, and

Portland. In 1950 Eugene was added and in 1970, Coquille. By court rule, sessions may be held at any other place in the district as directed by the court.[10]

In most of the locations outside Portland, the federal court utilizes courtrooms in post office buildings, or arrangements are made for temporary use of county courthouses. In 1976 a federal courthouse was built in Eugene.

∾

# PROCEDURE AND PRACTICE

The constitutional tradition of separation of powers between the legislative, executive, and judicial branches of government has caused much controversy concerning the quesiton of whether the power to make rules of procedure is inherently legislative or judicial. To some extent the question was mooted when Congress authorized the Supreme Court to promulgate rules for practice in equity, and by the Conformity Acts Congress directed the federal courts to follow the state practice in actions at law. But the state practice varied, and the result was a lack of uniformity among the different federal courts.

## The Federal Rules Of Civil Procedure

In 1934 Congress authorized the United States Supreme Court to prescribe rules of procedure for the federal courts; and after extensive consideration, the Supreme Court promulgated the Federal Rules of Civil Procedure, which took effect on September 16, 1938. Rules of criminal procedure were adopted in 1946.

The civil rules made profound changes in the previous practice and became the model many states followed in changing practice in the state courts. However, in some respects, they were highly controversial and they engendered considerable criticism.

In Oregon, for example, the legal profession generally resisted the "new" procedure;[11] and responding to that concern, the legislature refused to give the Oregon Supreme Court general rule-making power for fear that the federal rules might be adopted. When limited rule-making power was finally given to the Council on Court Procedures, the legislature retained a veto power over the rules.[12]

Any in-depth discussion of the Federal Rules of Civil Procedure is beyond the scope of this work, but some of the more significant changes should be mentioned:

1. *One Form of Action*—Previously, the distinction was observed between law and equity; and procedure in law actions followed that of the states under the Conformity Act, while equity cases were under the Equity Rules. The new rules combined both into one form of action.

2. *Notice Pleading*—As mentioned above, the federal courts followed state procedure in law actions, and the states generally utilized "code pleading," which required a pleading to state facts sufficient to constitute a cause of action or defense. The new rules substituted a "claim for relief," which merely notified the other party of the existence of a claim but did not require allegation of facts to support any particular legal theory. This change was—and still is—highly controversial, and it was the source of other problems.

3. *Expanded Discovery*—The adoption of notice pleadings made it necessary to use methods other than the pleadings to get at the facts of a case; therefore the new rules expanded pretrial discovery by means of depositions, inspections, interrogatories to parties, requests for admission, etc. This, again, was a controversial change, and Oregon still has not adopted the device of interrogatories to parties.

4. *Pretrial Conferences*—With the change from "fact" pleading to "notice" pleading, it also became necessary to have a new method of defining the issues to be decided. This need was filled by the pretrial conference, in which the attorneys conferred with the court and agreed on a pretrial order that stated the agreed facts, the contentions of the parties, and the issues to be decided and listed the witnesses and exhibits to be used. In many cases, the pretrial order was, in effect, a consolidated pleading.

Thus, the effect of the new rules was virtually to eliminate the pleadings as a device for the formulation of issues, and to substitute discovery and the pretrial conference as a means of performing the function previously served by the pleadings. The new procedure was intended to reduce the element of surprise in a lawsuit and to eliminate the so-called "sporting theory of justice."[13] It was challenged, however, by those who contended that in an adversary system of justice, the element of surprise is often an important tool for discovering the truth.[14]

Judge Fee, who was then chief judge of the U.S. District Court for Oregon, was not happy with this turn of events; and while he approved of the idea of court-made rules of procedure, he warned of the danger of reducing the effectiveness of pleadings.[15]

Nevertheless, he applied the rules vigorously and let it be known that in his view the best way to get the rules changed was to enforce them "up to the hilt," so as to demonstrate their error. One of the cases in which he explored the limits of the new procedure, and in the process set records for the length of a pretrial conference and a pretrial order, was *Montgomery Ward & Co. v. Northern Pacific Terminal Co., et al.*[16]

## The *Montgomery Ward* Case

The *Montgomery Ward* case originated with a labor dispute between Ward and its employees that resulted in a strike and picket lines at Ward's Portland store and mail-order house. The labor dispute gave rise to the decision in *N.L.R.B. v. Montgomery Ward,*[17] which enforced a National Labor Relations Board (NLRB) order holding that Ward had been guilty of unfair labor practices.

*A new federal courthouse was built in 1932-33 at 620 S.W. Main Street in Portland. It featured elegant art deco designs in bronze in the interior. (Oregon Historical Society Negative #ORHI26520)*

Ward's plant was normally served by a number of common carriers, both rail and truck. While the strike was in progress, the carriers were unable to serve the Ward plant because their unions refused to go through the picket lines of Ward's employees in the face of violence and threats of violence. As a result, Ward was unable to receive or ship its merchandise.

Because of the failure of the carriers to serve the plant, Ward initiated action for damages against six railroads and numerous truck lines. While many legal theories were involved, the gist of the action was breach of the common carrier obligation to serve the public. The lawsuit involved many parties, numerous shipments, and complex issues.

The case was filed in 1942 and came before Judge Fee for initial pretrial conference in May 1944. During the several days of pretrial conference, Judge Fee indicated that the attorneys would be expected to devote substantially full time to pretrial proceedings until a pretrial order was agreed upon. It was further decided that it would be desirable to stipulate as many facts as possible in order to save trial time, but it would obviously be inconvenient to do the detailed work of agreeing upon facts in open court.

The attorneys therefore suggested, and the court approved, a plan whereby they agreed to work on the order among themselves, but outside of court, and to report their progress to the court from time to time. This was done, and the attorneys worked continuously until June 1948, taking recesses during sessions of the Oregon Legislature (with respect to which they had extensive responsibilities). At that time, Judge Fee directed that thereafter, the attorneys engaged in such work should remain in the city and in conference, observing working hours similar to those of the court until the court excused them from doing so.

Under this regimen, a pretrial order was completed on June 4, 1951, it was signed, and the trial began on the following day. The pretrial order contained over 3,500 pages of agreed facts and schedules and over 100 additional pages dealing with the issues of fact and law raised by the parties. In addition, the parties filed briefs of several hundred pages. As a result of the extensive pretrial proceedings, the trial, which was originally estimated to take 18 months to two years, was in fact accomplished in nine days.[18]

At its conclusion, Judge Fee rendered two decisions: one on liability and one on damages. With respect to liability, he held that the carriers had violated their common law and statutory duties by failing to serve Ward during its strike.[19] With respect to damages, he held that the liability was individual, not joint,[20] and awarded damages in separate amounts against 34 of the defendants. The case was not appealed, probably because the individual judgments against the various defendants were not large enough to warrant the very substantial expense of such an appeal. Some thought that Judge Fee planned it that way.

The immensity of the pretrial effort is indicated by the following excerpt from Judge Fee's first opinion:

*When it is appreciated that the result was accomplished by examinations, tabulation and calculation of tariffs, connecting rates, history of shipments, plotting of mercantile and carrier operations, investigations into labor relations and the history of particular incidents, besides innumerable other factors, the magnitude of the task begins to take form. Many years of arduous work by the leading counsel for the carriers and the company in taking depositions, fixing statements of fact which all counsel could agree upon, and then making changes required to make them acceptable to opposing counsel required devotion hardly conceivable.[21]*

Present-day lawyers, experienced with the so-called "big" case and using computerized document control, may wonder why any case could require seven years of nearly continuous pretrial conference. But those involved at the time considered it a major accomplishment to hold it down to that!

## Change Of Venue

At common law under the doctrine of *forum non conveniens* a court has discretionary power to decline to hear a case, properly brought before it, if the case could as well be brought in another court that could handle it more conveniently. Usually, the first court would have no power to transfer the case to another court, and the result would be a dismissal, followed by a re-filing in the other court.

To alleviate the harshness of this rule, Congress amended the Judicial Code in 1948 to provide:

*For the convenience of parties and witnesses, in the interest of justice, a district court may transfer any civil action to any other district or division where it might have been brought.*[22]

A somewhat similar provision in Rule 20 of the Federal Rules of Criminal Procedure authorized the transfer of a criminal case when the defendant requested it and had expressed a desire to plead guilty in the new district.

Judge Fee regarded these procedures as involving jurisdiction as well as venue and, in several instances, declined to transfer cases to another district and declined to receive cases transferred here from other districts.

For example, in *United States v. Bink*,[23] the defendant—who was indicted in South Dakota and arrested in Oregon—requested that her case be transferred to Oregon so that she could plead guilty in Oregon. When the original indictment was sent from South Dakota, Judge Fee refused to accept the case on the ground that the criminal rules could not confer jurisdiction on the court to try a defendant for an offense not committed in the district. In the companion case of *In re Schwindt*,[24] Judge Fee permitted the defendant to withdraw her approval of the transfer and directed the clerk to transmit the papers back to South Dakota. The *Bink* case has since been disapproved in other circuits.[25]

In the companion cases of *United States v. Bishop* and *United States v. Tollett et al.*,[26] four defendants were indicted for robbing banks at Oakland and Sweet Home, Oregon. All were arrested outside of Oregon, but two were held in California, one was held in Oklahoma, and one was returned to Oregon. A material witness was arrested in Oklahoma and held there. The two defendants in California were tried and sentenced in the California state courts; the one who had been returned to Oregon pleaded guilty and asked to be sentenced in Oregon; and the one in Oklahoma asked to have his case transferred there.

Judge Fee expounded on the need to have all defendants tried and sentenced at the same place and scheduled all four trials concurrently in Oregon. However, he directed the clerk to forward to Oklahoma certified copies of the papers relating to the defendant who was being held there, while retaining the original indictment in Oregon and asserting the right to try all defendants in Oregon regardless of the action taken in other courts.

In a number of civil cases, Judge Fee refused to accept transfer of the cases from other districts unless the party requesting transfer obtained personal jurisdiction over the other party in this district, typically by serving and filing a motion or petition asking that the case be docketed in Oregon. His reasons were set forth in an opinion dated August 21, 1950, which dealt with several cases.[27]

∾

# THE GREAT DEPRESSION AND THE NEW DEAL

The economic depression that began in 1929 and continued into the mid-1930s did not afflict Oregon as much as some other areas because of Oregon's lack of much heavy industry. Nevertheless, the Depression and the "New Deal" legislation it spawned inevitably gave rise to litigation in the Oregon federal court. A complete catalogue would be impractical, and probably not very enlightening, but the following cases are illustrative.

## Bankruptcies

Of the many cases under the bankruptcy laws that came before the Oregon federal court, perhaps the most prominent was the reorganization of the Portland Electric Power Company (PEPCO).[28] The debtor was a public utility holding company, characterized by Judge Fee as follows:

*During the whole course of its largely colorful career until reorganization, its management has been marked by the financial manipulations in the grand style so characteristic of the period.*[29]

The reorganization began in 1934, a subsequent petition was filed in 1939, and it was not concluded until 1951. The proceeding was successful in that out of a well-nigh defunct holding company there emerged operations that still perform vital functions in the community. Its electrical system became Portland General Electric Company, its freight railway became Portland Traction Company, and its passenger system was eventually taken over by the Tri-County Metropolitan Transportation District, or Tri-Met.

The story is told at length in the many opinions of Judge Fee, cited in the endnotes, and in subsequent opinions of the Oregon appellate courts.[30] Because of the many local citizens and institutions involved, the PEPCO reorganization and its subsequent ramifications were a significant chapter in the economic history of the Portland area.

Other bankruptcies or reorganizations, although not as spectacular as that of PEPCO, revealed the severity of the times. These included: Portex Oil Company,[31] Ostlind Manufacturing Company,[32] and Western Bond and Mortgage Company.[33]

## New Deal Legislation

In an attempt to cope with the Depression, Congress passed a number of Franklin D. Roosevelt's "New Deal" measures, prominent among which were the National Industrial Recovery Act (NIRA) and the Agricultural Adjustment Act (AAA). These acts led to historic court challenges, in which the Oregon federal court participated.

Under the National Industrial Recovery Act, the president was authorized to adopt codes of rules governing various businesses and industries, and eventually more than 700 such codes were promulgated. In an attempt to allow all mills to carry on operations and to give employment to a maximum number of employees at a self-sustaining wage, the code for the lumber industry of western Oregon established a production quota and allocated that quota among various mills.

In the case of *Willamette Valley Lumber Co. v. Watzek*,[34] Judge McNary held that the act was valid, and he reversed a temporary restraining order that would have prevented its enforcement. However, he did not dismiss the case, but continued it pending further investigation. Subsequently, in *Schechter v. U.S.*,[35] the United States Supreme Court held the NIRA to be unconstitutional.

The Agricultural Adjustment Act authorized the secretary of agriculture to issue orders curtailing production so as to increase farm prices. Such an order, as applied to walnuts, was challenged in *Hudson-Duncan v. Wallace*,[36] and Judge Fee held that while the Act was not unconstitutional, the order as applied to the plaintiff was confiscatory and invalid. On appeal, that decision was reversed by the Ninth Circuit.[37]

Subsequently, the act was invalidated by the United States Supreme Court in *U.S. v. Butler*.[38]

∿

# WORLD WAR II

The entry of the United States into World War II brought vast changes in society and corresponding changes in the types and volume of litigation in the federal court. For example: (1) resistance to the Selective Service Act resulted in many prosecutions for draft evasion; (2) alleged violations of the economic regulations of the Office of Price Administration resulted in both criminal prosecutions and actions for civil penalties; and (3) greatly expanded ship construction in the Portland area gave rise to litigation over industrial accidents and occupational disease (*e.g.*, from welding fumes) not then covered by workers' compensation. Some of the wartime litigation was of major importance.

## The Japanese Exclusion Cases[39]

On December 8, 1941, Congress declared that a state of war existed between Japan and the United States, following the attack by Japan on Pearl Harbor and other Pacific bases on December 7, 1941.

From December 11, 1941, through the first half of 1942, a series of orders by the secretary of war and his delegate, General John DeWitt, made Oregon, Washington, and California military areas. Within portions of those areas, General DeWitt established a curfew requiring all persons of Japanese ancestry, both citizens and aliens, to remain in their homes between 8 p.m. and 6 a.m. In addition, by exclusion orders, all persons of Japanese ancestry were kept from entering designated areas and were required to report to assembly centers for eventual deportation to specified inland relocation centers. In Oregon, what is now the Multnomah County Exposition building was remodelled to serve as an assembly center. Ultimately, over 110,000 persons of Japanese ancestry—many of them U.S. citizens—were detained at the relocation centers, losing most of their possessions in the process.

The constitutionality of the orders was promptly challenged in several cases in the Pacific Northwest. One of the first was *U.S. v. Gordon Hirabayashi*.[40] Hirabayashi, an American citizen of Japanese ancestry, was a senior at the University of Washington when he decided as a matter of principle to resist the curfew and evacuation orders of General DeWitt.

*The treatment of Japanese Americans during World War II forms one of the darkest chapters in American history. Requirements that these individuals observe special curfews and report to "relocation centers" like the one pictured above led to several court challenges, known as the Japanese exclusion cases.* (Oregonian *photo*)

He surrendered to the FBI, and in September 1942 his case was heard before Judge Black in the western district of Washington. The court held the Army's orders to be valid, and the jury quickly found that Hirabayashi was a Japanese, that he was subject to those orders, and that he had failed to comply with them. He was sentenced to three months imprisonment on each of two counts, the sentences to run concurrently.

The next reported opinion on the validity of General DeWitt's orders was rendered by Judge Fee in the case of *U.S. v. Minoru Yasui.*[41] Yasui was born in Hood River in 1916 of Japanese parents. He graduated from the University of Oregon undergraduate and law schools and held a commission in the Officers Reserve Corps. Shortly after his admission to the bar, he was employed by the consulate general of Japan in Chicago and registered as a propaganda agent for Japan. When the United States declared war, he promptly resigned from the consulate and returned to Portland. Believing the curfew and evacuation orders to be unconstitutional, he walked into Portland police headquarters on March 28, 1942 and asked to be jailed as a curfew violator. The next day his action was reported in *The Oregonian* under the heading "Jap Spy Arrested." Yasui was released on bond and tried before Judge Fee without a jury in November 1942.

*An assembly center for Japanese Americans is surrounded by barbed wire and guarded by the military. For many individuals and families, relocation meant the loss of their homes and possessions.*
(Oregonian *photo*)

The *Yasui* case was prosecuted by U.S. Attorney Carl C. Donaugh and Assistant U.S. Attorney J. Mason Dillard, both of Portland, and Charles S. Burdell, special assistant to the attorney general, of Seattle, Washington. Yasui was defended by Earl F. Bernard, a respected Portland trial attorney. At the request of Judge Fee, eight other Portland lawyers (including Gus J. Solomon, later to be a federal judge for Oregon) were designated *amici curiae*, or friends of the court. In addition, Earl Warren, then attorney general of California, later to be chief justice of the United States, and his deputy, Herbert E. Wenig, appeared as *amici curiae*. Judge Fee held that the curfew order was invalid where citizens were concerned, but that it was valid for enemy aliens; and he found, as a matter of fact, that Yasui had upon attaining majority elected Japanese citizenship. This finding was based largely on the fact that he had for a time been employed in the Japanese consulate and was registered as a Japanese propaganda agent.

Yasui was held guilty, fined $5,000, and sentenced to one year imprisonment. He promptly appealed to the Ninth Circuit Court of Appeals and, according to the author of a history of the Japanese American Citizens League, "spent the next nine months in solitary confinement in Multnomah County jail, denied a haircut, a razor or even a typewriter."[42]

The *Hirabayashi* and *Yasui* appeals were treated in the Ninth Circuit Court of Appeals as companion cases. The court did not decide the cases but sent them on to the United States Supreme Court, certifying questions of law upon which the Ninth Circuit court desired instructions for the decision of each case. The Supreme Court decided both cases on June 21, 1943.

Hirabayashi had been convicted both of failure to report to the Civil Control Station and of violating the curfew. However, since the sentences on the two counts were identical and were to run concurrently, the court chose to consider only the curfew violation. It held the curfew order to be valid and sustained the conviction, but it did not decide the validity of the exclusion order.[43]

Yasui had been convicted only of curfew violation, so the Supreme Court treated the issue as identical to that in the *Hirabayashi* case, which the *Yasui* case followed. However, because the court held that the curfew order was valid for citizens, the question of whether Yasui had forfeited his citizenship became irrelevant. Therefore, while the Supreme Court sustained Yasui's conviction, it remanded the case to the district court for resentencing and to afford that court the opportunity to strike its findings concerning Yasui's loss of United States citizenship.[44] On remand, Judge Fee struck any finding to the effect that Yasui was not a United States citizen, and his sentence was reduced to 15 days imprisonment.[45]

While the *Yasui* and *Hirabayashi* cases dealt only with the curfew order and not with the exclusion order, the Supreme Court in *Korematsu v. U.S.*,[46] by a six to three decision, did uphold the exclusion order, on the ground that the same military considerations that justified the curfew also justified the exclusion.

On the same day that it decided *Korematsu*, the court also decided *Ex Parte Mitsuye Endo*,[47] in which it granted a writ of habeas corpus directing that Endo be released from detention at the Central Utah Relocation Center.

In the *Endo* case, the government conceded that Endo was a loyal American citizen, although of Japanese ancestry. The court distinguished *Endo* from *Korematsu* on the basis that *exclusion* was different from *detention*, and that the former was justified by military necessity, while the latter was not. On December 17, 1944, the day before the *Endo* case was decided, the Army lifted its mass exclusion order.

Notwithstanding the Supreme Court's decisions in *Hirabayashi*, *Yasui*, and *Korematsu*, it was widely felt that the wartime treatment of Japanese Americans was unjust; and the subject continued to fester in the national conscience.

In 1948 Congress authorized the attorney general to determine claims for loss of real or personal property that were "a reasonable and natural consequence of the evacuation or exclusion" of persons of Japanese ancestry;[48] and in 1956 his monetary authority was increased.[49]

In 1980 Congress established the Commission on Wartime Relocation and Internment of Civilians to review the facts and circum-

189

stances surrounding the executive order and the military directives and to recommend appropriate remedies.[50] The Commission submitted its report in 1982, entitled "Personal Justice Denied."

In 1982 a researcher at the National Archives discovered that the original report of General DeWitt regarding the Japanese evacuation contained statements indicating that the exclusion was based on racial animosity rather than true military necessity. Although the report was revised in the War Department so as to tone down those statements, neither the original nor the revised version was provided to the Justice Department at the time of the 1943 cases in the Supreme Court. When this became known, Hirabayashi, Yasui, and Korematsu each petitioned for a writ of error *coram nobis* to vacate his wartime conviction. *Coram nobis* is an ancient writ by which a court can correct errors in criminal convictions where other remedies are not available. Each of the three men alleged that in his previous case the government had suppressed or destroyed evidence that, had it been known, could have altered the result.

In both *Hirabayashi* and *Korematsu* the convictions were vacated.[51] In Yasui the government moved to dismiss the indictment, vacate the conviction, and dismiss the petition for writ of error *coram nobis*. The district court granted the government's motion, and Yasui appealed, but the appeal was dismissed for procedural reasons and remanded.[52] While the case was pending, Yasui died, and the appeal was dismissed as moot.[53]

Thus ended the litigation, but the strong feelings surrounding the exclusion orders continued, and in 1990 survivors of the Japanese-American internees reunited in Portland, and a memorial garden was dedicated.[54] As of that time, funds had still not been provided with which to pay their claims, but the first distribution began in the fall of 1990.

## Naturalization Cases

The Japanese Americans were not the only groups affected by the war mood. In a number of naturalization cases involving people of German extraction, Judge Fee referred to the person's racial and cultural background as a factor to be considered in determining whether or not he or she was in fact attached to the principles of the Constitution of the United States for a period of five years prior to taking the oath of allegiance (such attachment being a requirement for naturalization).

The situation was complicated by the fact that under the naturalization procedure then in effect, the examination of applicants by an administrative officer was somewhat perfunctory, and the great number of applicants made it impractical for the judge to examine them individually in open court. Nevertheless, when circumstances brought a particular case to Judge Fee's attention, he scrutinized it thoroughly.

For example, in *United States v. Scheurer*,[55] which was a proceeding to cancel a naturalization that had been granted to a German national in 1934, Judge Fee concluded that the prior *ex parte* proceeding was not *res judicata* (judicially binding) but was subject to reexamination; and based on Scheurer's background and activities, his certificate of naturalization was canceled. On appeal, that decision was reversed by the Ninth Circuit[56] on the ground that the government had not proved its case by "clear, unequivocal and convincing" evidence, as required by decisions of the United States Supreme Court.[57]

And in the case of *In Re Oppenheimer*,[58] which was a petition for naturalization by a German woman married to a Jew, Judge Fee discussed the Nazi philosophy and then postponed a decision until the applicant was in a position to produce further evidence that she had abandoned the principles of the German government. He made an important distinction between a naturalization proceeding, where the burden of proof is on the applicant, and a cancellation proceeding, in which the burden is on the government.

The opinions in the *Scheurer* and *Oppenheimer* cases and the first *Yasui* case reveal the importance Judge Fee attached to the obligations of citizenship, and his willingness to deny or cancel citizenship when he felt those obligations had been violated. This attitude may have been influenced by his own service in World War I.

## Sabotage of Italian Ships

Another example of war-time litigation the District of Oregon shared with other federal courts was a series of cases involving Italian merchant vessels. While Italy was at war on the side of the Axis powers, but before the United States entered the war, a number of Italian ships in United States ports were sabotaged by their own masters and crews. This was apparently according to a plan of the Italian government to prevent the ships from being used by the Allied powers.[59]

One such vessel was the Italian motorship *Leme*, which was in Portland harbor, where it had been seized by the U.S. marshal pursuant to several libels (at that time, a libel was the procedure for commencing an action in admiralty). While the ship was in custody, the master and crew were allowed to live on board and were able to damage its engine, navigation instruments, and other equipment. The master and crew were convicted in the Oregon federal court of the offense of damaging the vessel, and the conviction was affirmed.[60]

Meanwhile, the government libelled the ship, but possession was eventually released to the Maritime Commission, which either sold or lend-leased the ship to the British government. Subsequently, in an extensive opinion, Judge Fee ordered the ship forfeited to the U.S. government.[61]

Successive changes in possession of the ship and procedural complications prompted Judge Fee to say in the opinion:

*Such an outré drama would be intelligible only if the locale were that Wonderland in which Alice sojourned.*

## Selective Service

The Selective Training and Service Act that accompanied World War II was the subject of extensive litigation, particularly by those who resisted the draft for religious or conscientious reasons. Many attempted to challenge the act or the classifications made by the local draft boards, but the United States Supreme Court in the case of *Falbo v. United States*[62] held that in defense of an indictment for failure to obey an order of the board, the actions of draft boards could not be challenged.

However, the writ of habeas corpus was available when it was claimed that the action of the local draft board was arbitrary, capricious, or not based upon substantial evidence; and numerous petitions for habeas corpus were filed in the Oregon federal court.

For example, in the case of *Harold E. Robinson*, reported in the local press,[63] but apparently not having a published opinion, Judge McColloch discharged the defendant on a writ of habeas corpus when he found that a member of the local draft board who reclassified Robinson was a personal enemy of his and had prejudged the case.

However, in *Ex Parte Kelley*,[64] Judge McColloch permitted the petitioner to put on his case but denied the writ on the ground that the petitioner had not sustained the burden of proof.

In a third case, *United States v. Chiarito*,[65] the defendant was classified as a conscientious objector and assigned to a public service camp at Elkton, Oregon, and thereafter ordered to report to a camp in Colorado. When he failed to appear, he was indicted in Colorado, but Judge Fee denied his removal to Colorado for trial, on the ground that the Colorado court had no jurisdiction over the defendant.

## War-Time Economic Regulation

Probably no subject occasioned more litigation in the Federal courts during and immediately after World War II than the economic regulations promulgated by the Office of Price Administration (OPA) under the Emergency Price Control Act. In a footnote to the case of *Bowles v. Hudspeth*,[66] Judge McColloch said: "toward the end of the war, OPA cases were being filed in the Federal District Courts alone at the rate of 2,750 per month." In *Bowles v. Richards*,[67] he pointed out that during fiscal 1944-45, twenty-eight thousand OPA cases were filed in those courts.

In the Oregon federal court, most of these cases came before Judge McColloch, who made it clear that he usually had little regard for the government's position. For example, in *Bowles v. Dashiel*,[68] he described the OPA cases as "a discreditable chapter in law enforcement."

One aspect of OPA litigation that Judge McColloch found most offensive was the statutory provision that denied the courts the power to consider the OPA regulations' validity and required such questions to be taken to the Emergency Court of Appeals in Washington, D.C. In *Porter v. Fleishman* (see Note 69), McCulloch referred to this as an "infamous provision", and in *Bowles v. Richards*, as a "legal hoax (see Note 67)."

The OPA cases typically were for treble damages for violation of price control regulations,[69] for injunctions,[70] for investigative subpoenas,[71] and in some instances for criminal penalties.[72]

Some of the cases did not reach a decision stage until after the war had ended or the enabling act had expired, and on that basis the cases were dismissed.[73]

∾

# ANTITRUST LITIGATION

Oregon has not had a large volume of anti-trust cases, as compared with the more industrialized states, but some of the cases tried during this period have been significant.

Perhaps the most highly publicized one was *United States v. Oregon Medical Society*,[74] in which the government charged that the Oregon Medical Society, eight county and regional societies, and a number of individual doctors conspired to restrain and monopolize prepaid medical care, in violation of the Sherman Antitrust Act.

In a sense, the events that gave rise to the case were an outgrowth of World War II. Prior to the war the medical profession had been divided as to the merits of "socialized medicine," and some doctors had been expelled from medical societies, or resigned under pressure, for participating in prepaid or contract medical plans. With the war came the shipyards, which employed vast numbers of people, and with the shipyards came an increase in prepaid medical plans that were privately owned and operated. In response, and in order to meet that competition, the doctors in 1941 set up their own prepaid systems, such as Oregon Physicians' Service (OPS) and other doctor-owned county and regional plans. The government's case attempted to tie together pre-1941 activities with the subsequent operation of OPS.

The case was heard by Judge McColloch, who after a lengthy trial dismissed the case with findings of fact and conclusions of law that completely exonerated the defendants. He distinguished between the period before 1941, which he described as unhappy and unfortunate but in any event having no legal or causal relation with later events, and the period of OPS activity, which he held was a legitimate attempt to meet competition and to provide a socially needed service. His decision was affirmed on a direct appeal to the Supreme Court of the United States.[75] This decision was a major factor in the subsequent development of pre-paid medical plans.

Another anti-trust case of considerable significance was *Columbia River Packers Assoc. v. Hinton*.[76] In that case, the defendant fishermen's union required all packers and canners contracting with it to agree not to buy fish from anyone not a member of the union, and it forbade its members to sell fish to anyone not under contract with the union. The plaintiff was a fish packer and canner and was not under contract with the union, although all other fish packers and canners in Oregon were. As a result, the plaintiff was effectively denied a source of fish.

In the plaintiff's suit to prevent the union from interfering with its purchase of fish from any source, the principal question was whether the Norris-LaGuardia Act, which prohibited injunctions in labor disputes, applied. Judge McColloch held that the purchase and sale of fish was not a labor dispute and granted the injunction. His decision was reversed by the Ninth Circuit,[77] but that decision was in turn reversed by the U. S. Supreme Court, which held that no labor dispute was involved.[78] On remand, the Ninth Circuit held that the union was not exempt from the anti-trust laws and affirmed the injunction.[79]

In another case, Judge McColloch held that a farmers' cooperative, acting alone and not in concert with others for the purpose of mutual help, could not be prosecuted criminally under the Clayton Anti-Trust Act.[80]

∾

# WATER LITIGATION

In the West, where water is often the equivalent of life, it is natural that water should be the subject of much litigation. Most of the controversies about water rights, as such, have been heard in the state courts, under Oregon's statutory system of "prior appropriation,"[81] but the Oregon federal court also had its share of water-related litigation.

## Malheur Lake

Malheur and Harney Lakes in southeastern Oregon are shallow bodies of water that are situated in relatively flat country, and fluctuate widely in size, depending on weather conditions. In wet years Malheur Lake may exceed 60,000 acres, and in dry years there may be practically no water at all. Malheur Lake drains into Harney Lake, which has no outlet. In 1877 the U.S. government had a meander line established around the lakes by a surveyor named Meldrum, and in 1895 a second meander line was established by a surveyor named Neal. (The Neal line was generally inside the Meldrum line.)

From time to time, lands around the lakes were patented under the Homestead and Desert Land acts. However, in 1908 President Theodore Roosevelt, by executive order, set aside the lands within the Neal meander line as a bird refuge, subject to existing rights.

When the State of Oregon was admitted to the Union in 1859, the area within the meander line was part of the U.S. public domain. Under the established law of that period, title to the bed of the lakes would pass to the state, upon admission to the Union, as long as the lakes were navigable. If the lakes were *not* navigable, title would remain in the United States and portions would pass to the various patentees of the adjoining upland, each of whom would then presumably own a more or less triangular piece to the center of the lake.

To determine whether or not the lakes were in fact navigable, the United States brought an original suit against the State of Oregon in the United States Supreme Court to quiet title to the lands within the Neal meander line. The Supreme Court referred the case to a Special Master, who made a personal examination, took extensive testimony, and determined that the lakes were not navigable. His report was adopted by the Supreme Court, which found that the State of Oregon had no title, except to limited areas that were not in dispute.[82]

195

United States v. Oregon did not determine the rights of the patentees, and the government subsequently filed a condemnation suit and a declaration of taking to acquire the properties along the Neal survey line, including the rights of the owners to land within the Neal line.[83] In that case, certain of the landowners raised questions of title and to settle such issues, the government filed the suit of United States v. Otley.[84]

While the Otley suit was nominally brought to quiet title, it was characterized by the Ninth Circuit as an attempt to cancel portions of the patents of the upland owners and, as such, the government had a high burden of proof. The government took the position that the Neal line was not a true meander line, but only a boundary, and that the patents did not convey title to the bed of the lake. The government even suggested that Malheur Lake was not truly a lake.

Judge Fee took extensive testimony, made a personal examination of the meander line, and concluded that (1) Malheur Lake was in fact a lake; (2) the Neal line was a true meander line of the lake, (3) the shore was the true boundary of the patents; and (4) because the patents went to the shore, they included adjoining parts of the lake bed to its center. With minor modifications, his decision was affirmed by the Ninth Circuit.

As if the situation were not complicated enough, another element entered the picture. One Edward N. Brown, who was an officer of the Harney County National Bank, embezzled some $416,000 from the bank and invested a portion of it in Malheur Lake real estate. The bank was taken over by the Federal Deposit Insurance Corporation, which claimed a constructive trust (i.e., a judicially created trust to prevent unjust enrichment) on the land purchased with embezzled funds, and the FDIC thereby became a party to the condemnation proceedings.

On a similar theory the FDIC claimed, and was allowed, a constructive trust on the proceeds of certain life insurance, the premiums for which had been paid with funds Brown had embezzled from the bank.[85]

The Malheur Lake litigation not only settled numerous questions of land title that had been in controversy for many years[86] but clarified the law with respect to ownership of land under non-navigable waters.

## The Vanport Flood Cases

Wartime brought increased industrial activity to the Portland area, particularly in ship construction; and train loads of shipyard workers were recruited from other parts of the country. In an attempt to cope with the housing shortage that resulted, whole communities of government-assisted residences sprang up. The largest of these was Vanport, located in the lowlands between North Portland and the Columbia River. Vanport was built by the government and leased to the Housing Authority of Portland, which continued to manage it after the war. Soon Vanport became one of the largest cities in Oregon, complete with its own community college, which later became Portland State University.

On May 30, 1948 (a memorable Memorial Day), the Columbia River flooded and reached a height of approximately 30 feet above mean high water. An embankment supporting the SP&S railroad track, which was used by other railroads under contract, restrained the flood for a time but eventually gave way. The flood completely wiped out the City of Vanport with its population of approximately 16,000 and caused tremendous property damage, as well as the loss of 15 or 16 lives.

Following the flood, over 700 lawsuits, involving several million dollars of property damage, were filed against the United States. At the time, the railroads were in the government's possession under executive order to avoid a strike, and one of the principal charges of negligence in the damage cases was that the government had failed to prevent a break in the railroad embankment or to warn inhabitants that a break was imminent. The government tendered its defense to the railroad companies, which was declined, and at one point the government asked to bring the railroads in as third-party defendants, a request the court denied.

The trial court (Judge Fee) found no negligence on the part of the government, and this was affirmed by the Ninth Circuit.[87] In his opinion, Judge Fee relied on a part of the Flood Control Act, which provides that, "No liability of any kind shall attach to or rest upon the United States for any damage from or by floods or flood waters at any place...."[88]

For their part, the railroads took the position that their fill was not intended to be a flood control levee. However, because the government was held not liable in the principal case, there was never any occasion to determine the railroads' liability.

## Owyhee Flood Cases

The Owyhee Dam and Reclamation Project, which was built in 1935, was a major source of irrigation water for a sizable area in Malheur County and it converted a largely arid region into rich agricultural lands. But it was not without problems. In 1946 there were breaks in one of its main canals, which caused extensive damage. At the time the government was in control of and operating the canal, and 193 landowners filed suit against it.[89]

The claims fell into two classes: (1) damage resulting from failure to deliver water because of the breaks, causing crops to be lost (*White*); and (2) damage directly resulting from the flooding of plaintiffs' lands (*Ure*).

With respect to the claims of failure to deliver water, the cases were based on negligence under the federal Tort Claims Act and the trial court (Judge Fee) held that no negligence was established on the part of the government. This finding was affirmed by the Ninth Circuit.

With respect to the claims based on direct water damage, the question turned on whether the government, as owner and operator of the canal, was liable absolutely, or only for negligence. Under the Tort Claims Act the government is liable "under circumstances where the United States, if a private person, would be liable to the claimant in accordance with the law of the place where the act or omission occurred."[90]

Under the English common law, determined by the famous case of *Rylands v. Fletcher*,[91] one who stores water on his land is absolutely liable if the water escapes and damages another. If that law applied, then the government was absolutely liable. Judge Fee held that Oregon had adopted

*On Memorial Day 1948 the city of Vanport, home to 16,000 shipyard workers and their families, was inundated by a flood. In its wake, over 700 lawsuits were filed against the United States in the district court. (Oregon Historical Society Negative #68808)*

the rule of *Rylands v. Fletcher*, so the government was liable for the direct water damage, regardless of negligence.

On appeal, the Ninth Circuit reversed the *Ure* case, holding that regardless of the Oregon law, the Tort Claims Act imposed liability on the government only for negligence. In so holding, the Ninth Circuit relied on *Dalehite v. U.S.*,[92] (the Texas City explosion case), which had not been decided when the *Ure* case was in the trial court.

The *Owyhee* cases not only disposed of a large number of claims, but the opinion of Judge Fee, although reversed on other grounds, was a classical exposition of the law of Oregon with respect to escaping waters, which has been followed in other cases.[93]

∾

# AGRICULTURE

Traditionally, agriculture has been one of Oregon's principal economic activities and it has also been a source of litigation in the federal court. The following cases illustrate some of the ways in which the federal court has affected Oregon's agriculture.

## The Hop Crop

At one time, a substantial portion of the entire hop production in this country came from the Willamette Valley, and hop yards, driers, and camps were a familiar sight. Typically, the hop buyer would advance funds to the grower to defray production costs and the grower would agree to sell the crop when harvested, charging the advance against the contract price. In years when the crop was poor or the market changed, there was frequent litigation between grower and buyer.[94]

With the advent of irrigation, much of the hop raising moved to eastern Oregon and eastern Washington, where the drier climate made the hops less susceptible to fungus-type ailments. In 1947 Willamette Valley hops were affected by mildew, and some of the buyers used that as an excuse to reject crops they had previously contracted to buy. Several of the growers sued the buyers for the contract price, less advances, and three of the cases came before Judge McColloch for consolidated trial without a jury.

The crucial issue in these cases was whether the hops were of merchantable quality, within the meaning of the contracts. This was determined by examination of samples of the crop extracted at random from

*Hops samples became key evidence in three cases that came before Judge Claude McColloch after buyers refused to honor contracts to purchase crops damaged by mildew. Long after the cases were concluded, the pungent aroma of the hops lingered in the clerk's office. (Oregon Historical Society Negative #70400)*

the baled hops after drying. A key factor was the aroma of the hops, as judged by experts on the subject. At the trials a vast number of hop samples in the form of paper-wrapped packages were introduced in evidence. While on the stand, witnesses examined and smelled the samples and then expressed their opinions.

In all the cases, Judge McColloch found in favor of the grower and all were affirmed.[95] The cases were long remembered in the clerk's office, which had custody of the hop samples, and the pungent aroma of the hops lasted long after the cases were concluded.

The hop litigation illustrated the interplay between agricultural conditions and economic forces, with the judicial system as the final arbiter of disputes.

## Aluminum Fume Damage

One of the results of the construction of Bonneville Dam and consequent abundant electricity was the development of the aluminum industry in the Portland vicinity. But the production of aluminum involves the emission of fluoride particles which are deposited on adjacent lands and vegetation. When cattle eat from pastures on which fluoride has been deposited, their health is adversely affected. From this set of circumstances a long series of cases developed, in which farmers sued the aluminum companies for damages to their crops, livestock, and sometimes themselves. Some of the cases also attempted to shut down the aluminum plants, and one of them inspired a counterclaim for defamation based on a signboard erected on the plaintiff's land.[96]

Damage to cattle was usually correlated with stains on their teeth, and in order to determine damage, both the farmers and the aluminum companies conducted periodic examinations of the herds and kept extensive dossiers on each animal. Trials often involved "battles of the experts," with veterinarians expressing opinions as to whether the condition of the cattle was caused by fluorides or something else.

In some respects the aluminum fume cases foreshadowed a later era of environmental litigation.

∾

# INDEMNITY AND INSURANCE

The Oregon federal court has produced several decisions in the field of indemnity and insurance that have had far-reaching effects.

In *Oregon Auto Ins. v. U.S. Fidelity and Guaranty*,[97] Judge Solomon started the line of decisions that subsequently became known as the "Lamb-Weston" rule in Oregon, whereby insurance policies whose "other insurance" clauses are repugnant, are required to pro-rate.

That case arose out of an automobile accident in which the driver of one of the cars, who was held to be liable for the accident, was driving a car borrowed from an automobile dealer. The driver's own policy provided that it would pro-rate with other insurance, except that with respect to the use of other automobiles than his own, its coverage would be excess only. The dealer who owned the automobile had a garage liability policy which covered a permissive driver and which provided that it would pro-rate with other insurance, except that with respect to anyone other than a named insured, it would not apply if there were other insurance.

Thus, each of the policies would cover the driver's liability, if it were not for the other; and if both policies were applied literally, neither would cover. It was a typical case of "which came first, the chicken or the egg?"

In the trial court, Judge Solomon held that the garage liability policy was primary, and the driver's policy was excess. On appeal, the Ninth Circuit reversed the judgment and held that because the two policies were irreconcilable, the only rational solution was to require them to pro-rate in proportion to the amount of insurance provided by each.

The Oregon Supreme Court followed that decision in the case of *Lamb-Weston v. Oregon Automobile Ins. Co.*,[98] and it subsequently became known as the "Oregon rule," which is not generally followed by other courts. In fact, a number of insurance companies, by intercompany agreement, decided that in dealings between themselves in similar situations they would treat the owner's policy as primary and the driver's policy as excess.[99] Thus, the insurance industry, by voluntary agreement, has chosen to follow Judge Solomon's original holding rather than the rule adopted by the Ninth Circuit and the Oregon courts.

In *Booth-Kelly v. Southern Pacific*,[100] and *Union Pacific v. Bridal Veil Lumber Co.*,[101] the court dealt with indemnity clauses common in railroad spur track agreements. In *Booth-Kelly*, a railroad employee was injured when he was caught between the side of the caboose and a wood cart that the industry had left too close to the track. He sued the railroad under the Federal Employers' Liability Act and recovered a judgment which was settled. The railroad then sued the industry for reimbursement, under a contract which provided that the industry would indemnify the railroad against loss from any act or omission of the industry, and that if the claim arose from their joint or concurrent negligence, the loss would be borne by the industry and railroad equally.

In the trial court, Judge Fee held that there was some negligence on the part of the railroad, and he therefore gave judgment for only one-half the damage. But on appeal the Ninth Circuit held that any negligence of the railroad was only passive and secondary, while that of the industry was active and primary, and it modified the judgment so as to allow full indemnity.

In *Bridal Veil*, a railroad employee was injured while riding on the end of a freight car that was struck by a lumber carrier operated by the industry. As in *Booth-Kelly*, the employee sued the railroad under the Federal Employers' Liability Act and recovered a judgement which was settled, and the railroad sued the industry for reimbursement. The contract language was the same as in *Booth-Kelly*, but the case was tried to a jury instead of the court.

In a special verdict the jury found that the railroad was negligent, but it could not agree on an answer to one of the questions dealing with the industry's negligence. Using the jury's answers as a basis, Judge Solomon absolved the industry of negligence and denied reimbursement to the railroad. On appeal the Ninth Circuit held that the jury's failure to answer a crucial question left a gaping hole in the verdict, and the court reversed the judgment and sent the case back for a new trial.

In doing so, the Court of Appeals re-affirmed the *Bridal Veil* ruling with respect to construction of the contract, *i.e.*, that full indemnity applies only if the industry is guilty of active or primary negligence, with any negligence of the railroad being only passive or secondary. These cases have been followed in subsequent decisions of other courts.[102]

# DECEDENTS' ESTATES

Ordinarily, the federal courts do not get involved in probate matters; and in the case of *Jackson v. U.S. National Bank,*[103] visiting Judge Mathes, in a scholarly opinion, declined to accept jurisdiction over a contest of the will of Maria C. Jackson.

However, in *Howell v. Deady,*[104] Judge Fee found it necessary to construe the will of Lucy A. H. Deady, widow of Judge Matthew P. Deady, who was Oregon's first federal district judge.[105]

The suit related to the income from a block of downtown Portland business property, which was desposed of in Mrs. Deady's will. The controversy revolved about the construction of a paragraph in the will which provided that if her son Henderson Brooke Deady "die without issue," the undivided two-thirds of the property would vest in her grandsons.

Questions were also raised as to whether a provision for accumulation of the income for an indefinite period violated the rule against perpetuities and whether a provision prohibiting an encumbrance on the property for a period of 25 years violated the rule against restraints on alienation.

The following chart, taken from the briefs in the case, illustrates the family tree.

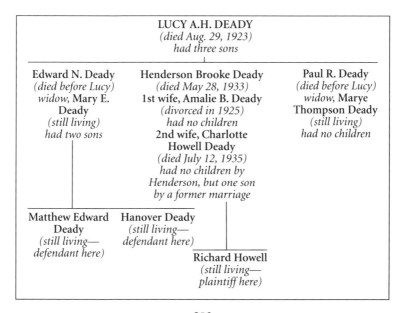

Judge Fee rendered three decisions: the first overruled a motion to dismiss the complaint; the second ruled on various questions regarding the evidence presented; and the third determined the merits of the case and made findings largely in favor of the plaintiff. In so doing, the judge expounded at length on the rules of law involved, and his opinions are classic with respect to the construction of future interest provisions. The defendants appealed and the plaintiff cross-appealed, but the case was settled by agreement after it was argued before the Ninth Circuit Court of Appeals and before a decision was rendered.

∾

# ADMIRALTY

While probate matters are rarely brought before the federal courts, admiralty cases are standard fare, as we saw in Chapter 2. Of the many admiralty cases handled by the Oregon federal court in this period, one of the most dramatic was *The Iowa*.[106] The *Iowa* was a vessel of the States Steamship Company, which had its headquarters in Portland. On January 11, 1936, she left Portland, loaded lumber at Longview, Washington, and proceeded down the Columbia River, bound for California. On the following day, in a terrific storm, she struck Peacock Spit, a shoal extending out from the Washington shore at the mouth of the Columbia, and was lost. It was the type of accident that has caused the mouth of the Columbia to be called "the graveyard of the Pacific."

Federal statutes provide that a shipowner is not liable for faulty navigation or perils of the sea if the owner has exercised due diligence to make the vessel seaworthy.[107] In such cases, the owner's liability may be limited to the value of the vessel and its pending freight charges if the loss results from acts done without the owner's knowledge.[108]

In the case of the *Iowa*, the owner of the vessel petitioned for exoneration from and limitation of liability. The *Iowa* case was referred to Robert F. Maguire, who was later to be a judge at the Nurnburg War Crimes Trials, as commissioner. Maguire conducted an extensive trial with over 5,000 pages of testimony and found that the ship was seaworthy in all respects except two: (1) the master did not have the up-to-date local Notices to Mariners showing condition of the aids to navigation at the Columbia Bar, and (2) the ship lacked a communicating system with its emergency steering gear, as required by a recent order of a federal board.

Maguire denied the *Iowa*'s owner exoneration because lack of seaworthiness prevents exoneration, even if it has no causal connection with the accident. However, he allowed limitation of liability because the cause of the accident was the master's negligence in taking his ship across the bar under the circumstances, and this was without the knowledge of the owner. The items of unseaworthiness that prevented exoneration did not prevent limitation of liability because they were not the cause of the loss. The report of the commissioner was adopted in an opinion by Judge Fee, and no appeal was taken.

Another prominent admiralty case of this period was *Babbidge & Holt v. The Hawaiian Planter*.[109] The *Hawaiian Planter* was a steamship owned by Matson Navigation Company that was heading down the Columbia River on its way to Honolulu. The *Columbia Queen* was a tug represented by Babbidge and Holt that was heading upstream in the Columbia, pushing the barge *Racquette*, which was loaded with artillery shells being taken to the Umatilla, Oregon Ordnance Depot. At a point about 15 miles above Astoria, the vessels had collided and the barge had broken loose from the tug, turned over, and sunk. The tug and barge interests sued the *Hawaiian Planter* and its owner, who cross-sued for damages to the ship. The United States, which was owner of the barge's cargo, proceeded against all vessel interests, as well as the pilot of the ship, for cargo damage.

At the time of the collision, the vessels had been able to see each other. The *Hawaiian Planter* had signalled for a port-to-port passing (*i.e.*, each on the left of the other), but the *Columbia Queen* had not responded because its whistle was out of order. Instead, the tug had veered across the course of the ship, and the starboard side of the barge had struck the bow of the ship, which had come to a stop.

The evidence concerning the vessels' positions relative to the channel was in conflict, but in a comprehensive opinion Judge Solomon determined that the collision was solely the fault of the *Columbia Queen*, which was guilty of gross negligence, and that the faults of the *Hawaiian Planter*, if any, were trivial and not a cause of the collision.

A different type of admiralty case was *Spokane, Portland & Seattle Rwy. v. The Fairport*,[110] which arose out of a collision between the ship and the plaintiff's railroad bridge across the Columbia River. The ship had been moored at Vancouver, Washington, and it was being moved to a dock in Portland, which required passing through the draw of the bridge, downstream from the Vancouver moorage. The tug *Portland* was assisting in the move, and because of confusion in orders from the ship to the tug, the ship was being taken stern first through the bridge instead of being turned so as to proceed bow first. In this position, it struck and damaged the bridge. The case was tried by Judge Solomon, who found that the negligence of the ship (through its master and pilot) was the cause of the collision.

A significant part of maritime litigation involves injuries to or death of workers on or about the water. The Jones Act[111] makes applicable to seamen the same federal laws as apply to injuries of railway employees (*e.g.*, the Federal Employers' Liability Act);[112] the Death on High Seas Act[113] gives a remedy for death occurring beyond a marine league from shore; and the Longshore and Harbor Workers' Compensation Act[114] provides an administrative compensation system for certain maritime employees. The line between maritime and land-based injuries is not always clear, and from time to time questions have arisen as to the interplay of federal law and state law such as the Oregon Employers' Liability Act[115] or the Oregon Wrongful Death Act.[116]

In *Sanderson v. Sause Bros.*,[117] a man, apparently a longshoreman, died on navigable waters within the territorial limits of the State of Oregon, due to the unseaworthiness of a barge. The dead man was employed by the defendant corporation but not by the defendant partnership, which was insured under the Longshore and Harbor Workers' Compensation Act and thus was immune from suit. In deciding the case, Judge Solomon held that the dead man's personal representative could recover damages from the corporation under the Oregon Wrongful Death Act, but not under the Oregon Employers' Liability Act, which could not constitutionally be applied because it had a higher standard of care than the general maritime law.

In *Hess Adm'n. v. United States*,[118] several workers who were engaged in repairing Bonneville Dam as employees of an independent contractor, died when their tug and barge capsized in the turbulent waters below the dam. The administrator of one of them sued the United States under the Federal Tort Claims Act,[119] claiming that the operators of the dam should have diminished the flow or warned the contractor of the extreme danger the situation entailed. The case was tried before Judge Solomon, who held (as he had in the *Sanderson* case) that the Oregon Employers' Liability Act did not apply, but that the Oregon Wrongful Death Act could be invoked. He held, however, that the plaintiff had failed to prove negligence on the part of the government. This opinion was affirmed by the Ninth Circuit, but the United States Supreme Court, by a divided opinion, held that there was no constitutional inhibition against applying the Oregon Employers' Liability Act in a maritime death. On remand, the Ninth Circuit held that there was a co-mingling of functions between the deceased and employees of the government, so that the Employers' Liability Act did apply, and the case was remanded to the district court to determine whether the government had fulfilled the duty of care required by that act. Judge Solomon took additional testimony, but before he announced a decision, the case was settled by agreement.[120] Some years later, the rationale of the *Hess* case was repudiated by the United States Supreme Court in *Moragne v. States Marine Lines.*[121]

∿
# TRANSPORTATION

Oregon's geographical location makes transportation of great importance. The markets for its products and its sources of manufactured goods are frequently distant by half a continent or more. And because much of the relevant transportation is in interstate commerce, the law of transportation is usually federal in character.

## Rate Cases

During this period, there was a substantial business in hauling grain from interior points in eastern Oregon to Portland. Initially most of the grain moved by rail, and a part then was shipped overseas or to points in other states. Typically the intrastate rail rate was lower than the interstate rate, and when the shipment was originally billed at the intrastate rate and later moved into interstate or foreign commerce, the railroads sometimes sued to recover the difference between the two rates.

In a series of cases, Judge Fee held that the question of whether the shipment was interstate commerce or not depended on the intent of the shipper at the time of the initial shipment, which was a question of fact. In other words, if the shipper knew from the start that a shipment was ultimately destined for interstate commerce, the interstate rate was due; but if the shipper did not know the ultimate destination and the grain was to be held in Portland to fill orders not then known, only the intrastate rate could be charged.[122]

When the Bonneville Dam and Locks opened the upper Columbia River to water transportation, the barge lines captured much traffic that had formerly moved by rail. The typical barge movement involved hauling petroleum products upstream and grain from the interior to down-stream ports (using separately compartmented barges). The two-way haul was necessary for economical operation. The grain from elevators or farm storage was hauled to river ports by truck — either private or common carrier.

In an attempt to meet this competition, the railroads filed tariffs with reduced rates on petroleum, and the barge and truck lines protested the reductions. Under federal law, the Interstate Commerce Commission (ICC) had power to regulate both maximum and minimum rail rates,[123] but it had no power over water carrier rates on petroleum because of the exemption for bulk commodities,[124] nor over motor carrier rates on grain because of the exemption for agricultural commodities.[125] The rates of private or proprietary carriers were of course not subject to regulation.

The ICC had power over railroad *intrastate* rates, insofar as they affected *interstate* commerce,[126] but it had no power over *intrastate* rates of motor carriers.[127] Likewise, the ICC had no power over intrastate rates of water carriers,[128] but in the case of *Inland Nav. Co. v. Flagg*,[129] Judge Solomon in an unreported decision held that the barge traffic in petroleum and grain on the Columbia River was in interstate commerce, so as to be beyond state jurisdiction in any event.

The result was that the rail rates were subject to complete regulation, while those of water carriers were completely unregulated. The rates of common carrier trucks were subject to regulation for petroleum, but not for grain. However, most of the petroleum was moving by unregulated private or proprietary trucks. Therefore, the trucks and barge lines were able to protest the rail rate reductions and obtain their suspension, without being subject to similar action where their own rates were concerned.

In the case of *Scandrett v. United States*,[130] reduced railroad rates on petroleum were protested, and the ICC first suspended them and then ordered them canceled. While the ICC found that the rates were fully compensatory and did not find a violation of any particular provision of the Interstate Commerce Act, it required a higher rail rate in order to protect the water carriers from rail competition. The railroads appealed to a three-judge court (District Judges Fee and McColloch and Circuit Judge Haney), which affirmed the commission, with Judge Fee dissenting. On appeal, the United States Supreme Court affirmed *per curiam* (without a signed opinion).

In the meantime, a major oil company built a pipeline from Salt Lake City, Utah, to Pasco, Washington, which was later extended to Spokane,

Washington. In an attempt to meet the competition of the pipeline, as well as that of the barge-truck combination, the railroads again tried to reduce their rates, and again the reduced rail rates were protested by the barge operators and the motor common carriers.[131]

Initially, the rates were suspended by the ICC, and the suspension was voluntarily extended by the railroads. After a hearing, Division 2 held the rates to be reasonable, but just before they were to go into effect the truck and barge companies obtained a temporary restraining order from Judge McColloch, in the case of *Pacific Inland Tariff Bureau, et al v. United States, et al,*[132] enjoining the railroads from using the lower rates. Thereafter, the full commission sustained the new rates, and that order was attacked by a supplemental complaint in the injunction case. Judge Solomon, writing for a three-judge court consisting of Circuit Judge Pope, Judge McColloch, and himself, made the injunction permanent, largely on the ground that the ICC order was not supported by adequate findings concerning the National Transportation Policy.

Thereafter, a motion for reconsideration was made, which was denied by an opinion dated September 12, 1955, also written by Judge Solomon.[133] The final decree, entered December 9, 1955, affirmed the ICC with respect to the westbound rates, but as to east-bound rates the proceeding was sent back to the ICC for further consideration. As to the latter rates, the restraining order was kept in effect until 15 days after further Commission action. After additional consideration, the ICC again held the rates to be reasonable — by an order dated November 4, 1957.

In the meantime, the railroads had faced a dilemma because the only rates lawfully on file had been enjoined and if new rates were filed, the whole proceeding could become moot. Therefore, the railroads continued to charge the old, higher rates. After the new, lower rates were finally sustained, at least one shipper claimed as reparations the difference between the higher rate paid and the lower rate which was on file at the time of its shipments. Reparations were allowed by the commission and were sustained by the U.S. District Court for Montana in *Humble Oil Co. v. Great Northern, et al.*[134]

Meanwhile, on the state level, the railroads had also tried to reduce their *intrastate* rates on petroleum. At that time, the public utility commissioner of Oregon claimed and exercised the power to suspend railroad rate reductions. By successive orders during the period 1930–1940, he had suspended numerous rail rate reductions, although in no case were the rates held to be improper. Finally, in *Union Pacific RR v. Bean,*[135] it was held that the public utility commissioner did not have power to suspend rail rate reductions; and in *Southern Pacific v. Heltzel,*[136] it was held that the commissioner had no power to prescribe minimum rail rates. However, during most of this time, the railroads were prevented from charging the lower rates that were ultimately held to be proper and, as a result, lost much of the petroleum and grain traffic to the barge lines.

## Railroad Line Extensions

For many years it was the dream of some people to have an east-west rail line across central Oregon. In the 1880s this vision sparked the ill-fated venture of T. Egenton Hogg to build a line across the Cascade Mountains (near the butte which still bears his name at Santiam Pass) to connect with his line from Corvallis to Newport.

When the Southern Pacific and Union Pacific were under common ownership, they planned that the Southern Pacific would build eastward from Eugene to a connection with the Union Pacific, which was building westward from Ontario. This plan was aborted when the U.S. Supreme Court in 1913 divorced the Union Pacific and Southern Pacific on anti-trust grounds,[137] although the Southern Pacific did build its Natron cut-off over the Cascade Mountains from Eugene to Klamath Falls by way of Crescent Lake.

The Transportation Act of 1920[138] empowered the Interstate Commerce Commission to require a rail carrier to provide reasonable and adequate facilities and to extend its lines, provided that such facilities and extensions were reasonably required in the interest of public convenience and necessity and would not impair the ability of the carrier to perform its duty to the public.

Proceeding under this act, the Public Service Commission of Oregon (predecessor of the present Public Utility Commission) filed a complaint with the ICC against various railroads to compel the construction of a line connecting the Union Pacific line at Crane, Oregon (near Burns in Harney County) with the Southern Pacific line at or near Crescent Lake. The Idaho Public Utilities Commission intervened in support of the application. The railroads objected on the grounds that the central Oregon territory would not produce enough traffic to warrant the investment and that they had not previously undertaken to serve that territory.

After investigation and hearing, the ICC ordered the Oregon-Washington Railroad & Navigation Company (a part of the Union Pacific system) to extend its line from its station at Crane to a connection with the Southern Pacific line at or near Crescent Lake, a distance of some 185 miles; and it authorized the Union Pacific to finance the construction.[139]

The OWR&N and SP objected and appealed the decision to a three-judge district court consisting of Circuit Judges Rudkin and Wilbur and District Judge McNary. That court enjoined the ICC order[140] on the grounds that the 1920 act authorized the ICC to require a railroad extension only into such territory as it had already undertaken to serve, and if an extension into new territory were required it would be an unconstitutional taking of the carrier's property.

The Interstate Commerce Commission appealed the case to the United States Supreme Court, which affirmed the district court, with Justices Cordozo, Brandeis, and Stone dissenting.[141] The majority of the Supreme Court held that the Commission was not authorized to require

*Plans to build an east-west rail line across central Oregon became the subject of disputes between the Public Service and Interstate Commerce commissions and the railroads. The resulting court case reached the district court, whose decision was appealed to the U.S. Supreme Court. (Oregon Historical Society Negative #25883)*

a rail carrier to extend its line into new territory not previously served and to do so would raise constitutional questions that should be avoided. The dissenting justices thought that Congress had given power to the ICC to require a rail carrier to extend its lines into new territory, so as to effect a national transportation system, even though the carrier was unwilling to do so. They also thought that deference should be given to the commission's finding that the extension was economically justified. So ended the dream of a cross-state rail line.

∾

# CHOICE OF LAWS

In 1938 the Supreme Court decided the landmark case of *Erie Railroad v. Tompkins*,[142] which held that when exercising jurisdiction based on diversity of citizenship and not acting in matters governed by the federal Constitution or acts of Congress, the federal courts should apply the laws of the states in which they sit. This made a fundamental change in federal jurisprudence and many times required the federal courts to anticipate what a state court would decide on questions that had never been presented to it.

One such case came before Judge McColloch in the case of *Harris v. Traglio*.[143] Mrs. Harris, her husband, and minor son (all residents of California) were involved in a collision with a truck in Oregon. The son was driving and there was some evidence of negligence on his part.

The car was community property of Mr. and Mrs. Harris and under California law the husband was the manager of the community property and the cause of action for the wife's injury was also community property. Oregon was not a community property state, and under Oregon law a wife was fully emancipated and could recover for her injury in her own right.

The defendant contended that the son's negligence was imputed to the father (for whom he was an agent) and that because the father was the manager of the community and would share in the proceeds of the cause of action, the son's contributory negligence should bar her recovery of damages (contributory negligence being then a complete bar). Judge McColloch refused to submit to the jury the question of the son's contributory negligence, and the jury returned a verdict for Mrs. Harris. Judge McColloch then denied a motion for new trial.

On appeal, the Ninth Circuit (Judges Garrecht and Haney) affirmed McColloch's decision on the grounds that: (1) Oregon law determined whether or not there was a cause of action, and under Oregon law the son's negligence would not be imputed to the mother unless she exercised control over him; and (2) Oregon law also governed the ownership of the cause of action, which under Oregon law was hers alone.

Judge Stephens dissented on the ground that even though under Oregon law the husband's negligence (through his agent) would not bar the wife's recovery on the basis of the marital relationship alone, nevertheless the Oregon courts would apply the rule that one may not profit by his own wrong and would bar recovery where the husband would be a direct beneficiary of the cause of action.

∾

# CRIMINAL CASES

Before the Eighteenth (Prohibition) Amendment was repealed in 1933, prosecutions for violation of the National Prohibition Act were a significant part of the federal court business. But when the Eighteenth Amendment was repealed by the Twenty-first Amendment, there was no savings clause, which would preserve pending cases, and the Supreme Court of the United States held that pending prosecutions for acts committed prior to repeal were automatically rendered invalid.[144] This brought such prosecutions to an abrupt end, if they had not already been discontinued.

Even with the repeal of prohibition, criminal cases still constituted a significant part of the court's work. Relatively few such cases resulted in published opinions, but several were of more than passing interest.

In *United States v. Vlahos*,[145] Judge Fee discussed at length the right of officers to search premises in connection with arrests for operating an unlicensed distillery and possessing untaxed liquor; he also denied all the motions to suppress the evidence and convicted all the defendants.

In *United States v. Boylen*,[146] the defendant was indicted for selling sheep that had previously been mortgaged to a Production Credit Association. He claimed that because of a brain disorder (arachnoiditis), he had suffered a complete loss of memory of events occurring during the period covered by the indictment and for several years before. On a motion for stay of proceedings, Judge McColloch ordered a full hearing on the question of the defendant's competency to stand trial. When the hearing was subsequently held, the defendant was discharged.

In *United States v. DeMaurez*,[147] Judge Fee considered and denied an application for a reduced sentence by a man who had a long record of offenses and who had pursued "a deluge of correspondence, petitions and pleas for executive clemency addressed to the United States Attorney and to the court, besides numbers of motions, petitions for writs of habeas corpus, motion for a correction of sentence and numerous other legal proceedings in every available court."

∾

# INDIAN LITIGATION

The Oregon federal court has been the scene of much litigation over matters relating to the Indian tribes, particularly with respect to hunting and fishing rights under the early treaties,[148] property rights after the termination acts,[149] and criminal cases involving questions of state, federal, or tribal jurisdiction.[150] Some of these cases are discussed elsewhere in this work, and not many of them occurred during the period covered by this chapter (1927 to 1950). However, a few such cases fell within this period, and they helped to set the stage for much of the later litigation over Indian rights.

## Fishing Rights

By a series of treaties commencing in 1855, various tribes relinquished title to their aboriginal lands, and in return they were guaranteed the right to take fish "at all usual and accustomed places," in common with citizens of the territory or of the United States. One of the traditional fishing sites was at Celilo Falls on the Columbia River. By a series of conveyances, legal title to the property at that location was acquired by Brookfield Fisheries, Inc.

At a particular point in the Celilo Falls, where a portion of the river was compressed into a narrow channel, Brookfield constructed a fish wheel with a fishway and wing dams to concentrate the migrating salmon into their trap. A major fishing industry developed, and the Indians were excluded from the site.

In *United States v. Brookfield Fisheries, Inc.*,[151] the United States, as trustee and guardian for the Indians, brought suit against Brookfield to restrain it from prohibiting access by the Indians to the fishing site and from preventing the Indians from taking fish there in common with other citizens.

Judge Fee weighed the extensive evidence, including testimony of elderly Indians and early settlers; concluded that Indian usage of the particular site was established; and prescribed a line of demarcation between the exclusive property of defendants and that on which the defendants and the Indians had fishing rights in common.

## Sale of Tribal or Allotted Lands

In the post-World War II era the policy of the United States toward the Indian tribes went through one of its many changes,[152] and Congress enacted laws terminating federal control over various tribes and reservations. For example, as applied to the Klamaths in southern Oregon, the termination act gave each adult member of the tribe an election between withdrawing from the tribe and having his interest in the tribal property commuted to money to be paid to him or, on the other hand, remaining in the tribe and participating in a non-governmental tribal management plan. The tribal property was to be appraised and sufficient sold to pay the claims of the withdrawing Indians, and a management plan was to be prepared for the remaining Indians and property.[153]

A substantial number of Klamath Indians elected to withdraw, and some of them, being unaccustomed to handling much money, were taken advantage of and squandered their new-found wealth.[154]

Even before the termination acts, Indian lands were targets for the unscrupulous. Under the general allotment acts,[155] certain tribal lands could be allotted to individual Indians, and such lands could then be sold, subject to some restrictions. One of the restrictions was that allotted land could be sold to an Indian at its appraised value, but a non-Indian could buy it only after it had been offered at public sale.

In the case of *Siniscal v. United States*,[156] allotted lands with extensive timber had been appraised at a figure the court found to be grossly inadequate. An arrangement was made for an Indian to purchase the land at the appraised value from the heirs of the original allottees, and immediately to deed it over to a non-Indian, with the Indian "straw-person" to be paid well for her services. This scheme having been carried out and discovered, the government, in its capacity as trustee for the heirs of the allottees, sued to set aside the transactions and recover the lands.

Judge Solomon set aside the transactions as void because of fraud and ordered return of the consideration to the white purchasers. On appeal, the Ninth Circuit affirmed Judge Solomon insofar as the transactions were cancelled; but it held that the government would not be required to restore the consideration, and any refund would have to come from the Indian beneficial owners.

Subsequent attempts by the white purchasers to recover their payment were only partially successful.[157]

# CONCLUSION

In the period covered by this chapter, the country and the state of Oregon were experiencing great turmoil, and profound changes were taking place. It was inevitable that this turmoil and these changes would be reflected in the work of the federal court, as this chapter illustrates.

History does not always divide itself into neat pigeonholes, but it is fitting that this chapter spans the service of Judge Fee on the district court. He was a dominant figure from the standpoint of both the force of his personality and his contribution to the jurisprudence of the court. He was truly a legend in his own time, as well as in the history of the court.

## NOTES

1. H. H. McCown, Article in *Oregon Benchmarks*, the bulletin of the U.S. District Court of Oregon Historical Society, hereinafter cited as *Benchmarks* (Fall 1988).

2. W. M. Dale, Article in *Benchmarks* (Fall 1986).

3. M. Montague, Article in *Benchmarks* (Winter 1987).

4. *The Oregonian*, June 6, 10, 12, and 27, 1950.

5. See articles by O. M. Panner and S. H. Munro in *Benchmarks* (Spring 1987).

6. See article by C. E. Coulter in *Benchmarks* (Winter 1987).

7. Excerpted in part from remarks by R. B. Kester at the rededication of the federal courthouse, reprinted in *Benchmarks* (Fall 1985).

8. Article in *Benchmarks* (Summer 1989).

9. 28 U.S.C. sec. 117.

10. Local Rule 105-1.

11. Oregon State Bar, *Report of Committee on Federal Practice and Procedure*, 1950, at 50-59.

12. Ch. 890, Or. Laws 1977.

13. See *Byers v. Clark & Wilson*, 27 F. Supp. 302 (D. Or. 1939); *Burton v. Weyerhauser*, 1 F.R.D. 571 (D. Or. 1941).

14. Bar report, *supra* note 11.

15. J. A. Fee, *The Proposed New Rules for Uniform Procedure in the Federal District Courts*, XVI Or. Law Rev. 103-120 (1937);

Fee, *The Lost Horizon in Pleading Under the Federal Rules of Civil Procedure*, 48 Colum. L. Rev. 491 (1948);

Fee, *Justice in Search of a Handmaiden*, II U. Fla. L. Rev. 175 (1949).

16. *Montgomery Ward v. NP Terminal Co.*, 128 F. Supp. 475 (D. Or. 1953) and 128 F. Supp. 520 (D. Or. 1954).

17. *NLRB v. Montgomery Ward.* 133 F.2d 676 (9th Cir. 1943).

18. See 128 F. Supp. at 483, n. 2.

19. 128 F. Supp. 475.

20. 128 F. Supp. 520.

21. 128 F. Supp. at 483-84.

22. 28 U.S.C. sec. 1404(a).

23. *United States v. Bink*, 74 F. Supp. 603 (D. Or. 1947).

24. *In re Schwindt*, 74 F. Supp. 618 (D. Or. 1947).

25. *Levine v. United States*, 182 F.2d 556, 558 (8th Cir. 1950), *cert. denied*, 340 U.S. 921 (1951); *United States v. Gallagher*, 183 F.2d 342, 345 (3d Cir. 1950), *cert. denied*, 340 U.S. 913 (1951); *Earnest v. United States*, 198 F.2d 561, 562 (6th Cir. 1952); *Hilderbrand v. United States*, 304 F.2d 716, 717 (10th Cir. 1962); *Yeloushan v. United States*, 339 F.2d 533, 535 (5th Cir. 1964).

26. *United States v. Bishop*, 76 F. Supp. 866 (D. Or. 1948); *United States v. Tollett*, 76 F. Supp. 871 (D. Or. 1948).

27. *Supernant v. Great Northern*, J.R. 27278; *Putnam v. Southern Pacific*, J.R. 27280; See also *Petition of Mundorff*, 8 F.R.D. 7 (D. Or. 1948).

28. *In Re Portland Electric Power Co.*, 97 F. Supp. 857 (D. Or. 1951) *aff'd sub nom. White v. Portland Electric Power Co.*, 162 F.2d 618, 624 (9th Cir. 1947). For opinions dealing with other aspects of the same matter, see: 97 F. Supp. 873 (D. Or. 1940); 97 F. Supp. 875 (D. Or. 1943); 97 F. Supp. 877 (D. Or. 1943); 97 F. Supp.885 (D. Or. 1943); 97 F. Supp. 886 (D. Or. 1944); 97 F. Supp. 887 (D. Or. 1944); 97 F. Supp. 889 (D. Or. 1944); 97 F. Supp. 895 (D. Or. 1946); 97 F. Supp. 896 (D. Or. 1947); 97 F. Supp. 897 (D. Or. 1947); 97 F. Supp. 899 (D. Or. 1947); 97 F. Supp. 903 (D. Or. 1947); 97 F. Supp. 918 (D. Or. 1948); *Delzell v. Flagg*, 97 F. Supp. 877 (D. Or. 1943); *Portland Gen. Electric v. Raver*, 97 F. Supp. 892 (D. Or. 1946); *Delzell v. Raver*, 97 F. Supp. 893 (D. Or. 1946).

29. 97 F. Supp. at 857-58.

30. See for example: *Morgan v. Portland Traction Co.*, 222 Or. 614, 331 P.2d 344 (1958); *Portland Traction Co. v. Hill*, 222 Or. 636, 352 P.2d 552 (1960); *Portland Traction Co. v. Hill*, 231 Or. 354, 372 P.2d 501 (1962); *Rose City Transit v. City of Portland*, 18 Or. App. 369, 525 P.2d 1325 (1974), *aff'd as modified*, 271 Or. 588, 533 P.2d 339 (1975).

31. *In re Portex Oil Co.*, 30 F. Supp. 138 (D. Or. 1939), *aff'd sub nom. Clark Bros. v. Portex Oil Co.*, 113 F.2d 45 (9th Cir. 1940).

32. *In re Ostlind Mfg. Co.*, 19 F. Supp. 836 (D. Or. 1937),

33. *In re Western Bond and Mortgage Co.*, 44 F. Supp. 89 (D. Or. 1941), *aff'd sub nom. Bank of California v. McBride*, 132 F.2d 769 (9th Cir. 1943). See also *McBride v.*

*Farrington,* 60 F. Supp. 92 (D. Or. 1945) aff'd, 156 F.2d 971 (9th Cir. 1946).

34. *Willamette Valley Lumber Co. v. Watzek,* 5 F. Supp. 689 (D. Or. 1934).

35. *Schechter v. U.S.,* 295 U.S. 495 (1935).

36. *Hudson-Duncan v. Wallace,* 21 F. Supp. 295 (D. Or. 1937).

37. *Wallace v. Hudson-Duncan,* 98 F.2d 985 (9th Cir. 1938).

38. *U.S. v. Butler,* 297 U.S. 1 (1936).

39. Excerpted in part from articles by T. B. Stoel in *Benchmarks* (Fall and Winter 1988).

40. *U.S. v. Hirabayashi,* 46 F. Supp. 657 (W.D. Wash. 1942).

41. *U.S. v. Minoru Yasui,* 48 F. Supp. 40 (D. Or. 1942).

42. B. Hosokawa, *JACL: In Quest of Justice* 257 (1982). See also L. Kessler, *A Legacy of Success,* The Oregonian, Dec. 7, 1988.

43. *Hirabayashi v. U.S.,* 320 U.S. 81, 85 (1943).

44. *Yasui v. U.S.,* 320 U.S. 115, 116 (1943).

45. *United States v. Yasui,* 51 F. Supp. 234 (D. Or. 1943).

46. *Korematsu v. U.S.,* 323 U.S. 214 (1944).

47. *Ex Parte Mitsuye Endo,* 323 U.S. 283 (1944).

48. Ch. 814, 62 Stat 1231 (1948).

49. Ch. 531, 70 Stat 513 (1956).

50. Pub. L. No. 96-317, 94 Stat 964 (1980); text reprinted in note following 50 U.S.C.A. sec. 1981.

51. *Korematsu v. United States,* 584 F. Supp. 1406 (N.D. Cal. 1984); *Hirabayashi v. United States,* 828 F.2d 591 (9th Cir. 1987).

52. *Yasui v. United States,* 772 F.2d 1496 (9th Cir. 1985).

53. See *Hirabayashi v. United States,* 828 F.2d 591, 594 n. 4 (9th Cir. 1987).

54. See stories in *The Oregonian,* July 30 and Aug. 4 and 5, 1990.

55. *United States v. Scheurer,* 55 F. Supp. 243 (D. Or. 1944).

56. *Scheurer v. United States,* 150 F.2d 535 (9th Cir. 1945).

57. *Schneiderman v. United States,* 320 U.S. 118 (1943); *Baumgartner v. United States,* 322 U.S. 665 (1944).

58. *In Re Oppenheimer,* 61 F. Supp. 403 (D. Or. 1945).

59. See for example: *The Pietro Campanello* and *The Euro,* 44 F. Supp. 348 (D. Md. 1942), 47 F. Supp. 374 (D. Md. 1942), 73 F. Supp. 18 (D. Md. 1947); *The Mongoia,* 73 F. Supp. 17 (S.D. Tex. 1947); *Bersio v. United States, Pieraccinni v. United States, Schiaffino v. United States,* 124 F.2d 310 (4th Cir. 1941); *Marchese v. United States,* 126 F.2d 671 (5th Cir. 1942); *United States v. Scaleggeri,* 126 F.2d 1023 (3d Cir. 1942); *Guigni v. United States,* 127 F.2d 786 (1st Cir. 1942); *United States v. Antoinetta,* 153 F.2d 138 (3d Cir. 1945).

60. *United States v. Polonia,* 77 F. Supp. 768 (D. Or. 1941) *aff'd sub nom. Polonia v. United States,* 131 F.2d 679 (9th Cir. 1942).

61. *The Leme,* 77 F. Supp. 773 (D. Or. 1948).

62. *Falbo v. United States.* 320 U.S. 549 (1944).

63. *The Oregonian,* Dec. 16, 1943, at 7.

64. *Ex Parte Kelley,* 48 F. Supp. 816 (D. Or. 1943).

65. *United States v. Charito,* 69 F. Supp. 317 (D. Or. 1946).

66. *Bowles v. Hudspeth,* 62 F. Supp. 803 (D. Or. 1945).

67. *Bowles v. Richards*, 63 F. Supp. 946 (D. Or. 1945).

68. *Bowles v. Dashiel*, 72 F. Supp. 219 (D. Or. 1946), *rev'd*, 161 F.2d 612 (9th Cir. 1947).

69. See *Bowles v. Wheeler*, 152 F.2d 34 (9th Cir. 1945); *Bowles v. Richards*, *supra* note 67; *Porter v. Wright*, 69 F. Supp. 46 (D. Or. 1946); *Porter v. Rushlight*, 69 F. Supp. 58 (D. Or. 1946); *Porter v. Fleishman*, 71 F. Supp. 33 (D. Or. 1947); *Bowles v. Dashiel*, *supra* note 68; *Bowles v. West Side Lumber Co.*, 72 F. Supp. 218 (D. Or. 1945).

70. See *Bowles v. Hudspeth*, *supra* note 66; *Bowles v. Levy*, 66 F. Supp. 97 (D. Or. 1946); *Porter v. Rushlight*, *supra* note 69; *Porter v. Wright*, *supra* note 69.

71. See *Bowles v. NW Poultry & Dairy Products Co.*, 153 F.2d 32 (9th cir. 1946); *Bowles v. Bronson*, 63 F. Supp. 189 (D. Or. 1945); *Bowles v. Abendroth*, 64 F. Supp. 704 (D. Or. 1946), *cf. Bowles v. Abendroth*, 151 F.2d 407 (9th Cir. 1945); *Porter v. Roach*, 69 F. Supp. 56 (D. Or. 1946); *Cook v. United States*, 69 F. Supp. 445 (D. Or. 1946).

72. *United States v. Evans*, 69 F. Supp. 676 (D. Or. 1947); *United States v. Sagner*, 71 F. Supp. 52 (D. Or. 1947), *rev'd*, 331 U.S. 791 (1947).

73. *Cook v. United States*, *supra* note 71; *Porter v. Wilson*, 69 F. Supp. 447 (D. Or. 1947); *United States v. Evans*, *supra* note 72; *Bowles v. West Side Lumber Co.*, 72 F. Supp. 218 (D. Or. 1945).

74. *United States v. Oregon State Medical Society*, 95 F. Supp. 103 (D. Or. 1950). See *Oregonian*, Sept. 29, 1950, at 1.

75. *United States v. Oregon State Medical Society*, 343 U.S. 326 (1952).

76. *Columbia River Packers Ass'n v. Hinton*, 34 F. Supp. 970 (D. Or. 1939).

77. *Hinton v. Columbia River Packers Ass'n*, 117 F.2d 310 (9th Cir. 1941).

78. *Columbia River Packers Ass'n v. Hinton*, 315 U.S. 143 (1942).

79. *Hinton v. Columbia River Packers Ass'n*, 131 F.2d 88 (9th Cir. 1942).

80. *United States v. Dairy Co-op Ass'n*, 49 F. Supp. 475 (D. Or. 1943).

81. But see *California-Oregon Power Co. v. Beaver Portland Cement Co.*, 73 F.2d 555 (9th Cir. 1934), *aff'd*, 295 U.S. 142 (1935).

82. *United States v. Oregon*, 295 U.S. 1 (1935).

83. *United States v. Carey*, 143 F.2d 445 (9th Cir. 1944).

84. *United States v. Otley*, 34 F. Supp. 182 (D. Or. 1940), *aff'd* in part, 127 F.2d 988 (9th Cir. 1942); see also 116 F.2d 958 (9th Cir. 1940).

85. *Brown v. N.Y. Life Ins. Co.*, 58 F. Supp. 252 (D. Or. 1944), *aff'd*, 152 F.2d 246 (9th Cir. 1945); for related litigation, see *Fine v. Harney County National Bank*, 181 Or. 411, 170 P.2d 365 (1947).

86. See *French-Glenn Live Stock Co. v. Springer*, 35 Or. 312, 58 P. 102 (1899), *aff'd*, 185 U.S. 47 (1902).

87. *Clark v. United States*, 109 F. Supp. 213 (D. Or. 1952), *aff'd*, 218 F.2d 446 (9th Cir. 1954).

88. 33 U.S.C. sec. 702(c).

89. *Ure v. U.S.* and *White v. U.S.*, 93 F. Supp. 779 (D. Or. 1950), *aff'd*, as to *White*, 193 F.2d 505 (9th Cir. 1952), *rev'd* as to *Ure*, 225 F.2d 709 (9th Cir. 1955).

90. 28 U.S.C. sec. 1346(b).

91. *Rylands v. Fletcher*, LR 1 Exch. 265; LR 3 HL 330 (1868).

92. *Dalehite v. U.S.*, 346 U.S. 15 (1953).

93. See, e.g., *Union Pacific R.R. v. Vale Irr. Dist.*, 253 F. Supp. 251 (D. Or. 1966).

94. See, e.g., *Livesley v. Johnston*, 45 Or. 30, 76 P. 13 (1904); *Livesley v. Heise*, 45 Or. 148, 76 P. 952 (1904); *Lachmund v. Lope Sing*, 54 Or. 106, 102 P. 598 (1909); *Daniels v. Morris*, 65 Or. 289, 130 P. 397 (1913); *Wigan v. La Follett*, 84 Or. 488, 165 P. 579 (1917); *Seidenberg v. Tautfest*, 155 Or. 420, 64 P.2d 534 (1937); *Steiner v. Hill*, 191 Or. 391, 226 P.2d 307 (1951).

95. *Loewi v. Geschwill*, 186 F.2d 849 (9th Cir. 1951), *cert. denied*, 342 U.S. 817 (1951); *Loewi v. Smith*, 186 F.2d 858 (9th Cir. 1951), *cert. denied*, 342 U.S. 817 (1951); *Haas v. Wellman*, 186 F.2d 862 (9th Cir. 1951).

96. *Martin v. Reynolds Metals*, 135 F. Supp. 379 (D. Or. 1952), *aff'd*, 258 F.2d 321 (9th Cir. 1958), *cert. denied*, 358 U.S. 840 (1958); *Wand v. Reynolds Metals*, 195 F. Supp. 730 (D. Or. 1961), *rev'd* 308 F2d 504 (9th Cir. 1962); *Reynolds Metals v. Lampert*, 316 F.2d 272 (9th Cir. 1963), 324 F.2d 465 (9th Cir. 1963), *cert. denied*, 376 U.S. 910 (1964); See also 25 F.R.D. 175; *Martin v. Reynolds Metals*, 224 F. Supp. 978 (D. Or. 1963), *aff'd*, 337 F.2d 780 (9th Cir. 1964); *Fairview Farms v. Reynolds*, D. Or. (unpublished); See also *Martin v. Reynolds*, 221 Or. 86, 342 P.2d 790 (1959), *cert denied*, 362 U.S. 918 (1960).

97. *Oregon Auto Ins. v. U.S. Fidelity & Guaranty*, 195 F.2d 958 (9th Cir. 1952).

98. *Lamb-Weston v. Oregon Auto*, 219 Or. 110, 341 P.2d 110 (1959).

99. See *Mutual of Enumclaw v. Hambleton*, 84 Or. App. 343, 733 P.2d 948 (1987) n. 1.

100. *Booth-Kelly v. Southern Pacific*, 183 F.2d 902 (9th Cir. 1950).

101. *Union Pacific v. Bridal Veil*, 219 F.2d 825 (9th Cir. 1955), *cert. denied*, 350 U.S. 981 (1956).

102. See, e.g., *Southern Pacific v. Morrison-Knudsen*, 216 Or. 398, 338 P.2d 665 (1959).

103. *Jackson v. U.S. National Bank*, 153 F. Supp. 104 (D. Or. 1957).

104. *Howell v. Deady*, 48 F. Supp. 104 (D. Or. 1939); 48 F. Supp. 116 (D. Or. 1941); 48 F. Supp. 123 (D. Or. 1941).

105. See Chapter 2, *supra*.

106. *The Iowa*, 34 F. Supp. 843 (D. Or. 1940).

107. Harter Act, 46 U.S.C. secs. 190-95; Carriage of Good by Sea Act, 46 U.S.C. secs. 1300-15.

108. Limitation of Liability Acts, 46 U.S.C. secs. 181-95.

109. *Babbidge & Holt v. The Hawaiian Planter*, 123 F. Supp. 394 (D. Or. 1954).

110. *Spokane, Portland and Seattle Rwy. v. The Fairport*, 116 F. Supp. 549 (D. Or. 1953).

111. 46 U.S.C. sec. 688.

112. 45 U.S.C. secs. 51 *et seq.*

113. 46 U.S.C. sec. 761.

114. 33 U.S.C. secs. 901 *et seq.*

115. O.R.S. 654.305 *et seq.*

116. O.R.S. 30.020 *et seq.*

117. *Sanderson v. Sause Bros. Ocean Towing*, 114 F. Supp. 849 (D. Or. 1953).

118. *Hess Admin. v. United States*, 259 F.2d 285 (9th Cir. 1958); *rev'd*, 361 U.S. 314 (1960), *on remand*, 282 F.2d 633 (9th Cir. 1960).

119. 28 U.S.C. sec. 2674.

120. For further detail, see article by C.C. Cory in *Benchmarks* (Spring 1989).

121. *Moragne v. States Marine Lines*, 398 U.S. 375 (1970).

122. *Oregon-Washington R. & Nav. Co. v. Srauss*, 73 F.2d 912 (9th Cir. 1934), *cert. denied*, 294 U.S. 723 (1935); *Oregon-Washington R. & Nav. Co. v. Farmers Nat. Grain Corp.*, 25 F. Supp. 667 (D. Or. 1937); *Oregon-Washington R. & Nav. Co. v. Pacific Continental Grain Co.*, 38 F. Supp. 230 (D. Or. 1940).

123. Former 49 U.S.C. sec 13-4.

124. Former 49 U.S.C. sec. 903-b.

125. Former 49 U.S.C. sec. 303-b.

126. Former 49 U.S.C. sec. 13-4.

127. Former 49 U.S.C. sec. 316-e.

128. Former 49 U.S.C. sec. 903-k.

129. *Inland Nav. Co. v. Flagg*, Civ. No. 5503. unreported (D. Or. 1951).

130. *Scandrett v. United States*, 32 F. Supp. 995 (D. Or. 1940), *aff'd per curiam* 312 U.S. 661 (1941).

131. *Petroleum in North Pacific Coast Territory*, I & S 6062, 291 I.C.C. 101, 292 I.C.C. 317, 302 I.C.C. 219.

132. *Pacific Inland Tariff Bureau v. United States*, 129 F. Supp. 472 (D. Or. 1955).

133. *Id.* 134 F. Supp. 210 (D. Or. 1955).

134. *Humble Oil Co. v. Great Northern Rv.*, 212 F. Supp. 747 (D. Mont. 1962).

135. *Union Pacific R.R. v. Bean*, 167 Or. 535, 119 P.2d 575.

136. *Southern Pacific v. Heltzel*, 201 Or. 1, 268 P.2d 605 (1954).

137. *United States v. Union Pacific*, 226 U.S. 61 (1912), opinion on form of mandate, 226 U.S. 470 (1913).

138. Ch. 91, sec. 402, 41 Stat. 456, 476 (former 49 U.S.C. sec 1 (21)).

139. 159 I.C.C. 630.

140. *OWR&N v. United States*, 47 F.2d 250 (D.C., Or 1931).

141. *Interstate Commerce Commission v. Oregon-Washington Railroad & Navigation Co.*, 288 U.S. 14 (1933).

142. *Erie Railroad v. Thompkins*, 304 U.S. 64 (1938).

143. *Harris v. Traglio*, 24 F. Supp. 402 (D. Or. 1938), *aff'd sub nom. Traglio v. Harris*, 104 F.2d 439 (9th Cir. 1939), *cert. denied*, 308 U.S. 629 (1939).

144. *United States v. Chambers*, 291 U.S. 217 (1934).

145. *United States v. Vlahos*, 19 F. Supp. 166 (D. Or. 1937).

146. *United States v. Boylen*, 41 F. Supp. 724 (D. Or. 1941).

147. *United States v. DeMaurez*, 54 F. Supp. 102 (D. Or. 1943).

148. See, for example: *Klamath & Modoc Tribes v. Maison*, 139 F. Supp. 634 (D. Or. 1956), related case 338 F.2d 620 (9th Cir. 1964); *Confederated Tribes of Umatilla Indian Reservation v. Maison*, 262 F. Supp. 871 (D. Or. 1966); *Confederated Tribes of Umatilla Indian Reservation v. Maison*, 186 F. Supp. 519 (D. Or. 1960), *aff'd*, 314 F.2d 169 (9th Cir. 1963), *cert. denied*, 375 U.S. 829 (1963); *Sohappy v. Smith*, 302 F. Supp. 899 (D. Or. 1969); *Kimball v. Callahan*, 493 F.2d 564 (9th Cir. 1979), *cert. denied*, 419 U.S. 1019 (1974); related case, 590 F.2d 768 (9th Cir. 1979), *cert. denied*, 444 U.S. 826 (1979); *Klamath Indian Tribe v. Oregon Dep't. Fish & Wildlife*, 729 F.2d 609 (9th Cir. 1984), *rev'd*, 473 U.S. 753 (1985).

149. See, for example: *Crain v. First National Bank*, 206 F. Supp. 783 (D. Or.

1962), *aff'd*, 324 F.2d 532 (9th Cir. 1963); *Foster v. First National Bank*, 213 F. Supp. 884 (D. Or. 1962); *Reed v. U.S. National Bank*, 213 F. Supp. 919 (D. Or. 1963).

150. See, for example, *Anderson v. Gladden*, 188 F. Supp. 666 (D. Or. 1960), *aff'd*, 293 F.2d 463 (9th Cir. 1961), *cert. denied*, 368 U.S. 949 (1961), related case, *Anderson v. Britton*, 212 Or. 1, 318 P.2d 291 (1957), *cert. denied*, 356 U.S. 962 (1958).

151. *United States v. Brookfield Fisheries, Inc.*, 24 F. Supp. 712 (D. Or. 1938).

152. S. Beckham, *Federal-Indian Relations*, in *The First Oregonians* 39 (C. Buan & R. Lewis eds. 1991).

153. 68 Stat. 718 (1954), 25 U.S.C. sec. 564 *et seq.*

154. See Oregon State Bar, *Report of Committee on Legal Rights of Indians*, 1956 and 1957.

155. 24 Stat. 388 (1887), 25 U.S.C. sec. 331 *et seq.*

156. *Siniscal v. United States*, 208 F.2d 406 (9th Cir. 1953), *cert. denied*, 348 U.S. 818 (1954).

157. See *Taylor v. Grant*, 204 Or. 10, 279 P.2d 479 (1955); related case, 220 Or. 114, 349 P.2d 282 (1960).

# CHAPTER 5

# A PERIOD
# OF
# COMPLEXITY
# 1950–1991

BY LAURIE BENNETT MAPES

*T*he 1950s ushered in a period of rapid growth and increasing complexity in American life that spilled over into the federal courts. Between 1950 and 1990, the number of cases filed in federal district courts nationally trebled, due in great part to the social legislation of the post-World War II era. As the laws became more intricate, the cases they spawned became more complex and difficult to manage. In addition, the class action suit became commonplace and added to case-management burdens. As government agencies took on more responsibilities, the courts had to review their actions more closely and more often.

To accommodate the increase in court load, Congress approved more positions for judges, which in turn dramatically increased the number and kinds of support personnel. Still, the courts were forced to streamline their procedures and develop time-saving measures for case management. The judges in the District of Oregon performed admirably in this respect, and many of their case-management innovations were adopted in other districts.

*As the number of judges and other court personnel increased, the influence of individual personalities naturally decreased. The District of Oregon had at most two judges until 1949, whereas by the end of 1991, there were six active judges, two senior judges, and four full-time magistrate positions. The judge whose influence was strongest throughout this period was Judge Solomon, who, at his death in 1987, had served longer than any other federal judge in Oregon's history. In 1989 Congress named the Portland courthouse after him.*

∾

# THE CONTEXT

### Increasing Case Load

Until the 1950s, the growth in the number of cases filed in the federal courts was slow and steady. Beginning late in that decade, however, the number of cases surged and continued to grow rapidly during the next 30 years. Despite additional judges and court staff, the workload of the courts fostered increasing congestion, delay, and expense in federal litigation. By 1988 public concern had prompted Congress to create a Federal Courts Study Committee to report on the U.S. courts and recommend revisions to their structure and administration. The committee reported that the caseloads had reached "crisis" proportions, which could not be resolved simply by adding judges.[1] The committee cited, as one reason for the surge in cases, the many new federal rights created by Congress and by the courts through their interpretation of the Constitution.[2]

The situation in the District of Oregon was typical. In 1950 only 709 civil and 109 criminal cases were filed.[3] By 1990 these numbers had increased to 1,964 and 392 and the number of cases per judge had nearly doubled. Between 1950 and 1990 the kinds of cases represented by these numbers also changed markedly. Most of the civil cases filed in 1950 involved land condemnation and other property issues or the Tort Claims Act. There were no civil rights cases. In 1990 there were 355 civil rights cases, 106 prisoner habeas corpus petitions, and very few real property actions.

On the criminal side, the types of cases changed to reflect the problems of the day. In 1950 auto theft, juvenile delinquency, liquor laws, and even white slave traffic consumed the attention of the district court, while only nine cases involved illegal drugs. By 1990, with the war on drugs in full swing, one-third of the criminal cases were based on drug violations; the number of immigration law cases had grown, and one out of eight cases filed involved robbery.

However, these statistics do not reveal the most important change in the workload and responsibility of the district court. As environmental issues and discrimination grew in importance and as Congress passed more laws to govern them, the court found itself deeply entrenched in the management of Oregon's forests, fisheries, freeways, and employment practices. Prisoner complaints—nearly unheard of before 1950—led the court into prison management, as well. In some circumstances, the court kept cases open so that the parties could turn to a judge immediately as management disputes arose. Thus, by 1990 judicial control of government agencies—a small part of the court's responsibility before 1950— had become a significant part of the court's work. Judge Alfred T. Goodwin observed in 1986:

> Nobody ever thought in the 1950's that a person who lost his job as a city police officer or lost her job as a deputy county clerk would have a federal court case to review that personnel decision, but that's a routine kind of litigation in our court today.... All governments need to be challenged frequently and early and often. But it's being done quite a bit now in federal courts by litigation when it used to be done by campaign speeches.[4]

## More Judges

Biographies for each of the judges who served after 1950, except Judges James Alger Fee and Claude McColloch, appear at the end of this chapter. (Biographies of those two judges appear in Chapter 4.) The placement of the biographies reflects only editorial convenience; the personalities and backgrounds of the judges influenced greatly their individual work and the atmosphere in the courthouse. Briefly, the composition of the court changed during this period as follows.

As of 1950 the court consisted of Judges Fee, McColloch, and Solomon. William G. East joined the court in 1955 after Judge Fee moved up to the Ninth Circuit Court of Appeals. John F. Kilkenny succeeded to Judge McColloch's seat in 1959, after Judge McColloch took senior status.

225

When Judge East took senior status in 1967, Robert C. Belloni replaced him. Judge Kilkenny was elevated to the court of appeals in 1969. Alfred T. Goodwin replaced him, but followed him just two years later to the appellate bench.

Shortly before Judge Goodwin left the district court, Judge Solomon took senior status, leaving two openings to be filled. Otto R. Skopil, Jr. and James M. Burns filled these spots. At this point, the court still had three full-time judges, but also two on senior status (Judges East and Solomon). The makeup of the court stayed the same until 1979, when Judge Skopil joined the court of appeals. The year before, Congress had approved two new judgeships for Oregon. But the two new judges, and Judge Skopil's replacement, did not arrive until March 24, 1980. On that date, Helen J. Frye, Owen M. Panner, and James A. Redden joined the district court.

Judge Belloni took senior status in 1984; his replacement was Edward Leavy. Judge Leavy joined the court of appeals in 1987 and was replaced by Malcolm F. Marsh. After Judge Burns took senior status in 1989, Robert E. Jones joined the district court. After Congress approved a sixth judgeship for Oregon, Michael R. Hogan became district judge in 1991. Thus, at the end of this period, the court was composed of six active judges (Judges Panner, Redden, Frye, Marsh, Jones, and Hogan) and two senior judges (Judges Belloni and Burns).

## The Role of Class Actions

The procedural device called a "class action" changed the kinds of cases typically brought before the court. This device allows large numbers of plaintiffs to sue as a group, represented by only a few, or even just one of them. Likewise, a plaintiff may sue a large group of defendants as a class. The theory is that as a practical matter, there are too many members of the class to join and appear in the case. Only the representatives and their lawyers appear before the court, but whatever success or failure they achieve applies to the whole class.

Changes to the Federal Rules of Civil Procedure in 1966 made class actions easier to effect and, as a result, they became a very powerful tool, particularly in civil rights cases. The class action also enabled large groups of consumers to join together in product liability cases and securities litigation. In many of these cases, an individual plaintiff could not otherwise afford the expense of litigation, the emotional cost, and, in some cases, the retribution that might follow.

The class action is one of the reasons for the rising workload of the federal courts. Such cases usually are complex and involve both the battle of the experts and the battle of the statistics. In the District of Oregon, one class action took nine-and-a-half months to try and required 487 pages for the judge to explain the result.[5]

## Efficiency Measures

When Judge Solomon joined the court in 1949, he discovered that Judge Fee spent a lot of time handling cases in other districts. Judge McColloch was ill and therefore absent from the courthouse a great deal. To keep up with the caseload, Judge Solomon held court six days a week and spent Sunday reading files to prepare for Monday.

Perhaps as a result of this trial by fire, and certainly because of his intolerance for wasted time, Judge Solomon changed many of the local procedures after Judge Fee left for the court of appeals. Whereas Judge Fee had lawyers spend every Monday morning in court waiting to report on the progress of their cases, Judge Solomon scheduled time-certain appointments with the lawyers every 30 or 60 days, depending on the requirements of their cases. He made certain that he had read every file completely, and local lawyers came to understand that they must be prepared.

Judge Solomon thought that lawyers spent far too much time in "discovery," the period of time before trial when the parties exchange and gather information about their case. Soon after a case was filed, he would hold a conference with the attorneys to find out what they intended to prove and which, if any, facts were in dispute. In this way, he could get the parties to admit many facts, thereby reducing the discovery time they would have to spend finding them and the trial time proving them.

Judge Solomon had many techniques to speed trials. He required lawyers to prepare all of the direct testimony of expert witnesses in writing. The written testimony went to the opposing lawyers several days before trial so that they could limit their cross-examination of the expert to points that truly mattered. As a result, testimony that otherwise might take two or three days could be dealt with in an hour or two of trial time. In non-jury trials, he often had non-expert witnesses submit their testimony in writing, as well. In cases that did require a jury, he demanded that the lawyers have their witnesses ready to take the stand without a second's delay, and he never permitted lawyers to read back the transcript of the last question before a recess.

Judge Solomon's speedy trial techniques earned him the title "Fastest Gavel in the West," and he was frequently invited to handle case calendars in other districts, where he would finish trials in far less time than had been allotted for them. Once, when he took over a case in Carson City, Nevada, that was scheduled for five to six days, Judge Solomon started at 9:30 in the morning, quickly picked a jury, and had a verdict before noon on the first day.[6]

*When Gus J. Solomon joined the court in 1949, he streamlined many of its procedures, earning the title "Fastest Gavel in the West." (Oregon Historical Society Negative #ORHI87138)*

Other judges, both within the district and without, adopted Judge Solomon's case-management techniques. In 1962 the Oregon court had fewer pending cases three or more years old than any other district in the Ninth Circuit.[7] The *Oregonian* reported two years later that the district tried more civil and criminal cases than the two districts in Washington combined, and as many as the districts of Montana, Idaho, Hawaii, and Alaska combined.[8] The court maintained its relatively clean docket even though every year each of the judges spent three or four months apiece sitting in other districts to help them clear their calendars. The court in Oregon is aided by its practice of scheduling dates for the pretrial order and trial on the date a case is filed. This practice is rare, if not unique, in the country.

Despite these innovations, however, the district court in Oregon did not escape the burdens of increased caseload. In 1978 filings had reached 1,600 per year, but Oregon still had only three judgeships. Although Congress approved two more judgeships for Oregon that year, these positions were not filled for two years. In 1979 the court faced a particularly bad time when Judge Skopil left the district court for the court of appeals. For a brief time, Judges Burns and Belloni were alone at the courthouse; Judge Solomon, then on senior status, was out of the district. Worse still, Judge Burns was stuck trying fourteen heroin defendants in a trial expected to last nine or ten weeks. U.S. Attorney Sidney Lezak acknowledged that his office did not bring some of the cases it otherwise might because of the court backlog at that time.[9] By then, the court and the federal prosecutors were under the gun of the Speedy Trial Act, which required all defendants in custody to go to trial within 100 days of their arrest.

Pressures eased dramatically in 1980 when Judges Panner, Frye, and Redden joined the court and increased the number of active judges from two to five.

## Magistrates

Beginning in 1793 the federal courts operated under a commissioner system which allowed the circuit judges to appoint persons trained in the law to handle certain court matters, such as taking bail and affidavits.[10] Over the years, the duties of commissioners were expanded by statute and by local custom.

In 1968 Congress abolished the commissioner system and set up in the Federal Magistrate's Act[11] a system of officers to assist district judges. Magistrates may handle a wide variety of civil and criminal court matters. These include hearing any pretrial matter, making findings of fact and proposals for the disposition of a case, acting as special master to orchestrate complex cases and conducting certain trials. The magistrates wear robes and are addressed as "judge," although parties to a case may have their findings and recommendations reviewed by a district judge. Magistrates must have been members of a state bar in good standing for at least five years. They are appointed for eight-year terms by a concurrence of a majority of the judges of a district.

Judges Skopil and Belloni worked hard to get the Magistrate's Act passed and to convince other judges across the country that magistrates could be of great help to the courts. The District of Oregon used magistrates to the fullest, beginning in 1971 when George E. Juba, a former FBI agent and state judge in Multnomah County, was appointed Oregon's first magistrate. He was joined by Michael R. Hogan in 1973, who started as half-time magistrate, half-time bankruptcy judge and had no prior judicial experience. Edward Leavy became Oregon's third magistrate in 1976, and when he became district judge in 1984, William M. Dale took his place. Judge Dale had been a circuit court judge in Multnomah County. The district court added a fourth magistrate, John Jelderks, in 1991. Judge Jelderks had been presiding circuit judge of the Seventh Judicial District of Oregon since 1972, serving five eastern Oregon counties.

The federal districts vary widely in how much, and in what ways, they use magistrates. In Oregon the local court rules specify that magistrates may perform any tasks permitted by the Magistrates Act. Oregon's magistrates are treated as colleagues of the district judges and have significantly eased the workload of the court. Cases are assigned to the magistrates in the same manner that they are assigned to the district judges, a practice that is unusual in the nation. By the late 1970s, the district of Oregon was the most advanced court in the country in the use of magistrates.[12] Congress made changes to the Magistrates Act based upon how the magistrates were used in Oregon.[13]

Three of Oregon's magistrate positions are based in Portland; one is in Eugene. There are part-time positions in Pendleton, Coquille, Bend, and Medford.

∿

# CIVIL RIGHTS

The 1950s marked the beginning of significant changes in the laws governing civil rights. The landmark *Brown v. Board of Education*[14] Supreme Court decision mandated desegregation of U.S. schools. The Civil Rights Act of 1964[15] codified the new social consciousness of the early 1960s as well as the civil rights guaranteed in the U.S. Constitution, the Bill of Rights, and the Civil War Amendments.[16] In Oregon, employment discrimination cases and prisoner civil rights cases comprised the bulk of civil rights litigation, and freedom-of-expression cases made their mark both on the sidewalks of Portland and in the halls of the U.S. Supreme Court.

## Job Discrimination
Oregon does not have a model record where treatment of women and minorities is concerned. The black population of Oregon at the beginning of the twentieth century was no more than 2,000, and hostility toward black immigrants continued to keep that population low.[17] The Ku Klux Klan has had a significant presence in Oregon, and even during World War II, when labor was in short supply, blacks from the South were greeted by segregation in unions and fewer benefits and privileges than whites.[18] A report by the United States Commission on Civil Rights in 1959 found that Oregon's laws on discrimination in education provided less protection than the laws of other states.[19]

Women did not fare much better. Disputes over maternity leave, promotion, and pay pushed women into litigation in increasing numbers from the late 1960s on.[20]

**Race Discrimination.** There were very few employment discrimination lawsuits brought by blacks in Oregon after the passage of the Civil Rights Act of 1964. At least one author has suggested that the hostility of the industry and citizenry of Oregon toward blacks prompted them to choose to leave the state or to suffer rather than to litigate.[21]

Nevertheless, racial discrimination suits in Oregon brought changes to employment practices and the laws governing them. In *Gibson v. Local 40, Super-cargoes & Checkers of International Longshoremen's and Warehousemen's Union*[22], the Ninth Circuit Court of Appeals lowered the barriers for civil rights plaintiffs who wanted to bring their cases in federal court. The case originated in the district court in Oregon, which had held that black "casual clerks" had not exhausted their state remedies, which was required before a plaintiff could bring a job discrimination case in federal court. The appellate court gave the exhaustion requirement a liberal interpretation and concluded that only "modest deference" must be given to a state agency's disposition of a complaint about discrimination.[23]

In *Gibson*, the plaintiff casual clerks brought a class action suit in 1968 under Title VII of the Civil Rights Act of 1964, which prohibits discrimination in employment on the basis of race, sex, color, religion, or national origin. (Casual clerks performed on-call clerical duties at shipyards, including receiving, delivering, checking, and tallying cargo.) One black casual clerk, who had not been dispatched for any work, learned that white applicants had been dispatched for work even though they had filed applications after he did. The clerk, a man named Gibson, filed a racial discrimination charge with the federal Equal Employment Opportunity Commission and the Oregon Bureau of Labor. The day after he filed these complaints, the union dispatched him for work, then never dispatched him again.

The state agent in the Bureau of Labor made a single phone call to the union on Gibson's behalf and then told Gibson there was nothing more that the agency could do. Judge Belloni heard the case and found that the state agency had not followed Oregon law in handling Gibson's complaint. Nevertheless, because the state agency could have taken further action and because Gibson had not pushed the agency to do so, Judge

Belloni believed that the exhaustion doctrine precluded Gibson from bringing his case in federal court. When the court of appeals reversed the decision, it clarified this murky area of the law and explained that "[i]f…state representatives choose to do nothing with a complaint duly filed with them and accordingly terminate state proceedings—whether with a helpless shrug of the shoulders or a turning out of pockets, or with no explanation whatsoever—the federal purpose [of exhaustion] has been fully met."[24]

On remand to the district court, visiting Judge Walter E. Craig heard the case. He denied the plaintiffs any relief, both on procedural grounds and on the merits of their case. However, the plaintiffs eventually convinced the court of appeals that the union's failure to dispatch the black clerks and its eventual removal of them from the list of available clerks was racially motivated.[25] The final *Gibson* decision was important for Oregon's black community because it showed that a minority worker could win a job discrimination claim.[26]

At about the same time that Gibson and his fellow casual clerks were deprived of work, Jeannette Gates applied for work with the Georgia-Pacific Corporation in response to a newspaper ad. Georgia-Pacific had four vacancies in a cost-accounting department. The company filled three of the vacancies from its own ranks; the fourth new hire was a male agency referral. Gates, a 43-year-old black woman, did not receive a job offer. She brought a Title VII action against Georgia-Pacific and claimed that the company failed to hire her because of her race.

Gates was well qualified. She had a Masters of Business Administration degree, had taught accounting, and had worked as an accountant both for the federal government and for the City of Portland. One of the Georgia-Pacific employees who was hired over her had no academic preparation for an accounting job, and his background was, in Judge Goodwin's words, "conspicuously unimpressive in comparison with that of the plaintiff."[27] During his interview, the company told him to telephone the next day to find out whether he would get the job; in contrast, the company never told Gates how to follow up after her interview.

Judge Goodwin found that the discrepancy in qualifications between Gates and the people hired and the discrepancy in treatment during the hiring process were enough to allow him to infer that the company had violated Title VII. Georgia-Pacific argued that it had sound management reasons for hiring from within, but Judge Goodwin held that this was not enough to overcome the charge of discrimination. "A company policy of recruiting all cost accountants from among accountants and clerks already employed by the company would result in de facto exclusion of Negroes from the better jobs whether the policy is intended to have that result or not."[28] Judge Goodwin ordered Georgia-Pacific to offer Gates a position as a cost accountant as soon as another position was open and to pay her one year's salary and her attorney fees. The court of appeals affirmed that decision.

The *Gates* decision was important because it made clear that unintentional as well as intentional discrimination could result in violation of the civil rights laws.

**Sex Discrimination.** Perhaps the most significant sex discrimination case in Oregon ended up in the U.S. Supreme Court and established the principle that an employer may violate Title VII by paying women less than men even if the men and women are not performing similar duties. The case originated when Alberta Gunther and three other women who worked in the Washington County jail charged the county and the sheriff with sex discrimination. The women, who guarded and transported female prisoners, also alleged that the county had paid them less than it paid male jailers for similar work and that the county had fired them when they complained.[29]

Judge Solomon found that the women actually performed very different duties than the male jailers. They guarded only one-tenth as many prisoners as the men because the jail did not house many female prisoners. During slack times, they performed clerical work. Because the women did not have as much responsibility as the men, Judge Solomon held that they were not entitled to equal pay under the Equal Pay Act of 1963.[30] The court of appeals affirmed this holding, and the plaintiffs pursued their equal pay claim no further.

But Judge Solomon also dismissed the women's claim that their low pay was due in part to sex discrimination, in violation of Title VII of the Civil Rights Act. The women contended that the differences in pay were much greater than the differences in the difficulty of the work. Nevertheless, Judge Solomon held that the women could not substantiate a Title VII discrimination case because they had failed to show that their work was equal.

The *Gunther* case thus presented a new issue: can Title VII of the Civil Rights Act support a claim for discrimination in pay even where the requirements of the Equal Pay Act are not met because the plaintiffs are not performing substantially equal work? On appeal, the Ninth Circuit Court of Appeals noted that there were no appellate-level decisions on this question. The court also struggled with an amendment to Title VII that provides it is not unlawful for an employer to discriminate in pay on the basis of sex "if such differentiation is authorized by the provisions of the [Equal Pay Act]."[31]

If the effect of the troublesome provision was to incorporate the equal-work standards of the Equal Pay Act, then Title VII could reach no further, and the women's discrimination claim would fail. If the provision simply incorporated the defenses of the Equal Pay Act (that the discrimination was based on factors other than sex), Title VII could reach further than the Equal Pay Act and provide relief even when work duties were not equal. Because the intent of Congress was not clear, the court followed the broad, remedial purposes of the Civil Rights Act and held that its protection against sexual discrimination could apply even where the Equal Pay Act did not.[32]

In the Supreme Court the county argued that the court of appeals' holding would subject virtually every employer's pay structure to the scrutiny of the federal courts. However, in a five-to-four decision, the Supreme Court affirmed that holding.[33] This case is noted for expanding the equal pay for equal work doctrine to "fair pay for productive work."[34] It established the precedent that women could bring successful pay discrimination claims even when their duties differed substantially from the duties of men in similar positions.

Another job discrimination case set no precedent at all but still left its mark because of its size and emotional content. In *Penk v. Oregon State Board of Higher Education*[35], the 2,200 women faculty members of Oregon's higher education institutions brought a class action sex discrimination case against their employer. Twenty-two individual plaintiffs brought "disparate treatment" charges—or charges that male faculty were treated differently—and the class as a whole charged that the institutions engaged in a "pattern or practice" of discrimination against women faculty. The trial, in front of Judge Frye, began on February 4, 1984; more than nine months later when it finally ended, there were 25,000 pages of transcript, 220 witnesses had testified, the state had spent an unprecedented $3 million defending the case, emotions were high, and the plaintiffs had lost on almost all counts.

The decision was particularly difficult for the plaintiffs to accept because of the massive amount of anecdotal evidence that they had put forth. An observer reported that "[w]itness after witness recounted for Judge Frye and those in attendance detail after detail of discriminatory practices and unfair working conditions at all eight state-run institutions of higher learning."[36] Anna Penk, the lead plaintiff, told how she was required to share space with secretaries, while male faculty members had private offices. Another plaintiff testified that she did not receive a raise when her male colleagues did; when she asked why, she was told that she simply did not need the money.[37]

Despite the amount of evidence, the class action failed, and Judge Frye was able to find discrimination in only 3 of the 58 specific charges of disparate treatment. The length of her opinion—487 pages—reflects the difficulty of the case. The decision itself illustrates the extreme difficulty of proving class action suits such as *Penk*. The *Penk* plaintiffs had to prove their case by statistics in order to establish that the institutions had treated women, as a group, differently from men, as a group. The plaintiffs took objective factors such as level of education, years teaching, and age and showed that male faculty members were paid about $2,300 per year more than similarly situated female faculty members. The state responded that the plaintiffs' statistics were flawed because other factors were used in making salary, promotion, and tenure decisions, such as teaching ability and scholarship. Because these latter factors are subjective, the plaintiffs could not quantify or refute them.

The burden of proof plays a large role in a sex discrimination case. Once the plaintiff makes a "prima facie" case—or puts forth enough evidence to create an inference of discrimination—the defendant must articulate legitimate, non-discriminatory reasons for its actions. If the defendant does so, the plaintiff has the burden to persuade the judge or jury that the defendant is lying. If, as in *Penk*, the question is which side to believe, the plaintiff is likely to lose because of this burden of persuasion.

The outcome of *Penk* was not unlike the outcomes of other sex discrimination cases of its day. The impact of *Penk* was its polarization of the educational community and of representatives of state government, some of whom believed that the state should settle the case and make changes in the institutions.[38]

One other class action employment case deserves note as a national "first." Although the case did not include an allegation of discrimination, it reflected some of the problems faced by Hispanic migrant laborers in Oregon and elsewhere. In 1969 migrant laborers from New Mexico and Texas sued a Washington County farm-labor contractor, Ronald

Tankersley, for fraud and breach of contract.[39] They alleged that they came to Oregon in response to radio advertisements that Tankersley's berry farm produced plenty of berries and that his camp met state health and labor requirements. They arrived to find that neither assertion was true.

The radio advertisements were the basis for Judge Goodwin's decision that Tankersley had a contract with the workers, which he had breached by overrecruiting. "When a farm-labor contractor by promises induces needy persons to travel to a distant state to labor in the harvest, he makes an implied covenant not to hire more workmen than can earn a reasonable wage...."[40] Judge Goodwin also suggested that assertions of indifference and insensitivity to the workers that the plaintiffs raised during the trial might be matters for social legislation.

## Freedom of Expression

During the period covered by this chapter, a major First Amendment case originated in the District of Oregon. Particularly during the Vietnam War, freedom of speech and of other forms of expression became political, as well as legal, issues. Some of the most troublesome First Amendment issues involved freedom of expression on private property held open to the public. In these quasi-public areas, First Amendment free-expression rights clash with Fifth Amendment private-property rights.

The Oregon case arose in 1968 when three Vietnam War protesters entered the Lloyd Center mall in Portland and quietly distributed handbills inviting the public to a "Resistance Community" meeting to protest the draft and the war. Although the protesters did not interfere with any of the mall's businesses or activities, security guards threatened them with arrest unless they stopped handing out the fliers. Lloyd Center—one of the first large shopping malls in the country—had posted signs warning that the mall was not a public way and that permission to use any of its areas could be revoked at any time.

The protesters left the mall, but filed suit against the Lloyd Corporation, Ltd. for depriving them of their constitutional right to free speech. They attacked the mall's policy of permitting the American Legion and other select groups to carry on activities unrelated to the retail trade but denying use of the facility to other parties, including Governor Tom McCall, who had wanted to make a political speech there. The policy also prohibited the distribution of handbills in the mall.

The Supreme Court had decided two closely related cases that did not give Judge Solomon clear guidance to decide *Tanner v. Lloyd*

*Corporation, Ltd.*[41] In *Marsh v. Alabama,*[42] the Court had held that a company town—where all of the homes, stores, utilities, and other services were owned by a company—was in essence a public place where the company could not restrict speech. Later, the Court upheld the right of union members to picket on private property directly in front of a supermarket in a shopping center.[43] In this latter decision, the Court found the shopping center to be the functional equivalent of a business district, where free speech could not be unreasonably restricted, and noted that the picketers had no other location to effectively convey their message, because the supermarket was the target of the picket. But the Court carefully limited its decision to cases where the speech was related to the activities within the shopping mall.

Neither of these decisions described the law that should govern when private property that is not as "public" as a company town is used for free speech purposes unrelated to the regular activities on the property, as in *Lloyd.* Judge Solomon considered the large size of the mall (50 acres and 60 commercial tenants), its connection to public streets, which ran along and into the mall, and the fact that it was open to the public and concluded that the Lloyd Corporation could not restrict the distribution of handbills. "In my view," he wrote, "an owner who opens his land to the general public for business purposes, to the extent that the land becomes the functional equivalent of a public business district, gives up the right to prohibit the distribution of literature or to decide which literature may be distributed."[44] Otherwise, he noted, the public's need for information could be frustrated.

The Supreme Court did not agree. Because the handbills were not related to the uses of the Lloyd Center mall and because the protesters could convey their message effectively on public streets or other public areas, the Court distinguished the union picketing case and reversed the district court's decision.[45] The Supreme Court case clearly established the concept that property does not lose its private character for all purposes just because it is open to the public. Mall owners can, at a minimum, place reasonable restrictions on signature gatherers and leafleters. Modern mall shoppers probably do not even notice the absence of interest-group advocates, but the reason traces to three Vietnam War protesters at the Lloyd Center mall.

Freedom-of-expression issues became volatile and emotional again during the 1980s, when the controversy over abortion reached a new pitch. Anti-abortion protests at clinics where abortions were performed were common across the country. In Oregon, clinics in Portland were the center of attention. The Lovejoy Surgicenter was the target of blockades, sit-ins, and scuffles. At Emmanuel Hospital, 450 protesters gathered one day in 1986 because the hospital allowed abortions and yet was the state's leader in neonatal care.

Anti-abortion activities at the Portland Feminist Women's Health Center on Foster Road (PFWHC) made the news most often. PFWHC is a nonprofit corporation that provides family planning and health services, including abortions. Beginning in 1984 and continuing through 1991, Advocates for Life, Inc. organized demonstrations in front of the PFWHC on days when abortions were performed there; anywhere from a handful to 150 persons participated. Demonstrators crowded around the entrance, blocking patients from the door, waving signs, and yelling comments such as "Murderer!" at the staff and patients. The activists called these events "rescues." There were physical scuffles and vandalism. The staff and volunteer escorts formed body barriers to help patients into the clinic. Some patients were too intimidated to enter, and the staff asserted that noise from the demonstrators on the street interfered with the provision of medical services.

In 1986 the PFWHC and individual women filed an action in the district court against Advocates for Life and 12 individuals, asking for compensation for damages and for an injunction against further protests. They alleged that the defendants conspired to disrupt and harm PFWHC's clinic, inflict emotional distress on its clients, and prevent women from exercising their right to a safe and legal abortion.

The case went first to U.S. Magistrate Dale. In trying to balance the demonstrators' free-speech rights with the women's constitutional right to an abortion, Judge Dale recommended a "no-picket corridor" extending from the clinic door into the street, and 12¹/₂ feet on either side of the doorway. His recommendation included a prohibition against excessive noise, trespassing, damage to property, and interference with the clinic's utility services. Judge Frye adopted the recommendations and issued them in the form of a preliminary injunction, pending a jury trial on the claim for damages. Pro-choice representatives praised the injunction and suggested that it might set a precedent for other clinics in the nation.[46]

But the injunction did not quell the controversy, even temporarily. The protesters had filed suit challenging Portland's noise ordinance against the use of bullhorns and a proposal for a city ordinance restricting protests near hospitals and clinics. U.S. Magistrate Juba dismissed the suit, in part because the proposed ordinance was not yet in effect.[47] Meanwhile, the demonstrations continued. PFWHC returned to court as protesters violated the injunction. In August 1986, just two months after imposing the injunction, Judge Frye found six protesters in contempt of court and fined each $500. She suspended the fines for so long as the protesters complied with the injunction. In 1987 she required two of the protesters to pay the fine when they violated the injunction for the second time. Later, she ordered the protesters to pay the more than $17,000 in attorney fees PFWHC had incurred.

The case did not go to trial until 1990. By then, some of the protesters had been arrested and convicted in state court for interfering with pedestrian traffic. The PFWHC had moved to the Holladay Park Professional Building and successfully urged Judge Frye to transfer the effect of the preliminary injunction to the new location. The jury found in favor of the clinic and the individual plaintiffs and awarded them damages. Based on the jury verdict, Judge Frye converted the preliminary injunction into a permanent injunction on March 5, 1991.

After five years of overseeing the demonstrators, Judge Frye brought the case to an end. The permanent injunction could not control the behavior of the demonstrators any better than the preliminary one, but a protester had suggested earlier that the fines and assessment of fees had reduced their numbers.[48]

## Prisoner Actions

In 1950 prisoner petitions requesting relief from sentences or from jail conditions were practically unheard of in the federal courts. But in 1963 the United States Supreme Court rendered a decision that made more available to prisoners the writ of habeas corpus, by which a prisoner may challenge the lawfulness of his detention. In *Fay v. Noia*,[49] the Court held that a prisoner who did not appeal his conviction in state court nevertheless could challenge his conviction later in federal court. Noia had been convicted of felony murder in 1942 but did not appeal his conviction; later, he asserted that his confession was coerced, in violation of his constitutional rights. The federal district court in New York had declined to hear his petition because by failing to appeal his conviction, Noia had not exhausted all of his state-court remedies first.

Fay and its progeny opened the door for prisoners to use habeas proceedings. At the same time, along with the growth in civil rights actions generally, prisoners began to challenge the conditions of their confinement. In 1970 there were 39 habeas corpus petitions filed in the District of Oregon and no prisoner civil rights cases; from the late 1970s on, habeas petitions averaged 100 per year and prisoner civil rights actions 200 per year.[50] Thus, at the end of this period, one-seventh of the court's civil case load was prisoner petitions. Many of these cases have presented difficult issues and some have fostered heated political debate about crime and punishment. In the end, they required the district judges to roll up their sleeves and become prison managers.

For example, in 1968 Vincent Capitan was convicted of larceny and sent to the Oregon State Penitentiary (OSP). A few months later, his sentence was stretched to life imprisonment after he was convicted of murdering a prosecution witness before the larceny trial. Three years later, the superintendent of the OSP, who believed that Capitan was involved in the drug trade within the prison, transferred Capitan to the federal penitentiary in Leavenworth, Kansas, 2,000 miles away from his family and his home. Capitan had no hearing or chance to refute his involvement in the drug trade. He sought habeas corpus relief in the district court.

*Beginning in the late 1970s, prisoners began to challenge the conditions of their confinement, including prison overcrowding. Since then, prisoner civil rights actions have averaged 200 a year. (Photo by Steve Dipaola)*

Judge Solomon noted that the new spurt in litigation over the constitutional rights of prisoners had made clear the requirement that a serious change in a prisoner's confinement must meet due-process requirements. "The task of administering a modern penal institution is a difficult one," he wrote. "I do not pretend to assume the role of warden. I only hold that Capitan was entitled to a hearing before the prison authorities either prior to or a reasonable time after his transfer."[51]

Not long after this due-process decision, the district court struck down Oregon's "civil death" statute, which provided that a felon lost all civil and political rights.[52] Because of the case's importance, the court convened a three-judge panel (of Judges Goodwin, Solomon, and Burns) to decide it. The plaintiff, Wendell Delorme, suffered a work-related injury two years before he was convicted of a felony in state court and sentenced to ten years in prison. After he went to jail, Delorme requested a Workmen's Compensation Board hearing to contend that the award for his job injury was inadequate. The hearing officer rejected Delorme's request because of the civil death statute. The panel struck down the statute under the Equal Protection Clause, because its provisions were not rationally related to the rehabilitation of prisoners.

In *Capps v. Atiyeh*,[53] Judge Burns's role came closer to that of warden than Judge Solomon's had in Capitan's case. In 1980 prisoners at the OSP, at a satellite facility called the Farm Annex, and at the Oregon State Correctional Institution (OSCI) filed a class action suit against the governor, the administrator of the Corrections Division, the superintendents, and the parole board members. The prisoners contended that the institutions were unconstitutionally overcrowded. The OSP held 370 more inmates than its capacity; OSCI was overloaded by 300 inmates, and the Farm Annex held nearly twice as many inmates as it was designed for. Inmates were doubled up in small cells, dayrooms had been converted to dormitories, and extra beds had been brought in. Judge Burns found that the crowded conditions resulted in health hazards, reduced medical care, increased potential for violence, friction between staff and inmates, and less effective rehabilitation efforts. He had visited the facilities to observe their conditions first hand. He concluded that the conditions constituted cruel and unusual punishment and therefore violated the prisoners' constitutional rights.

However, rather than issuing an injunction against the conditions, Judge Burns told the state to reduce the prison population by 500 and gave the state an opportunity to come up with a plan to achieve this goal. Governor Vic Atiyeh was not pleased with the order. He called the decision "preposterous" and asserted that Oregon's prisons were among the finest and most humane in the country.[54] The order, he said, would force the state to turn loose 500 convicted felons, an action he called irresponsible.[55]

Nevertheless, the state spent months coming up with several proposals, including shortening the time served for minor offenses, moving some women prisoners to a vacant work release center, reactivating forest-camp cabins, and building new prison space at a cost of $120 million; this last proposal would have required voter approval. Without specifically ordering implementation of any of these proposals, Judge Burns ordered the state in August 1980 to reduce the prison population by 500 inmates by the end of 1980 and by 250 more as of March 31, 1981, and to make progress reports to him monthly in the meantime. This flexible order generally pleased the governor, but he still chose to appeal the finding that conditions were unconstitutional.[56] Meanwhile, the state adopted an early release formula to free 13 percent of the prison population, primarily non-violent criminals convicted of property crimes.

While the appeal was pending, the Supreme Court held that double celling was not unconstitutional where it did not lead to deprivation of food, medical care, or sanitation, or to increased violence.[57] The Ninth Circuit Court of Appeals therefore vacated Judge Burns's decision and sent the case back to him to make findings about any specific, quantifiable deprivations. Ironically, by this time the state had reduced the prison population by 487, just 13 short of the original goal.

On this second round, Judge Burns held hearings at which dozens of inmates, as well as prison staff and expert witnesses, testified. In a lengthy opinion he explored many of the details of life in the prison system. Although he found unsatisfactory conditions related to violence, segregation, and isolation, idleness, sanitation, and mental-health care, he found specific Eighth Amendment violations only with respect to medical care, fire safety, and pasteurization of milk. For example, although the inmates described instances in which they did not receive mental-health care for serious mental illness, they could not show systematic deficiencies in care.

"I do not wish to have this opinion interpreted as a favorable report on Oregon's care for its mentally ill inmates," Judge Burns wrote. "This is not the first time mental health care in Oregon's prisons has been found wanting.… Because the inmates have not established the existence of a constitutional violation for me to remedy, I fear this will not be the last time a court will be called to do that which the executive and legislative branches will not."[58]

The Umatilla County Jail in Pendleton raised similar concerns about the conditions of confinement. In 1981 prisoners there filed a class action suit to challenge poor security systems that fostered attacks, injuries, and "cell bosses;" staff indifference to illness; skin diseases caused by filth; severe overcrowding; and certain prison policies.[59] The county had plans for new facilities and renovation that would remedy many of the complaints, but the county resisted Judge Redden's attempts to settle the case. During the trial, Judge Redden visited the jail. He also noted that Umatilla County grand juries had reported a lack of towels, unlocked knife drawers, knee-deep laundry, uncovered garbage, crusted bars, "gross" toilet areas, and an inability of the staff to respond to a fire, escape, or riot. Judge Redden found many constitutional violations in the conditions, which in combination produced even more serious violations. He ordered the county to devise a plan to remedy the conditions.

Perhaps the most colorful of the prison cases were those filed by Harry Franklin, who proved that one man in a prison cell could, single-handedly, generate enough cases to "bedevil" the court.[60] He filed so many cases that they became known as the "Franklin Docket." Within five years of his 1978 conviction for burglary and assault, he had filed 100 cases in the district court. Among allegations that Yamhill County jailers ransacked his cell and took personal papers were these complaints:

• Officers failed to take him for walks. (In other complaints, Franklin alleged that he was crippled.)
• Prison guards wore "clopping heels" on their boots.
• A Portland television station caused him mental frustration when it misidentified a fourteen-wheel tractor/trailer rig as an "eighteen wheeler" (Franklin sought $3 million in damages for this).
• Train whistles woke him early in the morning.
• A seat belt requirement should apply to horses and bicycles as well as cars (Franklin sought $8.9 million for this and named President Ronald Reagan as a defendant).
• He was subject to "harassment by water," or the over watering of prison lawns left him without a dry spot to lie down on.
• The food service baked desserts in aluminum rather than stainless steel pans.
• Franklin wanted to be governor, and the Oregon law forbidding

felons from running for or holding office during incarceration was unconstitutional.

Judge Burns dismissed most of Franklin's complaints as frivolous or malicious or because Franklin had not followed through with them. After Franklin appealed one set of dismissals, the Ninth Circuit Court of Appeals reversed some of the dismissals. Judge Burns's opinion on remand begins:

> This in another chapter in the Harry Franklin saga. No longer am I tempted to call it the final chapter, as desirable as that would be to me. I mention mournfully that only the finality of death—his or mine— would enable the other of us to use the term "final" in that way.[61]

Judge Burns again dismissed most of Franklin's complaints; the appellate court again sent a few back, including Franklin's complaint that he could not run for governor. The appellate court noted that Judge Burns was "understandably weary of Mr. Franklin," but suggested that the Oregon statute was arguably unconstitutional.[62] Judge Burns also limited Franklin to six *in forma pauperis* actions per year; Franklin would have to pay the filing fee on any others. The appellate court agreed that six was probably enough.

∾

# THE VIETNAM WAR

The term "go west, young man" took on new meaning during the United States' involvement in the Vietnam War, as draft evaders learned that the judges in the District of Oregon gave lenient sentences. In the early 1960s, young men who refused induction into the armed forces could expect a jail sentence of three to six months there, at a time when most federal judges imposed one- to two-year sentences.[63] The maximum sentence for draft evasion was five years. While some southern judges were sending draft dodgers to federal penitentiaries for the maximum term, a common sentence in the District of Oregon was a short stay in a coastal forest camp. By 1971 Oregon topped the nation with 1,000 conscientious objectors performing alternative civilian service in the state.[64]

The reasons for this leniency may have been the personal views of the judges or perhaps the consensus of the court. Judge Solomon, who handled many of the draft evasion cases in Oregon and some in California, was personally opposed to the war but adamant about upholding the law. He was concerned that young men were being sentenced to prison for an act of conscience and that some would be shunned from their religious groups if they submitted to service. "I am more disturbed by these cases than I am by any other," he said.[65]

However, Judge Solomon did believe in the selective service, in part because he believed that a voluntary armed forces led to public scorn of those who did not enlist. All of the Oregon judges agonized over the sentencing of young men who were following their consciences but could not qualify for conscientious-objector status because they were not opposed to all wars, just the Vietnam War.

The most perplexing draft cases that came before the court—and there were many of them—were those against Jehovah's Witnesses. The government typically granted conscientious-objector status to Jehovah's Witnesses and ordered them to civilian service, but the men did not show up to perform their service. Thus, the charges against them were not failure to submit to induction but rather failure to report to civilian work. Each time a Jehovah's Witness appeared before the court, he would explain that civilian service—such as work in hospitals or other domestic organizations—was against his religious beliefs. Because the young man would not report to civilian work, the judge was forced to find him guilty and sentence him. Typically, the sentence would be 18 months in prison with the option to report to civilian work after 6 months. When the 6 months expired, the young man would not choose civilian service.

Judge Solomon once asked a Jehovah's Witness whether he might not prefer work in a hospital to a stay in prison. The young man replied that the hospital work would compromise his principles. "The work you are doing now at the ESCO Corporation contributes to the war effort," Judge Solomon said to him. "I do not see why you won't accept this hospital work which has less involvement with the war and is of great national importance."[66]

Judge Kilkenny did not understand the religious restriction on civilian service either. Before sentencing one young man, he told him, "In my opinion, if all of our American citizens took the same position you take, our American nation would disappear in a very short period of time."[67] Another young man pointed out to Judge Kilkenny that other countries allowed Jehovah's Witnesses to avoid draft obligations because they contributed to society in other ways. "What would happen to your high principles if they fall under the heel of a conqueror?" the judge asked him.[68]

Judge Solomon told the story of the young Jehovah's Witness who appeared before him in 1967 and finally brought understanding to the court. The young man had a Bible in his hand. The judge asked him if he was willing to work in the hospital where he had been ordered to report, and he said "No." The judge then asked, "Suppose that the warden of the penitentiary tells you to cut the lawn. Will you cut the lawn?" The young man said "Yes," and Judge Solomon asked why. "Romans XIII," he said.

"Just a moment," the judge responded, and he called a recess. He phoned a minister friend and asked him what this section of the Bible provided. The minister explained that Romans XIII directs that the orders of civilian authorities must be obeyed.

The judge returned to court and explained to the young man that judges are civilian employees, not part of the military. "As a civilian authority, I am ordering you to go to the hospital in Kansas City, Missouri for a period of two years. You are required to go by law and by the very section of the Bible to which you referred me." The young man was satisfied and left for Kansas City.

Within a few days, Judge Solomon was receiving calls and letters from judges across the country who also did not want to send the Jehovah's Witnesses to penitentiaries. Judge Solomon sent them transcripts of the young man's trial. Apparently the Jehovah's Witnesses had disobeyed the orders to civilian service because they were given by military personnel; when the order came from a civilian employee, their religious principles were not offended. Rather than send these young men to prison for their disobedience, some judges began simply to re-order them to the civilian work they had avoided.

Judge Solomon was sympathetic to draft dodgers who were sincere about their convictions. He acquitted one young man who had tried unsuccessfully to claim conscientious-objector status on the basis of philosophical and educational grounds rather than religious beliefs. Judge Solomon ruled that the draft board could not deny the man this status just because his views were not traditional religious views; the Supreme Court had recently held that conscientious objector status did not require membership in an organized religion. The young man said that his religious beliefs came from the writings of Ralph Waldo Emerson, Henry Thoreau, Herman Melville, and Robert Ardrey.[69]

Judge Solomon was not sympathetic when he thought a draft dodger's position was untenable. One young man came before him and simply asserted that he would fight to save his own life, but not someone else's. "That is the law of the jungle," the judge replied.[70] Another admitted that he carried anti-draft pamphlets to his induction and refused to turn them over, knowing that this act would stop his induction. "I just can't get excited about a young man who does these things," Judge Solomon said. "I have all the sympathy in the world for a conscientious objector, but no sympathy for people who rely on technicalities to avoid their obligation."[71] Young men who tried conscientious-objector status as a last-ditch effort after failing to avoid the draft for financial or educational reasons faced similar resistance from Judge Solomon.

❧

# INDIAN FISHING RIGHTS

The United States government and the Indian tribes of the Pacific Northwest have had a long and troubled history together that cannot fairly be explored here. The Stevens Treaties of 1855 between the United States and each of the major Northwest tribes ended some disputes but started many others. Because of the importance of salmon to the subsistence and culture of these tribes, fishing rights became, and continue to be, a source of friction between Indian and non-Indian interests, particularly since hydropower facilities and increased ocean and inland fishing have depleted stocks. Ironically, when these disputes landed in court, the United States government joined on the side of the Indian Tribes in their battle to strike down state regulation of their traditional fisheries.[72]

Each of the 1855 treaties provided the tribes "the rights of taking fish at all usual and accustomed places, in common with citizens of the Territory." After 1855 the title to many of the off-reservation usual fishing places passed to private ownership. In addition, the state governments tried to subject the Indians to the same fishing regulations that covered non-Indians, including restrictions on how and when fish could be caught. In *United States v. Winans*[73] in 1905, the Supreme Court interpreted the 1855 treaties to not "restrain the state unreasonably, if at all, in the regulation of [the] right" to fish at the usual and accustomed places.[74] In two later cases the Supreme Court clarified this language from *Winans* only slightly: the state regulations on the time and manner of fishing must be necessary for the conservation of fish[75] and meet "appropriate standards."[76]

In this ambiguous state of the law, Judge Belloni faced *Sohappy v. Smith*[77] in 1969, in which individual members of the Yakima Indian Nation sought a decree defining their treaty fishing rights on the Columbia River system. The court joined a second, similar case brought by the United States, together with the Yakima, Umatilla, Walla Walla, Cayuse, Nez Perce, and Warm Springs tribes. Judge Belloni rejected the State of Oregon's argument that the treaties gave the Indians only the same fishing rights that other citizens had. "Such a reading would not seem unreasonable if all history, anthropology, biology, prior case law and the intention of the parties to the treaty were to be ignored," he wrote.[78]

While declining to prescribe the specific details of permissible regulation, Judge Belloni added two important points to the Supreme Court guidelines: the Indians are entitled to a "fair share' of the Columbia's fish, and their interests should be considered and promoted when the state adopts regulations.[79] Judge Belloni kept jurisdiction over the fishing issues in order to ensure prompt judicial review as disputes arose over future regulation. As "fishmaster of the Columbia River," he supervised the fishery for the next 12 years.

The *Sohappy* decision added to a growing body of law in which the district courts of Washington also played a large role. In *United States v. Washington*,[80] the district court in western Washington extended the *Sohappy* decision and held that the Indians were entitled to 50 percent of the fish runs. The Supreme Court agreed with the *Washington* decision, finding that the "in common with" language of the treaties was consistent with a 50-50 division with non-Indians.[81]

The *Sohappy* decision also prompted the state governments of Oregon and Washington, the federal government, and the Indian tribes to work together on a plan to manage the fisheries of the Columbia River and its tributaries.[82] During the next seven years, the parties appeared before Judge Belloni several times to resolve their continuing disputes over fishery regulations. In the meantime, the State of Washington intervened. Finally, in 1977, the parties presented to the court a five-year "Plan for Managing Fisheries on Stocks Originating from the Columbia River and its Tributaries." The plan set conservation goals for each species of fish and regulations governing their capture. The court approved the plan, but the life of the Northwest salmon only became more complex.

For one thing, Congress had passed the Fishery Conservation and Management Act of 1976,[83] which created a Pacific Fishery Management Council to manage ocean fisheries out to 200 miles off the West Coast. Many Columbia River fish species make annual round-trip migrations to the sea; therefore, the management of the ocean fishery is a critical factor in preserving Indian fisheries.

*The Stevens Treaties of 1855 guaranteed Northwest Indians the right to fish "at all usual and accustomed places" (such as Celilo Falls, pictured here 100 years later). However, balancing fishing rights with environmental and other concerns has become an extremely complex problem, and the district court has found itself becoming a manager of the region's fisheries. (Oregon Historical Society Negative #CN007237)*

For another thing, more players joined the battle over fish. The State of Idaho intervened in the continuing *Sohappy* case; together with the Shoshone-Bannock Tribe and the Makah Tribe, it objected to a revised management plan that the original parties put forth in 1988.[84] Once again, the judge—this time Judge Marsh—was forced to roll up his sleeves, become an expert on the biology and management of salmon and steelhead, and determine whether the proposed plan fairly allocated the fish while ensuring their survival. Judge Marsh affirmed the plan and rejected arguments that not all interests had been adequately represented in the planning process.

Other decisions made clear that a right to 50 percent of the fish was meaningless if there were no fish. The district courts of Oregon and of other western states therefore have held that the 1855 treaty rights can be invoked to preserve wetlands and minimum streamflows, limit diversions for irrigation, stop construction of dams, and restrict how dams are operated during periods of peak power demand.[85] The fishing rights of the Indians have become entangled in many federal environmental laws, including the Endangered Species Act.[86]

Through the interpretation of the courts, a short and ambiguous treaty provision has had profound effects. And by retaining jurisdiction over these disputes, the courts have, in effect, managed the fisheries for many years.

# CRIMINAL CASES

## Drug Cases

During the 1950s and 1960s, auto-theft cases comprised about one-fourth of the court's criminal docket. These cases were prosecuted under the National Motor Vehicle Theft Act,[87] also known as the Dyer Act.

By the 1970s, federal prosecutors had turned their attention to a much more pressing problem: illegal drugs. By the end of the 1980s, more than 140 drug indictments were being heard each year.[88] Whereas the civil case load had merely tripled, the rise in drug cases helped the criminal docket to nearly quadruple.

Oregon has had more than its share of drug cases because of its many small ports, where drugs can be brought into the state undetected, and its large expanses of remote country, in which marijuana production can be hidden. By 1976, the amount of cocaine smuggled into Portland had increased, and a local Drug Enforcement Administration agent predicted that Portland could become a major route for drug smuggling.[89]

But the drug problem was not limited to Oregon's largest city; even remote areas of the state were plagued with marijuana, tar heroin, and other drugs. In 1986 *The Oregonian* reported that there were as many as 30,000 marijuana growers throughout the state and that their estimated $1 billion annual crop may have been Oregon's second largest cash crop.[90] In addition, tar heroin was believed to be coming into the region with illegal immigrant farm workers, and southern Oregon had many methamphetamine laboratories.[91] In Multnomah County in 1985, there were more than twice as many deaths from heroin overdoses as in Seattle and San Francisco combined.[92]

As they did across the country, state and federal authorities in Oregon increased their efforts to fight the drug problem. In 1982 the U.S. attorney's office in Portland teamed up with Oregon state prosecutors to share resources and expertise. In 1987 Oregon got nine more DEA agents, increasing their forces by 60 percent; at that time, U.S. Representative Les AuCoin (D-Ore.) described the Oregon coast as "a virtual sieve."[93] In 1990 the U.S. Department of Justice tripled its annual grant to Oregon to nearly $5 million for drug enforcement, education, and treatment programs. Also that year the U.S. Army was added to the multi-agency forces trying to eradicate Oregon's marijuana crop.

The increasing drug traffic led to more than a large number of federal drug indictments to be tried in the District of Oregon. It also led to many more bank robbery cases. By the late 1980s, the district judges estimated that 80 percent of bank robbery cases were related to drugs, either because they were committed by people under the influence of drugs or because they were committed to get money for drugs. In 1986 Oregon ranked third in the nation in the rate of bank robberies, and by 1988 the state averaged more than one bank robbery per day.[94]

In order to efficiently handle the resulting load of criminal cases, each judge of the district began a practice of setting three to six criminal trials to begin at the start of each week. Usually, at most one or two actually go to trial; others disappear as a result of plea bargaining. As soon as the criminal trials are completed, the judges switch to civil cases. The judges also carefully screen criminal cases in advance in order to predict the likelihood that they will go to trial.

## United States v. Loud Hawk

The District of Oregon had one of the longest-running criminal cases in the nation's history. It is also a case that received much public attention across the country. The case involved Dennis Banks, leader of the American Indian Movement, whom the FBI was tracking after the 71-day siege at Wounded Knee in 1973. Incidents at the Custer County Courthouse there on the Pine Ridge Indian Reservation led to rioting and assault charges against Banks.

Two years later, Banks was still a federal fugitive. FBI agents believed that Banks and several others were in Washington, planning to take explosives and firearms back to Wounded Knee. Officials wanted to catch Banks as he crossed the Columbia River into Oregon, so that he could be tried in federal court for illegal weapons violations (which required that the weapons be transported in interstate commerce). Federal agents tipped off the Oregon State Police, but no one saw Banks enter Oregon. Then, when the suspect vehicles reached the Snake River at the Idaho border near Ontario, an over-anxious state trooper stopped them on the Oregon side. Banks and another allegedly fled, but police arrested Kenneth Loud Hawk, Russ Redner, Anna Mae Aquash, and Kamook Banks, Dennis's wife. Police also seized seven cases of dynamite, six firearms, and other devices.

In December 1975 a grand jury returned an indictment with three explosives counts and two firearms counts against Banks and his party. But meanwhile, state police had destroyed the dynamite for safety reasons. Judge Belloni granted the defendants' motion to suppress all evidence of the dynamite because they did not get a chance to examine it. On the date set for trial, the courtroom was packed, but the U.S. attorney refused to go forward with the case until the court of appeals decided the suppression issue, which the government had appealed. Because the government would not proceed, Judge Belloni dismissed the indictment.

Meanwhile, Governor Bob Straub faced a different problem related to Banks. Officials in South Dakota had sent requests for extradition of Banks to both Governor Straub and Governor Jerry Brown of California. Banks had asked for asylum in Oregon, and Governor Straub had in his office 500 letters from Oregonians and 2,000 letters from Californians— more mail than he had received on any other issue. Most of the letters opposed extradition. Governor Straub did not have to decide about extradition because Banks left Oregon for California.[95]

The government's Oregon case languished in the court of appeals for three years. The appellate court asked Judge Belloni to find out whether federal agents helped destroy the dynamite and then finally reversed the dismissals.[96] The government's new indictment in 1980 added two counts against the defendants that did not appear in the first indictment. Judge Redden, who had the case this time, found that the government's more serious indictment constituted vindictive prosecution against Banks's wife but not against the others. He dismissed the charges against her only. Both sides appealed, and the case sat in the court of appeals for another two years.

In 1982 the court of appeals sent the case back. The prosecutor, it said, had legitimate reasons to broaden the indictment. After several continuances of the trial, Judge Redden dismissed the case again on the grounds that the eight-year delay between the indictment and the trial violated the defendants' constitutional right to a speedy trial and their right to due process.

Yet another appeal followed. This time, the court of appeals affirmed Judge Redden's dismissal of the case, but the government found sympathetic ears in the U.S. Supreme Court, which held that because the defendants had been free most of the time, their right to a speedy trial had not been violated. By then, Banks was in South Dakota on parole from the charges he faced after Wounded Knee.

But Judge Redden refused the case yet again. The Supreme Court decision, he said, did not affect his dismissal on the alternate due process grounds; it merely resolved the speedy trial issue. On the case's next trip to the court of appeals in 1987, that court interpreted the Supreme Court's decision as reversing Judge Redden's entire opinion and reinstating the indictment. By this time, witnesses had died.

Still, Banks did not go to trial. The lawyers disputed whether the government had to turn over certain information, and this delayed the trial more. Finally, in 1988—more than 12 years after the incidents at the Idaho border—Banks pleaded guilty to a single explosives charge upon the government's agreement to drop all of the other charges against Banks and his co-defendants. Before a packed courtroom, Judge Redden sentenced Banks to five years probation and ended, in the judge's words, "an unhappy chapter in our history."[97]

## Sentencing
The judges of the District of Oregon who served between 1950 and

1991 were not recognized as more harsh or less harsh generally in sentencing than judges of other districts. However, the Oregon judges made every effort to achieve consistency in sentencing through their Monday morning sentencing conferences. In these conferences, all the judges meet with the probation officers; all have read the presentence investigation report of every convict scheduled for sentencing and have considered the probation officer's recommendation. The meetings allow the judges to discuss the sentences and the philosophy behind them. Ultimately, the sentencing judge determines the sentence, but the views of the other judges weigh heavily. This practice, which avoids disparate sentences, is rare in the nation.

Before 1984 a system of indeterminate sentencing was in effect in the federal courts. Although statutes provided the penalties for different crimes, the judges had wide discretion, and there were striking disparities in sentences. In 1984 Congress passed the Sentencing Reform Act of 1984.[98] In that act, Congress rejected the theory that imprisonment promotes rehabilitation and provided instead that punishment should promote retribution, education, deterrence, and incapacitation. Under the act, the United States Sentencing Commission promulgated Sentencing Guidelines from which a judge may stray only if there are aggravating or mitigating factors.

Although this has reduced disparities in sentences across the nation, the effect in the District of Oregon was less apparent because the judges there already had achieved a great deal of consistency through the sentencing conferences. However, the guidelines have given prosecutors greater power to encourage pleas, and some defendants may be pleading guilty who would have elected trial before the guidelines took effect.

∾

# ENVIRONMENTAL ISSUES

Oregonians as a whole have a strong tradition of appreciation for the natural resources and beauty of the Pacific Northwest. Even before the environmental movement took hold nationally in the late 1960s, Oregonians were cleaning up and protecting their surroundings. Oregon was one of the first states to enact water-use regulations, and the inauguration of Governor Tom McCall in 1967 marked the beginning of significant changes in the state's attitude toward development.

Under Governor McCall's direction, the state cleaned up a filthy, fishless Willamette River, adopted a plan for a "greenway" belt of scenic park areas along the river, held hearings across the state on water-quality standards, passed a "bottle bill" which required beer and soft drinks to be sold in returnable containers, and started the first comprehensive state land-use planning program in the country. The program required every county to comply with statewide goals in creating a plan to control development far into the future. The program also created the Land Conservation and Development Commission to review the plans and oversee land-use decisions.[99] Later, in 1983, Oregon became the first state to enact a law that required everyone in the state to be provided an opportunity to recycle.[100]

But not all Oregonians shared the same interests. The abundant and rich natural resources of the Oregon Territory brought settlers to the West and provided many with their jobs. Later, as the state adopted more and more conservation measures, the tension among jobs, development, and protection of the environment grew stronger. At the same time, public interest in the environment spawned environmental legislation at the federal level, beginning with the National Environmental Policy Act of 1969 (NEPA).[101] NEPA was followed by an explosion of other far-reaching federal acts, such as the Clean Water Act,[102] the Clean Air Act,[103] the Coastal Zone Management Act,[104] the National Forest Management Act,[105] the Resource Conservation and Recovery Act,[106] and the Endangered Species Act.[107] Because of the vast natural resources of Oregon and the keen interest in preserving them, it was inevitable that some of the most difficult and important cases in the district court would decide environmental issues. And as with the prison, fish, and employment cases, the judges were forced to become experts in technical fields and to act as managers.

## Herbicides in the Siuslaw National Forest

Judge Skopil heard one early, significant NEPA case filed in the District of Oregon. Two environmental groups—Citizens Against Toxic Sprays, Inc., and the Oregon Environmental Council, Inc.—together with an organization of forest workers sought in 1976 to stop the United States Forest Service from spraying phenoxy herbicides in the Siuslaw National Forest. Two of the herbicides (2,4-D and 2,4,5-T) comprised Agent Orange, the defoliant used during the Vietnam War that damaged humans, animals, and plants.

255

The plaintiffs charged that the environmental impact statements (EIS's) prepared by the Forest Service, as required by NEPA, failed to address the substantial health hazards posed by the herbicides. They also asserted that application of the herbicides violated the Act for the Protection of Bald and Golden Eagles[108] because the herbicides could harm the eagles who fed and nested in the forest. The Forest Service used the herbicides to kill plants that competed with conifers for light and nutrients.

In order to resolve this case, Judge Skopil had to become intimately familiar with long, highly technical EIS's, review and understand the history of herbicide research, and explore mountains of expert testimony. By this time, 2,4,5-T had been shown to cause birth defects in rats and mice, and the government had prohibited use of the compound in home products and on human food crops.

Judge Skopil found that use of the herbicides did not violate the Eagles Act because the Forest Service did not spray near any known or suspected nesting sites. However, he did find that the most recent EIS did not adequately address potential hazards to humans and to nearby farm crops posed by herbicides containing "TCDD," one of the most toxic chemicals known to man; in fact, the EIS did not even mention the controversy over Agent Orange. Judge Skopil enjoined—or prohibited—the Forest Service from using the herbicides 2,4,5-T and silvex until it had prepared and filed an adequate EIS.[109] Judge Skopil made clear that he was not deciding whether it was a good idea to use the herbicides, but only whether the EIS required by NEPA adequately addressed scientific information necessary to make an informed decision.

Ultimately, Judge Skopil approved a later EIS prepared by the Forest Service, which indicated that 2,4-D was a relatively safe herbicide compared with other compounds. Although the plaintiffs did not succeed in completely stopping the Forest Service from spraying herbicides, the injunction bought them time and a mandate to the Forest Service to more carefully evaluate the effects of their forest management practices.

## The Mount Hood Freeway

Although not based on environmental laws, Judge Burns's 1977 decision to set aside federal approval of the proposed Mount Hood Freeway in east Portland concluded a lawsuit that resembled environmental cases in that citizens instituted it to protect their surroundings. Nineteen individuals and one association asserted that the proposed location of the freeway would either displace them or irreparably damage their neighborhood. In doing so, they identified 12 legal bases for their claims, including constitutional rights.

The freeway was to be constructed under the Federal-Aid Highway Act.[110] The act and its implementing regulations required public hearings before a state highway department could be committed to a location for a freeway corridor. Because Judge Burns found that the State of Oregon was committed to the specific location in east Portland before it held hearings, he found that state officials had failed to comply with the act.[111]

After this decision, the state abandoned its proposal for the freeway. But the case continued in order to determine who would pay the $360,000 in attorney fees incurred by the plaintiffs. The federal defendants were immune by law from any duty to pay the fees. However, the state defendants were not. Judge Burns estimated that 75 percent of the plaintiffs' fees related to their case against the state, but the state appealed this split, in part on the grounds that it was imprecise. The Ninth Circuit Court of Appeals, which could not identify any more precise method for figuring the amount of fees, affirmed Judge Burns's decision that the state had to pay 75 percent.[112]

## Elk Creek Dam

Oregon's many waterways have been a constant source of friction because of the many competing interests they serve: aesthetic, wildlife, irrigation, fishing and boating, hydropower, drinking water, and commerce. The construction of the Elk Creek Dam in the Rogue River Basin in southern Oregon—a $119 million project—brought one of these controversies before the district court and eventually before the U.S. Supreme Court.

Congress authorized construction of the dam in 1962 as part of the Rogue River Project. The two other dams in the project—Lost Creek Dam and Applegate Dam—had already been constructed in the basin to control flooding when in 1985 four groups sought to stop construction of the third and final dam in the project, Elk Creek Dam. The Oregon Natural Resources Council, the Oregon Guides and Packers Association, Inc., the Rogue Fly-fishers, Inc., and the Rogue River Guides Association contended that the Army Corps of Engineers failed to consider important effects the dam would have. They asserted that the Corps violated the National Environmental Policy Act by failing to weigh the cumulative effects of the three dams or to include a "worst case analysis" of uncertain effects. Increased water temperature and turbidity, they contended, would harm water quality in general and fish in particular.

Judge Burns rejected each of their six contentions. First, he held that preparation of a retrospective EIS covering all three dams would be illogical; the first two were complete, and the Elk Creek Dam was one-third complete. Second, the Corps adequately considered the susceptibility of the soil to slides and the impacts on the Wild and Scenic stretches of the river 57 miles downstream. Third, the Corps' mitigation measures were adequate because for every adverse environmental effect, it had or was developing plans to alleviate damage. Fourth, the Corps' cost-benefit analysis of the project was not defective because it gave Congress a realistic assessment on which to decide whether to proceed with the dam. Fifth, the Corps was not required to conduct a worst-case analysis of uncertain impacts because its state-of-the-art modelling techniques made the impacts predictable. Finally, the Corps did not need to prepare a supplemental EIS based on a soil study and an Oregon Department of Fish and Wildlife study which indicated that the dam would reduce fish populations; Judge Burns found that the new information was not significant.[113]

The court of appeals reversed that ruling and instructed Judge Burns to halt construction on the dam. It held that the Corps should have looked at the cumulative environmental impacts of the three dams. The Corps did not challenge this holding, but it did seek review in the Supreme Court of the appellate court's holding that the Corps must conduct worst-case analysis and must consider the two new studies.[114]

Based on a companion case, the Supreme Court quickly dismissed the contention that NEPA required the Corps to conduct worst-case analysis. However, the Court used the Elk Creek Dam case to clarify when NEPA requires supplemental EIS's based on information discovered after a decision has been made to go forward with a project. This case established the concept that agencies must apply a "rule of reason" and supplement an EIS based on new information when any action that remains to be taken on a project would be environmentally significant and the new information indicates risks the agency had not considered.[115] The Court concluded that under NEPA, the Corps was not required to supplement the EIS for Elk Creek Dam because the new information was insignificant.

The controversy over construction of the dam continued, as did environmental studies. The Corps' court-ordered draft environmental impact statement recommended that the dam be completed but that Elk Creek be allowed to flow through it, except for flood control. The U.S. Fish and Wildlife Service then became involved to determine whether using the dam for flood control would threaten the Northern Spotted Owl. As of this writing, the dam stands only partially completed. Environmental groups continue to fight any further construction. The district court case remains open, and Judge Burns continues to supervise the project.

## Timber Cases

Perhaps no environmental issue has so polarized Oregonians as the controversy over timber. Oregon's economy has been highly dependent on timber throughout the state's history, and many thousands of Oregonians continue to depend on the forests for their jobs. But other Oregonians grew increasingly alarmed at the rapid rate at which the timber lands were being cut, particularly in the national forests. The environmental legislation of the 1970s gave citizens and watchdog groups new tools with which to protect the forests for wildlife and recreation; as a result, by the end of the 1980s, the federal court was enmeshed in oversight of the U.S. Forest Service and the Bureau of Land Management (BLM).

A particular difficulty with these cases is the myriad of complex statutes, regulations, and legal principles that govern whether agency action may be reviewed by the court, and when. Thus, when Judge Burns had to decide in *Oregon Natural Resources Council, Inc. v. United States Forest Service*[116] whether the reoffer of the North Roaring Devil timber sale amounted to a "decision" by the Forest Service subject to appeal, he had to look beyond applicable statutes and regulations to the ambiguous congressional reports behind them. He concluded that Congress did not contemplate full review of the Forest Service's original decision to sell a stand of timber when a later reoffer of the same stand was challenged, a point on which he was reversed.

In an unusual move in that case, Judge Burns decided to view the 61-acre sale area in the Willamette National Forest so that he could understand the maps received in evidence. Not surprisingly, the plaintiff environmental groups endorsed the view and the defendant timber company, which had purchased the timber, objected. A two-hour trek along muddy and partially snow-covered logging roads followed, led by a district ranger. Judge Burns allowed members of the media to accompany him and the attorneys and to ask questions before and after the view. In his written opinion in the case, Judge Burns described the area as "a river

*Forests managed by the U.S. Forest Service and the Bureau of Land Management have been the subjects of several district court cases in which environmental concerns must be balanced against Oregon's timber-dependent economy.*
(Oregon Historical Society Negative #ORHI85287)

gorge of heart-stopping magnificence,"[117] but denied the plaintiffs' assertions that the sale violated several environmental statutes.

Tension between environmentalists and industry reached new heights with the controversy over the Northern Spotted Owl. The owl requires for its survival old-growth forest, which has been an important part of the Pacific Northwest's economy. The Pacific forest has the largest, oldest trees in the world, some of which reach 300 feet in height and 50 feet in circumference.[118] The spotted owl is considered an "indicator species" whose condition gives a reading of the overall health of a forest.[119] The owl requires extensive territory—up to 2,500 acres per pair. As early as 1973, an interagency committee suggested that the spotted owl should be considered for protection under the Endangered Species Act.[120]

Concern over the spotted owl pushed environmental groups to challenge the harvest of old-growth timber in the forests of the Northwest and California. The resulting decrease in timber supplies threatened mill closures and lost jobs. Loggers and millworkers marched in protest, and the controversy stretched across the country to Washington, D.C., where President Bush stressed the human consequences of protecting the owl, and Oregon's Senator Bob Packwood promised to seek a waiver if the owl was listed as a threatened species.[121]

Most of the spotted owl cases were handled in the federal court in western Washington, but Judge Frye heard a significant owl case, which covered old-growth timber in seven BLM management districts. In *Portland Audubon Society v. Hodel*,[122] the plaintiff environmental groups challenged all of the BLM's proposed old-growth sales within 2.1 miles of known spotted owl habitat. The plaintiffs asserted that the timber sales violated NEPA, the Oregon & California Lands Act,[123] the Federal Lands Policy and Management Act,[124] and the Migratory Bird Treaty Act.[125]

Judge Frye dismissed the case under a federal statute that prohibited challenges to comprehensive timber-management plans on the basis of new information brought forth after the plan had been completed. The court of appeals reversed because the plaintiffs nevertheless had a right to challenge individual sales, even though the overall effect was to challenge the BLM's entire plan. On remand, Judge Frye again denied relief on the NEPA claim on the grounds that the suit challenged the overall plan and not particular activities, and she dismissed the non-NEPA claims on the grounds that the plaintiffs had waited too long to bring them. Because Judge Frye would not stop the sales pending another appeal, the plaintiffs secured a stay of the sales in the court of appeals.

This time the appellate court agreed that the plaintiffs could not challenge the sales under NEPA because the BLM already had considered the impact on the owls when it originally drafted the management plan. But the court sent the claims under the other acts back to the district court, noting that environmental cases should be dismissed for delay only sparingly.

Meanwhile, Congress was busy working on the "Northwest Timber Compromise," which took effect October 23, 1989 and required the Forest Service and the BLM, during fiscal year 1990, to sell 5.8 billion board feet of timber in Oregon and Washington, none of which could come from identified spotted owl habitat. In a case unrelated to *Portland Audubon Society*, Judge Panner ruled that the Timber Compromise did not require the Forest Service to sell exactly that amount, but only so much of it as the Forest Service could sell and still comply with environmental restrictions.[126] And the Ninth Circuit Court of Appeals struck down another provision in the Timber Compromise because it violated the separation-of-powers doctrine.[127] In that provision, Congress attempted to dictate the outcome of *Portland Audubon Society* and a related Washington case by declaring that the BLM's timber-management plans adequately considered the impacts on owls.

Back in Judge Frye's court, the plaintiffs pursued their non-NEPA claims and reasserted the NEPA claim on the grounds that the Timber Compromise barred it only temporarily. Judge Frye rejected each of the plaintiffs' contentions, but the Ninth Circuit Court of Appeals revived the NEPA claim in December 1991.[128] As a result of this and related Washington cases, the Forest Service sold only one billion board feet of timber in Oregon and Washington in 1991.[129] The spotted owl had been listed as a threatened species in June 1990, and the battle between the owls and the timber industry was destined to continue in the courts.

◌

# THE BHAGWAN SHREE RAJNEESH

One of the most volatile Oregon issues of the 1980s followed the development in Wasco County of Rancho Rajneesh, a religious commune. The district court decided two key cases that hastened the demise of this eastern Oregon community run by followers of the Bhagwan Shree Rajneesh.

*In the early 1980s approximately 5,000 followers of the Bhagwan Shree Rajneesh established a commune in Wasco County, took over the town of Antelope, and filed to incorporate it as Rajneeshpuram. This action triggered a series of suits in district court involving questions about the separation of church and state, charges that the commune had poisoned 750 people with salmonella bacteria, allegations of immigration violations, and rumors of threats to kill the governor and the U.S. attorney. (Photo by Claudia J. Howell,* The Oregonian)

The Bhagwan began his religious movement in India in the late 1960s. In 1981 his organization purchased what was then the Big Muddy Ranch, a 64,229-acre spread east of the Warm Springs Indian Reservation, and renamed it Rancho Rajneesh. That same year, the guru flew to the United States, purportedly for back surgery, but his motives were questioned when he then moved to Rancho Rajneesh, the new headquarters of his international religion.

The Bhagwan and his followers proclaimed that Rancho Rajneesh was a peaceful, crime-free, utopian society. Eventually, approximately 5,000 followers joined the commune. At first, most Wasco County residents did not oppose the Rajneeshees. But the guru's followers overwhelmed the tiny town of Antelope, within the ranch's borders, and tension mounted in 1982 when the Rajneeshees incorporated the town as Rajneeshpuram.

Soon the Rajneeshees began to butt heads with federal, state, and county authorities. The U.S. Immigration and Naturalization Service

263

(INS) investigated the Bhagwan's immigration into the United States and marriages between disciples who were U.S. citizens and disciples who were not. Informants alleged that Rajneeshees caused a huge outbreak of salmonella poisoning in The Dalles in 1984 by planting bacteria in the salad bars of restaurants that infected approximately 750 people. The alleged purpose of the poisoning was to test whether the city's water supply could be tainted with bacteria to make residents so ill that they could not vote in the election for the Wasco County Court, and the Rajneeshees could swing the election with thousands of homeless bussed in to vote.[130] On the basis of these allegations, Secretary of State Norma Paulus imposed emergency voter registration rules that required a hearing before a new voter could be registered.

The commune faced internal strife as well. The Rancho purportedly had a massive electronic surveillance system to supervise the disciples. The Bhagwan's personal secretary, Ma Anand Sheela, and two other Rajneesh women were charged with trying to poison the guru's personal physician. There were reports of power struggles within the organization. As a result of these internal struggles, as well as charges brought by government authorities, many court cases arose, both civil and criminal, both state and federal. Some were brought by the Rajneeshees.

In 1984 the State of Oregon filed an action in the district court for a declaration that the incorporation of Rajneeshpuram violated the constitutional requirement of separation of church and state. The state asked specifically for the court to declare that the incorporation was invalid and that therefore the state need not provide public money or services to the community. The Rajneeshees sued Governor Vic Atiyeh and other officials on the grounds that they were conspiring to eliminate the religion of Rajneeshism and the community of Rajneeshpuram. The Rajneeshees also sued to stop the ongoing INS investigation of possible immigration-law violations.

The suit against the governor originally went to Judge Panner. When the Rajneeshees asserted that Judge Panner was biased because he was friends with the governor and one of the defense lawyers, the judge denied any bias but ordered the case reassigned anyway. Meanwhile, informants alleged that a group of Rajneeshees led by Ma Anand Sheela kept a "hit list" that included the governor and U.S. Attorney Charles Turner.

The end of 1985 brought two major blows to the commune. On November 14, the Bhagwan appeared before Judge Leavy in response to

35 immigration charges that the government had brought against him. Security was unusually tight in the courtroom because of the government's concern about assassination attempts against the guru, and police had to cordon off streets around the courthouse to hold back the many spectators who awaited a chance to view the bearded Bhagwan. In a surprising move, the Bhagwan pleaded guilty to two of the charges. His plea bargain agreement with the U.S. attorney, which Judge Leavy approved, gave him five days to leave the country. The Bhagwan also had to pay $400,000 in fines and agree to stay out of the United States for the five years he would be on probation. The Bhagwan left for India.

Less than one month later, Judge Frye ruled that the incorporation of Rajneeshpuram violated both the state and federal constitutions because the governance of the city was closely tied to the religious teachings of the Bhagwan. Her ruling voided the city's incorporation. The Rajneeshees had protested that such a ruling would place urban development in the city in violation of state land-use laws.

But the disciples already had begun to dismantle the commune, and financial woes took them to bankruptcy court. In 1986 Oregon Attorney General Dave Frohnmayer announced that the Rajneeshees had agreed in a settlement to pay approximately $5.6 million to victims of Rajneesh crimes, most of which would go to victims of the Salmonella poisonings in The Dalles.[131] Members of the commune were selling off assets, and the ranch was on the market for $28 million.

As the era of the Rajneesh faded, Wasco County residents began a fundraiser to erect a life-size bronze statue of an antelope as a tribute to Oregonians who resisted the Rajneesh.[132]

∾

# LIFE IN THE COURTHOUSE

It is not easy to be a judge. A judge may hear cases all day long and then spend the evening preparing for the next day's calendar. A lawyer can select cases and limit them to a certain area of expertise, perhaps one the lawyer has studied for many years. In contrast, a judge must accept and decide a wide range of legal issues, many of which are complex and technical.

The judges who served in the district of Oregon between 1950 and 1991 met these demands admirably and were known for their hard work and diligence.[133] In the federal system, Oregon was considered a strong district with good administration.[134] These factors, together with the exacting attitude of Judge Solomon toward lawyers, led to a well-prepared and ethical local bar.

The judges tried to achieve consistency in their application of the law by circulating written opinions among themselves for comment before they were released to the public. They encouraged one another to go over the opinions carefully and comment not only on the legal analysis, but also on the writing. Judge Solomon took this invitation seriously. He had a reputation for his insistence on clear, concise writing and plain English. Judge Belloni recalled asking Judge Skopil how he was getting along soon after Judge Skopil joined the court. "You know," the newer judge replied, "I write these opinions, and they seem logical and well written and to correctly state the law, and I am quite confident in them. It never worries me to get them past the circuit without reversal, but I have trouble getting them past Judge Solomon."[135]

The judges were very friendly and collegial among themselves, which is not true of every district. Judge Solomon's great heart and outgoing nature came as a surprise to some of the newer judges, who knew only his reputation for eating lawyers for breakfast. Judge Goodwin confessed that he did not sleep the night before appearing as a lawyer in Judge Solomon's court,[136] and Judge Belloni had expected to have "no more than polite conversation" with him.[137] But Judge Solomon welcomed each new judge with friendship and the offer of whatever assistance might be needed. A warm atmosphere pervaded the courthouse and remains among the judges today.

Judge Solomon epitomized the human side of being a judge. He was famous in the courthouse for saying that in a close, difficult case, he would "rule on the side of God." "That way," he said, "if the court of appeals reverses you, at least you know which side they're on." He had been impressed by a New York judge who jabbed himself with a pin before sentencing a person, to remind himself that he was human and bled like everyone else. As a result, on his way to each sentencing, Judge Solomon would stop and look at a painting in the anteroom of his court that depicted the artist's concept of death.

Judge Solomon also changed the court's naturalization ceremony to make it more meaningful to new citizens. Before, the ceremony had involved no more than a quick oath read by the clerk and acknowledged by the applicants. When Judge Solomon was asked to take over the ceremony in the early 1950s, he had all of the applicants state their names and the countries from which they came, repeat the oath, and then pledge allegiance to the American flag.

When they reach retirement age, federal judges are entitled to stop working and continue to receive full pay for life. If a judge continues working on "senior status," he or she is entitled to receive any increases in pay awarded to active judges. A senior judge may choose cases rather than receive them on random assignment. The senior judge system has come under attack, but very few judges abuse the privilege of deciding how much work they will take, and many continue working full time until death.

Almost all of the Oregon judges who retired from active service during this period took senior status and continued to work nearly full time; the exception was Judge McColloch, who retired because of ill health. Judge East took senior status in 1967 for health reasons but continued working and hearing cases, many in other parts of the country. Judge Solomon took senior status in 1971 but continued hearing as many cases as his health would allow until his death in 1987 at age 80; at that time, he had served 37 years on the federal bench. Judge Belloni also continued a hectic schedule after he became a senior judge in 1984, as did Judge Burns following his retirement from active service in 1989.

In some districts, senior judges lose their chambers or otherwise become less than full colleagues in the way they are treated. In the District of Oregon, senior judges traditionally have been treated no differently than active judges, although on occasion they have voluntarily moved their chambers for the convenience of an active judge.

Although the occasional pay raises are an incentive for taking senior status rather than full retirement, one might wonder why a federal judge would continue pursuing a difficult job at an advanced age when full pay would accompany a more relaxed life. For example, in 1988 Judge Belloni—while he was handling 3,000 asbestos cases in Hawaii— received the same amount he would have received had he completely retired five years before he took senior status. At that time, he had been a judge for 32 years and still looked forward to work every day. "[M]y feeling is this," he said. "I've spent half my life trying to become a United States District Judge; why in the heck should I quit it?"[138]

❧

# PHYSICAL FACILITIES

The District Court for Oregon has occupied a block-size, seven-story building at the corner of Sixth Avenue and Main Street in downtown

Portland since 1932. However, the growing pains of recent years forced some court-related personnel—including the U.S. attorneys—to find other Portland locations, and the bankruptcy court has space in a privately owned building across the street from the United States Courthouse.

In the early 1980s the Portland courthouse underwent a $7.5 million renovation that included new courtrooms for the increased number of judges. Legislation introduced in Congress by Representative Les AuCoin and passed in 1989 renamed the building the "Gus J. Solomon United States Courthouse," in recognition of Judge Solomon's long and dedicated service on the district court bench. The renaming ceremony on April 28, 1989 required a video simulcast into a second courtroom to accommodate the many federal and state judges, legislators, lawyers, and friends of Judge Solomon in attendance. Officials at the ceremony unveiled a $100,000 Carrara marble statue that now graces the steps to the courthouse. The sculpture, titled "Ventana al Pacifico" and created by Manuel Neri, is an appropriate tribute to Judge Solomon's support of the arts.

Even before the renaming ceremony, plans were under consideration for a completely new, larger federal courthouse in downtown Portland. The existing building likely will not meet space needs as the district court enters the twenty-first century.

The federal courthouse in Eugene was built in 1976 and ended U.S. Magistrate Hogan's tenancy in a tiny office in an old post office and his need to borrow the bankruptcy judges' facilities in order to hold court. There are also United States courthouses in Pendleton and Medford. The courthouse in Pendleton is named after Judge John F. Kilkenny.

# OTHER COURT PERSONNEL

Like every other aspect of the court's business during the last half of the twentieth century, the number of court personnel exploded. By 1990 the court's staff included more than 100 persons, including the judges' secretaries, law clerks, and courtroom deputies, the staff of the clerk's office, librarians, and probation officers. In addition, bankruptcy judges, U.S. attorneys, federal defenders, and U.S. marshals play important roles in the judicial system. Regrettably, the scope of this chapter does not permit exploration of the contributions these people have made in the District of Oregon. Chronological listings of the people who have held some of these positions appear in Appendix B.

# BIOGRAPHIES OF THE DISTRICT JUDGES

### Gus Jerome Solomon

Judge Solomon was a native Portlander. He was born on August 29, 1906, to parents who had emigrated from eastern Europe in the late 1800s. His father owned an apartment house on Caruthers Street in which he later opened a store that carried work clothes.

Judge Solomon attended Lincoln High School. He graduated from the University of Chicago in 1926 and from Stanford Law School in 1929. He also attended the University of Washington, Reed College, and Columbia University Law School. He was a Republican until he became a Democrat in 1938, but he described himself as a liberal throughout his life.

He practiced law in Portland from 1929 until his appointment to the federal court in 1949. He was a strong force in the public power movement in Oregon.

In 1936 he took a free speech case to the U.S. Supreme Court and won a unanimous decision. His client, Dirk De Jonge, had been arrested for speaking at a public meeting called by the Communist Party during a period of labor strife on the Portland docks. The Supreme Court held that De Jonge could not be prosecuted for speaking at a public meeting where no laws had been broken and no one was incited to break the law.[139]

During World War II, he defended local Japanese Americans by publicly opposing their internment, protesting the boycott of their produce, and intervening on their behalf with labor and farm groups. He helped organize the Committee to Aid Relocation when Japanese Americans were allowed to return to the area.[140]

Judge Solomon was active in opening up private clubs, such as the Arlington Club and the University Club, to Blacks, Jews, and Hispanics. He organized the first Legal Aid Society in Oregon and the first state chapter of the American Civil Liberties Union (ACLU). He also was active in the Oregon Commonwealth Federation, a political organization to which several unions belonged. His liberal views were, in part, an outgrowth of the discrimination he experienced as a Jew throughout his life.

At the age of 43, Judge Solomon was appointed to the district court by President Truman. The date was October 15, 1949—during the McCarthy era. Senate approval was slow because of allegations that he was a

Communist. These allegations stemmed, in part, from his active participation in the ACLU and Legal Aid. Among his accusers was Daniel C.
Mahoney, then Judge McColloch's law clerk, who traveled to Washington,
D.C. to testify that two ex-investigators told him that Judge Solomon had
attended Communist meetings. In addition, the American Bar Association issued an unfavorable report about him, which they later withdrew
after an onslaught of angry letters from many lawyers in Oregon who
supported him.

Judge Solomon denied that he was a Communist, and several prominent Oregonians, including General Chester McCarty, testified in his
behalf. Eventually, he was confirmed without a dissenting vote and joined
Judges Fee and McColloch on July 5, 1950.

Judge Solomon worked hard and loved his job. He once said, "When
President Truman appointed me to this job, I thought I'd enjoy it. But it
has been wonderful beyond my wildest dreams."[141] He later advised, "If
you're offered a job as a judge, take it. It's a damn good job."[142]

Judge Solomon replaced Judge McColloch as chief judge in 1958.
While chief judge, he wrote the court's first set of local rules. He
remained chief judge until he took senior status in 1971 to allow the
appointment of another judge to help with the increased caseload. As a
senior judge, he spent much of his time sitting by designation on cases
before the Ninth Circuit Court of Appeals. He was twice considered for
vacancies on that court.

Judge Solomon was known for his control of the courtroom, for fin-
ishing cases quickly, for lashing out at attorneys who were unprepared,
and for helping along young attorneys with sometimes painful lessons.
He encouraged lawyers to write clearly, using short words and plain
English instead of long words and "legalese."

Many of Judge Solomon's most noted opinions involved individual
rights. He wrote the opinion for a three-judge panel that struck down tax
exemptions for the Portland Elks Lodge on the grounds that the lodge
discriminated against minorities in its membership policies. He also
struck down as unconstitutionally vague a state statute that allowed dismissal of a teacher on grounds of immorality; the teacher had been dismissed because she was a lesbian. He barred Martin-Marietta Corp. from
firing three Seventh-Day Adventists who cited religious reasons for refusing to pay union dues, saying that it was reasonable for the workers to pay
an equivalent amount of money to charity instead.

In 1976 he restricted state fish and wildlife officials from imposing hunting, fishing, and trapping regulations on Klamath Indians on the former Klamath Reservation. Even though the reservation had fallen out of tribal ownership between 1957 and 1961, Judge Solomon held that descendants of the 2,000 Klamath Indians on tribal rolls in 1957 were entitled to continue hunting, fishing, and trapping.

Judge Solomon handled the case of a young black woman accused of hitting an FBI agent over the head with a rolling pin to help her brother escape. (He was wanted as a military deserter.) Judge Solomon tried her as a juvenile and sentenced her to 18 months in prison in San Diego, but delayed the start of her sentence to allow her to finish high school. The case caused an uproar in Portland, as black organizations protested that her conviction was unjust. Her conviction was affirmed on appeal.

In 1965 Judge Solomon received the E.B. MacNaughton Civil Liberties Award for outstanding contributions to the cause of civil liberties. He also received the 1966 Annual Brotherhood Award of B'nai B'rith for his dedication to brotherhood and human rights. He was the first vice president of the American Jewish Congress, president and member of the board of the Boys and Girls Aid Society of Oregon, member of the National Civil Rights Commission, and former chairman of the Oregon Anti-Defamation League. In 1970 he was named First Citizen of Portland by realtors for his broad role in the community and for his active dedication to the removal of class and social barriers.

Judge Solomon married Elisabeth Miller, another strong liberal, in 1939. They had three children: Gerald, Phillip, and Richard. Judge Solomon died February 15, 1987, at age eighty, having served longer than any other district judge in Oregon. At his death, *Oregonian* Editor William A. Hilliard commented, "Equality and justice were not empty words to Judge Solomon.... All of us are freer today because of the courage and strength of this wonderful man."[143]

## William G. East

Judge William G. East was born in Lecompton, Kansas, on April 25, 1908. His family moved to Salem, Oregon, in 1910, where his father was a banker. The family also spent one year in Portland and one year in St. Helens.

Judge East lettered in football at Salem High School, from which he graduated in 1927. He studied pre-medicine at the University of Oregon, but then decided on law school. He graduated from the law

271

*Judge William G. East was appointed to the district court in 1955 by President Dwight D. Eisenhower. East's most famous case was the Frank Sinatra, Jr. kidnapping case, which he was given in 1964, while he was on assignment in Los Angeles. (Oregon Historical Society Negative #ORHI87767)*

school there in 1932 and was admitted to practice in Oregon that year.

After graduation, Judge East worked with the law firm of Harris, Smith & Bryson in Eugene. In 1937 he took over the practice of Charles A. Hardy. In 1940 he was elected to the Board of Governors of the Oregon State Bar, but he had to resign during his second year to enter the military. He earned several medals during World War II, including a purple heart.

After the war he opened a law office with Sidney A. Milligan in Eugene and specialized in lumber company cases. He served as city attorney for Eugene and counsel for the local water board. In 1949 he was appointed state circuit judge for Coos, Curry, and Douglas counties.

President Dwight Eisenhower appointed Judge East, a Republican, to the district court in 1955. East took his oath of office on June 24, 1955, at the age of 47. His appointment filled a position that had been vacant for one year—since Judge Fee had been appointed to the Ninth Circuit Court of Appeals.

Part of the delay resulted from an FBI recheck of Judge East after he was involved in a car accident in Reedsport. Judge East was driving, and two other state judges were in the car with him. After the editor of a Reedsport newspaper criticized the conduct of the judges during the investigation of the accident, the FBI rechecked Judge East's qualifications.[144] The recheck cleared Judge East of any blame for the accident.

Judge East was known for his no-nonsense approach to the administration of justice. He had a reputation for handing down stiff penalties, and he disliked newspaper pictures of trial scenes. He believed that this concept of a free press encroached on the concept of a fair trial.

While on an assignment in Los Angeles in 1964, Judge East was given the "Sinatra Kidnapping" case. The case involved the trial of Frank Sinatra, Jr.'s kidnappers. The trial lasted four weeks and received enormous publicity. In fact, Judge East cautioned the jury daily not to view any news reports because the attorneys went before television cameras that often to give their impressions of what had happened in court. There were four motions for mistrial during the case. Ultimately, the kidnappers were convicted and Judge East gave two of them the maximum sentence: life in prison plus 75 years.

Judge East took senior status in 1967 for health reasons. He continued to hear cases regularly for many years, mostly in Los Angeles and San Francisco. Eventually, he established his chambers in Eugene.

Judge East married Louise Frances Wilhelm in 1933; they had one daughter, Sara Elizabeth. Judge East died on April 27, 1985.

## John Francis Kilkenny

Judge Kilkenny, a first-generation Irishman, was born in Heppner, Oregon, on October 26, 1901. He attended Columbia Preparatory School in Portland, which later merged into the University of Portland. He graduated from the University of Notre Dame Law School with an LL.B. in 1925. He played football at Notre Dame, under Knute Rockne, until he was sidelined by a knee injury. Much later, the Notre Dame Club of Oregon created the John Kilkenny Fellowship Fund at the University of Notre Dame Law School. The fund gives money for law school to promising students.

After law school, he worked for Raley, Raley, et al. in Pendleton. He was president of the Oregon State Bar from 1943 to 1944 and served on the Oregon State Bar Board of Governors and the Oregon Board of Bar Examiners. In 1952 he opened the firm of Kilkenny & Fabre in Pendleton, where he worked until his appointment to the federal bench.

President Eisenhower appointed Judge Kilkenny, a Republican, to the District of Oregon in 1959; he assumed the position on August 15 of that year and became the first Catholic to serve as a federal judge in Oregon. He replaced Judge McColloch, who had retired at the end of 1958.

In 1969 President Nixon appointed Judge Kilkenny to the Ninth Circuit Court of Appeals. Senate Judiciary Committeeman Hiram Fong held up his confirmation for three months; the senator had insisted that he would not support any nominee until someone from his home state of Hawaii was nominated. The Senate eventually confirmed Judge Kilkenny,

273

and he became the first Oregon representative to sit on the appellate court since Judge Fee served there in the 1950s. Judge Kilkenny took senior status in 1971.

The judge headed the move to restore the old Pioneer Courthouse in downtown Portland instead of constructing a new federal building for the Ninth Circuit Court of Appeals' Portland quarters. Restoration of the 1875 building was completed in the early 1970s. Judge Kilkenny received awards from the Oregon Historical Society and the Portland Beautification Association for his work on this project. Later, the court-house in Pendleton was renamed for him.

He also received the University of Portland Medal of Achievement in 1972. His colleagues on the federal bench established and endowed the John F. Kilkenny Book Fund at the school.

Judge Kilkenny received an out-of-the-ordinary honor for a judge: the Oregon Geographic Names Board gave an eastern Oregon rock forma-tion the name Judge Kilkenny suggested. The judge had a long interest in eastern Oregon history and had researched the story of Thomas Fitzpatrick, an early Oregon guide who had broken his hand in a battle with Indians. Judge Kilkenny proposed that an ice-torn volcano in Deschutes County be given the name "Broken Hand."

He served on the Judicial Conference Committee on Court Administration from 1971 to 1976. Judge Kilkenny married Virginia Brannock in 1931. They have two children: John Michael and Karen Kilkenny Sagner.

## Robert Clinton Belloni

Judge Belloni was born on April 4, 1919 in Riverton, Oregon (in Coos County). His heritage is Italian-Swiss. His father was a dairy farmer and later had a transfer company. His mother taught school and later ran the transport company.

Robert Belloni graduated from the University of Oregon with a degree in history in 1941. He had planned to attend medical school, but changed his mind while serving as a combat medic in the Army during World War II. He served in the Asiatic Pacific Theater until his discharge as a first lieutenant in 1946.

After being discharged, he returned to the University of Oregon for law school, graduating in 1951 with Judge Goodwin. During college, he had often sat in the courtroom when Judge Fee heard trials in Eugene; Judge Belloni found the judge to be very strict and learned a great deal from watching him. Judge Belloni later said that within his first month of law school, he knew that he wanted to be a judge because it would allow him to work in all areas of the law, not just particular subjects.

Judge Belloni was in private practice in Coquille from 1951 until 1952, when he moved to Myrtle Point and became one of two lawyers in town. There, he served as councilman and mayor; he also chaired the Coos County Democratic Central Committee.

In 1957, he was appointed Oregon circuit judge for Coos and Curry counties, serving in Coquille. Later, he was elected to that position. He was the president of the Oregon Juvenile Court Judges Association in 1963 and president of the Oregon Circuit Judges Association in 1966.

In addition to his duties as a trial judge, he presided over the juvenile court. He recognized the need for a local facility other than the state reform school to house and educate children who were in trouble with the law and had to be removed from their homes for the protection of society and themselves. During his service as a state circuit judge, he continuously urged Coos County to establish such a facility.

Upon his appointment to the federal court, a spontaneous movement began to construct the facility which he had been advocating during his ten years as state judge. Labor unions, businesses, and individuals donated labor, land, and money, and presented a completed, debt-free facility to Coos County. The County Board of Commissioners named it the Robert C. Belloni Boys Forest Ranch. The ranch's volunteer board of directors later added a girls ranch and a shelter care facility and renamed the enlarged facility Bob Belloni Ranches, Inc.

President Lyndon Johnson appointed Judge Belloni to the district court on April 4, 1967, the judge's forty-eighth birthday. He replaced Judge East, who took senior status. Belloni served as chief judge after Judge Solomon, from 1971 to 1976. Judge Belloni took senior status in 1984 after 17 years on the federal bench and 10 years on the state bench.

Judge Belloni was very effective in managing cases where large groups of people were injured or killed from a single cause. Mass filings of such cases were threatening to clog the dockets of all federal courts. One such group of cases was brought by women injured by the Dalkon Shield against the A.H. Robbins Company, manufacturer of the intrauterine device. Judge Belloni devised a plan for consolidating all of the Oregon Dalkon Shield cases, and all were tried promptly. The district court in Arizona then asked Judge Belloni to handle the Dalkon Shield cases there; he quickly tried or settled all of the Dalkon Shield cases pending in

275

Arizona before the defendant company declared bankruptcy. Because the lawyers were impressed with Judge Belloni's method for handling these cases, they waived juries.

Because of his experience in mass tort cases, Judge Belloni was assigned, and completed, approximately 3,000 asbestos-injury cases filed in Hawaii by individuals employed by the Pearl Harbor Naval Shipyard.

Judge Belloni recalled the era of the Vietnam War as the most difficult years of his judicial career. It was a period when many young men refused to serve because of their belief that the war was wrong, yet for technical reasons did not qualify for conscientious-objector status. The struggle all the judges faced was knowing that enforcement of the law meant imprisonment of some of the country's best youths. After sentencing three young men to prison for two years, Judge Belloni later, on his own motion and without any request by the defendants, reduced the term to 120 days. "I just feel that they have been punished enough," he said.[145]

Judge Belloni has two children: James L. Belloni and Susan Belloni Gray. He is married to the former Faye Johnson Dement.

## Alfred Theodore Goodwin

Judge Goodwin was born on June 29, 1923, in Bellingham, Washington. He was the son of a Baptist minister and the oldest of eight children. His father's work took the family all over the West Coast. In his teenage years before college, Judge Goodwin worked as a ranch hand near Prineville. He intended to be a cowboy, but changed his mind and pursued a journalism degree from the University of Oregon. A stint in the Army Reserve during World War II interrupted his education from 1943 to 1946.

Upon graduation from the University of Oregon in 1947, Judge Goodwin was named the "outstanding male journalism graduate of the year." He served as associate editor of the *Oregon Daily Emerald* and as a reporter and Sunday editor for the *Eugene Register-Guard*.

Judge Goodwin graduated from the University of Oregon Law School in 1951. He practiced with Darling & Vonderheit in Eugene and became a partner there in 1954. Governor Paul Patterson appointed him to the circuit court of Lane County in 1955. He served as associate justice on the Oregon Supreme Court from 1960 until his appointment to the federal court by President Richard Nixon in 1969. He replaced Judge Kilkenny, who was elevated to the Ninth Circuit Court of Appeals.

Judge Goodwin's tenure on the district court in Oregon was short. In 1971 President Nixon appointed him to the Ninth Circuit Court of

Appeals. Again, he replaced Judge Kilkenny, who took senior status on that court. Judge Goodwin's appointment made him the fifth Oregonian to join the Ninth Circuit Court of Appeals.[146] He served as a member of the Judicial Conference Committee on Court Administration from 1977 to 1983.

Perhaps as a result of his journalism background, Judge Goodwin's written opinions are clear and concise. By his own admission, he learned many time-saving trial techniques from Judge Solomon. Judge Goodwin has an easy, comfortable manner in the courtroom. He once caught a witness—an eastern Oregon rancher—smoking in his courtroom. The judge explained to the man that smoking was not allowed, but added, "Don't be nervous. Most of these lawyers in here would be just as nervous in a corral as you are in here."[147]

While on the district court, Judge Goodwin struck down a banking practice that resulted in interest rates higher than those allowed under Oregon's usury laws. In *American Timber & Trading Co. v. First National Bank of Oregon*,[148] borrowers joined in a class action to challenge First Interstate's practice of computing loan interest based on a 360-day year. The practice turned 10- and 12-percent interest rates—the legal limits— into returns to the bank that exceeded those percentages. Although First Interstate asserted that this was a common banking practice, Judge Goodwin concluded that the plain meaning of the words "per annum" in the banking laws was a 365-day year. Because of the importance of this decision to the banking industry, Judge Goodwin certified his holding for immediate appeal to the Ninth Circuit Court of Appeals, which affirmed.[149]

A Republican, Judge Goodwin is also a First Amendment fundamentalist who believes that the press has the right to print whatever it chooses. In his opinion, if the press commits libel, it can pay damages to the injured party. Judge Goodwin believes that government secrecy is far more dangerous than irresponsible journalists.

Judge Goodwin married Mary Ellin Handelin in 1949. They have four children: Karl Alfred, Margaret Ellen, Sara Jane, and James Paul. Judge Goodwin has one child, Michael Theodore Goodwin, from a previous marriage.

## Otto R. Skopil, Jr.

Judge Skopil was born on June 3, 1919, in Portland. In 1941 he graduated from Willamette University, where he played basketball for three years on a scholarship. He did not play in his final year because he entered Willamette's law school in a joint-degree program. The program allowed him to attend law school after completing his junior year in liberal arts.

His law school education was postponed by World War II. He served in the Navy from 1942 to 1946. While in the service, he attended the Harvard University Graduate School of Business through the Supply Corps. After the war, he returned to law school and graduated in 1946.

Judge Skopil then entered a 26-year stint in private practice in Salem. He shared an office with his uncle from 1946 to 1951 and was a partner in the firm that began as Williams & Skopil from 1951 until his appointment to the bench in 1972. He served on the Oregon State Bar Board of Governors from 1960 to 1963.

President Nixon appointed Judge Skopil, a Republican, to the district court in Oregon in 1972. Judges Burns and Skopil were appointed at the same time to fill vacancies created by the retirement to senior status of Judge Solomon and the promotion of Judge Goodwin to the Court of Appeals. The two new judges were especially welcome because the court was facing the first serious backlog of cases in its history. To handle cases more efficiently, Judge Skopil took most of the securities cases and Judge Burns took most of the criminal cases.

Judge Skopil was chief judge from 1976 to 1979, when President Carter appointed him to the Ninth Circuit Court of Appeals. His appointment filled one of ten new positions on that court. He took senior status in 1986.

Judge Skopil was honored as the 1986 Legal Citizen of the Year, an award sponsored by the Oregon Law-Related Education Project. In 1987 he received the Founders Award from the National Conference of U.S. Magistrates for his contributions to the federal magistrate system. He had been a member of the Magistrates Committee of the Judicial Conference of the United States from 1977 to 1987 and chairman of that committee from 1980 to 1987.

*Oregon Journal* writers accurately described Judge Skopil as "a congenial, square-built man whose deep, melodious voice soothes the courtroom to about the same degree that Solomon's tenor electrifies it."[150] He has an easy-going, warm, and respectful manner both on and off the bench.

Judge Skopil is married to the former Janet Rae Lundy and has four children: Otto Richard III, Casey Robert, Shannon Ida, and Mollie Jo.

On June 4, 1992 the U.S. district court judges (back row) and magistrate judges (front row) joined U.S. court of appeals judges for the ninth circuit (middle row) for this formal portrait. Pictured are (back to front, left to right) Michael R. Hogan, Helen I. Frye, Robert E. Jones, James A. Redden, Owen M. Panner, Robert C. Belloni, Malcolm F. Marsh, and James M. Burns; Diarmuid F. O'Scannlain, Alfred T. Goodwin, John F. Kilkenny, Otto R. Skopil, and Edward Leavy; William M. Dale, George E. Juba, Thomas M. Coffin, and John Jelderks. Judges Goodwin, Kilkenny, Skopil, and Leavy sat on the district court bench before being appointed to the court of appeals. (Photo by Evan Wilcox)

## James Milton Burns

Judge Burns was born in Portland on November 24, 1924. He attended Grant High School and received a B.A. in business administration from the University of Portland in 1947. His undergraduate education was interrupted by World War II, while he served in the Army infantry from 1943 to 1945. After the war, he attended Loyola University Law School and graduated from there in 1950.

Burns was in private practice in Portland from 1950 to 1952 and again from 1956 to 1966. Between those times, he was the Harney County district attorney. He served as a Multnomah County circuit court judge from 1966 until his appointment to the federal court in 1972.

President Nixon appointed Judge Burns, a Republican, along with Judge Skopil, to the district court of Oregon. Judge Burns took senior status in 1989 after 17 years on the federal bench and has since traveled around the Ninth Circuit helping overloaded courts. He had served as chief judge from 1979 to 1984.

He was president of the Oregon Circuit Judges Association, former chairman of the Continuing Legal Education Committee, an original member of the Criminal Law Revision Committee (which drafted a new criminal code), co-founder of the Multnomah County Diagnostic Center, and founder of the annual Sentencing Institutes in Portland.

Since 1972 he has been a member of the National Judicial College faculty. In 1978 he co-authored the college's sentencing handbook. He has been the chairman of the U.S. Ninth Circuit Committee on Sentencing Guidelines Training and Implementation since 1987. In 1985 he was selected "Legal Citizen of the Year" by the Oregon Law-Related Education Project.

Perhaps the best known of his criminal trials were those of seven defendants who pleaded guilty or were convicted of aiding Stephen Michael Kessler's notorious escape from the Rocky Butte jail in 1982. In 1989 he ordered mediation in a six-year-old lawsuit against the Forest Service's use of herbicides in the national forests. The resulting settlement marked the first time that major environmental litigation was concluded by mediation.[151]

Judge Burns is known for his bow ties and his flair with the pen; in his opinions, he has discussed anything from butterflies to Jimmy Buffet songs. A classic Judge Burns opinion begins:

> *Nearly two centuries ago, Samuel Taylor Coleridge began his epic "The Rime of the Ancient Mariner" in this familiar fashion:*

> *It is an ancient mariner,*
> *And he stoppeth one of three,*
> *By thy long grey beard and glittering eye,*
> *Now, wherefore stopp'st thou me?*

> *My reaction to the "Complaint in Admiralty" filed here is similar to that of the wedding guest accosted by the seemingly demented old salt in Coleridge's poem. I haven't the foggiest concept of the legal course plaintiff is attempting to navigate. He attempts to invoke the admiralty jurisdiction of this court through vague metaphors relating to his Oregon birth certificate as a "charter"...aboard a "ship of state"....*

> *While I must confess I have some admiration for plaintiff's literary talents...plaintiff creates only a sea of confusion and a case of judicial malde mer.... [T]his case can deserve nothing more than a judicial "deep six."*[152]

Judge Burns is highly respected but also has been referred to as the judge most likely to chuckle or crack a joke in court or appear without his robe.[153] He is also known for offering bits of history or commentary to the attorneys, clients, or juries.

Judge Burns married Helen Hogan in 1950. They have four children: Nancy, Beth, Mary, and Molly.

## Owen M. Panner

Judge Panner was born in Chicago, Illinois, on July 28, 1924. He spent his childhood in the small community of Whizbang in the oil fields of Oklahoma. His father was a petroleum engineer and geologist. He graduated from high school in Shawnee, Oklahoma.

From 1941 to 1943, Judge Panner attended the University of Oklahoma (Norman), where he played on the golf team. He then served as a commander of army personnel on troop ships during World War II. He returned to the University of Oklahoma (Norman) for law school and received his LL.B. degree in 1949.

He practiced law in Bend, Oregon, at Panner, Johnson, et al., from 1950 until his appointment to the district court in 1980. For approximately 25 years he represented the Warm Springs Indian Tribe.

While in private practice, Judge Panner received the Oregon Trial Lawyer of the Year award. He served on the Oregon State Bar Board of Governors from 1961 to 1963 and was the vice-president in 1963.

President Carter appointed Judge Panner, a Republican, to the

District of Oregon bench in 1980. He was sworn in along with Helen J. Frye and James A. Redden on March 24, 1980. The three new judges filled the vacancy left by Judge Skopil's appointment to the Ninth Circuit Court of Appeals and the two new positions Congress had given to Oregon.

Judge Panner has a reputation for working long hours and handling court matters as expeditiously as possible. He keeps tight control of his courtroom.

Judge Panner has been a member of the Judicial Conference Commit-tee on the Budget since 1985. He served as chief judge of the federal court in Oregon from 1984 until 1991. He is a life trustee at Lewis and Clark College, a director of the Oregon Historical Society, and an elder in the Presbyterian Church. A Portland Inns of Court chapter bears his name. For many years, Judge Panner has raised and shown Arabian horses.

Judge Panner married Agnes C. Gilbert in 1946. They have three children: Owen M., Jr., Kathleen Susan, and Rene Laurie Panner Leavy. He married Nancy Hanson in 1989 and has one stepchild.

## James Anthony Redden

Judge Redden was born in Springfield, Massachusetts, on March 13, 1929. He left high school at age 17 to spend two years with the U.S. Army in Japan from 1946 to 1948. He then completed high school and attended the Boston University College of Business Administration. Judge Redden received his LL.B at Boston College Law School in 1954. Before moving to Oregon, he practiced in Springfield, Massachusetts, for one year. He then practiced in Medford from 1955 to 1973.

Redden, a Democrat, served in the Oregon House of Representatives from 1963 to 1967. He was House minority leader in 1967. He then retired from politics, but his retirement was short lived, and in 1973 he became Oregon's state treasurer. Halfway through his term as state treasurer, in 1974, he ran for governor. He and candidate Betty Roberts lost a close race to Bob Straub. Redden completed his term as state treasurer and ran successfully for Oregon attorney general in 1976.

President Carter appointed Redden to the federal court in 1980. He was 51 years old when the president submitted his name, and he made the decision to abandon his successful political career in order to serve on the bench.

In 1990 Judge Redden ruled unconstitutional a Portland city ordinance that banned disruptive behavior and bad language in city parks. He considered sanctions against the city because it had continued to litigate the validity of the ordinance even though the city council repealed the law during an overhaul of the city code.

Judge Redden is married to Joan Johnson. They have two sons: James Anthony, Jr., and William Francis.

## Helen J. Frye

Judge Frye was born on December 10, 1930, in Klamath Falls, Oregon, where her father farmed grain and potatoes. She graduated from Klamath Union High School in 1949 and from the University of Oregon with honors in 1953. In 1960 she received a masters degree in English and education.

Judge Frye taught junior and senior high school in Eugene and had three children with husband William F. Frye before entering law school at the University of Oregon in 1963. She finished there in 1966, practiced with Riddlesbarger, Pederson, Brownhill and Young, and later joined her husband's firm (Husband, Johnson and Frye).

In 1971 Governor Tom McCall appointed Judge Frye to a newly created circuit court position in Lane County. She became the first woman to serve on the Lane County Circuit Court bench and the first woman circuit court judge in Oregon to hear criminal cases. She was reelected to this position in 1972 and 1978.

President Carter appointed Judge Frye, a registered Independent, to the District Court of Oregon in 1980, making her Oregon's first woman federal judge. She was sworn in along with Judges Panner and Redden.

Judge Frye married William Frye (former Lane County District Attorney) in 1952. Her children are Eric Max Frye, Karen Lynn Gustafson, Heidi Elizabeth Black, and Hedy Elizabeth Black. Judge Frye married Charles Perry Holloman in 1980.

## Edward Leavy

Judge Leavy was born in Aurora, Oregon, on August 14, 1929, the youngest of ten children of an Irish immigrant father. His parents were hop farmers, and all of the sons worked hard in the fields. Judge Leavy and other members of his family still own the farmland near Donald, Oregon; two of his three sons work part of it.

Leavy graduated from Woodburn High School in 1947, already convinced he wanted to be a lawyer. He became the first member of his family to attend college and graduated from the University of Portland in 1950 with a degree in business administration. From there he went to the

University of Notre Dame Law School. He received his law degree and was admitted to the Oregon Bar in 1953.

Judge Leavy worked as a deputy district attorney in Eugene until his appointment to the Lane County District Court in 1957. At 27 he was the youngest judge in Oregon. Four years later he was elected to the Lane County Circuit Court, where he served until 1976. For a short time during 1974, he was a temporary justice of the Oregon Supreme Court.

Leavy became a U.S. magistrate in 1976. In 1984 President Reagan appointed Judge Leavy, a Republican, to the district court bench in Oregon, where he succeeded Judge Belloni, who took senior status. Just three years later, President Reagan appointed Judge Leavy to the Ninth Circuit Court of Appeals.

Judge Leavy is known for his easy-going, down-to-earth nature. He spends much of his leisure time doing chores at the hop farm. He married Eileen Hagenauer, a high school classmate, in 1951. They have four children: Thomas, Patrick, Mary Kay, and Paul.

## Malcolm F. Marsh

Judge Marsh was born in Portland, Oregon, on September 24, 1928. He grew up in McMinnville, graduated from McMinnville High School in 1946, and served as a corporal in the U.S. Army. He graduated from the University of Oregon with a B.S. degree in 1951 and an LL.B. in 1954, which was substituted by a J.D. degree in 1971.

Marsh practiced law in Salem for more than 30 years, from 1954 to 1987, and focused on product liability and malpractice cases. He was an associate in the Salem branch office of the McMinnville firm of Marsh, Marsh & Dashney from 1954 to 1958 and a partner in Clark, Marsh, Lindauer & McClinton from 1958 to 1987. He was Salem's First Citizen for 1983 and is a member of the Oregon State Bar, the American Bar Association, the American College of Trial Lawyers, and the Oregon Law Foundation.

President Reagan appointed Judge Marsh to the federal district court of Oregon in 1987, when Marsh was 58. He replaced Judge Leavy, who was elevated to the Ninth Circuit Court of Appeals.

Although he had no judicial experience before his appointment to the federal bench, Judge Marsh quickly impressed lawyers with his hard work and skill in the courtroom. He also perpetuated Judge Solomon's tradition of a warm and meaningful naturalization ceremony; Judge Marsh greets and shakes hands with each of the new U.S. citizens.

Judge Marsh is married to Shari Long. They have three children: Kevin Richard, Carol Marsh Tolles, and Diane Marsh Lorenz.

## Robert E. Jones

Robert Jones was born July 5, 1927, in Portland, Oregon. While a student at Grant High School, he earned the title of state golf champion. After high school he entered the U.S. Naval Reserve and served on troop ships in the Philippines and in Italy. He remained in the U.S. Naval Reserve and retired as a captain in the JAG Corps.

Judge Jones attended the University of Portland and then moved to Honolulu, where he received his B.A. degree in 1949 from the University of Hawaii. He worked in Hawaii as an insurance underwriter and adjuster. He returned to Portland in 1949 and continued working in insurance while he attended Northwestern College of Law (now Northwestern School of Law of Lewis and Clark College). He received his LL.B. there in 1953.

Jones was a trial lawyer in Portland and, from 1959 to 1963, a partner in Anderson, Franklin, Jones, Olsen & Bennett. He served as president of the Oregon Trial Lawyers Association in 1959-60. In 1963 he served in the Oregon Legislature as a Republican member of the House of Representatives.

Governor Hatfield appointed Judge Jones to the Multnomah County Circuit Court in 1963. The judge served there for 19 years and was president of the Oregon Circuit Judges Association in 1967. Governor Atiyeh appointed him to the Oregon Supreme Court at the end of 1982. Jones was elected to a six-year term on that court in 1985.

President Bush appointed Judge Jones to the U.S. District Court in 1990 to fill the judgeship of Judge Burns, who took senior status in 1989. He initially served in Eugene, along with Michael Hogan, then a magistrate. At the end of 1991, after Hogan's appointment as a district judge, Judge Jones moved to the Portland courthouse.

Judge Jones received the Multnomah Bar Association's Award of Merit in 1978 and 1979; the Citizens Award from the National Conference of Christians and Jews for establishing Volunteers in Corrections; the Service to Mankind Award from the Sertoma Club of Oregon, and the Legal Citizen of the Year Award from the Oregon Law Related Education Project in 1988. He has served on the Lewis and Clark College Board of Overseers and has chaired the Oregon Court Historical Preservation Society, Inc. Since 1964 he has been an adjunct professor at Northwestern School of Law of Lewis and Clark College. Judge Jones married Pearl F. Jensen in 1948. They have two children: Jeffrey S. Jones and Julie Lynn Jones.

## Michael R. Hogan

Judge Hogan was born September 24, 1946 in Oregon City, Oregon. He grew up in Myrtle Point near his family's 200-acre dairy and cattle farm. Hogan wrestled and ran track for the Myrtle Point Union High School Bobcats and went on to complete a history degree at the University of Oregon Honors College in 1968.

Judge Hogan attended Georgetown University Law Center by day and worked nights as a Capitol Hill police officer in Washington, D.C. He finished there in 1971 and returned to Oregon to clerk for Judge Belloni. In 1972 he joined the Portland law firm of Miller, Nash, Anderson, Yerke & Wiener. However, he practiced only 18 months before accepting an appointment as half-time U.S. magistrate, half-time bankruptcy referee in Eugene in 1973. At that time there was no federal courthouse in Eugene, and only a handful of civil cases were pending there.

Judge Hogan became a full-time magistrate by appointment in 1980 and was reappointed eight years later. He sat in Eugene throughout this time but became well acquainted with the southern and central parts of the state, holding court in Klamath Falls, Medford, Grants Pass, Roseburg, Coos Bay, Coquille, Gold Beach, Salem, and Bend.

At the time of his appointment to the district court, Judge Hogan had been a Democrat for many years. (He is now a Republican.) Nevertheless, President Bush appointed him in September 1991 to serve on the district court in Oregon, and he was strongly backed by Oregon's two Republican senators, Mark Hatfield and Bob Packwood. He filled the newly approved sixth judgeship for Oregon and became Eugene's first permanent federal judge. As a judge, Hogan has received accolades from lawyers for his settlement ability.

Judge Hogan married Christine Campbell in 1970. They have three children: Matthew, Joshua, and Michelle.

## CONCLUSION

The district court in Oregon responded well to the demands placed upon it during the period from 1950 to 1991. The demands came from

Congress, which passed voluminous federal legislation, and human society, which became more intricate. The institution of local court rules and the heavy reliance on magistrates helped the District of Oregon to handle the increased load with efficiency. Sentencing conferences, regular meetings, and the circulation of opinions for comment fostered consistency in the results of cases even though the number of judges quadrupled and four full-time magistrates joined the court. A strong work ethic pervaded the Portland courthouse, and this, together with remarkable collegiality, helped the court transition manageably from a two-man bench into a very large organization.

These traits will serve the district court well as it faces uncertain future demands. A federal courts study committee charged with planning for the next several decades is unable to do so because the workload of the federal courts will depend on the will of Congress. Hotly debated proposals are under consideration to split the Ninth Circuit, which has more judges than any other federal appellate circuit, or to combine other circuits to make them as large as the Ninth and to permit joint administration. As the federal courts grow larger, management becomes an overwhelming task.

Although the future demands on the district court in Oregon are unclear, an increase in the size of the court is a virtual certainty. Collegiality and consistency will be harder to maintain, and individual personalities will be less pronounced. Physical accommodations will continue to be a challenge; the addition of a single judge requires many extra support staff. But the court has met each new demand with energy and skill, establishing a solid foundation for a graceful and competent entrance into the twenty-first century.

## NOTES

1. Report of the Federal Courts Study Committee 4 (April 2, 1990).

2. *Id.* at 5.

3. These statistics come from the Annual Report of the Director of the Administrative Office of the United States Courts for the years 1950 and 1990.

4. Interview with the Honorable Alfred T. Goodwin, U.S. Circuit Judge for the Ninth Circuit, in Portland (Aug. 15, 1986), at 508-10.

5. *Penk v. Oregon State Board of Higher Education*, 48 Fair Empl. Prac. Cas. (BNA) 1724 (D. Or. 1985).

6. Interview with the Honorable Gus J. Solomon, U.S. District Judge for the District of Oregon, in Portland (1984), at 184.

7. *Oregon Docket 'Cleanest,'* Oregon Journal, Sept. 11, 1962, at 3.

8. Ted Natt, *3 Hard-Working Federal Judges, 'Educated Bar' Credited With Keeping Calendar Clear,* Oregonian, Nov. 8, 1964, at 40.

9. Jim Hill, *Lack of Judicial Manpower Delays Justice,* Oregonian, Nov. 18, 1979, at E8.

10. For a discussion of the commissioner system, see Erwin C. Surrency, *History of the Federal Courts* Chap. 27 (1987).

11. Pub. L. No. 90-578, 82 Stat. 1112 (1968).

12. James Long and Jamie Duncan, *Power Wielded by Few,* Oregon Journal, Jan. 30, 1978, at 2.

13. *Id.*

14. 347 U.S. 483 (1954).

15. 42 U.S.C. secs. 2000e et seq. (1988).

16. M. Edward Holland, *Oregon Civil Rights Litigation, 1964-1984: The Struggle for Equal Opportunity in the Marketplace,* 25 J. of the West 28 (1986).

17. *Id.* at 29.

18. *Id.*

19. Report of the U.S. Commission on Civil Rights 264 (1959).

20. Holland, *supra* note 16, at 31.

21. *Id.* at 29.

22. 465 F.2d 108 (9th Cir. 1972), *appeal after remand,* 543 F.2d 1259 (9th Cir. 1976).

23. *Gibson,* 465 F.2d at 110.

24. *Id.* at 110-11.

25. *Gibson,* 543 F.2d 1259.

26. Holland, *supra* note 16, at 30.

27. *Gates v. Georgia-Pacific Corp.,* 326 F. Supp. 397, 398 (D. Or. 1970), *aff'd,* 492 F.2d 292 (9th Cir. 1974).

28. *Gates,* 326 F. Supp. at 399.

29. *Gunther v. County of Washington,* 20 Fair Empl. Prac. Cas. (BNA) 788 (D. Or. 1976), *aff'd in part and rev'd in part,* 602 F.2d 882 (9th Cir. 1979), *aff'd,* 452 U.S. 161 (1981).

30. 29 U.S.C. sec. 206 (1988).

31. 42 U.S.C. sec. 2000e-2(h) (1988).

32. *Gunther,* 602 F.2d at 890.

33. *Gunther,* 452 U.S. 161.

34. Holland, *supra* note 16, at 33.

35. 48 Fair Empl. Prac. Cas. (BNA) 1724 (D. Or. 1985).

36. Kay Durham, *The Meaning of Penk,* Willamette Week, Feb. 21, 1985, at 6.

37. *Id.*

38. *Id.*

39. *Moreno v. Tankersley,* Civ. No. 69-481 (D. Or. Aug. 13, 1970).

40. *Id.*

41. 308 F. Supp. 128 (D. Or. 1970), *aff'd,* 446 F.2d 545 (9th Cir. 1971) *rev'd,* 407 U.S. 551 (1972).

42. 326 U.S. 501 (1946).

43. *Amalgamated Food Employees Union v. Logan Valley Plaza, Inc.,* 391 U.S. 308 (1968).

44. *Lloyd,* 308 F. Supp. at 132.

45. *Lloyd,* 407 U.S. 551 (1972).

46. Holly Danks, *Magistrate's Plan Applauded,* Oregonian, May 22, 1986, at C3.

47. Joan Laatz, *Anti-Abortionists' Suit on Noise Rule Rejected,* Oregonian, June 7, 1986, at C2.

48. Most of the decisions in this case are not reported. A 1988 procedural ruling with some of the case's history is reported in *Portland Feminist Women's Health Center v. Advocates for Life, Inc.,* 712 F. Supp. 165 (D. Or. 1991). The March 5, 1991 decision granting the permanent injunction is available through LEXIS (*Portland Feminist Women's Health Center v. Advocates for Life, Inc.,* Civ. No. 86-559, U.S. Dist. LEXIS 2867 (D. Or. Mar. 5, 1991).

49. 372 U.S. 391 (1963).

50. These statistics come from the Annual Report of the Director of the Administrative Office of the United States Courts for the years 1950 through 1990.

51. *Capitan v. Cupp,* 356 F. Supp. 302 (D. Or. 1972).

52. *Delorme v. Pierce Freightlines Co.,* 353 F. Supp. 258 (D. Or. 1973).

53. 495 F. Supp. 815 (D. Or. 1980), *vacated and remanded,* 652 F.2d 823 (9th Cir. 1981), *on remand,* 559 F. Supp. 894 (D. Or. 1982).

54. Jim Hill, *Judge Orders State to Cut Prison Rolls,* Oregonian, June 28, 1980, at A1.

55. *Id.*

56. Jim Hill, *State Told to Reduce Inmates by 500,* Oregonian, Aug. 23, 1980, at A1.

57. *Rhodes v. Chapman,* 452 U.S. 337 (1981).

58. *Capps,* 559 F. Supp. at 921.

59. *Martino v. Carey,* 563 F. Supp. 984 (D. Or. 1983).

60. *Franklin v. State of Oregon,* 563 F. Supp. 1310 (D. Or. 1983), *aff'd in part and rev'd in part sub nom. Franklin v. Murphy,* 745 F.2d 1221 (9th Cir. 1984).

61. *Id.* at 1316.

62. *Franklin v. Murphy,* 745 F.2d 1221, 1231 (9th Cir. 1984).

63. *Judge Keeps Word, Sentences 6 Conscientious Objectors to 18-month Jail Terms,* Oregon Journal, Sept. 16, 1965, at 3.

64. Walli Schneider, *Portland Draft Group Demands 'Better Break' for Conscientious Objectors,* Oregon Journal, Apr. 22, 1971, at 4.

65. Gerry Pratt, *… That One Man Can Make A Difference,* Oregonian, Aug. 25, 1968, at NW6.

66. *Objector Gets Prison Term,* Oregonian, Aug. 4, 1967, at 29.

67. *Man Takes Jail Term,* Oregonian, Feb. 24, 1966, at 25.

68. *Three-year Jail Term Given Draft Violator,* Oregonian, Dec. 1, 1966, Sec. 2, at 21.

69. *Court Backs CO's Appeal on Philosophical Basis,* Oregonian, Feb. 4, 1971, at 28.

70. *Judge Rakes Draft Stand,* Oregonian, June 12, 1968, at 17.

71. *Draft Charge Guilt Fixed,* Oregonian, June 12, 1968, at 19.

72. The U.S. government appears in these cases because it oversees Indian affairs.
73. 198 U.S. 371 (1905).
74. *Id.* at 384.
75. *Tulee v. Washington*, 315 U.S. 681, 684 (1942).
76. *Puyallup Tribe v. Dep't of Game of Wash.*, 391 U.S. 392, 398 (1968).
77. 302 F. Supp. 899 (D. Or. 1969).
78. *Id.* at 905.
79. For a discussion of the *Sohappy* decision and related cases, see Jack L. Landau, *Empty Victories: Indian Treaty Fishing Rights in the Pacific Northwest*, 10 Envtl. L. 413 (1980).
80. 384 F. Supp. 312 (W.D. Wash. 1974).
81. *Washington v. Washington State Commercial Passenger Fishing Vessel Association*, 443 U.S. 658 (1979).
82. Landau, *supra* note 79, at 444.
83. 16 U.S.C. secs. 1801 *et seq.* (1988).
84. *United States v. Oregon*, 699 F. Supp. 1456 (D. Or. 1988), *aff'd*, 913 F.2d 576 (9th Cir. 1990).
85. Michael C. Blumm, *Fulfilling the Parity Promise: A Perspective on Scientific Proof, Economic Cost, and Indian Treaty Rights in the Approval of the Columbia Basin Fish and Wildlife Program*, 13 Envtl. L. 103, 141 (1982).
86. 16 U.S.C. secs. 1531-1543 (1988).
87. 18 U.S.C. secs. 2311-2318 (1988).
88. These statistics come from the Annual Report of the Director of the Administrative Office of the United States Courts for the years 1950 through 1990.
89. Steve Carter, *Increase Seen in Cocaine Smuggled to Portland*, Oregonian, Nov. 18, 1976, at A17.
90. *7-Part Series to Look at Rising Drug Problems*, Oregonian, Aug. 15, 1986, at A1.
91. *Id.*
92. Tom Hallman, Jr., *Family-Run Heroin Rings Difficult for Agents to Crack*, Oregonian, Mar. 17, 1986, at C2.
93. Foster Church, *State Due Nine More DEA Agents*, Oregonian, July 15, 1987, at B1.
94. John Painter, Jr., *High Bank-Robbery Rate in Oregon Laid on Drugs*, Oregonian, Mar. 31, 1989, at C4.
95. Ed Mosey, *Straub Drops AIM Extradition Case*, Oregonian, June 10, 1976, at A1.
96. *United States v. Loud Hawk*, 628 F.2d 1139 (9th Cir. 1979), *cert. denied*, 445 U.S. 917 (1980), *appeal after remand sub nom. United States v. Banks*, 682 F.2d 841 (9th Cir. 1982), *cert. denied*, 459 U.S. 1117 (1983), *appeal after remand sub nom. United States v. Loud Hawk*, 741 F.2d 1184 (9th Cir. 1984), *rev'd*, 474 U.S. 302 (1986), *appeal after remand*, 816 F.2d 1323 (9th Cir. 1987).
97. Dave Hogan, *Banks Case Ends With Guilty Plea*, Oregonian, Mar. 8, 1988, at A1.
98. 18 U.S.C. secs. 3551 *et seq.* (1988).
99. Or. Rev. Stat. secs. 197.075-197.095 (1991).

100. Oregon Recycling Opportunity Act, Or. Rev. Stat. secs. 459A.005-459A.785 (1991).

101. 42 U.S.C. secs. 4321-4347 (1988).

102. 33 U.S.C. secs. 1251 *et seq.* (1988).

103. 42 U.S.C. secs. 7401 *et seq.* (1988).

104. 16 U.S.C. secs. 1451-1464 (1988).

105. 16 U.S.C. secs. 1600-1687 (1988).

106. 42 U.S.C. secs. 6901 *et seq.* (1988).

107. 16 U.S.C. secs. 1531-1543 (1988).

108. 16 U.S.C. secs. 668 *et seq.* (1988).

109. *Citizens Against Toxic Sprays, Inc., v. Bergland,* 428 F. Supp. 908 (D. Or. 1977).

110. 23 U.S.C. secs. 101 *et seq.* (1988).

111. *Southeast Legal Defense Group v. Adams,* 436 F. Supp. 891 (D. Or. 1977), *aff'd and remanded,* 657 F.2d 1118 (9th Cir. 1981).

112. *Southeast Legal Defense Group v. Adams,* 657 F.2d 1118 (9th Cir. 1981).

113. *Oregon Natural Resources Council v. Marsh,* 628 F. Supp. 1557 (D. Or. 1986), *rev'd,* 832 F.2d 1489 (9th Cir. 1987), *rev'd,* 490 U.S. 360 (1989).

114. *Oregon Natural Resources Council v. Marsh,* 832 F.2d 1489 (9th Cir. 1987), *rev'd,* 490 U.S. 360 (1989).

115. *Marsh v. Oregon Natural Resources Council,* 490 U.S. 360 (1989).

116. 659 F. Supp. 1441 (D. Or.), *aff'd in part and rev'd in part,* 834 F.2d 842 (9th Cir. 1987).

117. *Oregon Natural Resources Council,* 659 F. Supp. at 1442.

118. Michael C. Blumm, *Ancient Forests, Spotted Owls, and Modern Public Land Law,* 18 B.C. Envtl. Aff. L. Rev. 605, 606 (1991).

119. *Id.* at 609.

120. *Id.*

121. Roberta Ulrich, *Packwood to Seek Waiver if Owl Listed as Threatened,* Oregonian, April 6, 1990, at A1.

122. Civ. No. 87-1160, 1988 U.S. Dist. LEXIS 2323 (D. Or. 1988), *rev'd,* 866 F.2d 302 (9th Cir.), *on remand,* 712 F. Supp. 1456 (D. Or.), *aff'd in part and rev'd in part sub nom. Portland Audubon Society v. Lujan,* 884 F.2d 1233 (9th Cir.), *on remand,* 1989 U.S. Dist. LEXIS 15299 (D. Or. 1989), *rev'd sub nom. Seattle Audubon Society v. Robertson,* 914 F.2d 1311 (9th Cir. 1990).

123. 43 U.S.C. sec. 1181 (1988).

124. 43 U.S.C. secs. 1701 et seq. (1988).

125. 16 U.S.C. secs. 703 et seq. (1988).

126. *Gifford Pinchot Alliance v. Butruille,* 742 F. Supp. 1077 (D. Or. 1990). See also *Gifford Pinchot Alliance v. Butruille,* 752 F. Supp. 967 (D. Or. 1990).

127. *Seattle Audubon Society v. Robertson,* 914 F.2d 1311 (9th Cir. 1990).

128. *Seattle Audubon Society v. Evans,* 952 F.2d 297 (9th Cir. 1991).

129. Kathie Durbin, *Court Backs Timber Sale Ban,* Oregonian, Dec. 24, 1991, at A1.

130. Scotta Callister, James Long, and Leslie Zaitz, *On the Road Again,* Oregonian, Dec. 30, 1985, at B1.

131. Joan Laatz, *Rajneeshees to Pay Millions for Poisonings*, Oregonian, Aug. 16, 1986, at A1.

132. *Statue of Antelope Would Honor 'Survivors' of Rajneeshees*, Oregonian, Mar. 12, 1986, at B4.

133. See, e.g., Ted Natt, *3 Hard-Working Federal Judges, 'Educated Bar' Credited With Keeping Calendar Clear*, Oregonian, Nov. 8, 1964, at 40; James Long and Jamie Duncan, *Lawyers Rate U.S. Court 'Superior,'* Oregon Journal, Feb. 2, 1978, at 2; Dave Hogan, *State's U.S. District Bench Sets High Standard*, Oregonian, Feb. 21, 1988, at C1.

134. Interview with Judge Goodwin, *supra* note 4, at 409.

135. Interview with the Honorable Robert C. Belloni, U.S. District Judge for Oregon, in Portland (1988), at 165-66.

136. Interview with Judge Goodwin, *supra* note 4, at 443.

137. Interview with Judge Belloni, *supra* note 135, at 160.

138. *Id.* at 129.

139. *De Jonge v. Oregon*, 299 U.S. 353 (1937).

140. *Judge Known for Civil Rights Work Dies at 80*, Pacific Citizen, Feb. 27, 1987.

141. Stephen Gillers, *'On the Side of God,'* The Nat'l L.J., Apr. 27, 1987.

142. Dale Folkerts, *Solomon Offers Legal Advice*, Oregonian, Jan. 11, 1984.

143. *Federal Judge Gus Solomon Dies*, Oregonian, Feb. 16, 1987, at A1.

144. *Judge East Due to Fill Vacancy On U.S. Bench*, Oregonian, Mar. 11, 1955, at 1.

145. Peter Tugman, *Judge's Feelings Lead to Reduced Terms*, Oregonian, May 23, 1971.

146. The other four were William B. Gilbert (1892), Bert Emory Haney (1935), James Alger Fee (1954), and John F. Kilkenny (1969).

147. Interview with Court Reporter Dale A. Ray, in Portland (March 1988), at 2-3.

148. 334 F. Supp. 888 (D. Or. 1971), *aff'd*, 511 F.2d 980 (9th Cir. 1973).

149. *American Timber & Trading Co. v. First Nat'l Bank of Or.*, 511 F.2d 980 (9th Cir. 1973).

150. James Long and Jamie Duncan, *U.S. Court Here Imperial?*, Oregon Journal, Jan. 31, 1978, at 2.

151. John Painter, Jr., *Herbicide Accord Signed for Lands of Forest Service*, Oregonian, May 25, 1989, at G1.

152. *Loe v. Frohnmayer*, 615 F. Supp. 54 (D. Or. 1985).

153. Jim Hill and Dave Hogan, *Senior Status Not Likely to Slow James Burns*, Oregonian, Nov. 20, 1989, at B4.

# APPENDICES

# APPENDIX A

# THE EARLY
# FEDERAL JUDICIAL SYSTEM

*Excerpted from* Creating the Federal Judicial System, *a publication of the Federal Judicial Center, issued in 1989 to mark the Bicentennial of the Federal Judiciary. Used by permission of the center.*

## The Judiciary Act of 1789

With the Judiciary Act of 1789,[1] Congress first implemented the constitutional provision that "The judicial power of the United States, shall be vested in one supreme court, and in such inferior courts as the Congress may from time to time ordain and establish." The federal court system is still shaped by the basic concepts of that statute, although subsequent legislation has altered many of its specific provisions, and the 1891 Circuit Courts of Appeals Act effected a major change. But the basic design of the 1789 Act has endured.

The Act's Provisions. The Act's boldest stroke was simply to create a system of lower federal courts to exist alongside the courts already established by each state. There was considerable sentiment for leaving trial adjudication to the state courts, perhaps with a small corps of federal admiralty judges.

The Act provided for two trial courts—and gave the circuit courts a limited appellate jurisdiction. It made specific provision for the Supreme Court created by the Constitution. It defined federal jurisdiction. It authorized the courts to appoint clerks and to prescribe their procedural rules.[2] It authorized the president to appoint marshals,[3] U.S. attorneys, and an attorney general.[4]

The Act created 13 district courts; one for each of the 11 states that had ratified the Constitution, plus separate districts for Maine and Kentucky, which were then parts of Massachusetts and Virginia. Each district was authorized one district judge. Section 3 directed each court to hold four sessions each year, in either one or two specified cities in each district. The district courts served mainly as courts for admiralty, for forfeitures and penalties, for petty federal crimes, and for minor U.S. plaintiff cases. To reflect the wide variations in federal caseload from one state to another, Congress authorized different salaries for the district judges. The judge in Delaware received an annual salary of $800, but his counterpart in South Carolina, with its longer coastline and presumably greater admiralty caseload, received $1,800.[5]

The Act placed each district, except Kentucky and Maine, into one of three circuits: an eastern, a middle, and a southern circuit, following the administrative divisions used in the first year of the Revolutionary War.[6] Circuit courts were to sit twice each year in either one or two specified cities of each district of the circuit. For each circuit session, the judges were to be the two Supreme Court justices assigned to that circuit plus the respective district judge. These circuit courts were the nation's courts for diversity of citizenship cases (concurrent with state courts, but with a limited removal provision), major federal crimes, and larger U.S. plaintiff cases. (There was no provision for suits against the United States.) They were also intermediate courts of appeal for some of the larger civil and admiralty cases in the district courts.[7] The Kentucky and Maine district courts exercised circuit jurisdiction.

The Act established the size of the Supreme Court: a chief justice and five associate justices. Section 13 implemented the Court's original jurisdiction as delineated in the Constitution; it was a provision of 13 that the Court declared unconstitutional in *Marbury v. Madison*.[8] The Act spelled out the Court's appellate jurisdiction: review of circuit court decisions in civil cases in matters over $2,000 (for some sense of perspective, in 1789 the salary of the Chief Justice was $4,000)[9]. A general criminal appellate jurisdiction did not come to the Supreme Court until the 1890s.[10] The Act's famous 25 authorized the Court to review state supreme court decisions that invalidated federal statutes or treaties or that declared state statutes constitutional in the face of a claim to the contrary.

It seems axiomatic today that no district or circuit boundary should cross a state line because (with one minor exception[11]) none does. The 1789 Judiciary Act set this precedent, just as it required the district judges to reside in their districts.[12]

**Circuit Riding.** To observers today, perhaps the most curious thing about the 1789 Judiciary Act was Congress's decision to create a major federal trial court but not to create any separate judgeships for it. Instead, the Act directed the two Supreme Court justices assigned to each circuit to travel to the designated places of holding circuit court, to be joined there by the district judge. This requirement, along with a sparse Supreme Court caseload in the early period, meant that the early Supreme Court justices spent most of their time serving as trial judges.

Circuit riding was common in the states. It was attractive to Congress for three reasons. First, it saved the money a separate corps of judges would require. In 1792, the Georgia district court reported that Congress declined to create separate circuit judgeships not only because "the public mind was not sufficiently impressed with the importance of a steady, uniform, and prompt administration of justice," but also because "money matters have so strong a hold on the thoughts and personal feelings of men, that everything else seems little in comparison.[13] Second, circuit riding exposed the justices to the state laws they would interpret on the Supreme Court, and to legal practices around the country—it let them "mingle in the strife of jury trials,"[14] as a defender of circuit riding said in 1864. Third, it contributed to what today we call "nation building." It would, so went the argument, "impress the citizens of the United States favorably toward the general government, should the most distinguished judges visit every state.[15] (In fact, they did more than visit. The justices' grand jury charges explained the new regime to prominent citizens all over the country, winning praise from the Federalist press and, increasingly, barbs from the Jeffersonian press.)[16]

Whatever logic supported circuit riding, the justices themselves set about almost immediately to abolish it. They saw themselves as "travelling postboys."[17] They doubted, in the words of a Senate ally, "that riding rapidly from one end of this country to another is the best way to study law."[18] Furthermore, they warned President Washington, trial judges who serve also as appellate judges are sometimes required to "correct in one capacity the errors which they themselves may have committed in another . . . a distinction unfriendly to impartial justice."[19] The 1789 Act prohibited district judges from voting as circuit judges in appeals from their district court decisions[20] but placed no similar prohibition on Supreme Court justices. The justices themselves agreed to recuse themselves from appeals from their own decisions unless there was a split vote[21] (a rare occurrence). Congress's only response to their complaints was a 1793 statute reducing to one the number of justices necessary for a circuit court quorum.[22]

## From the Founding to the Evarts Act

In 1801, as their era drew to a close, the Federalists brought to passage a bill that President Adams had proposed two years earlier. It established separate circuit court judgeships and expanded federal court jurisdiction to all categories of cases authorized by Article III.[23] The incoming Jeffersonians repealed the statute the next year,[24] abolished the judgeships it created, and then passed a new judiciary act.[25] It created six circuits where there had been three and re-established the justices' circuit-riding responsibilities—one justice per circuit, to hold one circuit court session each year in each district within the respective circuit. A quorum of one judge was sufficient to convene the circuit court.

This slight restriction on circuit obligations brought only temporary relief. As time passed, the federal courts' condition deteriorated as case overload swelled. A political stalemate over the role the federal courts should play in national life made resolution impossible until 1891.

**Westward Expansion.** Between 1789 and 1855 the number of states increased to 31, and U.S. territorial possessions grew as well. The logic of the 1789 Judiciary Act dictated that new states and territories have their own district and circuit courts. The justices, however, found the travel burden of even the existing circuits to be too great. Congress thus created new circuits and gradually increased the size of the Supreme Court to provide justices for them. The expansion was not a smooth process. Creating a new seat on the Supreme Court became entwined with the politics of filling the seat. Thus, new states were often left in limbo, with the district courts exercising both district and circuit court jurisdiction. Not until the Civil War was every district within a circuit served by Supreme Court justices. (The territories, moreover, were also served by separate territorial courts, established pursuant to Congress's power to provide rules for the government of the territories. The territorial courts were vital instruments of government during the nineteenth century.)

The number of circuits reached its nineteenth-century high point in 1855. To deal with a large number of land disputes in California, Congress created a separate, tenth, circuit for the state's two districts and, for the first time, authorized a separate circuit judge.[26] The Supreme Court reached its largest size in 1863, when Stephen Field of California took his seat on the Court, as the justice for the newly created Tenth Circuit.[27] (Although the Court had ten members, it appears that the ten never sat as a group because of the illnesses of Chief Justice Taney in 1863-1864 and of Justices Catron and Davis the next term.[28] An 1866 statute[29] sought to reduce the Court's size by forbidding replacement nominations until the Court consisted of seven members. Traditionally regarded as an effort to restrict President Johnson's power, the statute may well in fact have been aimed mainly at producing a Court of more manageable size, evidently with the justices' support.[30] The net effect was a nine-member Court after Justice Catron died in 1865, and an eight-member Court from Justice Wayne's death in 1867 until March 1870, when Justice Bradley was appointed pursuant to a statute raising the Court's authorized size back to nine.[31]

**Reorganizing the Federal Courts.** From the Civil War period until 1891, the nation engaged in an extended debate over how to reorganize the federal courts. The debate took place in the context of a broader argument over the proper role of the federal judiciary in national life.

In 1861, in his first message to Congress on the state of the union, President Lincoln warned that "the country has outgrown our present judicial system."[32] The problem as he saw it was that the circuit system as established in 1789 could not accommodate the growth of the country. In 1861 eight recently admitted states had never had "circuit courts attended by supreme judges." Adding enough justices to the Supreme Court to accommodate all the circuit courts that were needed would make the Supreme Court "altogether too numerous for a judicial body of any sort." His solution: Fix the Supreme Court at a "convenient number," irrespective of the number of circuits. Then divide the country "into circuits of convenient size," to be served either by the Supreme Court justices and as many more separate circuit judges as might be necessary, or by separate circuit judges only. Or abolish the circuit courts.

Adjusting the circuit system was not the only problem. Lincoln noted also that many federal statutes "have been drawn in haste and without sufficient caution...as to render it very difficult for even the best informed persons to ascertain precisely what the statute law really is." Furthermore, although Lincoln did not mention it, the Supreme Court and, apparently, the circuit and district courts were increasingly backlogged.

Before the Civil War, a growing economy and the emergence of the business corporation increased the federal courts' workload as their decisions created the legal conditions for commercial growth and expansion in maritime trade and in domestic commercial activity.[33] Congress steadily expanded the Supreme Court's jurisdiction.[34] After the Civil War came statutes to promote and regulate economic growth, the enforcement of which fell to federal courts through diversity or statutory grants of jurisdiction. Other laws expanded federal court jurisdiction to implement Reconstruction and to enforce the Reconstruction Amendments.[35] The budget offers one measure of the growth of federal court business. In

1850, the U.S. Treasury expended $500,000 on the federal courts, a figure that rose to $3,000,000 by 1875.[36]

Federal court business grew even more with the Judiciary Act of 1875,[37] doing essentially what the most ardent Federalists would have done in 1789: establish a general federal-question jurisdiction in the federal trial courts for cases involving $500 or more. It was adopted on the same day as the 1875 Civil Rights Act,[38] and, as one observer has said, the two statutes together "may be seen as an ultimate expression of Republican reconstruction policies. One recognized a national obligation to confer and guarantee first-class citizenship to the freedman. The other marked an expression of the party's nationalizing impulse and complementary concern for the national market."[39] Although the 1875 Civil Rights Act was invalidated by the Supreme Court eight years later,[40] the 1875 Judiciary Act made the federal trial courts, in Frankfurter and Landis's words, "the primary and powerful reliances for vindicating every right given by the Constitution, the laws, and treaties of the United States."[41]

This vast expansion of federal court jurisdiction, especially the 1875 Judiciary Act, had two effects. In the long term, it established the federal courts' preeminent role as protectors of constitutional and statutory rights and liberties and as interpreters of the growing mass of federal statutes and administrative regulations. In the short term, by imposing significant jurisdictional increases on a court system conceived in 1789, it created serious delay in the administration of federal justice. In fact, Hart and Wechsler referred to the post-Civil War period as "the nadir of federal judicial administration,"[42] a condition which makes all the more remarkable what another scholar has called "the unifying function of the federal courts" in promoting commercial growth during the period.[43]

Numerous proposals to revamp the system led only to tinkering with the number, size, and terms of the federal courts. As a result, the nation lost much of its dwindling federal appellate capacity. Appellate review was statutorily foreclosed in many classes of cases. The decisions of the circuit courts were final in almost all criminal cases and in all civil cases involving less than $2,000 (after 1875, $5,000).[44] And even with this limitation, the Court's docket grew steeply. In 1860, the Court had 310 cases on its docket. By 1890, the 623 new cases filed that year brought the docket to 1,816 cases.[45] The Court was years behind in its work and, unlike today, was obliged to decide almost all the cases brought to it.

Consequently, decisions of federal trial courts were, for practical purposes, almost unreviewable. Those courts, moreover, had their own workload problems. Even with a partial restriction on diversity jurisdiction in 1887,[46] cases pending rose from 29,013 in 1873 to 54,194 in 1890,[47] or 86 percent. The number of district and circuit judges grew only by 11 percent, from 62 in 1873 to 69 in 1890.[48] Congress in 1869 had created nine circuit judgeships, realizing that the Supreme Court justices could attend but a fraction of the circuit court sessions. These nine judgeships were far too few to accommodate the increase in filings. In addition, the 1875 Act shifted some of the original jurisdiction of the circuit courts to the district courts and broadened the circuit courts' appellate jurisdiction. In the 1870s, single district judges handled about two thirds of the circuit court caseload. In the next decade, the figure was much closer to 90 percent—and often the district judges were sitting on appeals from their own decisions, thus making "the single district judges to a considerable extent ultimate courts of appeals."[49]

In one sense, the growing post-Civil War inability of the federal courts to accommodate this increased jurisdiction was caused by the inability of the bench and bar and legislators to discover an effective scheme of judicial organization: one that could accommodate this new workload and still serve other values that some members of the bar and legislature thought important, such as circuit riding. Numerous proposals were offered. Some were for an intermediate court of appeals, echoing bills introduced even before the Civil War and anticipating the reorganization of 1891. Others seem more curious today. Some proposed an 18-member Supreme Court divided into three panels to hear common-law, equity, and admiralty and revenue cases, with constitutional cases going to the Court en banc.[50]

But inability to agree on a new form for the courts reflected a more basic conflict. As Frankfurter and Landis put it:

*The reorganization of the federal judiciary did not involve merely technical questions of judicial organization, nor was it the concern only of lawyers. Beneath the surface of the controversy lay passionate issues of power as between the states and the Federal Government, involving sectional differences and sectional susceptibilities.... Stubborn political convictions and strong interests were at stake which made the process of accommodation long and precarious.[51]*

The conflicts between Federalists and Anti-Federalists resurfaced a century later. One group, based mainly in the House of Representatives and drawing strength mainly from the South and the West, wanted to retain the traditional form of the federal courts but restrict their jurisdiction. They believed, not without some evidence, that federal courts were too sympathetic to commercial interests, too eager to frustrate state legislative efforts designed to help farmers and workers. An Illinois congressman argued that the post-Civil War "increase of...jurisdiction...grew out of the then anomalous conditions of the country and was largely influenced by the passions and prejudices of the times." To regard "Federal courts...as the safeguards of the rights of the people...is a great mistake and...lessens respect for State courts, State rights, and State protection.[52]

A separate coalition, with strength in the Senate and based in the East, wanted to broaden the federal courts' capacity to enable them to exercise the expanded jurisdiction created in the wave of nationalist sentiment after the Civil War. One proponent cited "prejudice" by state courts against corporation and "in the West...granger laws and granger excitements that have led people to commit enormities in legislation.... Capital ...will not be risked in the perils of sectional bitterness, narrow prejudices, or local indifference to integrity and honor." The solution: "Let us stand by the national courts; let us preserve their power."[53]

The culmination of this controversy was the Circuit Court of Appeals Act of 1891,[54] worked out by Senate Judiciary Committee Chairman William Evarts of New York. According to Henry Adams, Evarts prided himself on his ability to do the things he didn't like to do.[55] He had resisted the idea of separate courts of appeals for a long time. In accepting the concept, Evarts fashioned legislation that resolved the crisis in favor of the nationalists, although there were modest concessions to those who favored the old form.

What did the Act do? Essentially, it shifted the appellate caseload burden from the Supreme Court to new courts of appeals, and, in so doing, made the federal district courts the system's primary trial courts. It created a new court, the circuit court of appeals, with one for each of the nine circuits. Each court consisted, in effect, of two circuit judges and a district judge. It provided direct Supreme Court review of right from the district courts in some categories of cases and from circuit courts of appeal in others. It routed all other cases—notably criminal, diversity, admiralty, and revenue and patent cases—to the courts of appeals for final disposition. The appellate court could certify questions to the Supreme Court, or the Supreme Court could grant review by *certiorari*. The Act's effect on the Supreme Court was immediate—from 623 filings in 1890 to 379 in 1891 and 275 in 1892.[56]

Deference to tradition temporarily spared the old circuit courts, but the Act abolished their appellate jurisdiction. Until the courts themselves were abolished in 1911,[57] the nation still had two separate federal trial courts. Neither did the Act abolish the justices' circuit riding, but rather made it optional, thus quietly burying this anachronism in similar deference to tradition. The important legacy today of justices' circuit riding is 28 U.S.C. 42, which directs the Court to allot its members "as circuit justices."

## The Federal Courts After 200 Years

In their 200th year, the federal courts differed strikingly in size and structure from their forerunners in 1891, and even more from those of 1789. An expanding jurisdiction had generated a growing caseload, generating in turn a large increase in the size of the system. Since 1891, the number of authorized judgeships grew almost nine-fold, from 84 to 739[58] (compared with a five-fold increase in the first century from the 19 judges originally authorized). In 1925, the federal judiciary employed 1,284 persons, of whom 179, or 13.9 percent, were Article III judges.[59] In 1988, it employed 20,743 persons, of whom 1,034, or 4.9 percent were Article III judges.[60]

The Supreme Court's limited *certiorari* jurisdiction in the 1891 Act has been broadened by successive legislation, the most noteworthy being the Judiciary Act of 1925, and the most recent being Pub. L. No. 100-352 in 1989, which eliminated most remaining categories of the Court's mandatory appellate jurisdiction. The number of courts of appeals increased from nine in 1891 to 13 in 1989. The number of district courts increased from 68 in 1891 to 94 in 1989. The old system of bankruptcy referees was transformed in 1978 and 1984 into bankruptcy courts as units of the district courts.[61] Similarly, the system of U.S. commissioners—dating back to a 1793 statute authorizing circuit courts to appoint persons to take bail—was replaced in 1968 with the U.S. magistrate system.[62] A 1925 statute[63] created a probation system for the federal courts, and a 1982 statute created a permanent pretrial services system. And, in 1964, Congress authorized federal defenders' offices in the various judicial districts. Permanent staff attorneys and court executives have joined the personnel rosters.

Since 1891, the federal courts have achieved administrative autonomy from the executive branch. Legislation in 1939 shifted budgetary and personnel responsibility from the Department of Justice to the Judicial Conference of the United States and created the Administrative Office of the U.S. Courts as staff to the Conference. Circuit councils and conferences, also mandated in 1939, and the recognition of the office of chief district judge and chief circuit judge in 1948, have bolstered the concept of internal federal judicial administration. A separate federal court research and education agency was provided by a 1967 statute.

Many things that the First Judiciary Act required have been swept aside. But many other things it provided are so intrinsic to our system of justice that we rarely give them a second thought: a separate set of courts for the national government, deciding matters of national interest, and arranged geographically according to state boundaries.

When that Act of 1789 was approaching, not its third century, but its third year, Chief Justice John Jay, sitting as a judge of the circuit court for the eastern circuit, undertook in his charge to the grand juries of that circuit to describe something of this new system of federal courts. Those who created the federal courts faced a formidable task, he observed, because "no tribunals of the like kind and extent had heretofore existed in this country." In that environment of experimentation, Jay reminded the grand juries—and his words could well be a charter for contemporary efforts—that "the expediency of carrying justice, as it were, to every man's door, was obvious, but how to do it in an expedient manner was far from being apparent.[64]

## NOTES

1. Act of Sept. 24, 1789, 1 Stat. 73.
2. Act of Sept. 24, 1789, § 17, 1 Stat. 83.
3. Act of Sept. 24, 1789, § 27, 1 Stat. 73, 87.
4. Act of Sept. 24, 1789, § 35, 1 Stat. 92-93.
5. Act of Sept. 23, 1789, § 1, 1 Stat.72.
6. J. Goebel, Jr. *Antecedents and Beginnings to 1800*, vol. 1 of *The History of the Supreme Court* 472 (Oliver Wendell Holmes Devise History of the Supreme Court of the United States 1971).
7. Act of Sept. 24, 1789, §§ 21, 22, 1 Stat. 83-84.
8. 1 Cranch 137 (1803).
9. Act of Sept. 23, 1789, § 1, 1 Stat. 72.
10. F. Frankfurter & J. Landis, *The Business of the Supreme Court* 109-13 ( 1928).
11. The District of Wyoming, in the Tenth Circuit, reaches into Montana and Idaho, in the Ninth Circuit, in order to keep Yellowstone National Park in one judicial district. 28 U.S.C. § 131.
12. Act of Sept. 24, 1789, § 3, 1 Stat. 73, 74. The successor provision is 28 U.S.C § 134 (b).

13. Nathanial Pendleton to James Iredell, Mar. 19, 1792, in G. McRee, II *The Life and Correspondence of James Iredell* 344-45 (1857).

14. Newspaper editorial quoted in Hall, *The Civil War Era as a Crucible for Nationalizing the Lower Federal Courts*, Prologue, 177, 184 (Fall 1975).

15. This was Attorney General Randolph's characterization in his 1790 report on the judicial system; he went on to rebut the argument. Quoted in F. Frankfurter & J. Landis, *The Business of the Supreme Court* 19 (1928).

16. A helpful analysis of these charges is Lerner, *The Supreme Court as Republican Schoolmaster*, 1967 Sup. Ct. Rev. 127.

17. Justice Iredell, quoted in C. Warren, 1 *The Supreme Court In United States History* 86 (rev. ed. 1926).

18. Gouverneur Morris, in 1802, quoted in F. Frankfurter & J. Landis, *The Business of the Supreme Court* 17 (1928).

19. Letter of Nov. 7, 1792, to Congress in 1 *American State Papers (Class X) Miscellaneous* 51-52.

20. Act of Sept. 24, 1789, § 4, 1 Stat. 74.

21. Justice Iredell explained the practice in *Ware v. Hylton*, 3 Dall. 199, 257 n.2 (1796).

22. Act of Mar. 2, 1793, 1 Stat. 333.

23. Act of Feb. 13, 1801, "To Provide for the More Convenient Organization of the Courts of the United States," 2 Stat. 89.

24. Act of Mar. 5, 1802, 2 Stat. 132.

25. Act of Apr. 29, 1802, "To Amend the Judicial System of the United States," 2 Stat. 118 (1802). The Supreme Court upheld this act in *Stuart v. Laird*, 1 Cranch 299 (1803).

26. Act of Mar.2, 1855, "To Establish a Circuit Court in and for the State of California," 10 Stat. 631.

27. Act of July 15, 1862, "To Amend the Act of Third of March, 1837...," 12 Stat. 576 (1862).

28. This conclusion is based on the tables of justices and the reporter's prefatory notes in volumes 1 and 2 of Wallace's Supreme Court reports.

29. Act of July 23, 1866, "To Fix the Number of Justices of the Supreme Court of the United States, and to Change Certain Judicial Circuits," 14 Stat. 209.

30. S. Kutler, *Judicial Power and Reconstruction Politics* 49-63 (1968).

31. Act of Apr. 10, 1869, 16 Stat. 44. See also the front pages of volumes 2 to 9 of Wallace's Supreme Court reports.

32. Message to Congress of Dec. 3, 1861, in 5 *The Works of Abraham Lincoln* 41-42 (R. Basler ed. 1953).

33. T. Freyer, *Forums of Order: The Federal Courts and Business in American History* chs. 1-5 (1979); Hall, *Circuit Courts*, in *Encyclopedia of the American Constitution* 213-14.

34. Specific provisions are in Bator, Meltzer, Mishkin & Shapiro, Hart and Wechsler's *The Federal Courts and the Federal System* 36-37 (3d ed. 1988).

35. See generally H. Hyman & Wiecek, *Equal Justice Under Law, Constitutional Development*, 1835-1875, chs. 8-11 (1982).

36. T. Freyer, *Forums of Order: The Federal Courts and Business in American*

*History* 125 (1979).
37. Act of Mar. 3, 1875, 18 Stat. 470.
38. 18 Stat. 335.
39. S. Kutler, *Judicial Power and Reconstruction Politics* 159 (1968).
40. Civil Rights Cases, 109 U.S. 3 (1883).
41. F. Frankfurter & J. Landis, *The Business of the Supreme Court*, 64-65 (1928).
42. Bator, Meltzer, Mishkin & Shapiro, Hart and Wechsler's *The Federal Courts and the Federal System* 37 (3d ed. 1988).
43. T. Freyer, *Forums of Order: The Federal Courts and Business in American History* 114 (1979).
44. Act of Feb. 16, 1875.
45. F. Frankfurter & J. Landis, *The Business of the Supreme Court*, 101-02 (1928).
46. Act of Mar. 3, 1887.
47. F. Frankfurter & J. Landis, *The Business of the Supreme Court*, 60 (1928).
48. Table B.3 in R. Posner, *The Federal Courts, Crises and Reform*, 354-55 (1985).
49. F. Frankfurter & J. Landis, *The Business of the Supreme Court*, 79 (1928).
50. *Id.* at 82.
51. *Id.* at 85.
52. Congressman Moulton of Illinois, *quoted in id.* at 91-92.
53. Congressman Robinson of Massachusetts, *quoted in id.* at 91-92.
54. Act of Mar. 3, 1891, 26 Stat. 826.
55. H. Adams, *The Education of Henry Adams* 30 (1918).
56. F. Frankfurter & J. Landis, *The Business of the Supreme Court* 102 (1928).
57. Act of Mar. 3, 1911, § 301, 36 Stat. 1087, 1169.
58. R. Posner, *The Federal Courts, Crises and Reform*, Table B.3 at p. 355 (1985), and 28 U.S.C. §§ 1, 44, 133.
59. R. Posner, *The Federal Courts, Crises and Reform*, 27 (1985).
60. Administrative Office of the U.S. Courts, 1988 *Annual Report of the Director*, at 51.
61. *See* 28 U.S.C. §§ 151, 152.
62. McCabe, *The Federal Magistrate Act of 1979*, 16 Harv. J. on Legis. 342 (1979).
63. Act of Mar. 5, 1925.
64. Charge to Grand Juries in 3 *The Public Papers and Correspondence of John Jay* 387, 390-91 (H. Johnston ed. 1891).

## APPENDIX B

# OTHER COURT & COURT-RELATED PERSONNEL AFTER 1950

### U.S. Bankruptcy Court

*Bankruptcy petitions are handled by the U.S. Bankruptcy Court and not by the district courts. The following people served as judges of the United States Bankruptcy Court for the District of Oregon during the years indicated.*
Estes Snedecor 1936–69
Lester G. Oehler 1942–73
Folger Johnson 1955–84
Clarence E. Luckey 1961–83
Henry L. Hess, Jr. 1958–73 (part time); 1973–present (full time)
Donal D. Sullivan 1969–present
Polly S. Higdon 1983–present
Albert E. Radcliffe 1983–88 (part time); 1988–present (full time)
Elizabeth L. Perris 1984–present

### Clerk of the Court

*The main responsibility of the clerk's office is to maintain the records of the court, including all documents filed in cases, and to oversee the court docket. The clerk also handles many administrative details. The court appoints the chief clerk; deputy clerks serve under the chief clerk. The people who served most recently as chief clerk are:*
Lowell Mundorff 1943–53
Frank L. Buck 1953–55 (Acting Clerk)
Roswell J. DeMott 1955–61
Keith Burns 1961–65
Donal D. Sullivan 1965–69
George E. Juba 1969–71
Robert M. Christ 1971–90
Donald M. Cinnamond 1990–present

### United States Attorney

*The U.S. attorneys represent the United States government as prosecutor in criminal cases or as either plaintiff or defendant in civil cases. The U.S.*

attorneys for Oregon who served between 1950 and the present are listed below. The office of the U.S. attorney for Oregon also has many assistant U.S. attorneys.

Henry L. Hess 1946–54
Clarence E. Luckey 1954–61
Sidney I. Lezak 1961–82
Charles H. Turner 1982–present

## Federal Defender

Federal defenders provide counsel to indigent criminal defendants. The District of Oregon established its first community defender office in 1974 as Federal Defenders, Inc., a private nonprofit offshoot of the Metropolitan Defender's, Inc., which provided counsel for state court defendants in Multnomah County. From 1977 to 1983, the office operated under its own corporate charter. David S. Teske served as the head of both of these early incarnations of the office. In 1983 the program was replaced with a federal defender office under the control of the court. Since then, Steven T. Wax has served as the Federal Defender for the District of Oregon, supervising offices in Portland and Eugene.

## Probation Officers

The probation officers are employees of the court. Their responsibilities are to prepare presentence investigations and recommend appropriate sentences, to supervise persons placed on probation or parole, and to report to the court the conduct of persons under supervision. The chief U.S. probation officer for the District of Oregon is appointed by the district judges. Those who served as chief in recent years are:

John M. McFarland 1956–65
Walter Evans 1966–1978
Frank S. Gilbert 1979–91
David Looney 1991–present

# "SEA STORIES" FROM THE U.S. DISTRICT COURT FOR OREGON

## COMPILED BY WILLIAM F. WHITE

**Editor's Note:** *Retired Portland attorney William F. White has been one of the U.S. District Court of Oregon Historical Society's most active members. Some years ago, Bill became what he called a "Sea Story Committee of one" and set about collecting, from local lawyers, humorous anecdotes about their experiences in the district court. Some of these stories were published in the* Oregon State Bar *publication* For the Record; *some appeared in* Oregon Benchmarks, *the bulletin of the District Court Historical Society; and some have remained unpublished.*

*In November 1988, when Bill turned his file of anecdotes over to the historical society, he wrote:*

*I have exhausted my sources for "sea stories" and for that reason withdraw as chairman of the Sea Story Committee so you may "pass the torch" to another. It is my hope that our Society will continue the effort to collect and get published anecdotes about our great Court, as that is the only practical way that the unreported, interesting and human side of the Court can be spliced into its history.*

*Although we are not able to publish all of Bill's sea stories here, we offer several that illuminate the day-to-day life of the court.*

### The Better Part of Valor
By Sidney I. Lezak
*First appeared in* Oregon Benchmarks, *Winter 1990*

During much of the 1970s there were two judges named Goodwin sitting on the federal bench in the Northwest. One was Alfred T. "Ted" Goodwin, who sat on the District Court in Oregon and is now chief judge of the United States Court of Appeals for the Ninth Circuit. The other was William Goodwin, U.S. district judge for the Southern District of Washington, sitting in Tacoma. Although Ted Goodwin at approximately 6 feet 1 inch and 200 pounds was certainly no pygmy, he was dwarfed by Bill Goodwin, who—I've been told—played tackle on Washington State's Rose Bowl team in 1931. A former prosecutor and combative trial attorney, the latter judge carried himself in a manner reminiscent of his days of gridiron glory. With understandable humor, Ted and Bill were described respectively as the "good" Goodwin and the "bad" Goodwin.

Occasionally, Judge Bill Goodwin tried cases in Portland and while he was there would handle the criminal docket—which primarily involved the receipt of pleas from defendants.

On one occasion, it was reported to me, Judge Goodwin was engaged in running the criminal docket when a young man came before him as a defendant allegedly involved in the sale of narcotics.

As Judge Goodwin glared down at him and demanded, "How do you plead, guilty or not guilty?" the young man unhesitatingly responded, "Guilty, your honor."

His lawyer, appalled at this answer, grabbed the young man's arm and whispered loudly, "But you were supposed to plead NOT GUILTY!"—to which the defendant replied in a trembling voice, "Yeh, man, but did you see the HANDS on that judge?"

∾

### Operator of Jackhammer Could Have Ended Up in the Slammer
As told by John R. Brooke, partner in the Portland firm of
Wood, Tatum, Mosser, Brooke and Landis
*First appeared in the Oregon State Bar's For the Record, September 1988*

U.S. District Judge James Alger Fee was known for the importance that he placed on having jurisdiction to act in his federal courtroom.

Around 1950, I was before Judge Fee as an assistant United States Attorney trying a case in his courtroom, which was then located on the sixth floor of the Broadway Street side of the Federal Courthouse in Portland. It was a hot and humid August day, and with no air conditioning the sweltering heat in the courtroom was all but unbearable.

To bring some relief from the heat, Judge Fee asked his bailiff to open the windows which lined the Broadway Street side of the courtroom. The open windows did provide some relief from the heat, but brought in unbearable noise—one block down Broadway from the courthouse construction workers were breaking up the sidewalk with a jackhammer. The loud banging of the jackhammer pounded through the open window, making communications impossible inside. So Judge Fee ordered his bailiff to inform the operator of the jackhammer to stop work, as the noise was preventing the court from conducting its business.

Upon his return, the bailiff reported that the operator in no uncertain terms had indicated the judge could go to hell. Without hesitation, Judge Fee called for the U.S. marshal and instructed him to order the operator to stop the jackhammer, and if the operator refused, to arrest him for contempt of court.

As the U.S. marshal left to carry out Judge Fee's order, I could not help but ponder the upcoming clash between the territorial jurisdiction of Judge Fee and that of the jackhammer operator one block away. Had Judge Fee gone too far?

Fortunately, when the U.S. marshal informed the jackhammer operator of Judge Fee's order, he stopped work and we finished our hearing. Later I learned the construction worker turned off his equipment after receiving orders from his boss to do so. He passed down that order upon the advice of his attorney.

Since that event occurred, I looked at the law and found 18 USC NO. 401, which provides that a federal court has power to punish for contempt for the "misbehavior of any person in its presence or *so near thereto as to obstruct the administration of justice.*"
The case of *Nye v U.S.* (1941) 313 U.S. 33, at 49-50 indicates Judge Fee was probably within the outer limits of his territorial jurisdiction.

∾

## Pants Suits on Women Don't Cut It in Judge Solomon's Court
As told by M. Christie Helmer, a partner in the firm of Miller, Nash, et al.
*First appeared in the Oregon State Bar's For the Record, April 1988*

U.S. District Court Judge Gus Solomon certainly did provide good material for stories. I have two. In one of the episodes I was, fortunately, only a spectator. In the other, I was the victim.

Criticism is not the purpose of the following vignettes; I hope they are appreciated from the perspectives from which they are given— humor and history.

I was sworn into the bar of the United States District Court for the District of Oregon in 1974. Back then, Judge Solomon always handled the swearing-in. He took advantage of these occasions as opportunities to advise neophyte lawyers on the proper way to conduct themselves in federal court, and sometimes to check if the applicants knew their federal rules. He used the particular occasion of my swearing-in to advise a young woman lawyer about proper federal court attire.

"Young woman! You there in the second row! *What is that you are wearing?*" Judge Solomon bellowed.

"It's a pants suit, Your Honor," the young woman answered.

"A 'pants suit'? What is a 'pants suit'?" he questioned.

"It's…uh…well, it's a suit with pants, Your Honor."

"Casual dress is *not* appropriate in *this* courtroom, young woman. What is your name? Do you plan to *practice* in this court?"

"Yes, Your Honor…I…uh…it's_____(name withheld to protect the innocent, and due to the author's lack of memory), and this isn't…uh…casual, Your Honor."

"What do you mean it isn't *casual?* You are a woman, aren't you? And you're wearing pants! Women in this court wear *skirts*. Now, let that be a lesson to you young lawyers…."

That was in 1974—the same year the head secretary in my office chastised me for wearing jeans to the office on a Saturday, even though many of the male lawyers in the office wore them. For some reason, her attitude struck me as more discriminatory than Judge Solomon's. Or perhaps because I have always thought that Judge Solomon, civil libertarian that he was, would have treated men in skirts much the same, even if they were Scots.

Not long after I appeared before Judge Solomon to take my oath of office, I began handling "monthly call" before him for my law firm. For those of you who never had the opportunity to practice in the Oregon federal court before 1978, monthly call was a lawyer's opportunity to catch up with colleagues on all the gossip, and Judge Solomon's opportunity to catch up on all the pending cases. Woe be to those who did not know how many witnesses the lawyer handling the trial planned to call and the issues on which they would be called, even if the case had no trial date. Woe be to those who responded "I don't know, Your Honor."

I had handled call perhaps six times when one morning I was late—only by seven minutes—but late enough to have missed Judge Solomon's first call to the lawyers handling a case on which to report.

"And where is the lawyer from Miller?" I heard the judge asking as I entered.

"Here, Your Honor," I replied in a barely audible voice as I hustled my way from the entry doors to the front of the courtroom.

"Miller? Is that someone from Miller?" Judge Solomon questioned.

"Yes, Your Honor, and I'll be able to give you a status report if you will tell me who my client is."

Dead Silence.

Not a sound from any one of those 100 lawyers amassed in rows behind me. And I sensed incredulity from the bench.

"I mean, there was a log truck overturned on the freeway, and I was stuck for almost an hour…I haven't had time to go to the office to pick up my notes and files," I attempted to explain. "I came right here. Whoever the client is, can we have another 60 days?" I asked.

I suppose some lawyers preceding me had had the same problem and that is why Judge Solomon chose not to question the truth of my explanation. Clearly, those waiting 100 lawyers thought it was a miracle. When His Honor calmly gave me 60 days, together with the advice that I should call my office to have the files brought to me, I turned to a room of awestruck faces. I can still remember how weak my legs felt (about the same as when I tried my first case), and how blurred the 100 faces became as I made for the bar.

Was I ever glad I wasn't wearing a pants suit that day!

∾

### Knowledge of the Law Is No Excuse!
#### As told by Ted E. Runstein

I knew Judge Solomon liked me because he had recommended that his former law firm hire me. I also knew it just meant I had to be doubly careful. A couple of years after entering private practice I had a premonition that I was about to get in trouble. A lawyer from out of state asked for our firm to assist in obtaining an attachment for an Oregon creditor. The lawyer appeared at our office one morning to prepare for a federal court hearing before Judge Solomon, scheduled for that afternoon. He was working with a senior partner from our firm, Cliff Alterman. Mr. Alterman asked me to review the papers. I was appalled. The pleadings were full of legalese. We all know that Judge Solomon did not accept the legal gobbleegook forms. I told the out-of-state lawyer (who was much older and more experienced) that our district required short, concise, and clearly written papers. We provided him with a secretary and I pleaded with him to write his pleadings in the appropriate manner.

Mr. Alterman asked me to accompany him and the out-of-state lawyer to the hearing. I expressed a strong desire not to accompany them.

Mr. Alterman told me to accompany them. Since I didn't have much say in the matter I reluctantly traveled with them to see Judge Solomon. Judge Solomon considered the matter, in open court. The three of us stood at counsel table. I was at the end of the table and tried to distance myself as far as possible from the others. On the way to court I reviewed the revised pleadings. Approximately half of the offending language was still in the papers. I suspected what was coming. I was right.

Judge Solomon immediately singled me out saying "Runstein, what are these papers?" I attempted to explain that I was sitting in my office minding my own business when Mr. Alterman (the judge's former clerk and good friend) ordered me to accompany them to court, that I had little knowledge of the matter and nothing to do with the preparation of the pleadings. Of course, that response only increased Judge Solomon's anger. He said that I was there and therefore responsible for everything submitted to him. He appeared extremely angry.

At this point he asked Helen Bradley (his secretary) to give him a file of form documents which she kept for his use. Judge Solomon angrily ripped a form of affidavit and order for a writ of attachment from his form book, handed them to her, and told her to give them to me so I could see what a properly prepared request for attachment looked like.

I looked at the forms Ms. Bradley gave me and was surprised to see they were ones I had submitted a couple of years earlier. I smiled and looked up at the Judge and with poor judgment stated "thank you very much Judge Solomon." He asked what I meant and I told him that these were forms that I had submitted in an earlier case. Any lawyer who practiced before Judge Solomon knows what came next. He got even angrier at me and chastised me again. Since I had demonstrated that I knew how to do it properly, my error was doubly offensive and a waste of his time. As we left the court, I advised Mr. Alterman that it would take me years to forgive him for taking me along. It is now 20 years later; I have not yet forgiven him.

∿

## A Good Judge Keeps His Cool
As told by Portland Attorney Bernard B. Kliks
*First appeared in the Oregon State Bar's* For the Record, *February 1989*

When I was first admitted to practice, about 45 years ago, I had my first case before U.S. District Judge James Alger Fee. I was assigned to defend, absolutely gratis, an indigent federal criminal with a long criminal record, who had kidnapped at gunpoint a prominent Oregon man from a pioneer family and driven him across the border to Vancouver, Wash., thus involving the drastic Lindbergh Law.

The only solution I could figure out was to plead him guilty, argue that he had made a geographical mistake thinking that the Interstate Bridge crossed the Willamette River rather than the Columbia, and ask for leniency.

I well remember looking up at Judge Fee on his 25-foot-high dais appearing like an angry god, while I made the sociological arguments about my client having been raised in a ghetto, etc., and that he was now ready "to pay his debt to society." The judge immediately rose from his throne, to his full height of nine feet, seven inches, and screamed at me: "Young man, where did you take law and from whom?"

"The University of Oregon, under Dean Wayne L. Morse," I replied. Judge Fee then told me that that was no excuse, and that there was no such thing as a "debt to society"—that criminals are incarcerated to protect society from them, and not to pay any debt, and further, that he wished never to hear that argument in his courtroom again.

Properly humiliated and chastised, I withdrew sheepishly to my seat among the other unfortunate young lawyers, waiting for the chance to escape. (My client did get a reasonable sentence to a correctional institution where he could learn a trade, however.)

When the court was adjourned, a few of the older and wiser lawyers came around to console me and ask me what I thought of their judge. My back was to the bench, and I let my peers know that I thought Judge Fee was a mean old S.O.B. At that time, I received a swift kick in the shins and turned around to find that I was now facing Judge Fee, who had no doubt heard my comments.

The judge quietly and courteously extended his hand to me and said, "Mr. Kliks, the court thanks you for your time and efforts in this case, and your service to the court."

∾

### It Was Only an Earthquake
As told by Portland attorney Frank Pozzi
*First appeared in the Oregon State Bar's* For the Record

In 1983 I had occasion to file an action under the Jones Act on behalf of a seaman to recover damages for an injury while sailing aboard a ship. The action was against a shipowner who was represented by William F. White.

The seaman I was representing had been put off the ship to receive medical attention by a doctor in Valdez, Alaska. With only a medical report in hand, Bill White set up a deposition of the doctor in Valdez to be taken by telephone from an office of a court reporter in Portland. I cooperated in the taking of this deposition.

Bill opened the deposition on the conference telephone by taking the doctor through the substance of his medical report and then turned him over to me for cross-examination. I had no sooner propounded my first question when the doctor/witness said: "Hold the phone, we have an earthquake."

Bill, the court reporter, and I all waited two or three long minutes before the doctor/witness returned to the phone in Valdez and calmly stated, "The earthquake is over. Would you please repeat the last question?"

∿

### Hats Off for Judge James Alger Fee
#### As told by Portland Attorney Neva M. Elliott
*First appeared in the Oregon State Bar's* For the Record

My most vivid memory of Judge James Alger Fee is from the day I first appeared before him. I was dressed in the highest of label merchandise and privately thought I was at my best. On my head was a divine hat which, while modest in size, was thick with violets blooming riotous, springing from a delectable veil. I had spent an entire divorce fee on myself, much to the disgust of my then mentor (he was Frank Sever, Senator Guy Gordon's partner, and he had just taken me on as a kind of secretary-lawyer-janitor-helper).

"Now, Neva," Frank had warned me, "Alger doesn't like a lot of fuss; better dress down, not up."

Regarding Frank's advice as worthless when it came to female attire, I walked down the long aisle in the large courtroom, and when Judge Fee gestured me forward I thought it was to permit me to launch into some opening statement. Instead, there thundered throughout the court from the bench, "**WHAT IS THAT ON YOUR HEAD?**"

I reached up to see if the violets had faded, and gulped, "It's my new hat, your honor."

"Look around, Miss Elliott. Do you see any of the males in this courtroom wearing anything on their heads?"

"No, Your Honor."
"You will please leave this courtroom," the judge ordered, "and when you are minus the hat you may proceed with your motion. WE DO NOT WEAR HATS IN THIS COURTROOM AS LONG AS I AM SITTING." And we never did.

∾

## How Are Things on the Reservation?
By Malcolm Montague
*First appeared in the* Bulletin of the U.S. District Court of Oregon Historical Society, *Winter 1987*

When I was a very young man, I essayed forth from my family hearth to become a college man. During the course of my adventure through the cauldron of a four-year societal manhood initiation, I did what was expected of me and joined a fraternity—Beta Theta Pi by name. It was thus that in the first term of my freshman year I was by the fates propelled to commit the worst gaffe of my life, or so I thought.

Now to appreciate this story, you must understand that I knew of a man by the name of Chet See, an Indian agent who ran the country store on the Warm Springs Reservation. I knew that Mr. See was a special friend of my father, for he often arranged a permit that allowed Father to fish the glorious Warm Springs River, perhaps the greatest fly fishing stream in the world.

All of that I knew. But as you will soon see, I didn't know as much as I thought I did. One day at the fraternity house, where I was a pledge, I was summoned to entertain a distinguished visiting alumnus brother by an upperclassman who did not know what to say to him, either. What I did not know (until he told me) was that the honorable and imposing visitor was James Alger Fee, class of 1908 or so.

After telling me who he was, the gentleman inquired after my father. I answered him, and then there followed that most fearful moment in any conversation: silence. In desperation, I filled the gap by blurting out, "Well Mr. See, how are things on the reservation?"

I dread what ensued, even now. The alum became red faced, the veins in his neck protruding and twisted like those of some primeval vine. He huffed, choked, rose to his very considerable height (his black eyes staring through me all the while), and stalked majestically out of the fraternity house. I was crushed and knew not what I had done.

That evening, I called my father (collect) and told him the story, upon which he literally came unglued at the other end of the line—snorting and laughing and crying. He even had the ill grace to ask me to repeat the humiliating tale and then went into paroxysms and gales of laughter a second time.

Finally, my father told me the difference between Chet See, the Indian agent, and the Honorable James Alger Fee, the chief judge of the Big Court in the Sky, at least in Oregon. He said he felt hardly able to tell me the most curious thing about the encounter (but he struggled up to it amidst snorting and chuckling).

It seems that the judge was of Indian blood, his mother having been Indian.

That did it! I said I guessed I'd better come home or join the army, or suchlike. He said to take heart—that he would talk to "Alger" (if you will) in a few days and fix it. He did and reported later that Alger had thought the episode every bit as funny as Father had.

Nevertheless, I am more than glad that I never had to appear before Judge Fee. I am reasonably sure that I would have been in very, very big trouble.

# PRESIDENTS OF THE U.S. DISTRICT COURT OF OREGON HISTORICAL SOCIETY

### Randall B. Kester (1984–85)

Randall Kester graduate from Columbia University Law School in 1940 and began to practice law in that same year with the firm of Maguire,

 Shields & Morrison. During his time with the firm, Kester also served as general attorney for the Union Pacific Railroad Company, and from 1947 to 1956 he was an instructor at Northwestern College of Law in Portland. In January 1957, he was appointed associate justice of the Oregon Supreme Court and served until March 1958, when he resigned to become general solicitor for Union Pacific Railroad Company. In January 1979 he became senior counsel for Union Pacific, retiring from that position at the end of December 1980. Kester is now a partner in the Portland firm of Cosgrave, Vergeer & Kester.

In 1956 he became president of the Multnomah Bar Association and served as treasurer of the Oregon State Bar from 1965 to 1966. He was also a member of the Judicial Council of Oregon from 1970 to 1971 and has served on several state bar committees. In 1991 he received the Multnomah Bar Association's Professionalism Award. Kester's civic activities have included leadership roles in the Portland Chamber of Commerce and the City Club of Portland.

### Norman J. Wiener (1985–87)

Norman Wiener earned his law degree from the University of Oregon and in 1947 joined the six-attorney firm of King & Wood. Over the years, he helped the firm grow to the present-day Miller, Nash, Wiener, Hager & Carlsen, which employs 125 attorneys. Wiener is a general practitioner who emphasizes litigation and is recognized by both clients and the legal community for his expertise in environmental and natural resources law, as well as antitrust regulation.

An active American Bar Association member, Wiener has served on a variety of committees and was a member of the eleven-person ABA Standing Committee on Environmental Law. He has written numerous legal articles in the *Oregon Law Review*, *Willamette Law Journal*, *Environmental Law*, *Natural Resources Lawyer*, and the Oregon State Bar *Bulletin*. His community activities have included the presidencies of the Rehabilitation Institute of Oregon and United Way. During World War II and the Korean War, he was an agent for the U.S. Army Counterintelligence Corps.

### Wayne Hilliard (1987–89)

Wayne Hilliard graduated from Willamette University College of Law in 1951 and in the same year joined the law firm of Koerner, Young, McCulloch & Dezendorf—now Lane Powell Spears Lubersky. Hilliard was admitted to the partnership in 1958. During his professional life, he has specialized in civil litigation, with emphasis in later years on antitrust, securities, and general commercial litigation.

Hilliard's principal professional activities include membership on various Oregon State Bar sections and federal court committees, as well as membership in the American College of Trial Lawyers, with over 10 years of service on its Complex Litigation Committee. Hilliard is also a member of the International Association of Insurance Counsel, the National Association of Railroad Trial Counsel, a fellow of the American Bar Foundation, past state chairman of the U.S. Supreme Court Historical Society, and a member of various civic, business, and social organizations.

### Don S. Willner (1989–91)

Don Willner received his law degree from Harvard Law School in 1951 and has been a practicing attorney for 41 years. He has also been a part-time circuit court judge pro-tem for the State of Oregon and a part-time adjunct professor at the Northwestern School of Law of Lewis and Clark College, where he teaches Oregon constitutional law and an advanced labor law seminar. From 1957 to 1959 Willner was a state representative

for Multnomah County and from 1963 to 1973 he was an Oregon state senator, serving as assistant majority leader in 1972–73. He retired from the Oregon Senate to seek the Democratic nomination for United States Senate.

Willner's civic activities have included the chairmanship of the Governor's Commission on Youth in 1975 and of the Joint Legislative Task Force on Ethics in Government in 1982. He has also been president of the Northwest Regional Council of Boys' Clubs of America, a director of the Portland Chamber of Commerce, president of the Consumer Federation of America, and corporate secretary of the Portland Youth Philharmonic Association. He has been a member of the National Panel of American Arbitration Association since 1955.

## Katherine H. O'Neil (1991–93)

Katherine O'Neil began the study of law at Harvard Law School in 1961, leaving after one year to raise a family. She returned to her studies at the Northwestern School of Law of Lewis and Clark College and graduated in 1977. Today, O'Neil is a partner in Graff & O'Neil, maintaining a trial and appellate practice that includes work in business litigation and admiralty law.

A founder of Oregon Women Lawyers, O'Neil served as that organization's first president and remains an active member. In 1991 she was elected to the American Bar Association's House of Delegates and more recently became the first woman president of the Professional Liability Fund board of the Oregon State Bar. O'Neil has also been president of the alumni board of Northwestern School of Law and has sat on committees of the Oregon State Bar and the Multnomah Bar Association. Both organizations have presented her with their respective membership service awards. O'Neil's community activities have included membership on the board of directors of Chamber Music Northwest and boards of the Presbytery of the Cascades.

# INDEX

Project coordination and editing of *The First Duty* was handled
by Carolyn M. Buan, owner of Writing and Editing Services,
Portland, Oregon. Graphic design was provided by Jeanne E. Galick
of Portland. The two women have also collaborated on
*The First Oregonians*, an illustrated collection of essays
about the Indians of Oregon; *Oregon Humanities* magazine;
newsletters for the U.S. District Court of Oregon Historical Society
and Oregon Women Lawyers; and a variety of other publications
for business and nonprofit clients.

Typeset in Bembo and Minion by J.Y. Hollingsworth Company, Portland

Printing by Thomson-Shore, Dexter, Michigan